THE REMINISCENCES OF
Rear Admiral Robert B. Erly
U.S. Navy (Retired)

INTERVIEWED BY
Paul Stillwell

U.S. Naval Institute • Annapolis, Maryland

Copyright © 2015

Preface

This memoir emphasizes three principal legs of the tripod that dominated much of Admiral Erly's career: destroyer operations, amphibious warfare, and relations with other nations in the Americas. The memoir documents the ingredients that shaped a wayward youth who, with the benefit of a Naval Academy education, became a substantial contributor to the nation's military efforts. An individual who had a major influence on young Erly was his brother-in-law, Lieutenant Charles Wootten. Wootten provided the motivation and tutorship that landed Erly an appointment to the Naval Academy class of 1937. Erly absorbed the academy's ethic and demonstrated himself to be a go-getter.

Erly's attempt to become a naval aviator fizzled, but then he put together a solid career as a surface warfare officer. His baptism of fire—literally—came during the Japanese attack on Pearl Harbor in December 1941. Lieutenant (junior grade) Erly seized the initiative—and a fire hose—and proceeded to ward off the potential for an explosion of weapons on board the destroyer *Downes*, a sister of his own ship, the *Cassin*. He served in several destroyers during the war the followed, including commanding the USS *Phelps* in the conflict's closing months. Along the way, his knowledge of the Spanish language diverted him into a tour of duty helping the Mexican Navy beef up a couple of its warships for Atlantic antisubmarine duty. That international experience would serve him well later in his career.

The Korean War posed another combat challenge, in this case reactivating the destroyer *James C. Owens* from the mothball fleet, training a green crew, and then commanding her during gun duels with the North Koreans. In his shore tours he got a taste of Pentagon duty, working in the area of fleet operations and readiness. He also acquired a heavy seabag of amphibious warfare experience: on the staff of an Atlantic Fleet amphibious group, as first skipper of the attack transport *Paul Revere*, amphibious squadron commander, chief of staff to Commander Amphibious Force Pacific Fleet, and as developer of some of the riverine warfare doctrine employed in the Vietnam War.

Later he was on the OpNav staff for inter-American relations, working with Canada and Latin American navies. He subsequently served on the staff of Commander in Chief Atlantic Fleet, and then capped his career with another international assignment. He added Portuguese language capability to his knowledge of Spanish and served a tour as Commander Iberian Atlantic Command and chief of the Military Assistance Advisory Group Portugal. He continued to run NATO exercises even as the Portuguese Government was overturned in a bloodless revolution in 1974.

My association with the admiral came during his retirement years. Vice Admiral Charles Minter, one of his Naval Academy classmates, recommended Erly as an interviewee. I was able to interview him during his periodic visits to Annapolis for meetings of the Naval Academy Foundation.

Once the interviews were transcribed, I sent them to the admiral, who made a good many editorial changes that have been incorporated in this final version. I also did some additional editing for the sake of accuracy, clarity, and smoothness, and I inserted footnotes for the benefit of readers. My biggest regret is that, for a variety of reasons, the process took far longer than expected. My hope was to get the finished product to him as a present for his 100th birthday, but I fell short. Fortunately, the interviews were done when he was available and will now be a lasting legacy of his naval service.

Thanks go to Ms. Janis Jorgensen of the Naval Institute staff who has coordinated the printing and binding of the finished product. In completing this volume, the Naval Institute expresses its gratitude to the Tawani Foundation and the Pritzker Military Library of Chicago for their generous financial support of the oral history program that produced this memoir.

Paul Stillwell
U.S. Naval Institute
February 2015

REAR ADMIRAL ROBERT BROUSSARD ERLY
UNITED STATES NAVY (RETIRED)

Robert Broussard Erly was born in Washington, D.C., on 12 June 1914. He was the son of Alfred Angus and Estelle Beatrice (Harice) Erly. He attended Eastern High School and Bullis Preparatory School in Washington. He served as a seaman second class in the Naval Reserve prior to entering the U.S. Naval Academy, Annapolis, Maryland, on an appointment at large, 3 August 1933. As a midshipman he participated in football and boxing and was a member of the reception committee. He was graduated and commissioned ensign in June 1937 and subsequently advanced in rank to rear admiral, to date from 1 July 1965.

After graduation from the Naval Academy, he reported on board the battleship *New Mexico* (BB-40) and served in that vessel until detached in November 1938 for an assignment in the destroyer *Conyngham* (DD-371). He spent almost all of 1940 undergoing flight training at Pensacola and Opa Locka, Florida. In January 1941 he joined the USS *Cassin* (DD-372) and was attached to that destroyer during the Japanese attack on Pearl Harbor on 7 December 1941. For his actions during the attack, he received the Navy Commendation Medal with Combat "V." As an interim assignment due to the loss of the *Cassin*, he was battery commander of Naval Antiaircraft Shore Battery Number 4 at Pearl Harbor.

He returned to destroyer duty in July 1942 as gunnery officer and senior watch officer of the USS *Frazier* (DD-607). From January 1943 to January 1944, he served as assistant chief of the naval mission to Cuba. For services in connection with training the crews of Cuban naval units and sailing with them in antisubmarine operations, he was awarded the Cuban Order of Merit.

Between February and July 1944 he served as executive officer and navigator on board the destroyer *Laub* (DD-613), after which he commanded the destroyer *Phelps* (DD-360). He reported in January 1946 to the U.S. Naval Mission to Venezuela and later assumed the position as acting chief, where he remained until February 1948. For his service to the Venezuelan Navy he was awarded the Venezuelan Order of Naval Merit. Following duty afloat as executive officer of the destroyer tender *Yosemite* (AD-19), he reported in July 1949 as senior instructor in the antisubmarine warfare and combat information center courses at the General Line School, Newport, Rhode Island.

After the outbreak of the Korean War in June 1950, he was prospective commanding officer of the destroyer *James C. Owens* (DD-776) and became commanding officer when the ship was recommissioned that September. He was awarded the Bronze Star Medal for meritorious achievement "while commanding that destroyer during operations against enemy aggressor forces in North Korea from May 7 to May 10, 1952." During the period August 1952 to January 1953 he attended the Armed Forces Staff College, Norfolk, Virginia, after which he served as assistant operations officer, radiological defense officer, tactical officer, and senior watch officer on the staff of Commander Amphibious Group Two, Atlantic Fleet.

In February 1955 he was assigned to the Office of the Chief of Naval Operations, Navy Department, Washington, D.C., where he remained until March 1958. While there, he served successively as Operational Coordinator for Fleet Operations, Head of the Fleet Organization section, and finally as administrative aide to the Deputy Chief of Naval Operations for Fleet Operations, Readiness, Research, and Development. In September 1958 he assumed command of the newly commissioned attack transport *Paul Revere* (APA-248) and in July 1959 reported for duty as Planning Officer and later Assistant Chief of Staff for Operations, Plans, and Training, on the staff of Commander Amphibious Force Pacific Fleet. From February 1961 to August 1962 he commanded Amphibious Squadron Five, then had instruction in 1962-63 as a student at the National War College, Washington, D.C.

He reported in July 1963 as Chief of Staff and Aide to Commander Amphibious Force Pacific Fleet and was awarded a gold star in lieu of a second Navy Commendation Medal for meritorious service in that capacity from July 1963 through April 1965. In June 1965, as his first flag command, he reported as Commander Amphibious Group Three/Commander River-Coastal Warfare Group. He received a second gold star for his Navy Commendation Medal for his outstanding service in that assignment. While in this billet he initiated the doctrine for riverine warfare.

In the 1966-68 period Erly had duty as Director of the Pan-American Affairs, Naval Missions, and Advisory Group, Office of the Chief of Naval Operations. He was awarded the Legion of Merit for his meritorious service. The citation read in part, " . . . under the outstanding leadership and guidance of Rear Admiral ERLY, the Pan-American Affairs Division has reached an unprecedented high level of performance." While in Washington he was assigned additional duties as the Senior United States Navy Member of the Joint Mexican-United States Defense Commission; Senior United States Naval Member of the Joint Brazil-United States Military Commission; Senior United States Naval Member of the Permanent Joint Board on Defense, Canada-United States and United States Delegate of the United States Delegation, Inter-American Defense Board. For the latter he was awarded the Joint Service Commendation Medal for his meritorious service: "In this unique assignment requiring the finest sense of diplomacy, professional competence, and knowledge of Inter-American Defense Affairs, he made significant contributions to the successful conduct of United States policy in this international organization charged with planning the defense of this hemisphere."

Admiral Erly served from 1968 to 1972 on the staff of Commander in Chief U.S. Atlantic Fleet. He was Inspector General from March 1968 to June 1969 and from June 1969 to October 1972 was Deputy Chief of Staff for Plans and Operations. His last post prior to his physical disability retirement in September 1974 was that of Commander of the Iberian Atlantic Command, a major subordinate NATO command, and Chief of the Military Assistance Advisory Group to Portugal.

In addition to four awards of the Legion of Merit, Admiral Erly received the Bronze Star Medal with Combat V; the Joint Service Commendation Medal; Navy Commendation medal with two gold stars and Combat V; American Defense Service Medal with star; American Campaign Medal; European-African-Middle Eastern Campaign Medal with star; Asiatic-Pacific Campaign Medal with two stars; World War II Victory Medal; Navy Occupation Service Medal; National Defense Service Medal with bronze star; Korean Service Medal; United Nations Service Medal; and the Armed Forces Expeditionary Medal. His foreign awards included the Order of Naval Merit from Brazil; the Great Star of Naval Merit from Chile; the Order of Naval Merit from Venezuela; and the Order of Naval Merit from Cuba; and the Korean Presidential Unit Citation Badge.

He was active in retirement as president of the San Diego/Coronado chapter of the Naval Academy Alumni Association, president of the board of directors of the Coronado Community Theater, chairman of the Coronado chapter of the American Cancer Society, vice president for organization for the San Diego unit of the American Cancer Society, and board member of the California Division of the Society, western area Vice President of the Naval Academy Alumni Association, and trustee of the Naval Academy Foundation.

Admiral Erly was married to the former Lois Richards from 1944 to 2004. The admiral died 31 July 2014 in San Diego. He was survived by his second wife, Mrs. Thea Wallace Erly.

Authorization

The U.S. Naval Institute is hereby authorized to make available to individuals, libraries, and other repositories of its choosing the transcripts of six oral history interviews concerning the life and naval career of the undersigned. The interviews were recorded on 6 May 1987, 7 September 1988, 8 September 1988, 21 September 1989, 27 September 1990, and 1 April 1992 in collaboration with Paul Stillwell for the U.S. Naval Institute.

The undersigned does hereby release and assign to the U.S. Naval Institute the rights and title to these interviews, with the exception that the undersigned retains the right to use the material for his own purposes, as he sees fit. The copyright in both the oral and transcribed versions shall be the sole property of the U.S. Naval Institute. The tape recordings of the interviews are and will remain the property of the U.S. Naval Institute.

Signed and sealed this _____ day of _____ 1997.

_____
Robert B. Erly
Rear Admiral, U.S. Navy (Retired)

Interview Number 1 with Admiral Robert B. Erly, U.S. Navy (Retired)

Place: U.S. Naval Institute, Annapolis, Maryland

Date: Friday, 6 May 1988

Paul Stillwell: Admiral, just to begin at the beginning, could you please tell me something about when and where you were born and your parents and what you remember of your early life?

Admiral Erly: I was born in Washington, D.C., June 12, 1914, in a spot called Congress Heights. Don't ask me where it is; it's there in Washington. I was a home delivery by a Dr. Mudd, who for many, many years had the Navy dispensary at the old Navy Annex. My dad was a newspaperman and had worked with the Associated Press, the *Star*, and other newspapers. Then he became involved on Capitol Hill and very active in running campaigns. Evidently he took part in Taft's election.[*] I'm trying to think of some of the autographed photographs we had: "To Alf Erly for his help." He went to all the conventions. In fact, in some of the congressional trips to the Hawaiian Islands, Philippines, etc., he was the main coordinator of those junkets.

Paul Stillwell: Was this Dr. Mudd any relation to the one that treated John Wilkes Booth?[†]

Admiral Erly: That I don't know—possibly. I vaguely recall there could be some connection. But for anyone in the old-time Navy, World War I, he was number one in medical care. I remember going back to the Navy dispensary in 1945, and he was still holding forth. I was getting ready to go to Venezuela, and Lois, my wife, and I received our departure physicals from him. Everyone knew him. He knew my dad in connection with these congressional trips. My dad made many friends among the congressmen and senators. This was evidenced by my being named after Senator Robert Broussard from

---

[*] William Howard Taft was President of the United States from March 1909 to March 1913.
[†] In April 1865, in southern Maryland, Dr. Samuel A. Mudd treated the broken leg sustained by John Wilkes Booth after assassinating President Abraham Lincoln.

Louisiana.* He was my godfather. When he died, his brother Edgar Broussard then filled that Senate seat, which, in turn, I think, Huey Long took over.† I was christened Robert Foligny Broussard Erly, but I later dropped the Foligny.

Paul Stillwell: How did it happen that a Navy doctor would attend your mother at the birth?

Admiral Erly: I think he was a contract doctor, and I think it had to be the friendship with my dad. I think that was the connection. And promptly also that connection through the congressional bit and Capitol Hill bit is the way I remember it.

Paul Stillwell: Did you spend all your growing-up years in Washington?

Admiral Erly: Yes, just about. Let's see. I was sent to St. Joseph's. I'm trying to remember what grade and how many. This gets really involved. Way back when we were living on 14th Street in the Hudson Apartments, I was going to St. Paul's, a Catholic school. I went with my brother, who is about three and a half years older than I. I was only maybe first grade, and my brother Jack was in the third or fourth. We used to take off for school with our lunch, and we'd end up in the zoo. We got to know the zoo very well. We got away with this for about three months. As the end result of that, we were packed off to a Catholic boarding school in Manassas, Virginia. I'm trying to remember its name. Well, we were at a boarding school for, I guess, the next two years, and then came back.

I'm getting a little confused in my age and at what time. When I was about eight or ten, my father and mother were divorced. My brother and I went with my father and my sister, the eldest, went with my mother. My father and brother Jack became sort of a nomadic deal, from here, thither, and yon. For the fifth and sixth grades, I was at a

---

* Robert Foligny Broussard, a Democrat from Louisiana, served in the U.S. House of Representatives from 4 March 1897 to 3 March 1915. He was in the Senate from 4 March 1915 until his death on 12 April 1918.
† Edwin Sidney Broussard, a Democrat from Louisiana, served in the U.S. Senate from 4 March 1921 to 3 March 1933. Huey Pierce Long, a Democrat from Louisiana, served in the U.S. Senate from 25 January 1932 until his death on 10 September 1935.

Catholic school. Then I went to St. Joseph's through the sixth grade or seventh in Brookland, St. Catherine's Parish.

Paul Stillwell: Where's that?

Admiral Erly: That is on C Street in Washington, D.C., which I imagine is an all-black area now. It wasn't too far from the Capitol, actually.

Then I came down and went through the eighth grade at St. Mary's. My sister had married a lieutenant by the name of Charles Wootten, and I came down and went to St. Mary's over here in Annapolis for one year.[*] Then, of course, that whole year I was here, I saw all the boxing and everything that went on at the Naval Academy, and I imagine it was then the thought engendered that perhaps I would like to come to the Naval Academy, although my sister before—I can remember this when we were living on S Street, had dated midshipmen. In a little side note, I remember we were sweating out the sinking of the submarine *S-4*, because there was a little ensign on board by the name of Graham Fitch whom my sister had dated.[†] Of course, he was lost in the *S-4*.[‡]

Then, as I graduated from the eighth grade here in Annapolis, my sister and brother-in-law went on to China. I went on back to Washington, and the following fall entered Eastern High School. Man. Let's see. Bilged French, bilged algebra.

Paul Stillwell: Were you going to the zoo again? [Laughter]

Admiral Erly: [Laughter] I might as well have been. I became a high school dropout at that. We were in pretty bad times financially at this stage. I remember that I had signed up for the JROTC that we had in the high schools, and those were quite the things.[§] I was measured for a uniform, but we couldn't scrape together the money for it. Those were

---

[*] Lieutenant Charles T. Wootten, USN, was stationed at the Naval Academy.
[†] On 17 December 1927, as the submarine *S-4* (SS-109) was surfacing from a submerged run over the measured mile off Provincetown, Cape Cod, Massachusetts, she was accidentally rammed and sunk by the Coast Guard destroyer *Paulding*. The Navy tried unsuccessfully to rescue six survivors who sent a series of signals to divers by tapping from inside the hull. The *S-4* was eventually raised on 17 March 1928.
[‡] Lieutenant (junior grade) Graham N. Fitch, USN.
[§] JROTC – Junior reserve officers' training corps.

tough times. So we can just say that my high school education was a short one.

Paul Stillwell: How much attention was your father able to pay with this busy, demanding job he had?

Admiral Erly: Well, at this time my father had sort of slipped off the rung of a ladder. He was still up on Capitol Hill, and I'm sorry to say he didn't have a paying job, per se, and I guess he became sort of a sponger. I hate to say that, but that's exactly what was happening.

My brother, in this phase, was working in a patronage job, in what they called the folding room. This is where the congressional mass mail to constituents is reproduced and mailed. He did that for several years, so things were really rough. In some cases during this time frame, instead of eating, you just cinched your belt up another hole. Actually, my brother at his young age, through patronage jobs as a Capitol page and folding room employee, was the breadwinner of the family.

Paul Stillwell: Was the problem coincidental with the Depression, or did it start earlier?

Admiral Erly: Well, from '27. It was part of the Depression, and part of it earlier.* My dad had flushed it down the toilet drinking, really, too much alcohol, which was his downfall.

Paul Stillwell: Where does a youngster go for values and character building in an experience like that? Were you in Boy Scouts or church groups?

Admiral Erly: My brother was quite an entrepreneur and started a Boy Scout troop in Brookland, so I went over there. At the same time, there was a National Guard unit

---

* Following the crash of the New York Stock Exchange in late October 1929, the United States was plunged into the Great Depression, from which it did not recover until the nation geared up for World War II at the beginning of the 1940s. The Depression was marked by high unemployment and many business failures.

where I used to go and box and be sort of a mascot. So I wasn't getting any formal schooling. I got to be a Star Scout, I guess, and was senior patrol leader.

Then my sister came back from China, and her husband was executive officer at the Naval Home in Philadelphia.[*] I realized something had to be done, and they gave me the opportunity to come up there. I joined the Naval Reserve the day after I was 18, up there. Charlie, my brother-in-law, sat me down and, I forget, would it be Wentworth's geometry? I can't remember. But he gave me this geometry book, and I started with geometry. We went through it page by page. If I came to an original that I couldn't solve, Charlie would start me over again at the front of the book. I guess it took most of the year, and the end result was that there wasn't an original problem that I couldn't solve.

Charlie then started me on physics. He also taught Tom Washington, the son of Admiral Washington, who was the superintendent of the Naval Home.[†] Tom Washington went into the academy with my class and then slipped back a class, to the class of '38.[‡] So Charlie went through and covered physics with us. I realized that Charlie had corrected my math deficiencies, but I realized that I wasn't getting English and the history and everything else. It was now the fall of 1932, and I was 18. I knew that something else had to be done if I was to enter the academy in 1933, because I had a hell of a hurdle to get over.

Paul Stillwell: And you didn't have a formal transcript that you could hand in, either.

Admiral Erly: No, no way. No way. So I leaned on my father and said, "No way am I ever going to make it this way. I've just got too much to do. I need to get to prep school."

Well, Dad, with his congressional bit, had gotten Bill Bullis of Bullis School his

---

[*] The Philadelphia Naval Asylum, renamed the Naval Home in 1889, was a complex of buildings that served as a residence for retired sailors from 1834 to 1976.
[†] Rear Admiral Thomas Washington, USN (Ret.), was governor of the Naval Home.
[‡] Midshipman Thomas Washington Jr., USN, who eventually retired as a captain.

appointment to the Naval Academy, way back.* So the old man leaned on Bill Bullis, and I went to Bullis Prep School, along with Schnitzel Schneider, Tom Cunningham, Pinky Baer, Sid Bottomley, Owen Chambers, and probably some others.† I've forgotten how many of that class came in, but we went to Bullis. Most of them were domiciled, ate dormitory chow, and everything else at Bullis. I had a room about a block away.

Paul Stillwell: Why was that? Your influence didn't include room and board?

Admiral Erly: Did not include room and board. Did not include room and board. No way. I was lean and hungry most of the time.

Paul Stillwell: So who provided that, your dad?

Admiral Erly: Yes, spasmodically. Spasmodically. We'll get into that if you want. And it went on, evidently. Well, I got the algebra, physics, geometry, English, U.S. history, and ancient history.

Paul Stillwell: Would you describe yourself as highly motivated during that period?

Admiral Erly: Oh, yes. Yes, yes. Yes, indeed. I got even more highly motivated. We had five days of exams. I had to take an exam in every subject, and it was competitive. The day I started the exams, I got locked out of my room. I was motivated. Even though I felt I had geometry cold, I almost failed geometry. Not quite. I got a 3.98, but I got on the first problem, and this is even knowing better, having been coached. Old Bullis had said, "If you get hung up on a problem, go on to the next." I was so confident there

---

* William F. Bullis resigned his commission upon graduation from the Naval Academy in June 1924. He served as a second lieutenant in the Army, 1924-26, and subsequently earned a master's degree from George Washington University. In 1930 he founded The Bullis School in Washington, D.C., as a preparatory school for the service academies. He served on active duty as a Naval Reservist from 1940 to 1945 and eventually retired as a commander.
† Midshipman Frederick H. Schneider Jr., USN; Midshipman Donald G. Baer, USN; Midshipman Harold Sydney Bottomley Jr., USN; and Midshipman Owen A. Chambers, USN, graduated in the class of 1937.

wasn't anything anybody could throw at me, I got into this one and I just couldn't prove it out. When they yelled 30 minutes to go, I went through the other nine problems. My problem on the hang-up one was that I couldn't add, but I proved it down to that point. But I hadn't to my satisfaction. Charlie Wootten had given me a great foundation in math. The high marks I made in geometry, physics, and algebra were due to his tutoring. That high mark got me into the academy, because I made a bare 2.5 in English.

This was 1933; you've got to remember that this was the Depression. The U.S. Naval Reserve in those days had 25 appointments, and the fleet, I think, had 50 to 100. So many young men had joined the Naval Reserve to compete for the 25 reserve appointments to the academy. Some 600 took the exam for the 25 appointments; 190-odd passed. I finally went in the Naval Academy as number 23 out of 25. Incidentally, we went to drill one night a week, and I forget what we got paid. At the end of every three months we got a little check from the government.

Paul Stillwell: Where were the drills held?

Admiral Erly: Out at the old Naval Gun Factory.[*]

Paul Stillwell: What sorts of things did that cover?

Admiral Erly: Oh, basically they would have a practice loading machine. You'd do that as part of a gun crew. They had seamanship, knot-tying, close-order drill, and this type of business. I first joined in Philadelphia the day after I was 18 years old, and they had an old Eagle boat up in Philly that first year.[†] We'd go out and cruise to Cape May. I guess I was a quartermaster striker at this point, ended up as a seaman second in the reserves when I got my discharge papers.[‡] We were given a seabag of sailor's clothing. I

---

[*] The Washington Navy Yard is on M Street in southeast Washington, D.C. For many years it was an industrial facility known as the Naval Gun Factory.
[†] During World War I, the Ford Motor Company built dozens of steel-hulled antisubmarine craft known as Eagle boats. Each was 200 feet long and displaced 615 tons. None was in combat during the war.
[‡] A striker is a non-rated enlisted man or woman officially designated as being in training for a specific petty officer rating. The quartermaster rating is involved with navigation.

was just trying to remember other Bullis members in the reserve—Willie Dye, Tom Cunningham.*

Paul Stillwell: Was there a military atmosphere at Bullis? Did you wear uniforms or have military discipline?

Admiral Erly: Oh, no, no, no, no. There was another prep school just across the street. I forget its name. That building where we went is now the Fleet Reserve Association building on New Hampshire Avenue.† That's where Bullis was at that point. It was a big old handsome brownstone building. The Fleet Reserve put a lot of money in it, and I don't know whether they are saying it is a historical site or not, but it's on a triangle. Have you ever seen it? It's just below DuPont Circle.

Paul Stillwell: I'm sure I've driven by it.
    How demanding was the pace at Bullis?

Admiral Erly: As far as I was concerned, it wasn't demanding enough, particularly with the English teacher. I felt that was where my lack was, the ability to hook words together and do this type of thing, so I took it upon myself to get some extra tutoring, coaching, from him. I said, "I think this is one of my major weaknesses, and I need to work on it."

Paul Stillwell: How much was genuine learning, as opposed to just preparing for exams?

Admiral Erly: Well, I would say that first you've got to learn the subject before you can take the exam. Oh, sure, when you got into algebra and some of those problems—you know, if the bathtub's faucet coming is in with a flow and the drain is taking this long,

---

* Midshipman Willard J. Dye, USN, entered the Naval Academy with the class of 1937 but did not graduate.
† The Fleet Reserve Association is a non-profit organization that represents the interests of Navy, Marine Corps, and Coast Guard enlisted personnel, notably in dealings with Congress. The headquarters is now in Alexandria, Virginia.

how long will it take to fill up? We were drilled on that type, but you really had to know your math. I don't think you could just memorize the old exams and then go in and crack the new exam. So as far as for myself and what I learned from my brother-in-law Charlie Wootten on the drilling, I found that the physics and the geometry, and even the algebra, which I told you I'd bilged in high school, became an open book. It was no problem. Bullis had an intelligence test, and I think I stood fairly high on that.

Paul Stillwell: That helps.

Admiral Erly: All of these other kids at Bullis had already had four years of high school, and I didn't feel that I had to take any backwater from any of them in any of the subjects, really.

Paul Stillwell: How much interest did you have in the world at large—current events? Certainly Washington is like a textbook in national government.

Admiral Erly: Well, I guess there were some broadening experiences. When I was a youngster, I remember, the old man used to take me around, and you might say that I grew up in the Library of Congress. Again, with his oomph, I could go as a youngster into the library. I'd go back and wander through the stacks and come out with all kinds of books. This was where I spent a lot of time when I should have been in school. I guess you could call it my school.

There wasn't any exhibit in the Smithsonian Institution that was automated that I didn't know where it was. I could have been a tour guide. I knew the Senate, House Office Building, and the Capitol. I knew if you go to this corner and have someone stand over there and you whisper, then it would carry. I knew the paintings. So did I have worldwide interest? I don't know at that point, but I would say the interests were different than what I did miss out on, naturally, was, say, the high school athletics, but then I was boxing in my young teens with the National Guard team.

Paul Stillwell: How had that interest developed?

Admiral Erly: Well, I guess as a youngster I started when I was about 10 or 11. I then took a more active interest at 14 with the National Guard team and also with the Scout troop. In fact, I remember when I joined the Naval Reserve, the examining physician was going to disqualify me for a displaced septum, which I had repaired before I went in the Naval Academy. I had it chiseled out. That didn't last long before it got knocked back the other way. [Laughter]

Paul Stillwell: What became of your brother in this process?

Admiral Erly: He became a policeman up on Capitol Hill. Then he got started in running a school, of all things, and now has retired. He ended up really running the D.C. Police Boys Camp down below Patuxent Point, Point No Point, in that area. In fact, he's down there, and I shall go down and see him after the trustee meeting.* He had a debilitating stroke a year ago in March. How much longer he can hang on there I don't know. His formal education was also sporadic. He had been a Capitol page and did have some high school. In that time frame, the pages were sent out to Devitt Prep and had to go to night school.† He had some schooling, but he never attended college. He didn't go that way, but ended up very well. He was drafted during the war and was in the Army, came out a sergeant.

Paul Stillwell: How much social life were you able to have during your teenage years?

Admiral Erly: Zilch. Zilch.

Paul Stillwell: Did you have any part-time jobs to help support yourself?

Admiral Erly: The congressional mail needed addresses affixed to envelopes. This was farmed out and paid so much per 1,000. I had lots of writer's cramp. Also, I used to

---

* Admiral Erly was in Annapolis in conjunction with a meeting of trustees of the Naval Academy Foundation.
† The Devitt School, Washington, D.C., 1928-1951

work at Glen Echo in the summer months.* Again, the old man was pulling strings. He happened to know, I think it was a Mr. Slosh [phonetic], who headed Glen Echo for the Potomac Electric Power Company. That's how I got the job at Glen Echo for a couple of years in the summer months. I worked on the roller coaster, keeping everybody honest, and then sometimes I'd be on the brake and loading the cars and this type of thing. When I was 14, Dad got me a job at the botanical gardens at the foot of the Capitol. We kept the greenhouses clean and the plants watered.

Paul Stillwell: That was an interesting background to bring to the Naval Academy.

Admiral Erly: [Laughter] You wonder how in the hell I ever got there.

Paul Stillwell: What are your recollections once you reported in 1933?

Admiral Erly: I guess just like any other plebe coming in, being snowed with the horrendous task of all the equipment and clothing and the stenciling that takes place in the first few days.† Actually, I came in in August. Most of the other plebes had been in for a month or six weeks ahead of me. The problem was raising 150 bucks to get in.

Paul Stillwell: How did you go about that?

Admiral Erly: Well, the old man, again, did that.

Paul Stillwell: Was your mother a factor in the family at that time?

Admiral Erly: No, she had died when I was 13 of peritonitis from a gall bladder operation.

---

* Glen Echo amusement park, Montgomery County, Maryland.
† A midshipman in his or her first year is called a plebe; second year, youngster or third classman; third year, second classman; fourth year, first classman.

Paul Stillwell: How well did you take to the military discipline? I guess you'd had some advantage being in the Naval Reserve already.

Admiral Erly: Well, I had no problems, of course, with the drill routines. I thought I did very well. I'm trying to think in terms of demerits. I did very well, I would say, the first two years. I remember on youngster cruise I was okay but later ran into trouble. I had trouble academically; mechanical drawing had me thrown. I just had trouble visualizing three dimensions in mechanical drawing. Also, I wasn't doing too well in Spanish, but my roommate, Willie Dye, was good in Spanish and was a big help. He'd been at Bullis. He also came in through the Naval Reserve. Willie came in as number 21. His dad was a counselor in the State Department. We'd met at Bullis and opted to be roommates at the Naval Academy.

Paul Stillwell: You were going to tell me about your cruise.

Admiral Erly: Well, we went on youngster cruise, and coming out of youngster cruise, we had a grease mark, which was your aptitude-for-service mark. I stood number six in the class.

Paul Stillwell: That's very impressive.

Admiral Erly: Yes, considering as a second classman I think I stood practically anchor. I had ended up on the *Reina*.[*]

Paul Stillwell: What prompted that?

Admiral Erly: Alcohol.

Paul Stillwell: Do tell. I'm sure the statute of limitations has expired.

---

[*] USS *Reina Mercedes* (IX-25), captured during the Spanish-American War, served as a station ship at the Naval Academy from 1912 to 1957. Until 1940, midshipmen being punished for various disciplinary infractions slept and took meals on board the ship but continued to go to classes ashore.

Admiral Erly: Let's say I had consumed too much alcohol. That was rated as a class A offense, and I ended up with 30 days on the prison ship.

I climbed my way back up my first-class year. I went on the first-class cruise in 1936 and came back pretty well up in aptitude for service. I had a company officer, and I had an experience that I think is comical as I look back on it. When I was starting first class year, I came into the battalion office. After that second-class year had been so bad, the company officer said to me, "How many stripes did you get?" when I was scheduled to be a midshipman ensign in the first set.*

I said, "A midshipman ensign, sir."

He said, "If I had my way, you'd have three diagonals this way," which meant a first classman with second-class privileges.

That was old Hank Burford.† So I started the first-class year with my company officer not one of my strong advocates, but in the third set, I was recommended for midshipman lieutenant, ended up as a midshipman ensign again. So my grease mark first-class year came back, but that damage from the second-class year aptitude-for-service mark had a significant impact on my class standing.

Paul Stillwell: How well did you do in the academics?

Admiral Erly: Horrible. I never took a re-exam. I remember youngster year, I guess it was, I was reading *Gone with the Wind* during study hour, and then Willie Dye would hide the book so I'd study something else.‡ But I really had gotten to the point where I would wait till about ten minutes before we were to leave for class and then rapidly scan the lesson and have to draw a good question when we were told to man the blackboards.§

Paul Stillwell: Why was that, after all this effort you'd made to get into the Naval

---

* In order to provide opportunities to a greater number of midshipmen, the Naval Academy rotated positions so that there were three different "sets" of leaders in the academic year—autumn, winter, and spring.
† Lieutenant William P. Burford, USN.
‡ Margaret Mitchell's sprawling Civil War novel *Gone with the Wind* was published in 1936.
§ The format at that time called for the instructor to hand out questions about the current lesson on slips of paper, which the midshipmen then had to answer on the chalkboard.

Academy?

Admiral Erly: It doesn't make sense, does it?

Paul Stillwell: How would you explain it?

Admiral Erly: Sheer stupidity.

Paul Stillwell: Did you think you had it made?

Admiral Erly: No, not really. Not really. It's hard to believe, but—

Paul Stillwell: Did you pursue boxing here at the Naval Academy?

Admiral Erly: Yes. I was out for the boxing team, but I'd ended up with this [demonstrates].

Paul Stillwell: Your right bicep. What befell you?

Admiral Erly: Well, I had a shoulder separation youngster year. Second-class summer they went in, cut the tendon, drilled a hole through the end of the humerus, and then ran the tendon through. I had gotten my knee hurt also, so as an athlete that pretty well took care of that.

Paul Stillwell: Do you have any recollections of Spike Webb?

Admiral Erly: Oh, God, yes. Don't let me get into the some of the stories about Spike.[*]

Paul Stillwell: Well, please do. That's what we're here for.

---

[*] Hamilton W. "Spike" Webb was involved in Naval Academy athletics from 1919 to 1954, including service for more than 20 years as varsity boxing coach. For more on his history, see Jack Sweetman, *The U.S. Naval Academy: An Illustrated History* (Annapolis: Naval Institute Press, 1979), pages 181-182.

Admiral Erly: [Laughter] Well, I'm trying to think. I made a couple of speed runs with Spike to Baltimore.

Paul Stillwell: What was the purpose of these speed runs?

Admiral Erly: Just to barhop and see what was going on.

Paul Stillwell: Was this part of what led you to the *Reina Mercedes*?

Admiral Erly: No, no. This was after that. No, Spike had nothing to do with getting me to the *Reina Mercedes*. I'd been already. I started going over the wall as a youngster. They had it by the stadium. You'd climb up and down where they used to run the ferry on that one. So I guess as a youngster I started going over the wall and coming back in.

In fact, after the shoulder operation—you don't want to listen to all that crap.

Paul Stillwell: Sure, go ahead.

Admiral Erly: [Laughter] After the shoulder operation second class summer, Willie and I were then over in the third battalion, on the bottom deck, so we decided to French out.* I didn't have full use of this arm in the hospital, so what we did was take down our nameplates, take the mattresses off, and throw them in the vacant room across the hall. We put everything in there so our room appeared to be vacant. So out we'd go, right behind the chapel. We had it rigged so you could unhook that bottom wire. I guess this was about 10:30 at night; it was after taps anyway. Willie had to boost me up, because I only had one arm. So I'd drop on the other side, and when I looked down, and I could see it was an officer out for a walk and headed our way. I was telling Willie, "Hurry up." He was on top of the wall, and I said, "Hurry up! Hurry up!" He finally dropped on the barbed wire, and away we went. We came in just before daybreak and had to reverse the process. He had to get up and unhook and then jump down, get me up, and then I dropped.

---

* "French out" is midshipman slang for leaving the Naval Academy without authorization.

No sooner did I drop than this voice hollered from the other side of the roadway, "Halt!" At this point, where in the hell had we been? We'd been to Baltimore or Washington, I can't remember.

I said, "For Christ's sake, shut up. You'll get the jimmy legs and everybody up."* I walked up, and there was a Marine.

He looked at me and said, "Oh, my God, it's you."

"Yeah," I said, "well, what are you doing here?"

He said, "Well, somebody saw you all go, and they posted a Marine here to get you."

Well, he had been in the hospital when I was over there, and when they would dress my shoulder and he would be in for a dressing, we'd chat a little bit, and the corpsman would give us orange juice laced with a little medicinal alcohol. So he said, "You all get the hell out of here," so we took off, put our nameplates back up, moved our gear back in the room, and were ready to stand morning inspection.

Paul Stillwell: A little tired by the point?

Admiral Erly: Oh, yes, definitely.

Paul Stillwell: Was there some real attraction going on these night jaunts, or was it more the thrill of forbidden fruit?

Admiral Erly: I'd say the thrill of beating the system, so to speak, period.

Paul Stillwell: What could you do between 10:30 and daybreak?

Admiral Erly: I'm trying to remember. We went to Washington, I believe. Where did we go that particular night? I really can't remember.

Paul Stillwell: Did you hitchhike?

---

* "Jimmy legs" was the nickname for the Naval Academy's civilian policemen.

Admiral Erly: Oh, no, we had a car out in town. We had an old beat-up Chevrolet.

Paul Stillwell: Did you wear your uniforms?

Admiral Erly: Oh, no. When you went out, the rig was boxing shoes and dark trousers and a dark shirt so you'd blend with the darkness.

Paul Stillwell: What do you remember about your summer cruises? What ships did you go in?

Admiral Erly: The first one was in the *Arkansas*.[*] It was a great experience, really, because as a third classman you were doing the seaman and fireman work. The regular crew had been reduced. Then the middies, the third class, were basically the non-rated personnel, with the first class being the junior officer concept. So you shined brass, you kept notebooks. When you were in engineering, when you were in gunnery, that type of thing.

I would like to see regular midshipman cruises again, but with our commitment with the Navy today, I don't think that will happen. It also bonded together the classmates. Most importantly, it gave you a sense of appreciation of the men you were going to command later on, because you had to work really closely with the petty officers. You got to know the petty officers and realized that they were so essential to the organization.

Paul Stillwell: It gave you an appreciation also for what that enlisted man had to go through.

Admiral Erly: Oh, absolutely.

---

[*] USS *Arkansas* (BB-33), lead battleship of her class, was commissioned 17 September 1912. Following modernization in 1925-26 she had a standard displacement of 26,100 tons, was 562 feet long and 106 feet in the beam. Her top speed was 21 knots. She was armed with 12 12-inch guns and 16 5-inch guns. She was the oldest U.S. battleship in active service during World War II; she was decommissioned in 1946.

Paul Stillwell: What were the living conditions like on board the *Arkansas*?

Admiral Erly: They had at that point the mess tables stored up in the overhead, and they were lowered and set up for meals. Your group was together for all meals, both first and third classmen. The mess cooks went up to the galley, brought the chow back, and then it was served family style. The dining compartment also served as a sleeping area. As third classmen, of course, we were there, and we swung hammocks. The first classmen were permitted cots. I preferred to sleep outside. I'd normally go out and stake out a spot under one of the seaplanes on the main deck and sort of make my hammock into a sleeping bag.

You had one bucket of water, and then to heat that water you had the steam pipe. You stuck the pipe in your water and heated it from the steam jet. You brushed your teeth, shaved, did your face, and then if you wanted to wash anything else, you did it progressively. They did have the laundry that went out, but you still had to maintain your cleanliness. You wanted to keep your work whites and your inspection whites presentable. You still only had that little locker. They did allow you a big cruise suitcase, I guess what you'd call it, and that could be stowed down below, because your locker was about like this [demonstrates].

Paul Stillwell: Two feet by two feet, maybe.

Admiral Erly: Yes, no more. Just about two feet by two feet, as a third classman. Then you learned to make do. You learned to stand your watches, to be at a certain place at a certain time, and so forth. I thought the cruises were really necessary to drive home what shipboard life was all about.

Paul Stillwell: Did you find yourself enjoying that way of life?

Admiral Erly: Yes, sure did.

Paul Stillwell: Where did the ship go during that cruise?

Admiral Erly: I'm trying to remember. Did we go north first? I know we were in England. I'm trying to keep youngster cruise sorted out from first-class cruise, because we had two, and then second-class summer here. Oh, yes. Well, I'm sure we went north on our youngster cruise. We went into Plymouth, I'm almost sure, and then after England, went on down and came on into the Mediterranean and went along and did Nice, Cannes, Naples, and, of course, we stopped at Gibraltar on the way out.

Paul Stillwell: That's quite a treat for a 20-year-old guy.

Admiral Erly: Yes, you got to see a bit of the world, I must admit. A little bit more of a treat for me, because my mother's sister was married to the mayor of Brighton, which is south and on sea in England. Willie Dye and myself got leave and went down there. Spent three of four days there.

It gave you the opportunity to see the things that you'd read about in history. I'm sure we stopped in at Pompeii in Italy, the Parthenon in Greece. I think naval officers were more cosmopolitan because they'd been exposed a lot more cultures than the average Army officer in the pre-World War II phase. We didn't have all those troops stationed overseas the way they have now. So your average naval officer was much more a sophisticated individual than your average Army type for that reason.

Paul Stillwell: Which ship were you in for the first class cruise?

Admiral Erly: *Oklahoma*, which had reciprocating engines.[*]

Paul Stillwell: What do you remember from your engineering duty on shipboard as a midshipman?

Admiral Erly: That it certainly wouldn't be my choice. Hot going through the airlocks, then standing under the blowers in the firerooms. I was not really too impressed.

---

[*] USS *Oklahoma* (BB-37) was commissioned 2 May 1916. She had a standard displacement of 27,500 tons, was 583 feet long, and 95 feet in the beam. Her top speed was 20.5 knots. Her main battery comprised ten 14-inch guns.

I would have thought that, in looking around, that gunnery and—back to the youngster cruise—in the 12-inch guns, I was a pit powderman. They put the husky guys there, because you were hoisting these bags of powder up to the loading platform. I learned a very, very sharp lesson on that youngster cruise, which I never forgot throughout my naval career. I was a pit powderman, and when those guns elevated, you had to go all the way forward by the elevating screw. It was quite something. When you went in there you were damn careful. They rammed the practice shell into the barrel and then the dummy powder bags. Then they simulated firing.

To remove the shell and powder, the guns were elevated, and the shell and powder backed out. So each time they had to get the dummy load out, you had to get forward. After I'd been doing this for a while, it got more and more commonplace, and I found I could stay in place without going forward. I thought, "Oh, hell, nothing to this." So doing the practice ramming, I would stand below the loading platform and rest my left arm on a ledge. On one occasion of backing out the practice round, I was slow in moving my arm. There was a layer, and there was a ledge in here down under this deal. Well, as the gun was elevating, the first thing I knew, the loading tray support bar came down on my arm. I was going to have an arm in three pieces. But, thank goodness, the alert midshipman on the tray yelled, "Silence," the classic safety command.

Everything stopped. Then they depressed the guns. The injury didn't draw blood, but it really badly bruised that arm. But familiarity breeds contempt, and I don't care what kind of dangerous situation you're in, if you are going to be in and out of that situation, you've got to continually, continually stress constant vigilance. Don't relax when you are in a dangerous situation. If you dope off, you're going to get it, and this I preached to my crews, I preached to my people from then on, and would even cite my personal experience on how you can get trapped, particularly when I was a gun boss.

In those days as a gun boss, before any gunnery exercise you had to read the gunnery safety precautions. That was part of your check-off list. I would be very explicit and say, "Hey, guys, look. Every bloody one of these things is written in blood. That's why they're here, that someone, or quite a few, have been killed, and this is why we have this."

I tried to, if I could, interlace other things, to try to keep people on the step. Safety was one thing I never forgot and I never will. You can be low, and then look out, because in any dangerous situation, and going to sea in itself is dangerous. You'd better be alert and aware of everything that's going on, and don't get lulled into a sense of false security.

Paul Stillwell: Did this other man realize the problem before you did?

Admiral Erly: Yep. I didn't yell, "Silence." I was being forced down this way, and I think he was a second classman by the name of Foote, if I recall.[*]

Paul Stillwell: So he saved your arm?

Admiral Erly: Yep. Saved my arm, saved my career, and I hope in the process made me a much better leader and a proponent of safety, really.

Paul Stillwell: How much interaction did you have with the officers on board the ships during those cruises?

Admiral Erly: As a youngster, minimal. Of course, some of the interaction, some of the schooling was done by the junior officers. My first-class cruise, I remember, little Snuffy Smith, out of '35, had ended up as being out for a short time, damn if he didn't have a turret.[†] As a youngster, I would say minimal. As you came along and, of course, as a first classman much more. You stood watches with the officers and as a third classman, of course, when you were on the deck segment, you might end up doing the ship's bell or making entries in the rough log, whereas as a young first classman, you might even be required to write the log up for the officer of the deck to sign, things of that nature. Also, first classmen could function as division officers of other midshipmen.

---

[*] Probably Midshipman John J. Foote, USN, class of 1935.
[†] Ensign Russell H. Smith, USN, of the *Oklahoma*.

Coming into port, you would be going through the whole drill of the navigation, the plotting, this type of thing. Under way you would be doing celestial navigation. As a third classman, you're really basically performing what you would expect of the deck apes and the snipes. So you get that sense of appreciation, and then on your first-class cruise you were that of the junior officer type.

Paul Stillwell: We talked earlier about getting a sense of values when you were a youngster. What did the Naval Academy do to impart values to you?

Admiral Erly: I think that your word is your bond. That, I think, can sum it up for me.

Paul Stillwell: Not as formal apparently as it became later with the honor code.

Admiral Erly: Well, yes, but there was none in our time frame. The honor code didn't come in till after World Way II or later.

Paul Stillwell: 1950s, I think.*

Admiral Erly: Yes, '50s. But whether it was there or not, there was an unwritten code, so to speak, that you had.

Paul Stillwell: And, interestingly, there was this unwritten code that you would try to beat the system too.

Admiral Erly: Oh, sure. I'm trying to think, with the honor code today, it might be curious to talk to a midshipman. There's a little gal over here I'm going to talk to. She's cuter than a bug's ear, and her dad works with me in the American Cancer Society. I'm going to ask if some of the things that I did, would they be violations of the honor code?

---

* See the Naval Institute oral history of Vice Admiral William P. Lawrence, USN (Ret.). As a midshipman in the class of 1951, he played a prominent role in devising the Naval Academy's honor concept.

Paul Stillwell: That would be intriguing to know.

Admiral Erly: I'm going to do that. I'll bet it would be. I don't know. Because I didn't hurt anyone else. The only one's neck really was on the line was mine, except for that young Marine. I shouldn't have allowed him, as I look back on it, to put his neck on the line for some stupidity of mine.

Paul Stillwell: Was there a perverse pride among those who got sent to the ship?

Admiral Erly: Oh, hell, yes. All you've got to do is look at a *Lucky Bag* and see a black "N" with so many stars, certainly.*

Paul Stillwell: How did you spend your time in the *Reina Mercedes*?

Admiral Erly: I guess studying, talking, beating the system maybe by going to see the movies. I don't know. It went by. You marched, you went to class. You still had your classes. In fact, I guess I ended up studying more than I would have, because I had no outside diversion, so to speak.

Paul Stillwell: What do you remember about the camaraderie of Bancroft Hall?†

Admiral Erly: Oh, well, I think the friendships that you form there last forever, actually. I used to have a lot of fun when I got to be a first classman. I inherited, and I don't know where I got it, a big, old, beat-up French horn. So I would indoctrinate the plebes, and whenever that horn blew, they'd better come en masse. So one of my favorite things was to have somebody come up to the room, a classmate or whatnot, when they'd get ready to

---

* Each year's edition of the Naval Academy yearbook, the *Lucky Bag*, contained a boldface black N next to the photo and biography of each midshipman who had been confined to the station ship *Reina Mercedes* for a time as punishment.
† Bancroft Hall is the large multi-wing dormitory that houses Naval Academy midshipmen. It also contains the offices of members of the executive department, including the commandant, executive officer, and battalion and company officers.

leave, and I'd say, "Just a minute, I'll furnish your transportation." And I'd blow the horn and these plebes would come charging in, and I'd say, "Take him out." [Laughter]

And an interesting sidelight. When I was the western area vice president, I went up to install new officers in San Francisco.

Paul Stillwell: This is for the academy alumni?

Admiral Erly: Yes, Naval Academy Alumni Association. Lo and behold—and I can't remember who it was—they brought a French horn, and so I blew it. It was some of the plebes, I guess, who had remembered it. I'd forgotten it, but they hadn't. So I made some allusion to it, and of all things, I wrote Bill Busik, and I said, "I don't know too much about this honor system, and so forth and so on, and I'm not so sure that a lot of the older alumni, and which the preponderance, or quite a few of them, are up in San Francisco, and I'm going up to install the new alumni officers. I'd like to talk about the honor code."[*]

So he sent me some material, and I prepared something. That's what I talked to them about. There were then some younger officers in the audience, and we got a little question-answer. I'd say, "Okay, you were there and you were in it, now can you answer?" It turned out to be a very lively exchange, and I'm glad I had selected the topic.

Paul Stillwell: You're rare. Most people have much more vivid memories of being victims of this sort of thing rather than the perpetrators of the hazing. What was it like when you were a plebe to be at the receiving end?

Admiral Erly: Well, I sat on infinity, but that didn't bother me. I did pushups. It was all part of a system, what the hell. You blended and you took it, except there was really only one guy ever got to me, but I got back at him on 100th night. This business of that big serving spoon and whopping you with it, which concentrated all the force in a little spot

---

[*] Captain William S. Busik, USN (Ret.), was the executive director (redesignated president and CEO during his tenure) of the Naval Academy Alumni Association from 1971 to 1994.

like so [demonstrates]. Actually, the guy's right up here in Washington now, Doug Fuller, who was a first classman.*

Hundredth night, I took one of those big spoons out of the mess hall, went around and said, "Get your butt in the shower," wet him down, and said, "Take the position," and let him have it.

The guy was great, though. He said, "My God, I'd forgotten how much it hurt." He got the message.

Paul Stillwell: Apparently so.

Admiral Erly: After 100th night, he never hit me, never again, or anyone else. He'd just forgotten it. I never found a sadist, and I wasn't either. The broom bit was part of the whole game.

Paul Stillwell: What extracurricular activities were you in as a midshipman?

Admiral Erly: Basically I was a member of the committee that greeted the incoming visiting teams and sort of got them squared away and saw if they had any needs, this type of thing. I ended up coaching the battalion boxing, and I would help Spike Webb somewhat with the plebe team. One of my plebes was a heavyweight, Tom McGrath, and I'd be in his corner.† Looking back, I would think now what I would have liked to do would to have been in the debating bit like Dick Colbert.‡ I guess they called that the Quarterdeck Society.

Paul Stillwell: I've heard some very impressive things about him. What are your recollections of Colbert?

---

* Midshipman Harold Douglas Fuller, USN, class of 1934.
† Midshipman Thomas D. McGrath, USN, class of 1935.
‡ Midshipman Richard G. Colbert, USN, a classmate of Erly.

Admiral Erly: Well, I think that Dick, again, was one of those who, like Bud, was very gifted when it came to getting up and making a speech.* He really waxed eloquently at the Quarterdeck Society. I remember going and listening to Dick have one, and it was the Gran Chaco War down there between Paraguay and one of the other ones, and he went all through that. He was an imposing individual, just by stature alone, and he had an easy manner about him. He came up, I would say, pretty well with a silver spoon in his mouth. His father was very well off and had yachts and this type of thing. And Dick reflected some of that.

I worked with him when he came back and was deputy at SACLant for a while before he got his fourth star and went over to the Mediterranean as CinCSouth, and that's when I was leaving down there.† Oh, when I first went to Norfolk in '68 as Atlantic fleet inspector general, Dick was there as number three in SACLant. The prime thing that he was doing at that time was working on getting the standing naval force started, in which he did a great job.‡ I listened to him give a presentation up in the Pentagon, when I was in the Pentagon as director of Pan American affairs, when they were getting this thing set up. And through the years our paths have crossed. I was very fond of Dick.

Paul Stillwell: Sounds as if he had an interest in international affairs even as a midshipman.

Admiral Erly: Yes, he did. He started early on. Yes. Yes. Yes.

Paul Stillwell: To wrap up the Naval Academy discussion, how well do you think the education, the training, the instilling of values, and so forth, prepared you for a naval career?

---

* This is a reference to Admiral Elmo R. "Bud" Zumwalt Jr., USN, who served as Chief of Naval Operations, 1970-74.
† Admiral Richard G. Colbert, USN, served as Commander in Chief Allied Forces Southern Europe from May 1972 to November 1973. Before that he was on the staff of the NATO Supreme Allied Commander Atlantic in Norfolk.
‡ Standing Naval Force Atlantic, a multi-national group of ships that operated together under the auspices of NATO. Rear Admiral Richard G. Colbert, USN, initiated the concept paper on the subject in November 1966. NATO approved the concept, and the force of ships was activated in January 1968.

Admiral Erly: Considering what they had to work with, I think they did a hell of a good job. [Laughter]

Paul Stillwell: How many applications did you see later? Did you find shortcomings as the years passed, things that you might have wished for but didn't get?

Admiral Erly: Not really, but one thing that I have found—I'm thinking entropy, I'm thinking some of the steam stuff, some of those things, and I'm thinking Mark's handbook and Hudson's manual, in the fleet, how often, or if ever, were they used. Now, maybe the EDO types, yes, but I'm saying for some of the things that we got, we came out with a bachelor of science degree in electrical engineering.* I'm trying to think, in some of those subjects, was it overdone? Could we have had something else that would have been more meaningful?

How often did I use my slide rule? Not very. I took a torpedo course, yes, and a few other things, but I don't think I can equate that to the Navy that we went to, to the Navy that the youngsters are going to today. It's so much more highly sophisticated, and if you aren't up on your computer sciences, you're going to be behind the eight ball. I'm just trying to think of what subjects would have better prepared me than what I had. Maybe all these things were necessary as a training process.

I felt it was ridiculous when I was a midshipman, from what I saw that people had to do. I had a classmate, Jack Obermeyer, who stood number one in the class, but Obie was a brain to start with.† Hell, he'd been going to Columbia or somewhere and had maybe been there one or two years, yet he was forced to go through the same stuff he'd already been through, which was a waste of time. I strongly endorse what they're doing, and more forward-looking at the academy, that a youngster like Obermeyer could have come in and perhaps at least gone out with a couple of masters or something else, instead of holding him down. I still haven't answered your question, because I really don't know how to reply to what should I have gotten that would have better prepared me for the fleet.

_____
* EDO – engineering duty officer.
† Midshipman Jack A. Obermeyer, USN, stood number one of the 323 graduates in the class of 1937.

Paul Stillwell: Probably it's really not a fair comparison to talk about what they're doing today, because that wasn't the mission then.

Admiral Erly: Yes, but even then, I felt that it was ridiculous for people to have to go back over the same material, particularly when they probably had been Phi Beta Kappa. I think it'd been awful boring if it'd been me in some cases, I would have wondered what I would have done.

Paul Stillwell: Well, apparently, you decided to take that approach, even though you hadn't already had some of those courses. [Laughter]

Admiral Erly: [Laughter] Well, so be it.

Paul Stillwell: How well did the Naval Academy do at making a leader of you to go into the fleet?

Admiral Erly: Can you make a leader?

Paul Stillwell: Well, I don't know. Perhaps. You can emphasize—

Admiral Erly: You can emphasize certain things that a leader should be, but I think it has to come from within, and a leader has to have the desire to excel. A leader has to have some thoughts of what is expected of him as a leader, and to be able to communicate that to the people he's leading. I'm not so sure that the textbook will do it all. I think it has to come within. The fire of that, to make a leader, I think, depends on the individual.

Paul Stillwell: For example, before we started the machine, you were talking about the importance in leadership of taking care of your men, your subordinates. Where did you get that quality?

Admiral Erly: I would have to say the Naval Academy, I'm sure. That's one of the basic tenets; you take care of your troops first.

Paul Stillwell: That is particularly strongly instilled, from what I understand, in the Marine Corps, that you always make sure the enlisted men get fed first and that sort of thing.

Admiral Erly: Well, certainly. Sure. It's the same thing in the Navy, I would say: "Take care of your troops." That's what turned me off. Remember when I said when I went to the *New Mexico*, where I thought the troops were being subjected to really maltreatment, to win a lousy engineering "E."[*]

Paul Stillwell: We didn't get that on the record, so perhaps this would be a good place to insert that, what you encountered on the *New Mexico* to lead you to the conclusion.

Admiral Erly: Well, as a young ensign, first reporting aboard the *New Mexico*, I noticed that we had the engineering "E" and at least one or two hash marks, which meant consecutive winning of engineering excellence award.[†] I was assigned to the fourth division as a JO, and in going through the compartments of the fourth division, and having to make out hull reports and doing everything else, I could see that the lighting, I thought, was inadequate. In the living compartments, I noticed that the showers had been plugged so there was only a trickle of fresh water that would come out of the shower. I thought, "My God, what are we doing here?" It was pretty obvious that to save fresh water, which, in turn, meant that you didn't have to use as much fuel oil to make steam to run through the evaporators to distill your fresh water, that you were going to burn less oil, and therefore would help you on a good engineering score. I thought, what a hell of a way to run a railroad. I was quite perturbed with it.

---

[*] An "E," for excellence, is generally awarded to a ship or component of a ship as a result of top performance in competition with other ships during a given time period.
[†] The battleship *New Mexico* (BB-40) was commissioned 20 May 1918. She had a full-load displacement of 32,000 tons, was 624 feet long, and 97 feet in the beam. Her top speed was 21 knots. She was armed with 12 14-inch guns, 12 5-inch broadside guns, four 3-inch guns, and two 21-inch torpedo tubes. She served through World War II and was eventually decommissioned in 1946.

I was told that this energy-saving concept had come from one Lieutenant Rickover, who had been the assistant engineer and had only recently left from the USS *New Mexico*.* I would imagine a perusal of Rickover's record would show he probably got a letter of commendation for winning an "E." That I don't know, but I would presume, because this is what happened, that he as assistant engineer would have some recognition for that, as would the engineer, and it would also rub off on the captain and the exec. I remember grumbling and saying to myself—and even out loud at times, possibly where I shouldn't have been so outspoken—that the captain, exec, and the chief engineer and the assistant engineer all should be court-martialed for maltreatment of their troops.

Paul Stillwell: I imagine you couldn't say that very loudly.

Admiral Erly: No. [Laughter] But among classmates and other young officers, which brings me up to something else. Maybe not right now, but later we'll get into it from the attack on Pearl, where I was saying, "If we don't get rid of these old goddamned admirals, we're going to lose this goddamned war," which I said, which came back as a quote from me from Admiral Hank Miller.† I was really perturbed on that.

Paul Stillwell: We just jumped briefly there into the *New Mexico*. What do you recall about the graduation ceremony from the Naval Academy and the culmination of your four years' effort here?

Admiral Erly: Well, I guess it was one of sheer exultation that we were now being released from a monastery and were going to go out and become part of mainstream of life.

---

* Lieutenant Hyman G. Rickover, USN. Later, as a flag officer, Rickover ran the Navy's nuclear power program for many years.
† Rear Admiral Henry L. Miller, USN (Ret.), whose oral history is in the Naval Institute collection.

Paul Stillwell: How did you happen to wind up in that particular ship?

Admiral Erly: We were given our chance to select where we wanted to go to, and in talking with officers and looking at the long run for career enhancement, they seemed to think that a flagship was a good place to start for a young officer. I selected *New Mexico* because at that time it supposedly flew the flag of Commander Battleship Division Three; however, it was never aboard while I was aboard. That was one of the reasons I selected the *New Mexico*. Also, the other was, the bigger the ship and with the rotation through the various departments, you'd have a better grounding of what was going on and have a better sense of appreciation for the Navy.

Paul Stillwell: What were the perceived advantages of being in a flagship?

Admiral Erly: Perceived advantages were, I guess, that you were going to see a ship kept sharper and more on its toes, more attention to detail and these things than you would experience on another one. In other words, it was something that you should experience and learn what happens to prepare you for later on in your career where possibly a flag would be embarked in some ship that you commanded.

Paul Stillwell: Of course, with the advantage of hindsight, some of the things that seemed so important in the late '30s didn't prove important at all when the war came.

Admiral Erly: That's correct. A lot of the attention on the spit and polish in some cases went by the board, but in many cases, I'm saying that what we did in damage control and going through the weekly inspection of hull fittings and watertight closures and all these things that we were practicing then well paid off during the later years. But the flag wouldn't see that unless you were programmed for an inspection. Remember, we still had the basic inspections that went on for a young division officer, and particularly the JO in the division.[*]

---

[*] JO – junior officer.

Paul Stillwell: What sort of assignment did you get when you reported to your first ship?

Admiral Erly: In the *New Mexico* I was very, very fortunate, because I had a lieutenant (junior grade) as my boss, and he didn't like to do certain things. I'm getting away from the flagship now and back into being a JO. We had turret four, which meant we had the after catapult that the seaplanes were on. He didn't like to catapult, nor did he like to bring them back in on cast recovery.*

Paul Stillwell: That gave you something to do.

Admiral Erly: Well, sure. That was fine. I volunteered, and when I volunteered, he readily acquiesced to both. So I felt very fortunate. The guy just stepped back and let me do these things. I found it very broadening. I was a year, I guess, in turret four. We put an "E" on the turret and we had the port side of the quarterdeck aft. It was a great experience.

In addition to my division assignment, when I got aboard the *New Mexico*, I had to keep a journal, and that stimulated the learning process. You learned damage control, because as the JO, and you had a division officer, and the division officer wasn't going to go around and check all the fittings and make the whole report, so you did that.

Then you were rotated. I was rotated down into the engineering, where I was in B division. I crawled boilers, I helped punch tubes. I water tended, because these are some of the things that you had done on a midshipman cruise, which you've got to remember that some people hadn't done.† But as a young JO, I figured that to do hands-on, to really understand what you're doing, so if you ever have to tell somebody what you're doing, then you know what you're telling them. The same way of punching tubes. You want to be there.

I'm trying to remember the fourth division. We had a first-class boatswain's mate on there by the name of Solar. A DE is named after him. I've forgotten where, but he

---

* "Cast," which represented the letter C in the phonetic alphabet of the time, designated a recovery method whereby the airplane landed on the water, rode up on a sea sled, and was lifted aboard by a crane on the ship's fantail.
† Water tending involved making sure the boilers were operating properly and had sufficient feedwater to make steam.

was killed.* I learned a lot from him, some of the other ones. Even then, though, I was just thinking, a young division officer, and you watch, you don't get the attention to detail unless somebody checks. For a Saturday inspection, in the waterways along the side, I had to go along and, boy, here's a swab, would be part of one of the details. Even with Solar as the first-class boatswain's mate, say, "Hey, hey, look. Come on now." I learned early on that even though you had a lot of the experts, and you can learn from them, but again, attention to detail has got to be there. It's not going to happen automatically. Unless there's a demand and you continually insist, it isn't going to get done. So I found that being that JO in the fourth division paid off well for me.

Also, when I got orders to *Conyngham*, my classmates, Harvey Lanham, Roger Mehle, and all the rest of them, said, "Now that you're leaving, Bob, maybe we can get a decent fitness report."†

I started an exercise program in the ship. I got the boxing team going. I would have smokers. I'd have boxing before the movies. I did a lot of things in that ship as a young ensign that hadn't been done, and it was appreciated by the captain and the exec and, of course, reflected in my fitness report. In those days, we were on probation, and at the end of two years, your fitness reports were used as a basis and you'd jump numbers. I jumped numbers. I had done very, very well as a young ensign. Was it two years or three years?

Paul Stillwell: I think it was two, yes. That's when the prohibition against marriage expired also.

Admiral Erly: That's right. Yes. Yes.

Well, again, a selection of a battleship in those days was considered—and would you believe it or not, my gun boss whom I worked for, turned out to be the man who was

---

* The destroyer escort *Solar* (DE-221), commissioned in 1944, was named for Boatswain's Mate First Class Adolfo Solar, who was killed in action while serving on board the battleship *Oklahoma* (BB-37) when she was attacked at Pearl Harbor on 7 December 1941.
† Ensign Harvey P. Lanham, USN; Ensign Roger W. Mehle, USN.

my battalion officer at the academy. That was L. P. Padgett, whom we affectionately called "Flangehead."* [Laughter]

Paul Stillwell: Doesn't sound too affectionate to me.

Admiral Erly: Well, since I got fried on that drinking charge, it used to give me great pleasure to go to Lieutenant Commander Padgett's house out there in Long Beach.† We'd have some drinks and dinner, and he'd want to wrestle, and I could deck him. [Laughter] I would say, "Yeah, this is the guy that fried me." Not really, but he was a great guy. I really admired Lem. We'd be sitting in the JO mess, and a cap would come sailing through the door, and a voice said, "We challenge you for deck tennis," and that was with the quoits. He was really a great guy. I have fond memories of him.

We used to have what they called tactical school in the wardroom. A couple of times I was late, so he looked up one day as I came in, the same old play that you would expect with my name: "If Ensign Erly is late, he's going to be the late Mr. Erly." [Laughter] He was a great shipmate, really. I was quite impressed. And Lem Massey was there.‡ He was the senior aviator.

Paul Stillwell: Was he flying the SOCs?§

Admiral Erly: Yes. I went up with him. Because I was catapulting people off. God, I went up with Lem, and I'll never forget, here I was in the after cockpit, and a damn smoke bomb got loose, so I have to hold it in my feet—there was nowhere I could put it—until we had landed. [Laughter] That was one reason I put in for aviation. I was quite impressed with the aviators that I saw, with what I thought was their approach to

---

* Lieutenant Commander Lemuel P. Padgett Jr., USN.
† In the 1930s most of the fleet's battleships were home-ported at Long Beach, California.
‡ Lieutenant Lance E. Massey, USN, was officer in charge of Observation Squadron Three on board the *New Mexico*. He was killed in action as commanding officer of Torpedo Squadron Three during the Battle of Midway in 1942.
§ The Curtiss-built SOC Seagull was a biplane that first entered fleet squadrons in 1935, primarily in a floatplane version to perform observation and scouting missions for battleships and cruisers.

life and that type of thing.

Paul Stillwell: What about their approach to life appealed to you?

Admiral Erly: They seemed friendlier, not as reserved and stiff. Well, of course, they were younger too. When I'm saying that, I'm thinking of Ransom Fullinwider.* Wilbur Wright was another, a great guy.† I liked Wilbur, and he was quite senior to some of them. I guess it was youth, and therefore being younger, they could better relate to the younger JOs than some of the older ones. Although Wilby, I thought, did well, and Simpson, who was a juvenile at heart, was there.‡

I was just thinking some of the officers that made the big imprint. Lem was one, and he would have us out to the house, and it completes the circle. Lem Massey Jr., I recommended for the yacht club in Coronado. He's retired out there. I can tell him stories of his father, and I remember the son when he was about like so. So it's that camaraderie that I recall. We had a great JO mess.

Paul Stillwell: Was there any regret leaving there to go to the wardroom?

Admiral Erly: I never went to the wardroom. See, I didn't graduate up to the wardroom because I left in November of '38 to go to *Conyngham*.

Paul Stillwell: What sorts of things happened in the JO mess that you remember so fondly?

Admiral Erly: Oh, well, of course, you had acey-deucey games, you had the cribbage games, and the joshing that went on at meals and this type of thing.§ I was very fortunate there. I never got elected mess caterer for the simple reason I said, "Hey guys, you want

---

* Lieutenant Ransom Fullinwider, USN.
† Lieutenant William D. Wright Jr., USN.
‡ Lieutenant Rodger W. Simpson, USN, was the ship's communication officer.
§ Acey-deucy is a variation of the board game backgammon.

to elect me? I'm running for office. Elect me, because you're going to get rice and curry seven days a week." And they knew I wasn't joking.

Paul Stillwell: Why would you do that?

Admiral Erly: Well, because I really liked rice and curry. When the warrant officers' mess would have it, the stewards would go get me a ration. When the wardroom would have it, they'd go get me a ration, and when we had it, they knew it, and everyone knew that I really, dearly loved rice and curry. So I escaped that onerous job.

Paul Stillwell: Not too many people welcome that job.

Admiral Erly: Well, actually, people will like it once a month or something like that, but then you had that one or two persons in our mess—I guess we had around 30-some-odd in that mess—who did not want it in any way. You know, we're talking East Indian, with so-many-boy curry. They then would have scrambled eggs or something. There were one or two in the mess that just wouldn't take it.

Paul Stillwell: Did members of the JO mess go on liberties together?

Admiral Erly: Oh, yes.

Paul Stillwell: What were some of the attractions?

Admiral Erly: Well, let's see. The Pike was one spot, and then of course there was Hollywood up the way.* I'm just trying to think. Let's see. Margie Weaver at this point had married K. G. Did K. G. talk about Margie?

---

* The Pike was a popular amusement park near the fleet landing in Long Beach.

Paul Stillwell: Yes, and I heard from Slade Cutter the fascinating story about when K.G. got out of prison camp and found out that Marjorie Weaver was married to somebody else, and went to see her.*

Admiral Erly: Yes. Well, I guess they'd given him up.

Paul Stillwell: Apparently so.

Admiral Erly: Well, whereabouts are we at this point?

Paul Stillwell: We're talking about your liberty experiences in Hollywood.

Admiral Erly: Yes, we'd go up there. Marjorie was living with Judy. Tommy King was dating Judy, so we'd go up and go to some of the spots around Hollywood.† A lot of times we drove back in that cotton-picking fog to get to the ship. The other thing was the Pacific Coast Club in Long Beach, which we all belonged to. It was a great hangout. And then, maybe in the first year they were in the fleet, they all started a Navy club out there, and paid dues and this type of thing. It was in an old mansion right on the beach down towards Belmont Shores. A lot of time was spent there as a hub of activities.

Paul Stillwell: Sounds like an exciting, enjoyable life.

Admiral Erly: Oh, it was. It was. It was so enjoyable that I found that most of my ensign's magnificent salary of really 125 bucks a month plus 18 for subsistence was going into the Pacific Coast Club.

Paul Stillwell: It must have been one of the appeals of aviation, then, to get more money.

---

* Slade D. Cutter and Kenneth G. Schacht were submariners from the Naval Academy class of 1935. In March 1942, upon the sinking of the submarine *Perch* (SS-176), Schacht was captured and spent the remainder of the war as a prisoner of the Japanese. He had been married to Hollywood actress Marjorie Weaver in the late 1930s. In 1943 she married businessman Don Briggs when Schacht was still a prisoner. See the Naval Institute oral history of Captain Slade D. Cutter, USN (Ret.).
† Ensign Thomas Starr King Jr., USN, was in the crew of the *New Mexico*.

Admiral Erly: [Laughter] Yes. Exactly. I'm sure that's why a lot of people went into aviation, for more money.

Paul Stillwell: You mentioned the things that you did with Solar to keep him on his toes. What did you learn from him?

Admiral Erly: A respect for petty officers. In other words, I wouldn't go below the chain of command. Be careful of that, very, very careful. Stay in the chain of command. Don't break it.

Paul Stillwell: What do you remember about the quality of the enlisted men in that ship?

Admiral Erly: Oh, we had some real pros, and also you saw at this phase—this was now '37-'38—you were seeing people come in there with one, two years of college. For new inputs they weren't taking anyone in without a high school degree. So from what I saw and what further proved out after the war, with this hard core of your petty officers that had come in in this time frame during the Depression, that you had people that came to the top and became officers, which in some ways was just great, but in other ways, you sort of emasculated that hard core of professionals at that level. Then you found that you were having chiefs with four years' service.

Paul Stillwell: But trained by these prewar guys, though. So they had that benefit.

Admiral Erly: In some ways I wonder how much we lost by putting them up into the officer ranks. A lot of them, by choice, reverted back to chief at the end of the war. Some opted to go on. I'm remembering when I got to be exec of the "Yo-yo," *Yosemite*, I had chiefs coming out of my ears. Some of them had been officers and had reverted. I'd say the years of experience and what was coming in, the input that we were getting before, due to the Depression, really gave us that hard core we could pull on when we needed it for the rapid expansion we went through.

I just told you about getting a chief with four years, and then all of a sudden, it flashed through my mind, that you were getting a commander in eight, whereas the senior lieutenant, when I went to the battleship, had about ten years.

Paul Stillwell: I would have guessed even more than that.

Admiral Erly: Could be. Maybe you've got a better feel for that than I and my memory, but I'm trying to think. Ransom Fullinwider was class of 1926. Hede was class of '25, and I was '37, so we're looking at 11 and 12 years' difference.* These senior lieutenants had been in the fleet more than ten years, and with no prospect around the corner at that phase of being lieutenant commander.

Paul Stillwell: What do you remember about the business of making formal calls on your seniors?

Admiral Erly: I, again, thought that was an excellent idea. It gave you a chance to see your senior in a different setting. I think it also took some of the rough spots off of a young fellow doing the calling and so forth, to make him at ease with those above him. I think it's a great idea, and I would like to see the Navy continue it, and I'm not so sure they are on this business of leaving cards. I would like to see some of that go back, because I get the feel that some of these things are just going by the board.

Paul Stillwell: Well, that is certainly one of them.

Admiral Erly: I, in fact, have been a little aghast to go to a formal dinner, what we call June Week West, we have out there during June, with some of these youngsters coming in an open shirt and practically shorts for a formal sit-down dinner.† Now, damn it, they ought to know better.

---
* Lieutenant Adolph Hede, USN.
† June Week was the term at the time for the collection of festivities surrounding the graduation and commissioning of the first classmen. Naval Academy classes now graduate in late May during what is known as Commissioning Week.

One thing I do like which we didn't have then, they have formal mess nights, which are good. That I heartily endorse, but I'd like to see some of the others. I feel in some ways, too, that I had something to do with what goes on after watching the Army and the long grey line and what they did at one of their ceremonies. I wrote to Tom Moorer and, said for Navy Day, "Hey, you know what? We're looking too far out. Let's look inward. Let's look inward and among ourselves and have these mess nights and this type of thing."[*]

Paul Stillwell: Certainly the Marine Corps makes more of that than the Navy does.

Admiral Erly: The Navy is coming along, because when I was in Portugal, this thing came out from Chinfo saying, "Hey, celebrate and so forth."[†] It cited the context and the way to go, and it cited my recommendation to Moorer in that, and it has basically gone that way, to look and reevaluate ourselves and our pride in ourselves, and keep that flowing down a long blue line. The Army does it well, the West Pointers, because I happened to sit on one up north when I was in PhibLant.[‡]

Paul Stillwell: What specific memories do you have of the CO and XO of the *New Mexico*?

Admiral Erly: In my case, because I got what I wanted from them, one was to get the program going, I got the boxing team revved up, I got the exercise schedule going when we had everybody at quarters, they supported me wholeheartedly. I had read in the Naval Institute *Proceedings* an article about the facilities available up in the Puget Sound area, and the *New Mexico* was scheduled to go up there for overhaul. One was an old mine depot which had a barracks and galley and this type of thing. So I went and said, "I think that once we get there, to keep the crew off the streets of Washington and getting in trouble, I recommend that you give me a cadre that I can go over, and let's request this

---
[*] Admiral Thomas H. Moorer, USN, served as Chief of Naval Operations from 1 August 1967 to 1 July 1970. His oral history is in the Naval Institute collection.
[†] Chinfo–Chief of the Office of Information, basically the Navy's public relations and media relations arm.
[‡] PhibLant – Amphibious Force, Atlantic Fleet.

camp. I'll have a basic cadre there, and every Friday I will load up a couple of hundred men and take them over there and for the weekend where we will play softball, pitch horseshoes." And for those that wanted, I programmed to go over to Bainbridge Island to a place where they had a Scottish dance on the weekends.

So my weekends, when we were up there, were basically getting these people and taking them over there and watching them eat and feed and swim and have a ball, without being out exposed to all the other things that were available. I got supported in that. So anything I asked for, I pretty well got, because, again, what I was doing was looking out for the crew. I think that got appreciated. It was Walter Jacobs and "Jig-Jig" Brown, J. J. Brown.*

Paul Stillwell: What do you remember about the formal athletic competitions among ships?

Admiral Erly: Intense. [Laughter] Intense. Particularly the football and the boxing, because I became one of the fleet referees. If they'd have it on one of the other battlewagons, those of us who were in it would go and referee fights. I did it in the Y, on the beach, and if they had it on the ship, I'd go. So a lot of times my weekends were taken up doing those types of things.

Again, let's see. After I'd gotten to the *Conyngham*, along came a letter from the skipper of the *New Mexico* saying, "We, *New Mexico*, so and so, on such and such and such weight and so forth and so on, and Ensign Erly as the coach and so forth and so on, is to be congratulated." You know, that was the stuff, and that got included, I'm sure, in my fitness report somewhere. I never bothered to look for it, but it got included as a commendatory sort of thing.

Paul Stillwell: This builds up spirit of the ship's crew too.

---

* Captain Walter F. Jacobs, USN, served as commanding officer of the *New Mexico* from December 1937 to June 1939; Commander John J. Brown, USN, was the executive officer.

Admiral Erly: Oh, sure, intense. Not only that, but betting went on on the side, I'm sure. I never did it, but it was there. I'm sure there were, that thing.

Paul Stillwell: One thing that particularly fostered that was the Battenberg Cup race for the pulling whaleboats.

Admiral Erly: Oh, yes. And then the sailing bit, the sailing whaleboat. We used to have the races. I raced as coxswain of the *New Mexico* deal. That was a lot of fun, really, the sports, all of this, and you can see the good of it for ship's spirit.

What you had to watch, though, just like anything else, was that you couldn't bend too far over backwards, because, for those who were the non-athletes, you didn't want to keep them out, but you wanted them cheering the people on. You didn't want to be too flagrant in saying the athletes got extra privileges, because one of the extra privileges was that they used to leave the ship at 1:00 o'clock to go practice. That's football and so, but that was their duty.

Paul Stillwell: It can be resented by the guys who have to carry their shipboard load.

Admiral Erly: Yes, yes, and at times I think the first lieutenant grumbled a few times when I was taking this work force off the ship. We were leaving on a Friday early afternoon and coming back about mid-forenoon on Monday.

Paul Stillwell: He didn't have much choice, really.

Admiral Erly: No, not with the captain and the exec. Walter Jacobs had come on board as a new captain. The ensigns were required to call on him in his shipboard quarters. I went in and was introduced and we were talking, "Well, what do you think of so and so?"

I said, "Well, Captain, there's one thing and I really think we ought to go for," and that's when I banged him with the ship going up for overhaul, that we should do something for the crew and that I would like to get a letter off and reserve that to make sure we had it when we got there.

Paul Stillwell: What do you remember about the overhaul itself and the time spent at Bremerton?*

Admiral Erly: Again, that's one of those things that you encounter. It's a continual battle for two things: safety and cleanliness. Once you get in a yard atmosphere and you get all that clutter, it's so easy to fall in with, "This is the way it is," instead of saying, "It can't be this way." It becomes a continual thing that you have to watch.

I also really was up there to make sure I'd go out and run with my boxing team early in the morning, and then in the afternoon work out at the local Y. I remember that very vividly, being part of a routine, in addition to the weekends off at this old mine depot.

Paul Stillwell: I can see morale is a real tough problem when you've got the ship all torn up like that.

Admiral Erly: Sure. Well, any time that you interfere with set routines, you're bound to have people upset, and it makes it tougher. Of course, when you're in dry dock, in some cases you don't have the head services aboard ship, and these are limited, and other things are also. When the ship went in dry dock, everybody, including the ship's cooks, had to go down and scrape the ship's bottom.

In an all-hands maneuver, the division that could do the most and do it fastest and safest was the winner. A lot of it was good to bond people together. I just wonder in my own mind, when you talk bonding, in the bigger ships you've got to have some central activity to pull them together. Of course, the division being core number one, and even in those days, at Christmastime, what they would do was unbelievable. At this point they'd let them bring furniture in. You should have seen some of the crews' living compartments and the way they were decorated. I hope you've got that recorded in other histories.

Paul Stillwell: I don't, so I'd appreciate your description.

---

* Puget Sound Navy Yard, Bremerton, Washington.

Admiral Erly: Well, you take a cold, bare compartment with mess tables from the overhead, and all of a sudden you come into a gracious salon or living room, which was again a big morale factor at Christmas. The kids would pool their money, and you would see, again, that division competition. Not only ship competition, you had division competition, who could be best, and this was part of it.

Today there is no way you could do it, because berthing compartments aren't made up today as division messes also. It was something else for that division unity in a larger ship. They messed together. Again, your petty officers were there with the non-rated men, and they broke bread together.* Today with the mess lines and whatnot, t'ain't so. I think you got your first class off somewhere, then you've got your chiefs off somewhere, and the first thing you know, then the second class want their niche. But with the old division messes, that was a welding, and you really found division loyalty. You really did.

Paul Stillwell: That was the core unit.

Admiral Erly: Yes, sure. It really was, and there it was. You had three meals a day—together, everybody there except the chiefs. You had your first class, see, and old Papa Solar was the leading boatswain's mate.

Paul Stillwell: Another difference was that fewer were married.

Admiral Erly: Exactly. They couldn't afford to be married. What the hell were they getting—about 32 bucks a month? Or maybe less at that phase. As an ensign, I was drawing $125.00 base; what were they drawing base? And you couldn't get married even as a second class, without your CO's permission?

There was that type of a thing in there also. As we mentioned earlier, in our group of junior officers, you were on probation, couldn't get married for two years, although people did. Slade Cutter, for one, got away with it.† I've got a couple of

---

* Non-rated men are those who have not yet advanced to petty officer.
† Cutter discussed his early marriage in his oral history.

classmates who got away with it, and I've got a couple of classmates that had their commissions rescinded on account of it.

Paul Stillwell: But because they weren't married, the ship was their home.

Admiral Erly: Oh, absolutely. The same thing, again, for the young ensigns, the ship was home. Then we had time to work on our notebooks, and each place again, when you're in the gunnery department you had a gunnery notebook that you were working on. Engineering the same thing. You'd go to a movie. The ship was your home, your life. Really.

Paul Stillwell: It was a very paternalistic system.

Admiral Erly: Oh, sure.

Paul Stillwell: Anything you needed was supplied.

Admiral Erly: And with a flourish. You got your shoes shined, you got your bunk made up, you got your laundry taken, you were served three meals a day. If you wanted a snack, it was available. The whole thing was right there.

Paul Stillwell: How would you compare your personal bunking situation as an ensign in *New Mexico* with what it had been as a midshipman on the *Arkansas* where you had the hammock on deck and the bucket of water?

Admiral Erly: Well, it was the difference between daylight and darkness, the comparison. You go from the sublime to the ridiculous. Well, actually, I had a stateroom with two bunks in it, but I was the only one there. So I had beaucoup room.

Paul Stillwell: And a steward to clean up and make the bed.

Admiral Erly: Oh, sure. Make the bed. Absolutely. Take the laundry. Take your clothes for pressing, this type of thing. Shine your shoes. Indeed.

Paul Stillwell: What do you remember about the Marine detachment on board?

Admiral Erly: Well, again, there was another entity, and the competition to see who could be the better. They manned certain guns, and they wanted to have more E's than the bluejackets did. I didn't see any disharmony with the Marines, and I think that the Marines on board enjoyed it. They manned the 5-inch secondary battery guns; I used to check-sight some of their firings as a safety officer.

Paul Stillwell: In retrospect, the antiaircraft protection on those ships was not very impressive.

Admiral Erly: No. No, it's a wonder that they hit anything. They were 3-inch guns, and they could really bark. That's probably why I've got bum hearing, from check-sighting those guns. It was just like you were getting slapped in the face. Wham! Wham! A very sharp crack.

My brother-in-law had devised a system of setting up a pre-conceived barrage against incoming aircraft. This required that the fuzes be preset.

No, when you consider what's available today, or even what became available with the 40-millimeter and the 20 and the 5-inch/38—

Paul Stillwell: The proximity fuze.[*]

Admiral Erly: And the proximity fuze, yes. It's all the difference.

---

[*] Dr. Merle A. Tuve was instrumental in the development of the proximity fuze for 5-inch antiaircraft projectiles. It was also known as the VT, or variable time fuze. For a detailed account, see Buford Bowland and William R. Boyd, *U.S. Navy Bureau of Ordnance in World War II* (Washington, D.C.: U.S. Government Printing Office, 1953), pages 271-290.

Paul Stillwell: With that mechanical time fuze before the war, you just had to sort of set it and hope that the plane would be where it went off.

Admiral Erly: You would hope that the plane hadn't changed course, that you had properly tracked him, and the computer had turned it out that your lead time and time of flight and all of these are cranked in for that thing to go. Yes.

Paul Stillwell: What do you recall about the turret fire from your experience in that, and the main battery fire control?

Admiral Erly: Main battery plot was manned by an ordnance postgraduate gunner, and the ensigns who were part of his crew stood high academically. I never got near flag plot or main battery plot. [Laughter] Although I was always on the firing string as a trainer, it was sort of match or follow a system—

Paul Stillwell: Unfortunately, the tape recorder can't see what your hands are doing, so maybe you could describe that in words.

Admiral Erly: Well, when you're training those big turrets, see, these were 14-inch guns three of them in a turret, and you had a certain amount of slack. And, of course, the ship was moving and the target was moving, so you had to be real sure and steady as you kept coming. You didn't want to get too far ahead, and then going back, you wanted to be a slow, steady right on and hold it as best as you could to give the pointer a chance, too, as he was doing this to fire. It was great. I was always on the pre-firing string to calibrate. We'd go out for the short-range battle practice and see what the system was. You always had what they called that first run with an officer pointer trainer.

Paul Stillwell: Are there any specific incidents that you recall from the short-range or long-range battle practices when you were an ensign?

Admiral Erly: No, except you went and observed. They sent observers to you, and I would be on the firing string as a pointer trainer. Then as young ensigns we were down in the lower magazines, making sure the powder bags were delivered to the guns. That's where you ended up as a JO in a turret. So you were really down below on those runs, and you were pretty damn well limited. But you wanted to be sure that when the guns were firing that the interlocks were working in case there was a flareback or whatnot, so there would be no way the flame was going to get down to the powder bags in the magazine and blow up the turret.

Paul Stillwell: Safety was number one.

Admiral Erly: Yes.

Paul Stillwell: Especially from that experience you'd already had as a midshipman.

Admiral Erly: As a pit powderman.

Paul Stillwell: I came across a piece of paper recently from about 1938, as it happened. It said that the ships of the *New Mexico* class had an advantage in war games in not having the twin fire-control tops, because when they were hull down, it was more difficult to tell which direction they were going.

Admiral Erly: That's right, because she had the tripod mast. Okay. Yes, the *New Mexico*, *Idaho*, and *Mississippi* had that conversion done in Philadelphia Navy Yard. I remember seeing a battleship—I think it was *New Mexico*—because I used to go for my drills at the shipyard.* That's where the reserve unit drilled. I remember this battleship cut clear back to the main deck, and then they came up new with the tripod, just the forward spotting and control station.

---

* The Philadelphia Navy Yard modernized the *New Mexico* from 1931 to 1933.

Paul Stillwell: Visual was so much more important for fire control then, for the obvious reason that you didn't have radar.

Admiral Erly: You better believe it. But of course, the plane supposedly could be able to spot you over or under the target, but it was a Mark II, Mod II, eyeball all the way, for your range finder operators. Of course, when I was gun boss on the destroyer, it was the same thing—Mark II, Mod II eyeball.

When you would come in—we're getting a little ahead of it—in a destroyer, a night attack on the battle line simulated torpedo attack, Mark II, Mod II, eyeball, and all back emergency full. In fact, I remember on the *New Mexico*, I thought, "Isn't this great," watch those boys flash by, the small boys coming in. She backed down a couple of times on one of these things, it was that close.

Paul Stillwell: They hadn't broken off soon enough, I take it.

Admiral Erly: Well, how do you break off, and which way do you go? No one's got a plot. This ship here, this ship here. It's a wonder that there weren't collisions.

Paul Stillwell: What do you remember about night operations in that ship?

Admiral Erly: Well, again, it was the constant steaming. Are you talking darkened ship, or are you just talking night operations or just steaming? Are you talking wartime war games?

Paul Stillwell: Fleet problems, war games.

Admiral Erly: Yes, on a fleet problem, lookouts again were the eyeballs, and as a JO, of course, you were learning to do, in some cases, position-keeping with your binoculars, how much the field as being filled up. In those days, the ships were still steaming as part of a battleship division, and they might be in line. You were mainly concerned in maintaining position. Normally, as a JO, you ended off watch with your thumb up like this and your hand like that in a vise, because you were standing and taking stadimeter readings.* You quickly learned not to make any great changes in speed. You've got a tendency going, and then you sort of broke it to the officer of the deck, "We're drifting aft, we're drifting aft." You didn't tell him, "We've lost 400 yards," or anything like that. You got it in steps. [Laughter]

Paul Stillwell: Because that would indicate you hadn't been paying attention.

Admiral Erly: No, no, it was just that it got people all exercised, and you pretty well had a tendency which way it was going, and so you just eased the strain. You took part of that responsibility and strain on yourself; let's put it that way.

Paul Stillwell: How much did you learn about watch standing in that ship?

Admiral Erly: [Laughter] I'll never forget. Frank Jack Fletcher was the skipper.† I was the JO on the bridge, and the signal came out to cast to port. Old Frank Jack said, "Now, what in the hell does the batdiv commander mean?"

I said, "Well, sir . . ."

That wasn't it. What he was doing was questioning why he wasn't casting to starboard. I was going to tell him what cast to port meant.

Paul Stillwell: You were taking him literally.

Admiral Erly: Yes, I took him literally, but then I realized that, in fact, what he was asking. Laughter]

Paul Stillwell: Do you have any other memories of Fletcher?

---

* The stadimeter is a mechanical device for measuring the range to another ship when the height of her mast is known.
† Captain Frank Jack Fletcher, USN, commanded the *New Mexico* in from June 1936 to December 1937. He was later a prominent flag officer in World War II.

Admiral Erly: Yes. Well, of course I was impressed with him. Didn't he have a Medal of Honor from Veracruz, as I recall?*

Paul Stillwell: He and many others did, yes.

Admiral Erly: Yes, I know. Okay. Well, that very impressed the young ensign to see the Medal of Honor. Of course, I realized, as you say, quite a few got it for nothing. He impressed me as the veritable old sea dog. He really did. And he was, I thought, a good ship handler, from what I saw. He knew what it was all about, and I thought in his own way, interested in his young officers.

Paul Stillwell: What sort of personality did he have?

Admiral Erly: I didn't get to know Frank Jack as well as I did Walter Jacobs. I'm trying to remember how long Frank Jack was there; maybe he was only there about four or five months after I arrived. Except at ship's parties, I had a drink with him at the bar. I didn't get any sea stories from him, per se. I remember calling on him, but at this phase I was sort of feeling my way as the new kid on the block, along with the other group of ensigns.

Paul Stillwell: He got sort of a knock in World War II for being too cautious.

Admiral Erly: Yes, I read that. I have not formed a judgment on whether he did right or whether he did wrong, or whether he wasn't aggressive enough or whatever.

Paul Stillwell: There's sort of a revisionist view that's restoring his reputation on the ground that nobody knew all that much about how to operate carriers at that phase of the

---

* In April 1914 a U.S. Navy paymaster was detained ashore in Veracruz, Mexico. Rear Admiral Henry T. Mayo, USN, demanded an apology and amends. The situation worsened when a German ship approached with guns and ammunition for the Mexican government. The result was that a landing force of U.S. Marines and sailors went ashore at Veracruz on 21 April and fought a series of gun battles with Mexicans.

war, and it's hard to fault a surface officer, especially, who was thrust into that position.*

Admiral Erly: Well, that could well be. As I say, my impression of him, he was a good prototype, to my mind, of what a seagoing skipper should be. How he was going to do in flag rank and running a fleet were something else.

Paul Stillwell: What about Captain Jacobs? What are your recollections of him?

Admiral Erly: Well, a warmer personality, but you've got to remember that he had two daughters. [Laughter] And his wife. And the JOs flocked around more Captain Jacobs's house than Frank Jack.

Paul Stillwell: Did the daughters wind up marrying any of the ship's JOs?

Admiral Erly: No, I don't believe. I don't believe. But they were dated. In fact, there were two; one had been divorced and was home again.

Paul Stillwell: Anything else to finish up *New Mexico* before we move on to the destroyer *Conyngham*?

Admiral Erly: I remember *New Mexico* was involved in an amphibious landing off Lahaina Roads—a disaster.†

Paul Stillwell: When was that?

Admiral Erly: That had to be the summer of '38.

---

* John B. Lundstrom, *Black Shoe Carrier Admiral: Frank Jack Fletcher at Coral Sea, Midway, and Guadalcanal* (Annapolis: Naval Institute Press, 2006). Vice Admiral served as Commander Task Force Six for the Solomons operation in the summer of 1942. For a discussion of his role at Guadalcanal, see John B. Lundstrom, "Frank Jack Fletcher Got a Bum Rap," *Naval History*, Fall 1992, pages 22-28.

† Lahaina Roads is an area off the Hawaiian island of Maui. The U.S. Fleet often used it as an exercise area and anchorage in the years prior to World War II.

Paul Stillwell: What was disastrous about the landing?

Admiral Erly: Well, you went in, and you had that surf coming up on the beach there. Even though you rigged canvas on the stern of the motor launches, you got in there, and the way to hang onto a beach, you had to keep that engine driving and holding her in there. But we broached a motor launch, and then the only thing we could salvage out of it, we finally ended up was getting the engine out.

Those were the landing craft. That was how you were going to land the Marines on a landing. Our landing party per se composed of bluejackets and Marines. This was a holdover, as we were discussing earlier, from Veracruz days of 1914. Everybody had a landing party; they had an artillery piece. We'd go out to San Clemente and take the kids on the firing range out there and have them shoot the rifles and try to get them qualified and instructed, so that your landing force really was a landing force in fact.[*] Basically, your parade units, too, some of the ships we would also parade our landing force, when we would go up and down the coast—remembering again, we were still in Depression.

During the summer months they would take the battleships, and they would all go to various and different ports of call. I remember even going into Santa Barbara and dropping the pick off of there and sending people and then having visitors aboard. Up into San Francisco, all the way up to Seattle. In those days we would parade. The city officials or whatever group would put on a naval military ball, and all the officers would turn out in their dress railroad trousers and this, and the young debutantes of the area would show up. I'm sure there were several hundred marriages that resulted from that parade up and down the coast with the young officers and all their glitter, and the balls and everything that went with it.

Paul Stillwell: Very accommodating of the Navy to arrange that. [Laughter]

Admiral Erly: [Laughter] Well, I think it was a little bit more than the Navy. Remember, when those ships came in, it was normally timed around a payday, so that meant that many dollars were going into the coffers of the local economy, and, again, I

---

[*] San Clemente is an island off the coast of Southern California, southeast of Los Angeles.

imagine that our local senators and congressmen were highly in favor of this cruise up and down the coast for that reason.

Paul Stillwell: What was the social standing of a young naval officer in that era?

Admiral Erly: Oh, Lord. Well, they, I think, were very much sought after at that point.

Paul Stillwell: Did you experience that yourself?

Admiral Erly: Yes, yes. You were invited out, not only for the ball, and there would have been cocktails and then dinner or something of the nature. And you could reciprocate by having the young lassies aboard ship for dinner and that sort of thing. This is the way it went. It was great. Also, you've got to remember that the young ensigns in our group couldn't get married for two years. So you could really play the field and know that you couldn't be snared. [Laughter]

Paul Stillwell: Did you have any close calls in that time?

Admiral Erly: Well, don't we all? [Laughter]

Paul Stillwell: Enough said. [Laughter]

Admiral Erly: I went into engineering for a short span before I detached from *New Mexico* in November of '38.

Paul Stillwell: Had the Rickover practices been moderated any by then?

Admiral Erly: No, not to the best of my knowledge. Everybody was still after the hash mark and self-aggrandizement.

Paul Stillwell: And this didn't sit well with your concept of taking care of your men.

Admiral Erly: No, no. My thought that these practices were making liars and cheats out of everybody, instead of really increasing efficiency and economy in the use of oil. In gunnery it was the same thing. Just get the scores. Was it really reflecting battle readiness and a true picture of our effectiveness?

Paul Stillwell: Were there shortcuts or tricks to improve gunnery scores?

Admiral Erly: Yes.

Paul Stillwell: Such as?

Admiral Erly: Well, I'm just trying to think on which were the practices. You had to figure out from what angle you wanted to do. What is the best favorable approach? Any of those things. How to steady down first. How do you pick them up, get more tracking time? All of these things. And there's always the guy with that sharp sense of trying to get one-upmanship on somebody else in a better way.

Paul Stillwell: Well, some of that can be constructive.

Admiral Erly: Oh, yes, yes, it could be. Yes, yes, yes. It's not all bad, and for that matter of it, except, as I say, when you do anything that's going to impinge on your crew, you shouldn't do it, unless it's essential for the life of the ship.

Paul Stillwell: Is this a good point to break for lunch before we go to your destroyer?

Admiral Erly: It's a good idea. [Tape recorder turned off]

Paul Stillwell: We're just back from lunch, and you mentioned one thing I think would be worth including on the tape, and that was sort of an anti-Japanese alert in the fall of 1937. What do you recall of that?

Admiral Erly: I remember that we were required to man a launch and maintain a circle patrol around either a Japanese freighter or a tanker in Long Beach Harbor, on the San Pedro side.

Paul Stillwell: Was this a duty that rotated among the various battleships to provide the boat, or how did it work?

Admiral Erly: I know that we were tasked to do it. Now, who tasked us, I don't know. The batdiv commander or the Battle Force Commander, that I don't know. I don't think it lasted too long. Maybe a week at the most, if that.

Paul Stillwell: You can't trace it to any particular incident as a stimulus?

Admiral Erly: No, I can't, but in our discussion, I think you tried to fix it to the proclamation by Roosevelt.

Paul Stillwell: The quarantine speech.*

Admiral Erly: Quarantine maybe. But I don't specifically recall. I just know that this did happen.

Paul Stillwell: One more thing on the *New Mexico*. How much did you learn as an ensign about tactics and strategy in that ship?

Admiral Erly: I'd say very little. Very little. The battle line concept, I mentioned to you before, and I don't know whether we have it on tape about the destroyer attacks coming in. Even if you weren't on watch, all of a sudden you'd feel the ship backing down and you came topside to see what was going on, knowing that something was amiss. In those

---

* On 5 October 1937 President Franklin D. Roosevelt made a speech in Chicago in which he called for an international "quarantine of the aggressor nations," notably Germany, Japan, and Italy. He was attempting to change U.S. public opinion, which then favored neutrality and isolationism.

days, as I say, you really did station keeping with a Mark II, Mod II, eyeball, even if you had shielded stern lights or wake lights even, if you were running at darkened ship.

Paul Stillwell: What do you remember about operating in fog?

Admiral Erly: Operating in fog. Very hairy situation, and they'd string fog buoys and you kept position on the fog buoy. Everybody was very, very jittery and, I think, practically dreading fog, really. I remember, in fact, when we were en route, going up for our overhaul in Bremerton, we ran into fog and we dropped the hook. You just didn't want to proceed blind. It's a far different cry now with radar.

I remember leaving Narragansett Bay and I let go a buoy and backed away, and my exec grabbed me and said, "Captain, the ferry! The ferry!"[*]

I said, "No, that's the buoy we backed away from. Relax." And we had it on radar, and CIC was plotting and courses and checking. We couldn't visually see anything in the channel, and we proceeded out the channel to seaward.[†] No way could you have done it in the old days.

Paul Stillwell: Well, you went to the *Conyngham* after a relatively short tour in the *New Mexico*.[‡] Why were you transferred so soon?

Admiral Erly: I like to think that they were getting the cream of the crop to send to destroyers. I really looked forward to it, because, as I told you, I was really impressed with those night destroyer attacks that the greyhounds were making on the battle force. And I'd watch him come alongside to refuel during fleet exercises.

---

[*] This refers to a later tour of duty when Erly commanded the destroyer *James C. Owens* (DD-776) in the early 1950s.
[†] CIC – combat information center.
[‡] USS *Conyngham* (DD-371), a *Mahan*-class destroyer, was commissioned 4 November 1936. She had a standard displacement of 1,500 tons, was 341 feet long, 35 feet in the beam, and had a maximum draft of 10 feet. Her design speed was 36 knots. She was armed with five 5-inch guns and twelve 21-inch torpedo tubes. She was decommissioned in 1946 and used as a target in that year's atomic bomb tests at Bikini Atoll. She was eventually destroyed by sinking on 2 July 1948.

Paul Stillwell: How much underway replenishment was there in the late '30s?

Admiral Erly: A good bit during fleet exercises, but there was one way that we don't do that anymore, and it's probably just as well. The *New Mexico* had blisters on the sides.* Isn't that a nice way to pick up a little destroyer when you roll? They had the concept then of a sea painter, and the destroyer would come up, and they would pass over this 8-inch line, and the destroyer would then ride on it like a sea painter. I think that method was done away with for good reason, because there were some collisions. But this business of coming along and having no hindrance there and allowing the destroyer to maintain position, which they can do, alongside, they had much less kisses between the destroyer and the fueling ship, and I'd say less broken hoses too. But that was the way they did it: come in with a sea painter. You know what happens when you let go of your whaleboat and they come out on the sea painter; that was the same concept that they were using with the destroyer.

And you've got to remember, too, that the destroyers were getting bigger and heavier, not the little old 1,200-tonners. The *Conyngham* was a 1,500-ton gold-plater with the thyraton fire-control system.†

Paul Stillwell: What were your jobs when you reported to that ship?

Admiral Erly: Well, first I relieved Bert Orr out of '36; Bert was the commissary officer and assistant first lieutenant.‡ I remember in that turnover, Bert was a pipe smoker, and so was I, and we'd get under way, and we'd stand out. We were down in one of those forward holds, because in that day and age, we'd been reading some of the court-martial procedures where a young ensign was being court-martialed because when he'd taken over as commissary officer and signed for these crates of food and whatnot. He hadn't

---

* When the old battleships were modernized in the 1920s and 1930s, external compartments were welded onto the ships' hulls at the waterline to provide increased protection against torpedo damage. The compartments were nicknamed "blisters."
† The first of the "gold-platers," the modern destroyers designed in the 1930s, was the USS *Farragut* (DD-348), commissioned 18 June 1934. They replaced the old four-pipers as the front-line destroyers in the U.S. Fleet.
Thyraton is a type of gas-filled tube used as an electrical switch and rectifier.
‡ Ensign Ellis Burton Orr, USN.

hefted each one and opened it; some of them were empty. There was obvious malfeasance by the storekeeper. So as we went through this change, you'd better be sure that I checked each carton. We were both smoking, and I happened to look over at Bert and said, "Jesus, you're turning green."

He looked at me and he said, "You don't look any better." [Laughter] So we got out of there for the nonce and let the air clear, and then when we went back. Since there was no ventilation down there, we shouldn't have been smoking in the first place.

I relieved him. Then shortly thereafter, Bert went off to submarine school, and then Paul Van Leunen went in the next class.* Paul was communication officer and torpedo officer. I relieved him. I took over those functions.

I guess about this same time, Jack Raymer out of '38 came on board, and he took over the commissary and the other.† I became the torpedo officer, and I guess you would also say assistant gunnery officer.

Paul Stillwell: How much exposure did you get to the engineering department?

Admiral Erly: Part of my time in the destroyer *Conyngham* as the assistant engineer. We wiped a main bearing and had to replace it. Here were the chief engineer and the chief machinist's mate preparing to take bridge gauge readings. I was the young wet-behind-the-ears ensign, and I noticed that they were not taking the proper procedure prescribed by the bridge gauge manual. I was fresh in this destroyer engine room, which I didn't know one end from the other, but I'd read the book. It said, "Make damn sure before you put that bridge gauge in that you clean out the casing holes that you're going to set it in, or you'll get an incorrect reading." Finally, I said, "Wait just a minute. Clean it out."

Well, I became an engineering authority. So it's the thing of really getting hands on. I always liked to really get hands on, because I think you do better that way. And as I say, from that background, then you had a sense of appreciation. You got to know the guy down there on the floor plates, and the engine room personnel are just as important

---

* Lieutenant (junior grade) Paul Van Leunen Jr., USN.
† Ensign Jackson H. Raymer, USN.

as any other men on the ship, because if the engines don't turn, the ship doesn't move. It's that simple. They are a big part of the team, and don't ignore them. Let them know that you know that they're there, and let them know that they're important to the mission of the ship. You can't do that just sitting up on the bridge. You've got to go down and stick your head in and say, "Hey, what's going on?" and show up, let them know you have an interest. I've seen some skippers that thought all that you had to do was sit on the bridge, and that doesn't work.

But, as I say, with basic background and upbringing—I think a guy that exemplifies this, really this curiosity, and I hope that you've gotten him on tape, is Gene Wilkinson.* You know, that guy wants to know every nut and bolt and something else. He's a lot like John Bulkeley, who loves this InSurv job.† He just loves the nitty-gritty. I'm not that, I won't say, meticulous, because that means overly so. But those guys really, really go at it, and I admire them for it, and they do it with such enthusiasm.

Paul Stillwell: We don't have Wilkinson. He's on my wish list for interviewees.‡

Admiral Erly: I'll talk to him.

Paul Stillwell: Great.

Admiral Erly: Yes, you should. He'd be able to tell you a lot. And since the old man's passed away, he'll probably be more candid with you.§ He's a great guy. I like him. I call him Dennis the Menace, really. He just tickles the hell out of me. When I had my sailboat, we had him on board. They sailed around Catalina with us for a week.

Paul Stillwell: I would appreciate that.

---

* Commander Eugene P. Wilkinson, USN, became the first commanding officer of the USS *Nautilus* (SSN-571), commissioned as the world's first nuclear-powered submarine on 30 September 1954.
† Rear Admiral John D. Bulkeley, USN, began serving as president of the Board of Inspection and Survey in 1967, continued after his age-mandated retirement in 1974, and remained until he finally left active duty in 1988 and was promoted to vice admiral.
‡ The oral history of Wilkinson, who retired as a vice admiral, is in the Naval Institute collection. He was interviewed subsequent to this interview with Admiral Erly.
§ The "old man" referred to here was Admiral Hyman G. Rickover, USN (Ret.), who died in 1986.

Admiral Erly: I will.

Paul Stillwell: How sophisticated was damage control in that era?

Admiral Erly: Not too. We had a shallow-water diving outfit. We had, I think, some of the shoring plugs, and you had the old anti-collision hogging mat. You used to go through that drill, rigging it, which they don't do anymore, I'm sure.

Paul Stillwell: Was there an emphasis on it in training? Frequent drills?

Admiral Erly: Yes, yes. Well, it'd be collision and all that. Prepare to abandon ship, away the fire and rescue team—the whole bit. That gets me into something else about abandon ship when we get on another one. As I rewrote my ship's organization book when I later had command, the first thing I said, "The words, 'Abandon ship,' will never be used aboard this ship, and will only be used by the surviving senior. We will have debarking drills, but no abandon-ship drills," because I had to comply that far. "But the words will not be used." And you will find out later—when I was exec of the *Laub*—what happened to me over in the Med. But as a skipper, that's one of the things you will find in my ship's organization books.

Paul Stillwell: How much training was there in fire fighting?

Admiral Erly: Oh, you would usually run your drills on a Wednesday morning, because Wednesday afternoon was rope yarn normally.[*] There was a cycle. You would run through your emergency drills at least once a week, and when you were in port, you would want to run your duty section with a fire drill. This was very well maintained, because, again, fire on a ship is a terrible thing. You want to get there and get there fast and get it out.

---

[*] Typically, the Navy worked half a day on Saturday morning. To compensate, a free weekday afternoon, usually a Wednesday, was known as rope-yarn Sunday. The term comes from the old Navy, when sailors were given time off from their duties to make and mend uniforms.

Paul Stillwell: You mentioned your attention to detail and neatness on the *New Mexico*, and looking for that strand from the swab and so forth. How were the standards in the destroyer?

Admiral Erly: Similar. You religiously had to turn in your compartment check-off list every week, annotating any deficiencies, indicating those that existed more than a week. You had to comment on the cleanliness and everything else that went with it. All watertight fittings. The inspections, don't forget, regular as clockwork. Friday below decks. Saturday topside and personnel, come hell or high water. Which gets me into something dear to my heart. I did those, and at times I thought they were asinine to a degree, particularly with that requirement to do it on a Saturday morning after the ship has been deployed umpteen days and so forth. And my answer to that was, "Let's get the Navy regs changed so you can get it out of the Navy regs and not feel as you see the requirements laid on a commanding officer to hold this." Incidentally, a one-up for Bud and some of the other people to getting away from some of that trivia that griped a lot of us.* But, again, they went. You knew what you were going to have for lunch. The crew knew what the hell they were going to have for breakfast on Saturday morning. It was going to be baked beans—period.

Paul Stillwell: And cornbread.

Admiral Erly: Yes, certainly. Sure. I don't know whether that still goes on or not.

Paul Stillwell: I don't think so.

Admiral Erly: I don't think so, and it shouldn't.

Paul Stillwell: What training did you have to get as a line officer to be able to serve the supply function in that ship?

---

* In the early 1970s, as CNO, Admiral Elmo R. Zumwalt Jr., USN, sought to do away with what he called "Mickey Mouse" regulations.

Admiral Erly: You learned the hard way, and you really had to. I felt that I didn't really receive any training at the Naval Academy that qualified me to do that supply function. I had to rely heavily on the chief storekeeper and the cooks, and we'd go over the menus. And quantities, of course, you had to rely on what the breakout was and a constant check there. But there was nothing that I can recall as a midshipman that prepared me to be a commissary officer.

Paul Stillwell: Strictly on-the-job training?

Admiral Erly: On-the-job training, yes.

Paul Stillwell: Did the Bureau of Supplies and Accounts allocate a certain amount of money per man, per day, for food?

Admiral Erly: Yes, yes. I'm trying to remember some of the figures. For some reason, I'm thinking back at that time whether I was allowed about 48 cents per man, per day.

Paul Stillwell: Could be.

Admiral Erly: It was some low figure. It was less than a buck, I know that.

Paul Stillwell: But you could buy a lot more food for a dollar then.

Admiral Erly: Oh, sure, and don't forget that you were buying it in bulk, too. Every can was about so big, then you had sacks of beans and everything else, sure, and it was being bought under contract. I think we would get the milk on contract, which would be delivered to the dock, and then the whaleboat would pick it up and get it to the ship, and bread when we were in port. We got milk and bread that way, because we weren't doing that much baking, as I recall.

Paul Stillwell: How would you assess the quality of the food in that era?

Admiral Erly: Well, I would say it was substantial. When you look at the calories and knowing what we know about diet now, and realizing when you're putting out a lot of ham and pork and sausage and those things, and beef, they are not the most healthy, although I think beef is coming back a little bit more, but the emphasis was on—for health food would be turkey, chicken, fish. It was high in calorie count, and when you were working their little butts off, they needed a lot of protein.

Paul Stillwell: Probably not as much variety as today, either.

Admiral Erly: Oh, no, no. You've got to remember, in this time frame we're also saying there were no frozen foods, which is a way you can store it in your reefer and then you've got fresh frozen stuff. And some of the fresh stuff from the beach. But when you got out at sea, we normally would go out on a Monday and come in late Thursday. That was our operating schedule.

Paul Stillwell: Did you operate from San Diego?

Admiral Erly: San Diego, unless there was a fleet problem or we would go. Then we, of course, would have underway replenishment and underway refueling.

Paul Stillwell: We were talking about the division being a focus for men in the battleship. Did you have much more of a one-ship spirit in the *Conyngham*?

Admiral Erly: Yes, and although you bunked by divisions, the bunking areas could not convert for messing. Because at this time we'd gone to those one-two-three-tiered bunks with chain. The setup didn't allow you to be able to put a table, so you lost that three meals a day with the family gathered around the table, so to speak, and you went into a communal sort of mess hall where people didn't really always end up sitting as a division. If your buddy or the black gang wasn't all in one spot, and the deck force in another, they all got interspersed, which again in a small ship, gives you the hard core.

You get really to know everybody and the crew in a small ship. Now, you were in the *New Jersey*.*

Paul Stillwell: I was also in an LST, so I saw both extremes.†

Admiral Erly: Well, that's what I'm saying. I was going to come at you and say, "Okay, in that crew what did you have?

Paul Stillwell: About 1,600 men.

Admiral Erly: Okay. Of the 1,600, how many did you know personally?

Paul Stillwell: My division. Plus the JOs I saw in the wardroom.

Admiral Erly: Sure, that's what I'm saying. In a destroyer and in the LST, I'm sure that you knew all hands and the ship cook.

Paul Stillwell: Exactly right.

Admiral Erly: In that context, I think you can build a better morale in a smaller unit than you can in the bigger ones. I could see where carriers, particularly, when you slap an air group on there, get bewildering. You almost get lost in humanity, and no one knows each other except those little individual groups—like the flight deck crew or the people running CIC and so forth and so on. I just looked at a roster, and I was amazed to realize we had only five officers in *Conyngham*, as you showed me that. When I commanded destroyers, I had 15-16 officers.

Paul Stillwell: I'd be interested in how much you acquired in terms of ship-handling and tactical skills in the *Conyngham*.

---

* The interviewer served in the crew of the battleship *New Jersey* (BB-62) in 1969.
† The interviewer served in the tank landing ship *Washoe County* (LST-1165) from 1966 to 1969.

Admiral Erly: I think I acquired early on my feeling that the younger officers weren't given enough tactical experience. In other words, they weren't given the conn; they weren't permitted to come in and make the landing; they weren't permitted to pick up the buoy.* Of course, going along and building on that, seeing that lack of need in any ship that I ever commanded, you'd better believe that every one of them not only had the conn and station-keeping or other maneuvers, but were forced to bring the ship in and dock the ship.

The only way you're going to make a ship handler is through practice. I felt that I didn't get enough of that, so I made up for it in other ways. Even if I couldn't conn the destroyer, whenever I was in the whaleboat, I always took over and ran it, made the landings, and did that. Incidentally, that's something I continued even as a flag officer. I think it was disconcerting to many ships to find the admiral bringing his barge in alongside, or the captain always at the conn bringing his gig in alongside, or as a phibron commander, doing the same.† So I'm a firm believer in practice makes perfection. One of the things I learned starting in *Conyngham* was, okay, when I get my ship, my officers are going to get more ship-handling experience.

Paul Stillwell: Would you say that this lack of opportunity for JOs was typical of that period?

Admiral Erly: Yes. Well, from my observation, I don't think any of my classmates were getting to pick up the buoy or do it. Again, it was one of those things that everyone had their finger on their number. To wit, I remember in one incident in Pearl, we were going in. I had the deck, and I didn't like the way the helm was answering. I reported to the captain, "Look, sir, this ship is not responding properly to the helm."

Well, he got his chief quartermaster out there and asked him if the helm was okay. "No, the helm is fine, Captain."

Well, after we were going in alongside the nest and he'd wiped off three stanchions, he found that the rudder was not performing properly and so reported a

---

* The individual with the conn—normally an officer—directs the ship's movements in course and speed.
† Phibron – amphibious squadron.

rudder casualty as the cause for the damage. Being communication officer meant that I was the officer of the deck for special sea detail, coming in and leaving port, which gave me more time on the bridge, plus standing the watches at general quarters, than the average officer, because I was pulling the watch during the tense times. And I think you're well aware that in the open sea is one thing, but entering and leaving port is when you stand the greatest danger of having something go wrong and possibly ending up with a grounding.

Paul Stillwell: There was no operations officer billet in ships then. How was that function performed?

Admiral Erly: I would say basically the communicator was really the operations officer for part of it, and then the exec, being the navigator, was the other segment of that. So mainly the two together were fulfilling that function. Of course, there was no CIC.

Paul Stillwell: No electronic warfare.

Admiral Erly: No, you had a radio direction finder. [Laughter] We can tell a little joke here, and I don't mind if it goes on the tape. You know what you used to do when in a fog trying to find the entrance to the harbor at San Diego when you were coming in? You'd send for the young bridegrooms and put them on the bow and have pecker direction finder drill. [Laughter] And on it goes.

There's one thing that strikes me at this time. Once you've been in port a couple of days, people seem to get disoriented ship-wise, and when you go back to sea, there's a period of readjustment for them to become attuned to that. I would say, never, but never, have a competitive exercise on a Monday. Everyone is left-handed, and everyone is just a little off key. The teamwork isn't there. I think it's a dangerous time for a ship, too, until things simmer down. It isn't until Tuesday they start to swing around, and then Wednesday and then you've got your team. You've got them a little fine-tuned, and then you can swing in and expect the teamwork.

Paul Stillwell: The other side of that coin is, though, that the enemy, such as the Japanese, may elect to hit you on a Sunday, even before the Monday.

Admiral Erly: Well, if they're going to hit you—it's fine if you are at sea, but what I'm saying, this is just fact, whether it's Sunday or not, if you come into port and immediately go out, the crew is not thinking about the ship. They're ashore duty and with their families, and I imagine even in this day and age, they are thinking of more of that than in terms of thinking in terms of ship. I used to say, "You've got to cut the umbilical cord to the beach before you're going to really have that ship as a fighting entity and with the teamwork and with all the functions that have to be performed."

Paul Stillwell: The fleet concept of operations then was so different. You didn't have the six-month deployment and the workup and all that.

Admiral Erly: Well, there was no fleet underway-training group. See, that came along with World War II, and maybe we got the concept from the British. We do a lot of things now much better. We do this alongside, running through your drills alongside.

Paul Stillwell: It would be interesting to contrast communications then with today by radio. We've got these high-speed crypto Teletype things, and reams and reams of paper. How was it then?

Admiral Erly: Oh, well, jeepers. I remember on a fleet exercise and we had a shift and you went from maybe a blue forest to a red forest to a green forest to a yellow forest, and each time you did that you had to shift your communications, and these days you also were doing it by key.

Paul Stillwell: Morse code.

Admiral Erly: Yes, sure. That was how you received it. There was some fleet broadcast coming out, but it had to be typed. You had the log. When I was communication officer,

I'd go look at the log. Also, as communication officer you were a one-man coding board at that time. So anything that came in code you had to break until we started getting the first reserves around 1940.[*] Then they started augmenting the crew of the destroyers, and I had some help in the coding board.

Paul Stillwell: How much help?

Admiral Erly: We got the first TBS voice radio in DesDiv 5.[†] I think one of the reasons we got it was Jimmy Craig, because he was an ex-aviator and knew voice procedure.[‡] I think he got it, and then was to indoctrinate the division in the use of voice radio. Otherwise, it was Morse code, semaphore, and signal light.

Paul Stillwell: Did you operate tactically by Morse code?

Admiral Erly: Well, yes, you could do that, but basically you were operating tactically by signal light and flags. They liked flags. At night it had to be by flashing light. We had signals for emergency turn, we had speed lights, we used to use speed flags indicating our speed—any change. You had to know what standard speed was, and then a steady light was standard, and two blinks was two-thirds, and three blinks was one-third or something like that on the speed lights.

But at this time frame we're talking about, you had a gyrocompass and the magnetic compass. There was a DRT, dead reckoning tracer, which a navigator had, but it was mounted vertically, and then some smart soul got the idea to lay it out, and this became your basic surface plot when we started coming up with the CIC.

Paul Stillwell: How was it used when it was vertical?

---

[*] In this context, "break" means decrypt.
[†] DesDiv 5 – Destroyer Division Five.
[‡] Lieutenant Commander James E. Craig, USN, commanded the *Conyngham* (DD-371) from 3 March 1939 to 18 June 1940.

Admiral Erly: I've seen it used for one of the gunnery exercises. You've got the range to the tug and to make an approach of coming in to do it the same basic way you would have done it if it were laid down.

Paul Stillwell: How much antisubmarine warfare did you do in the *Conyngham*?

Admiral Erly: Very little. I'm trying to remember actual sonar ping time. How about the sonar and the sonar operators? Lord, if they had a day's ping time in a year, the emphasis really wasn't there. The emphasis really at this point was not so much ASW as delivering torpedo attacks on the battle line.

Paul Stillwell: You had seen it from the receiving end, from the battleship side. Can you describe it, please, from the destroyer side?

Admiral Erly: From the destroyer's side, it was sheer panic. You came charging in on a wing and prayer, straining your eyeballs out to see what you could see and to make sure what you could pick up, and having people on both wings of the bridge. Anytime you could pick up something, you made sure the word got in so the skipper knew what was around him and what he had, but he had no plot or anything to look at.

We had, of course, the maneuvering board for ship tactics.[*] Everyone had that. Most skippers, and I found that, were pretty good if you've been doing this, you almost see the, mentally, the maneuvering board and the solution. You figure, okay, I'm going to 20 knots, I need to come to course so and so to get from this relative movement point to that point. I found that even with my combat information center, when I got a tactical signal that was forcing me to move, I was gone. While combat was coming up with the solution, I would just say, "Combat, I'm coming course so and so, I'm coming to speed so and so. Check me." I was already headed out, and I was pretty close to what they're going to tell me to go on. I think you get a sensing for that.

---

[*] A maneuvering board was a sheet of paper containing a compass rose, concentric circles, and logarithmic scales. It is used for working out relative motion problems for ships that are maneuvering. In years past it was known as a "mooring board."

Jimmy Craig, of course, came with his old aircraft maneuvering board for the vectors, but if you do it enough and you have a lot of tactics, most skippers in the end come up with that, those that have any sensing and are good tactical people, will know immediately. We'll be within a couple of degrees of the course.

Paul Stillwell: Did you work on shore bombardment at all?

Admiral Erly: In those days, no. Basically we were doing a lot of surface shoots. There were antiaircraft shoots, because they had the thyraton control, and this was the 5-inch/38. It was an open-back, single mount, on the *Conyngham* and *Cassin* both. I can't remember a shore bombardment practice.

As I'm realizing now, from what we're saying in this history, as far as I'm concerned, in my memory, the two things that we were going to do most in World War II, except for the AA, antiaircraft, side of it, we did a lot of shore bombardment and we did a hell of a lot of ASW. Those were the points that we were lacking prior to Pearl Harbor.

Paul Stillwell: What surface targets did you envision shooting against?

Admiral Erly: You name it. As you would be going in for your torpedo attack, if you came under fire, and heading for the battle line, you could well expect to run into enemy destroyers, and that would have been a target of opportunity to take under gunfire. As I say, my feeling was that we were more concerned with torpedo attack on the main battle line than we were with ASW or shore bombardment. You had short-range battle practice, long-range battle practice, a lot of antiair, quite a bit of antiair and torpedo-firing practices. Actually, shooting the torpedo with an exercise head.

Paul Stillwell: And great care to see that you got the torpedoes back.

Admiral Erly: Oh, yes. Oh, yes. If you lost one, it was a mess of paperwork to explain to BuOrd the circumstances.[*]

---

[*] BuOrd – Bureau of Ordnance.

Paul Stillwell: How much maintenance had to be done on the torpedoes between shoots?

Admiral Erly: Really minimum, because the main thing was just to keep things greased, to make sure there was no corrosion. The exercise heads, of course, you really got from the tender for the scheduled shoot. You didn't keep them. They got rotated around for whoever was coming up for that. Then there was a periodic schedule of the torpedoes going to the tender for overhaul. You basically relied on the tender to do the overhaul. The major upkeep, of course, was on the mounts themselves, which kept the torpedomen busy.

Also there was a torpedo directors on each wing of the bridge, and there were receivers on the mounts that would take the input from the torpedo directors. One of the favorite devices, particularly when you were going for BTP A practice, you would centerline on the center bridge window and then mark about every 15 degrees.* Then you would take your two wing torpedo tubes, train them out 45, have a 45-degree gyro offset, and you aim the ship at the target, then have the skipper stand behind the helmsman and find out how much angle of lead which you know for—if he's dead on to you, you're going to give him no lead, and the more lead, of course, if he's broadside, then you're going to give him the most lead, and then you'd shoot your fish. Then the spread goes out this way, and you try to get him in the spread. So you were really aiming the ship.

The other way, of course, if you were cranking it in, you set up his target angle on the director, and if you just did one tube, then it computed the angle of lead and so forth, because the input from the gyro was giving your own ship's head, and when you crank in the target angle, that's also giving you his head, so it's solving the lead angle and taking in consideration of the spread. Then you would fire that way, from one side.

What did we have? We had two wing tubes and one centerline tube. Well, as I say, there were two ways to do it. One was to aim the ship itself and make your lead just like you were shooting skeet. The conning officer was sequestered from the bridge. All of a sudden he got the word, "Contact," and they let him out. Then he had to visualize the tactical situation really fast and analyze whether he was going to aim the ship or use

___
* BTP – battle torpedo practice.

the torpedo directors. He only had a certain length of time to do that, and the target ship was moving all the time.

Paul Stillwell: Did you get plenty of services in the way of targets?

Admiral Erly: Oh, yes, yes. You had plenty of targets, and it was amazing the number of targets we'd get when we went out for the aerial shoots. When we were getting ready for short-range battle practice and that type of thing, we used to rig a big cross line between the stacks. Then the division commander would designate one to be a target. The other destroyers would train on him and just practice the pointing and training.

Paul Stillwell: How much did you operate as a division or squadron in the *Conyngham*?

Admiral Erly: We did an awful lot as a division, not as much as a squadron. The *Clark* was the squadron flagship, which was an 1,850-tonner. Let's see, that was the *Clark*, the *Phelps*, the *Selfridge*. We had eight total of that class of the squadron leader, which was their official designation.* Every once in a while the squadron commander would get us out there with both divisions and we'd do "tictacs" and this type of thing, but mainly the basic unit being the division.†

Paul Stillwell: What maintenance and repair facilities were available for you operating out of San Diego?

Admiral Erly: You had the tender and then you had the des base. The des base is now known as the 32nd Street Naval Station over there now. Those days, we moored to buoys. It's a far cry from what you have today, and I'm glad to see what they have today. I was really a proponent and pushed for this strongly, to let the ships come in to be sure they could get fresh water and steam and electricity from the docks, to cool their plants down. In some cases now they cool down anyway, because they are gas turbine. In those

---

* The class comprised eight ships: *Porter* (DD-356), *Selfridge* (DD-357), *McDougal* (DD-358), *Winslow* (DD-359), *Phelps* (DD-360), *Clark* (DD-361), *Moffett* (DD-362), and *Balch* (DD-363).
† "Tictacs" is a nickname for tactical maneuvering drills by a formation of ships.

days we had steam plants. When we nested as a division, there was always a duty steamer that supplied steam to the other three in the nest. You needed it for cooking and you needed it for heating and for power.

I forget how they figured oil consumption for that if you were going to do for the engineering "E," but you had a duty steamer. In those days also, we had a duty officer of the nest, as we called it, who would take the duty and make sure that everything was fine on all four of the ships. You'd split the watch. A lot of times the officer of the deck was the petty officer of the watch, in other words. During working hours we had an officer of the deck on, but after working hours, no. It was petty officer of the watch.

Paul Stillwell: How was San Diego as a liberty town compared with Long Beach?

Admiral Erly: Oh, much quieter. Sidewalks really rolled up practically in San Diego when the sun went down.

Paul Stillwell: It's amazing to see what has become of it today.

Admiral Erly: That skyline changes every minute, every minute. I took some people out in my boat, oh, last Thursday. They had lived in Coronado, been in Palm Springs where they live now, and were just down for a visit, and they couldn't believe what they were seeing. Even on the Coronado side they're putting in, right on the bay, the Meridian, 600-room hotel, and all that area there that was devoted to Navy housing is now the hotel. There's a shopping mall. More and more things are going in there.

Admiral Erly: How long since you've been out there?

Paul Stillwell: I was there early '87, January.

Admiral Erly: This is all new. Really changed.

As I say, we were at a buoy. You've got to remember also in this time frame, the pier space was taken up mainly with four-pipers.* The des base was really a reserve fleet headquarters. They had all the old inactive four-pipers over there, and there was a tender there. I can't remember whether there was a tender in the stream or whether she was tied up over there, but they had, oh, quite a few of the old four-pipers and some of those, of course, went in. One of my old shipmates, Harry Richter, who was our exec, was detached to take command of one of those and put it in commission.†

Paul Stillwell: Well, they sort of rotated in and out of commission at times.

Admiral Erly: Yes, that's right, a certain amount, but as things got tense and as they went on—when did we make the swap with—?

Paul Stillwell: In 1940 we sent some to Britain.‡

Admiral Erly: Okay, well a lot of those, I think, came out of that pool at the des base.

I remember coming down for torpedo school in '39, and the first night I reported there, they had opened up some of these, and I spent the night in one of those old four-pipers. They were used as quarters for the torpedo school attendees.

Paul Stillwell: There's a movie with Walter Brennan, and he was tending one of these that got reactivated for World War II.§ He had been in it in World War I as a young enlisted man. So there's a lot of truth in that.

Admiral Erly: Oh, yes, yes. They'd seen lots of service, and they did quite well in World

---

* The four-stack destroyers, many out of commission by the late 1930s, had been commissioned in the 1910s and 1920s.
† Lieutenant Commander Henry E. Richter, USN, commanded the destroyer *Roper* (DD-147) in 1940-41.
‡ In September 1940 President Franklin D. Roosevelt concluded a deal with Prime Minister Winston Churchill of Great Britain whereby the United States transferred 50 destroyers to the Royal Navy for use against German submarines. In return the United States received 99-year leases to British bases in the West Indies, Bermuda, and Newfoundland.
§ Walter Brennan played Chief Yeoman Henry Johnson in the 1942 Warner Brothers movie *Stand by for Action*. Also featured were Robert Taylor and Brian Donlevy.

War II, and a lot of them were converted to APDs.*

Paul Stillwell: How did those ships ride, the *Conyngham* and her sisters?

Admiral Erly: I'll tell you, they were really the greyhounds of the sea. You know, the bigger they get, the slower they became. I remember going out on engineering full-power trials, and we'd clock over 39 knots.

Paul Stillwell: Wow.

Admiral Erly: Yeah, wow. With the new ones, you're lucky to break 30. The old ones were light, but you've got to remember by the time the war was over and you got through hanging all that gear on them, and putting more guns and 20 millimeters and 40 millimeters, that would increase weight. I'm just thinking—that was just a real light shield around those 5-inch/38 guns. Not that heavy thing that you found on the later destroyers coming out. They would move. I think they were some of our fastest, and actually what would the four-piper do? I think they were no slouches either. They were really, really thinking in terms of torpedo boats, weren't we? Seagoing slim and fast torpedo boats. When I commanded the *J. C. Owens*, I think I was lucky to get 32 or 33 full out.

Paul Stillwell: Did the *Conyngham* roll?

Admiral Erly: Yep. I remember we were getting ready for the start of a fleet exercise. We were anchored up in Long Beach, and a Santa Ana came through, and a general recall was put out.† I went back to the ship in our whaleboat. I was trying to get aboard *Conyngham* as she rolled. One minute the bilge keel was here, I was down here; the next minute the deck is here and I'm up here. I finally managed to jump aboard, but we couldn't pick up the whaleboat. Sent the whaleboat back in to the fleet landing. It was

---

* APD was the designation for a high-speed amphibious transport.
† Santa Ana is the term used for hot, dry winds that blow from the north, northeast, or east in southern California. In other words, these are winds that do not come in from the sea.

just freaky. I went forward to my stateroom to change clothes. I was in civilian clothes. This was a Sunday. And gee, I no sooner got to my stateroom and then, WHAM! "What in the hell is that?" So I ran for the forecastle. That's where the sound came from, and the anchor chain had parted. Thank God, the chief engineer and the captain were on board. They had gotten steam up. I got a crew up on the forecastle, and they were able to get another anchor down. Then they decided, "Well, let's get out of here. Let's go to sea." It was miserable.

We had a supply officer on board, and I'll never forget, I went into the wardroom. I hadn't had any chow, and I stuck my head in the little pantry. I said, "How about fixing me a sandwich," as we started out through the breakwater. She rolled, and I ended up on top of the wardroom table clutching like this [demonstrates]. [Laughter] I watched the supply officer, who was sitting in an armchair go from one end of the wardroom to the other. She must have rolled at least 50 degrees or more. We took some water over, and I was concerned whether it was going to come into the wardroom. Finally she leveled off and we went popping up and went up through an escape scuttle up to the next deck and on up to the bridge.

We had a hell of a miserable night. I remember the chief engineer and I heeled and toed it and we were out there just wallowing all night long and making about five knots just trying to stay out of harm's way, and came back the next morning.* We pretty well we knew where we had dropped the anchor. After things had moderated, we got the whaleboat out and started dragging grapnels. By golly, we snagged the chain and got the anchor back up on board.

Paul Stillwell: When was that chronologically, could you say?

Admiral Erly: That had to be a fleet exercise in '39 or '40.

Paul Stillwell: Are there any specific events that you can pick out from your life in that ship, essentially those two years, '39 and '40?

---

* "Heel and toe" meant the two of them were alternating the watch as officers of the deck.

Admiral Erly: No. Basically that was a learning period more than anything else.

Paul Stillwell: What about the increasing tension in relations with Japan?

Admiral Erly: I'm trying to remember when I went to flight training in March 1940. See, I left *Conyngham*, went to flight training and then got to *Cassin* in January '41.

Paul Stillwell: So that probably would have taken most of 1940.

Admiral Erly: Yes.

Paul Stillwell: Then you probably missed the fleet's big deployment to Pearl in the spring of '40, if you'd already gone to flight training.

Admiral Erly: Yes, I'm sure I did. I did not go in *Conyngham* to Pearl. No, I did not. I missed that. I also missed in *Conyngham* when they deployed to the East Coast. Remember that alert when a great portion of the PacFlt went through the canal, and they ended up in Guantánamo?

Paul Stillwell: The fleet was due to go up to New York for the World's Fair in 1939 and didn't make it.

Admiral Erly: I was in the naval hospital getting that knee worked on at that point.

Paul Stillwell: What had caused that problem?

Admiral Erly: Well, that was a football injury that finally gave way.

Paul Stillwell: How much of an extent did the destroyers participate in the fleet sports?

Admiral Erly: Boxing, you might have one entry in boxing, but you didn't have a whole team, or a wrestler. I'm trying to remember if that time the flotilla commander sort of got baseball players or something together or not. But it was not nearly the activity in destroyer sports that I encountered in the battleship. Actually, I didn't referee any fights down here. God, I'd been busy as hell up in Long Beach the whole time. I did referee one fight, but it was at the old Fifth Street landing. But there wasn't that degree. There was some activity, but there was no division team or squadron team, to the best of my knowledge.

Paul Stillwell: Any more to add on the *Conyngham*? Any of the individual officers or enlisted men that stand out in your mind?

Admiral Erly: I'm trying to remember, again, the little first-class boatswain's mate, and his name is escaping me at the time. He was the papasan for the deck force. His life was the Navy—you know, the old pro. Chief radioman was Hearst. I haven't thought of that name in 50 years. Now, whether he made officer, I've lost count, I don't know ever what happened to him, but I would have thought he would have been a prime candidate for officer material later on. Very knowledgeable, I'd say even a cut above the best CPOs. He really was, I thought, quite outstanding.

When I left *Conyngham*, they hadn't started to augment the fleet. We were not yet getting the first reserve officers. They started coming in in '40, but when I left, we hadn't received any in *Conyngham*.

Paul Stillwell: Please tell me about flight training.

Admiral Erly: We went through preliminary training in the "Yellow Perils" at Pensacola.[*] Those that were going to do seaplanes and the VP, the big boat, stayed on

---

[*] "Yellow Peril" was the nickname for the yellow-painted N3N trainer, a biplane equipped with a centerline pontoon. It was 26 feet long, had a wingspan of 34 feet, gross weight of 2,792 pounds, and a top speed of 126 miles per hour.

there. The rest of us, who were going to fighters and the other, went on to Opa Locka.* Opa Locka at that point had grass runways; that's how new that area was. It was really just opening up. Jerry Bogan, as I recall, was the skipper then. He made a good name for himself in World War II and retired as a vice admiral, as I recall. Bob Pirie was there, I think, as the head flight instructor and a big fellow, as big as Bob, called Bagdanovich, was down there as a lieutenant.† Spencer Butts was there; Bill Strickler, who was an aviator in *New Mexico*, was there.‡ This was basically advanced training at Opa Locka. Their operations point really was a tent on this trip.

Paul Stillwell: Did you enjoy flying?

Admiral Erly: Yes, I enjoyed it. Perhaps what you need to be a flier, you really need to have a swivel neck. You've got to be looking over your shoulder.

Roger Mehle had gone to Pensacola a class ahead of me. Roger Mehle, Butch O'Hare, Harvey Lanham, these were some of my shipmates out of *New Mexico*.§

Paul Stillwell: Do you have any recollections of O'Hare from the *New Mexico* days?

Admiral Erly: Oh, sure. We were in the same battalion for four years at the Naval Academy. Butch was just a nice affable guy—period. He had soloed as a youngster.

Paul Stillwell: Apparently he had a natural gift for aviation and a competitive spirit.

Admiral Erly: Yes, he played water polo. Evidently was a hell of a fine gunner. What

---

* Opa Locka Naval Reserve Air Base, northwest of Miami, functioned from 1931 to 1942. Miami Naval Air Station was commissioned 15 August 1940 with Commander Gerald F. Bogan, USN as the first commanding officer. The oral history of Admiral Bogan, who retired as a vice admiral, is in the Naval Institute collection.
† Lieutenant Commander Robert B. Pirie, USN. The oral history of Pirie, who retired as a vice admiral, is in the Naval Institute collection. Lieutenant Michael P. Bagdanovich, USN.
‡ Lieutenant Whitmore Spencer Butts, USN; Lieutenant Robert L. Strickler, USN.
§ Ensign Roger W. Mehle, USN; Ensign Edward H. O'Hare, USN; Ensign Harvey P. Lanham, USN.

did he get, those six big planes?* You know he was shot down by his own.†

Paul Stillwell: Yes.

Admiral Erly: That's too bad. His widow is married to a classmate.‡ They were back here at the 50th reunion, which we had last year. Butch's body, of course, was never recovered. He is on that memorial that we dedicated in front of the Naval Academy columbarium. That memorial is for those who were lost in the line of duty and bodies were never recovered.

Paul Stillwell: There's an airport in Chicago that honors him also.

Admiral Erly: Oh, I've been through there. Yes. I felt sorry for Butch when we were at Pensacola, and I was down there with him. His father was connected with Al Capone, and he was knocked off, was killed.§ Let's see. Did his sister marry one of our classmates? I'm trying to remember. She may have. When *New Mexico* was up in Bremerton, Butch's mother and sister came out and had an apartment there in Bremerton, while we were in. We were in about three months.

Paul Stillwell: What kind of a shipmate was he in the *New Mexico*?

Admiral Erly: Oh, great, you know, got along fine. I'm trying to remember who Butch roomed with, but I can't.

---

* On 20 February 1942, while a member of Fighting Squadron Three, Lieutenant (junior grade) O'Hare, USN, shot down five of nine Japanese bombers approaching the aircraft carrier *Lexington* (CV-2), thereby saving the ship. He was awarded the Medal of Honor for his exploit.
† Lieutenant Commander O'Hare was killed the night of 27 November 1943. He was the pilot of an F6F Hellcat while it was flying with a radar-equipped TBF. See Eugene Burns, "Butch O'Hare's Last Flight," *The Saturday Evening Post*, 11 March 1944, page 19. In the biography by Steve Ewing and John B. Lundstrom, *Fateful Rendezvous: The Life of Butch O'Hare* (Annapolis: Naval Institute Press, 1997), the authors made the case that a Japanese plane shot down O'Hare, in contrast to the earlier contention that a gunner on board the TBF had shot him down by mistake.
‡ After her husband's death, Rita O'Hare married Morton H. Lytle, class of 1937, who served until his retirement as a captain in 1967.
§ For details see the Ewing-Lundstrom biography of O'Hare.

Paul Stillwell: What was he also a student at Pensacola when you were there?

Admiral Erly: He was a class ahead of me. That meant that about halfway through he graduated and went off, as did Mehle and Lanham and some of the others that were there. They had gone in earlier. I think in those days they put in a class about every six months, so I think they were down there six months ahead of me. Or maybe it was every three months. I can't remember.

Paul Stillwell: What do you recall about the training at Opa Locka?

Admiral Erly: I had a problem in Opa Locka. I was doing all right at first, and then we got in the F4B-4s.[*] I was taxiing out—you know how you go boom, boom, boom, the old bit. We were all probably too close. The plane ahead of me stood on his brakes, his tail went up like this, and he dropped back down. I hit my brakes, and I just clipped his aileron with my right wing. So he pulled off.

There was a sailor on the line, an enlisted man. He checked my wing, and I said, "Okay?"

He said, "Yeah, you're fine."

So I took off on my flight and came back and found that I was on report for gross violation of safety—that I personally hadn't gotten out and double-checked instead of taking somebody else's word for it. Okay. Well, that brought me to the attention of the board somewhat.

Then I went up, and we had the dive-bombing with the F4B-4s. You roll, come in, and are supposed to pull out. Well, I wasn't getting lined up, and I hung in there, and I was going below the safety altitude. What the hell else happened? I don't think I ground-looped. But I got boarded.

---

[*] Boeing F4B-4 biplane fighters first entered fleet squadrons in 1932, and then were replaced by Grumman F3Fs in 1938. The F4B-4 was 20 feet long, wingspan of 30 feet, gross weight of 2,750 pounds, and top speed of 176 miles per hour.

Admiral Erly: Have you gotten Rear Admiral H. S. Matthews?*

Paul Stillwell: Yes.

Admiral Erly: Spence. He was the yeoman there at that time, and he tells me this story about when we came in. I didn't ask for reconsideration. I was being boarded, and he says—and I don't remember this—but Spence does, and he says that Commander Pirie said to me, "Look, for your safety, we think we should discontinue, because there's been this business of your not pulling out, and one of these days you're going to go all the way in, and we don't want that, and so forth and so on. I'm sure you're going to go back and make a great career in the surface Navy and probably be a flag officer." This is Spence. I'm quoting him.

Paul Stillwell: Mr. Silver Tongue. [Laughter]

Admiral Erly: I'm quoting him, okay? So I went back to the fleet. I'd left *Conyngham* for flight training, and after I left aviation then I went to *Cassin*.

Paul Stillwell: Well, let's not jump too far ahead.

Admiral Erly: Incidentally, I had orders to Fighting Six, really. Had my uniforms.

Paul Stillwell: Did you have your wings?

Admiral Erly: No, it was just a question of . . .

Paul Stillwell: You were close.

---

* Rear Admiral Herbert Spencer Matthews, USN (Ret.), has been interviewed by the Naval Institute oral history program.

Admiral Erly: Oh, yes, I was close. I had gone through the formation flying, the night flying, the VC. You know, I had done everything else. I'd flown the bomber. I'd flown the SNJ.[*] I ended up with over 200 hours.

Paul Stillwell: Did you feel a sense of disappointment when this decision was reached in your case?

Admiral Erly: Well, I had an option. I could have requested to appeal, but I was thinking that, "Well, why fight it. Just go ahead. Forget it."

But I'll tell you what I did do once the war started. I put in for it again, and didn't get it. I felt that that's where the action was going to be after seeing it. As it turned out, I was pretty right, wasn't I? But who knows? I might not be here now. I might be like some of the other ones that crashed or dove in or went into the deck, who probably shouldn't have gotten wings either. I don't know. Maybe I just didn't have what it took, but I was willing to try it again.

Paul Stillwell: Admiral Thach, in his oral history, said he made up a list of the guys in his squadron that he thought would be killed first, and after it started coming true, he threw his list away.[†] So probably it was good to go along with that judgment.

Admiral Erly: Yes, possibly. I lost quite a few that were operational.

Paul Stillwell: And even capable guys like O'Hare.

Admiral Erly: That's right. Well, he got shot down, but I'm saying that—

Paul Stillwell: But it can still happen.

---

[*] The SNJ Texan was a training aircraft manufactured by North American Aviation. The Navy first ordered a version of the airplane in late 1936; the Army designation was AT-6. Versions of the Texan continued in use for Navy training well into the 1950s.

[†] See the Naval Institute oral history of Admiral John S. Thach, USN (Ret.). At the beginning of World War II, as a lieutenant commander, Thach was the commanding officer of Fighting Squadron Three (VF-3), a squadron that also included O'Hare at the time.

Admiral Erly: Oh, sure, sure.

Paul Stillwell: We were talking earlier about your classmate John Boal, who was lost from the *Boise*.[*]

Admiral Erly: Yes, and I'm thinking some others that come to mind that just operationally crashed—period. One of my later roommates, Doc West, was a Marine aviator.[†] He ran into a damn hill in Korea coming back from a recreation tour over in Tokyo. You never know. Maybe it's fate.

Paul Stillwell: Maybe it is.

Admiral Erly: And there's no sense in fighting it.
    Are you running out of steam?

Paul Stillwell: Why don't we save the USS *Cassin* for the next time?

Admiral Erly: Okay.

---

[*] On 5 August 1942, Lieutenant John K. Boal, USN, was lost at sea while flying a scouting mission from the light cruiser *Boise* (CL-47) in the Western Pacific. For details, see Mike Stankovich, "The Hardest Choice," *Naval History*, Winter 1988, pages 30-33.
[†] Lieutenant Colonel Radford C. West, USMC, Naval Academy class of 1937, was killed in a plane crash in Korea on 8 February 1951.

Interview Number 2 with Admiral Robert B. Erly, U.S. Navy (Retired)

Place: U.S. Naval Institute, Annapolis, Maryland

Date: Wednesday, 7 September 1988

Paul Stillwell: Admiral, in the spring we got up to the point where you were about to report to the *Cassin* in January 1941.* I wonder if you could compare that experience, please, to the previous destroyer you'd served in, the *Conyngham*.

Admiral Erly: Well, I would say at the start it was quite similar, because at this phase I relieved a classmate of mine, Jack Whistler, who was the communication and torpedo officer in *Cassin*, so I really went back to the same job, initially.†

Paul Stillwell: Each ship, though, has her own personality. What differences did you observe?

Admiral Erly: Well, you sort of meld in and join the team. Dan Shea was the skipper at that point, and Rittenhouse was the exec.‡ Mell Peterson had gunnery, and Whitehurst was the engineer.§

Paul Stillwell: It looks from the April 1941 *Navy Directory* that you had the commodore on board then too.

---

* USS *Cassin* (DD-372), a *Mahan*-class destroyer, was commissioned 21 August 1936. She had a standard displacement of 1,500 tons, was 341 feet long, and 35 feet in the beam. Her design speed was 36 knots. She was armed with five 5-inch guns and twelve 21-inch torpedo tubes. She and the *Downes* (DD-372) were badly damaged in dry dock when the Japanese attacked Pearl Harbor in 1941. Both were eventually rebuilt and returned to service. See John D. Alden, "Up from the Ashes—The Saga of *Cassin* and *Downes*, *U.S. Naval Institute Proceedings*, January 1961, page 33.
† Lieutenant (junior grade) Jack C. Whistler, USN, who then reported for flight training at Pensacola.
‡ Lieutenant Commander Daniel Francis Joseph Shea, USN, commanded the *Cassin* from 17 January 1941 to 7 December 1941. Lieutenant Basil N. Rittenhouse Jr., USN. The ship was decommissioned as of 7 December, rebuilt at the Mare Island Navy Yard, and recommissioned on 5 February 1944.
§ Lieutenant Mell A. Peterson, USN; Lieutenant Edson H. Whitehurst, USN.

Admiral Erly: Well, we had Tom Keliher as ComDesDiv 5.* The *Cassin* was the flagship of Destroyer Division Five, and, of course, that was another responsibility when you were carrying the flag. Also, as I recall, as communication officer, our crypto machine was in the dining area and the office area of the commodore's quarters. If I'd get a coded message, I had to go into the quarters to decode it. The crypto machine had wheels in it, and I guess the code was hard to break. The decoding had to be done by a commissioned officer. At this phase, we had just gotten aboard some of the first group of the Naval Reserves that they were calling to duty. This was as a result of the buildup of the Navy by Roosevelt. As we were having more and more ships coming in, they were starting to call on the reserves. You can see from the ship's roster that we had Child and Moore, and then we had a couple more come on very shortly thereafter.†

Looking here, I can see that I had that job for communications, but then there was this acceleration, feeding in from the bottom, when they started bringing in a lot of the Naval Reserve ensigns. On the ship's roster of April '41, they had a postgraduate gunner, who was Mell Peterson, out of the class of '30. They had a postgraduate engineer in the ship, and by the time we shot our short-range battle practice, in a matter of some months, I became the gunnery officer and the senior watch officer. Shortly thereafter, young Culpepper, who was the assistant engineer, fleeted up and relieved Whitehurst, who was the engineer.‡ So you can start to see this buildup that was going on.

I got there in January, and in about June we took aboard a full complement of enlisted. We took on our wartime ammunition allowance. I was still, in this time frame, torpedo officer, because I had to go to the tender and receive instructions on the new magnetic exploder mechanism for the torpedoes, which was supposed to go off from the magnetic signature of the target. These were the same exploder mechanisms that impeded our submarine attacks. I had to go to the tender to get indoctrination. We got those ahead of anyone else.

We were getting ready to deploy. They were sending us out, and we sailed under sealed orders. We didn't know where the hell we were going at this point. But we had DesDiv 5. I don't know whether DesDiv 6 was with us or not. I don't know whether we

---

* Commander Thomas J. Keliher Jr., USN.
† Ensign Earl T. Child, USNR; Ensign Jack G. Moore, USNR.
‡ Ensign Frank M. Culpepper, USN, Naval Academy class of 1939.

had the full squadron of destroyers. We had one or maybe two cruisers and an oiler. We got under way with depth charges armed and torpedoes armed with electric impulse exploder mechanisms. I had to come back from the tender, and then they had to put canvas around me, and none of the torpedomen could see what I was doing. I had to personally put the exploder mechanisms in the torpedoes. This was how tight the security was on that.

Paul Stillwell: When did the deployment take place?

Admiral Erly: When was the Lend-Lease Bill passed? Because the day that the Lend-Lease Bill was passed, we entered Sydney Harbor and steamed in there.

Paul Stillwell: Well, just a minute. [Tape recorder turned off.]
    I just looked up a couple of references. The Lend-Lease was passed on March 11, 1941, and the history of the *Cassin* said that she made a deployment to the Western Pacific between February and April 1941.[*]

Admiral Erly: I may say that deployment evidently was, I gathered, and I've never been able to find out really, and maybe perhaps with the oral history and things that you have here at the Institute you can stitch this together. It was supposedly some type of signal to the Japanese, because we went out, we were in darkened ship, fully provisioned, wartime ordnance on board, wartime complement of personnel, which was unheard of with the manning levels, and we played ticktacking, steaming at night in darkened ship conditions, the whole bit, as if we were really going out as a naval force ready for surface action, not just as a show of force.[†]

Paul Stillwell: It would be important for the Japanese to see you doing that.

---

[*] The Lend-Lease Act, passed by the U.S. Congress, was a device that enabled the United States to provide military aid to Great Britain without intervening directly in the European war then in progress. The program was later expanded to include aid to other Allied nations as well.
[†] "Ticktacking" refers to conducting tactical maneuvers.

Admiral Erly: I guess, for the signal of that type. Once again, my memory becomes hazy, and which ports we hit and when, because—

Paul Stillwell: Well, you remember Australia, certainly.

Admiral Erly: Oh, I remember that because I can remember the cliffs and what a reception was given to a U.S. force coming in there. You've got to recall, at this time frame, of course, Australia was deeply committed in the war, and a lot of her troops had been sent overseas to England, and I gathered some had been in the desert warfare. I don't know whether they were caught in Dunkirk or not, with some of that, but their troops, their manpower had really been bled out.* As we were thinking about the rationale, the first port we would hit, of course, would be obvious that a U.S. naval force was out, and as I recall, and as you said, we hit the other ports of call. I'm trying to remember whether we hit them on the way out or the way back—Samoa, Fiji, that type of thing.

Paul Stillwell: Do you remember any encounters with Japanese forces?

Admiral Erly: No. No, we encountered none.

Paul Stillwell: But presumably they had some intelligence people.

Admiral Erly: Oh, I'm sure that in any port that you hit they probably had some, and so the fact that this force was there and heading that way, whether it was going to go on the long way and to reinforce the Asiatic Fleet or something of that nature would be conjecture. But, as I say, we went no farther than Australia, and then when we turned and came back we ticktacked again. As we were mentioning before, we had no radar, and all of us were steaming darkened ship. The way you did that and the way you

---

* As France neared defeat at the hands of Germany in the spring of 1940, a collection of small British naval vessels and private craft evacuated 338,226 British, French, and Belgian soldiers and delivered them safely to Britain. The operation, which took place in and near the English Channel port of Dunkirk, France, lasted from 26 May to 4 June.

maintained station was with your binoculars and how much of that ship you were maintaining station on filled the field of the binoculars.

Paul Stillwell: Obviously that was something the Japanese were very proficient at without benefit of radar.

Admiral Erly: Oh, indeed. If you will recall, they also had those—and I think the Germans also had those massive big binoculars, which we got later on, mainly for our signal gang, but I'm talking about your officers of the deck and the way they maintained position. Again, getting back into that business of what we did, of course, we were going in and doing again some of the exercises. The destroyers would come in on a night torpedo attack, as again by grace and by God.

Paul Stillwell: Did you have a feeling at that point that war with Japan was inevitable?

Admiral Erly: Yes. Yes, I had that feel. That goes back a little bit as a midshipman, and maybe I should see if they've got any file here. I wrote a thesis about the Philippines and what was going on—the feeling of the Filipinos versus the Japanese and what could be expected. I wrote that in the year I graduated, in '37, and for my own curiosity, I wonder if they have that on file here at the Naval Academy. It might be worth looking at and see what I came up with in regards to the Japanese in 1937.

But I had a feel, yes, and I think I mentioned to you before that that feeling was further fostered when I was in the *New Mexico*. I think if we go back through our oral history, we mentioned we were having picket patrols out there in Long Beach Harbor, and particularly on Japanese freighters, and, of course, again, the rumor rift about a lot of the fishermen and so forth and so on were really, in fact, Japanese naval officers getting information. So I would say, yes, the thought was ingrained that our potential enemy was Japan. And obviously with the deployment that we were then on, breaking out the super-secret new exploder mechanism for the torpedo warheads and having our depth charges armed, full complement of everything, well, what the hell are you doing it for? So the answer is definitely, yes, I did have a feeling that the Japanese were what it was all about. You remember also the bombing of the USS *Panay* by the Japanese in 1937.*

Paul Stillwell: Well, really, the United States had been preparing for that war for a couple of decades. Now there was a new immediacy to it.

Admiral Erly: Yes, because Japan was on the move to gobble up China and the Philippines.

Paul Stillwell: How was the atmosphere in the *Cassin* during that period different from what you'd experienced a year before in *Conyngham*?

Admiral Erly: Well, I think we just hit on it. Here you were really sort of girding for war. You were feeling that it was imminent; something was going to happen.

Before, mainly in *Conyngham* it had been really the Monday-through-Thursday routine, in and out of San Diego harbor. You didn't have that feel.

There was a feel of urgency. Again, as I mentioned, what happened later on, as all of a sudden what was happening in the fleet, relatively inexperienced people were replacing postgraduate specialists in the fleet in jobs. As this will come out a little later, I guess by June, I was the gunnery officer and Culpepper was the chief engineer. I replaced a man seven years senior to me, and Culpepper basically the same for the chief engineer, Whitehurst.

Paul Stillwell: An impression I've gotten of those early reserve officers was that they were extremely capable people, people who after the war went into very responsible positions in civilian life. What was your impression?

Admiral Erly: Oh, I think that they were eager to learn. They had a hell of a lot to learn. Quite a few of them, of those earlier types, not only did they go on in industry and

---

* On 12 December 1937 the Yangtze River gunboat USS *Panay* (PR-5) was attacked and sunk by Japanese aircraft near Nanking, China. Two crew members were killed and 43 wounded. Japan claimed it had made an error in identification and paid an indemnity for the incident.

whatnot after the war, a lot of them stayed on and made the Navy a career. I really think you were getting a good cream of the crop when you got them.

Paul Stillwell: There was a midshipman school, as it was called. For instance, there was the old *Prairie State* up at New York, the former USS *Illinois* that was used for training them, and often they came from the Ivy League schools.[*]

Admiral Erly: Right, and they had NROTC units, and a lot of these people were NROTC people, rather than the V-5 or whatever it was started after the attack on Pearl.[†]

Paul Stillwell: The V-5 was an aviation thing. V-12, I think, for surface officers.[‡]

Admiral Erly: Yes, the V-12 program. At this point I think that we were getting NROTC people, and quite competent—eager to learn, eager to learn. In looking at that list there, there was one youngster by the name of Cattermole. I guess he came later than the spring, a kid from North Carolina who did very, very well. I've run into him through the years. He finally retired as a captain, USNR.

Paul Stillwell: Do you remember any specific incidents from that cruise?

Admiral Erly: No. I remember training, training, training is what we basically did. Remember, of course, in Australia they really rolled out the golden carpet. It really became an endurance contest. They were trying to entertain almost too much, so you

---

[*] The pre-dreadnought battleship *Illinois* (BB-7) was commissioned in 1901. After her active service she was loaned to the New York Naval Militia in 1921 to serve as a training ship, stationed in the Hudson River west of New York City. In January 1941 she was renamed the *Prairie State* so the name "Illinois" could be used for a projected new battleship. Construction of the new ship started in January 1945 but was canceled in August of that year because World War II was about to end.

[†] NROTC – Naval Reserve Officers' Training Corps, a program that provides training leading to officer commissions at selected universities. V-5 was a naval aviation cadet program that procured and trained officer pilots. At the end of the six-stage program, individuals were commissioned as Naval Reserve ensigns or Marine Corps Reserve second lieutenants.

[‡] During World War II, V-12 was a Naval Reserve officer training program in which individuals received naval instruction at the same time they worked toward bachelor's degrees. The program, which was held at civilian colleges and universities, took about two years. See James G. Schneider, *The Navy V-12 Program: Leadership for a Lifetime* (Boston: Houghton Mifflin, 1987).

were glad when you had the duty so you didn't have to go to a duty party and show up, this type of thing. They were most hospitable.

Paul Stillwell: What do you remember about the skipper, Commander Shea?

Admiral Erly: I've got to hand it to Dan. Once we got under way, the poor guy was seasick most of the time. But he stuck with it. He stuck with it. He was a driver. I learned from him. He was a communication expert and, I guess, quite a damage control one.

I remember one of my skippers in *Conyngham* was Gadget Crawford.* I remember meeting Gadget in the head at the officers' club at Pearl Harbor after I'd reported to the *Cassin*. There was obviously no love lost between Dan and Gadget Crawford. Gadget was senior to Dan, and he said, "Well, if you have any trouble, you let me know." I didn't have that much of any problems with Dan Shea, Captain Shea.

Paul Stillwell: I don't think, though, that he would welcome it if you went to your former skipper if you did have problems. [Laughter]

Admiral Erly: No. Oh, hell, no. I don't whether they'd been on the same staff together or something, but there was obviously no love lost between the two. I was just a young jaygee, and you think to yourself, "Well, gee, that's sort of undermining the skipper to say something."

Paul Stillwell: That sort of tells you how deep it ran.

Admiral Erly: Oh, yes, to do that. Well, remember where I met him. I think Gadget liked his drinks and had probably had several drinks, which made him much more—probably if he hadn't had a drink would never have said what he said, because realizing that it could be undermining of morale. A terrible thing to do, really, but I think the setting explains what took place.

---

* Lt. Commander David C. Crawford, USN, commanded the *Conyngham* from June 1938 to March 1939.

Paul Stillwell: What sort of a routine did you get into around Pearl after you got back from the cruise?

Admiral Erly: Well, the same old bit—exercises. I remember as gunnery officer, then I got involved on the director, bore-sighting, going out for short-range battle practice, and I think that was it. That was a good one, because we put an "E" on every gun, which we'd never done that well before under the postgraduate gunner. In port it seemed that we had daily air-raid drills.

Paul Stillwell: What do you attribute the improvement to?

Admiral Erly: Training, training, and more training with the loading crews; this is where you sink it or make it. I just kept those loading crews practicing at every chance. Every time we would go to GQ, I would get permission from the CO to secure one mount and send them to the loading machine for more training.

In fact, if I had had my way, and I used to say about that time, "I'd like to have that first shellman carry a dummy projectile around the ship so it could almost become part of him," because that was the secret. It wasn't so much the powderman. It was that first shellman of getting that shell in there fast and secure—no bounce. If you're going to get your rate of fire, you can't have a jam. Your rammerman has got to be sure he's got that shell firm and steady in the tray, because if it's moving and the rammerman rams, it's liable not to go into the bore of the gun.

Paul Stillwell: You need a guy with some physical strength for that job, too, don't you?

Admiral Erly: Yes, your first shellman needed physical strength, but you also wanted him to be able to think. He had to be very observant, because he was right there. Also you had the gun captain, and you wanted to make sure that breechblock went all the way up or the gun wasn't going to fire. And every once in a while she might misfire. Then you had to come up under the breech and rap it with a rawhide hammer.

We would go through the motion of backing out guns, and this was a slow-motion depiction of what took place when the gun fired and recoiled. I would make the crew get there, and I'd say, "Hey, this is the way this thing works. You can't see it in action, but I'm going to show it to you in slow motion." I spent a great deal of time with the gun crews, telling them, "This is what happens and this is why you do this and this is why we're saying do that."

I think that helped a lot, although admit also that I must have bore-sighted the damn guns until my eyeballs came out—to make sure you were going to be on for the range. So that was quite a feather in our cap when put an "E" on every gun, and, of course, that meant—

Paul Stillwell: Prize money for the crew.

Admiral Erly: Yes, made them happy, not only for the money but because they got to wear that big white "E" on their uniforms.

Paul Stillwell: Was that as much a motivator as the international situation?

Admiral Erly: I really can't say. At this phase, remember, we'd done a cruise and we were back. However, we are still running with the torpedoes, warheads, depth charges, fully ready and ammunition in the ready lockers. We never stood down.

Paul Stillwell: Were you in task forces with the battleships and carriers?

Admiral Erly: Yes. Hell, this was leading up to December the seventh. We would go out on exercises, and I can remember the first bedspring radars, which is what we called the things on the battleships. The battleships would have a contact and send us out on a certain bearing to investigate and confirm and this type of thing. That was the first air search, I guess, that they had.

We did a lot of offshore patrol off Pearl. I'm trying to think when the antisubmarine nets went in across the entrance of the channel. I'm taking us up to

November now. As we were moored to buoys out in the harbor, there were an awful lot of air-raid drills, and so you would man and track as the planes would come in, and a lot of this was going on.

Paul Stillwell: You had your mechanical time fuzes on the antiaircraft shells?

Admiral Erly: Right, so the fuzes had to be set. The fuze-setter matched pointers. We didn't get the VT fuze until later on. We didn't have the VT at Pearl. That was why probably a lot of the shells that hit on the beach might have been even some 5-inch guns fired during the actual attack. There was ready ammunition in the ready-service lockers, but in port, in some cases, there was a lock on the ammo lockers.

Paul Stillwell: Did you feel Admiral Kimmel's influence as fleet commander in chief?[*]

Admiral Erly: Just how does a young jaygee feel his influence and what do you feel? Not really. I know that he raised hell a couple of times on something, in terms of military courtesy when he would come ashore and that not proper honors were being rendered and that type of thing, and, I mean, what you would call military smartness. I guess it happens people need to be jacked up quite often in terms of that. I guess he felt it was a laxness.

In terms of readiness, I felt that how could you be any more ready with no war than where we were. Here we had ammo at the ready lockers, we had our depth charges ready in the racks, with the exploder mechanisms in, okay? How in the hell else could you be any more ready? I felt that he had done everything that he could possibly do.

Paul Stillwell: I've even heard it to the point that the fleet was being run ragged during that period, that tongues were hanging out because of the pace that Admiral Kimmel was setting.

---

[*] Admiral Husband E. Kimmel, USN, served as Commander in Chief Pacific Fleet from 1 February 1941 to 17 December 1941.

Admiral Erly: Well, on the operations, let me tell you, again, as you pointed out and as we noted, that *Cassin* was the division commander's flagship. I don't remember the exact date. We had some fleet exercises in late November, maybe the last two weeks of November. As I alluded to, one of the battlewagons was out with the air-search radar. That was the first time we noted them from a destroyer, and then this particular exercise, the first time I had seen it, because when we had deployed, there was no radar in the cruiser that was with it, and I think it was the *Chicago*, if I recall.[*]

We had been on fleet exercise. I'm trying to remember what happened during the exercise. But there was a sense of awareness. We were sent back to set up the offshore patrol, DesDiv 5, and that was *Cassin*, *Downes*, *Conyngham*, and *Reid*. I had taken over the midwatch, and I guess maybe around about 1:00 o'clock in the morning, here came an emergency flash message directed to ComDesDiv 5. It said, "Seek out and destroy submarine at such lat and long."

So I woke up the commodore and the captain, we got full boilers on the line, and we went charging out. I guess about an hour down the pike, we got a message, "Cease and desist. Return. Continue your offshore patrol."

Then the fleet came in, and we went into port. This has got to be coming down the latter part of November now, and we went into dry dock in the shipyard, and, as I remember, even in the shipyard we had torpedoes on board.[†] I don't know whether I took the exploder mechanisms out. I think I probably did. The depth charges still had their exploder mechanisms in them, didn't take them off. We took the breechblocks out of all the 5-inch/38 guns and sent them up to have a modification made to them. The hull plating in some sections of the ship was taken off to be replaced by heavier plating, and we ended up in dry dock with *Downes* on our starboard side, and then *Pennsylvania* was astern of us.[‡]

---

[*] The heavy cruiser *Chicago* (CA-29) visited Australia and New Zealand in early 1941. Her commanding officer at the time was Captain Bernard H. Bieri, USN. The oral history of Bieri, who retired as a vice admiral, is in the Naval Institute collection.
[†] Ten-Ten Dock, which was part of the Pearl Harbor Navy Yard, was so named because it was 1,010 feet long.
[‡] The battleship *Pennsylvania* (BB-38) was officially the fleet flagship, though Admiral Kimmel and his staff had moved to offices ashore earlier in 1941.

Paul Stillwell: I've certainly seen pictures of that.

Admiral Erly: So that was your setup of what would happen. Of course, that's the way they were situated on December 7.

Paul Stillwell: I'd be interested in your recollections of the times ashore in those months leading up to December 7. How much opportunity was there for liberty?

Admiral Erly: Well, when we were in port, sure. I think we were catching liberty one in three.

Paul Stillwell: Was there a concern about Japanese agents in Hawaii?

Admiral Erly: About this time frame also occurred—whether it was Japanese agents, but the skipper of one of the tenders disappeared. You know, you're going back and trying to remember a mood. I think that was being brooded about, what happened to the skipper.[*] He was a hiker. There was conjecture then that he may have been stumbled on something that caused someone to do him in. I don't know whether I'm confusing that now with the tenor of the times or things that I have read or heard subsequently. That's the problem with that when you're trying to determine a mood.

Did we feel like war was imminent? I would say that for myself that particularly with that last incident of cease and desist offshore, patrol, proceed, seek out and destroy, that was telling me we were getting pretty damn close to something, that we were really on edge. If it was an enemy submarine, as far as I was concerned, the only type of submarine that I could think of that we would be worried about at this time frame—it sure as hell wasn't German—would be Japanese. So I don't know whether we would sit around the wardroom, or did we discuss that we thought it was imminent, what happened.

Our major concern, though, as I think that I can paint for you, and probably, even though we had the air raid drills, and had them quite frequently, and with the

---

[*] In July 1941 Commander Thomas C. Latimore, USN, the commanding officer of the destroyer tender *Dobbin* (AD-3), disappeared while hiking in the hills around Pearl Harbor. His body was never found.

antisubmarine nets across the entrance to Pearl, I think you get by painting of this picture and maybe Sunday quarterbacking it all, you would say, "Well, your primary concern was against, and the thought of any attack would be from, submarines." Therefore, if the attack was to come from submarines, you would think the safest spot for your heavies and your aircraft carriers would be in port where they were protected. I would even now say that was a pretty fair observation.

Paul Stillwell: It was not really conceivable that the Japanese could get that close undetected for an air attack.

Admiral Erly: Yep, that's what one would think, although, of course, we've all read about the fleet battle problem in the early '30s, when Americans had pulled a sneak air attack coming in from that side.* But I would say, in retrospect, and from what we were thinking, your major threat would be from submarines, and from anybody that intercepted that message that we received, they would, I'm sure, have thought the same thing. As I say, we'd been running around with our depth charges ready to go and, of course, our sonar gear manned the whole damn time.

Gee, did we have a chemical recorder at that phase on our sonar gear? I doubt it. The blips gave you the lead time, time to fire. I think that came later. We call them chemical recorders. And how well were our sonar operators at that point? We didn't get too much ping time on submarines, as I recall. Got a lot more after the war started than before. So the general mood—yes, something was going to happen. When? People were jumpy. I'm trying to think now if at this point whether or not people being ordered out there were permitted dependents.

Paul Stillwell: I don't know.

Admiral Erly: Because I think what was happening in the Far East, they were starting to ship dependents out.

---

* U.S. carrier planes made a sneak attack on Oahu during a war game in February 1932. See Admiral Arthur C. Radford, USN (Ret.), "Aircraft Battle Force," in Paul Stillwell, editor, *Air Raid: Pearl Harbor! Recollections of a Day of Infamy* (Annapolis: Naval Institute Press, 1981), pages 18-22.

Paul Stillwell: They were from the Philippines, certainly.

Admiral Erly: I don't know whether that had hit Pearl or not for people being ordered out there. It seems to me that in some cases, for those that were home ported there, I guess they could still have them. Of course, DesDiv 5, DesRon 3, actually, was home-ported out there.

Paul Stillwell: There were a number of ships, though, that were officially home-ported in Long Beach and de facto were in Hawaii. I think it was at the individual's expense to bring his family out.

Admiral Erly: Exactly. That's right, because their homeport was not changed, and some people couldn't afford that expense. So I'm sure in many ways this acted as a deterrent for dependents, because Honolulu was not cheap.

Paul Stillwell: Even to get there was not cheap.

Admiral Erly: No. *Lurline* of the Matson Line, and we had the Pan Am Clipper, also, I think, and that was it.[*]

Paul Stillwell: Do you have any other things to recall before the Japanese attack?

Admiral Erly: The general tenor, the general feel of the island—no, not really. Maybe if I sleep on it tonight, I might have some tomorrow.

Paul Stillwell: All right. What, then, are your recollections of that weekend?

Admiral Erly: That weekend I was not on duty. On that Sunday, I was with a group of people from Ewa, and we were down on the beach, maybe about five miles from Ewa.[†]

---

[*] The Pan American Clipper was a flying boat that was in transpacific service.
[†] Ewa was the site of a Marine Corps air station 17 miles west of Pearl Harbor.

We really became aware of ships at sea, firing. Really didn't fathom something was amiss, nothing really weird, but it solved itself, because "I Fly for Vengeance" Dickinson was coming in.* I saw his plane get shot down.

Paul Stillwell: He was from the *Enterprise*.

Admiral Erly: Well, from the *Enterprise* group, and they were flying in to Ewa, and from where we could see, we saw these two planes and then a plane behind them, and tracer fire, and then a parachute go, and then the other plane, we could see the rising sun. It was a Jap Zero fighter had shot them down.

Paul Stillwell: How did you react to something like that?

Admiral Erly: Well, the general reaction, once you saw the rising sun, "Oh, well, goddamn, here it is. What comes next?"

I had no wheels of my own, and so we started back from Ewa, and on the way overtook a car and forced the car over, stopped him, and I jumped out and got in the car with him. He was a sanitation worker from Honolulu, and he was getting the hell out of there. So I convinced him he was taking me to Pearl.

Paul Stillwell: You say you jumped out of something and got in the car. What did you jump out of?

Admiral Erly: The car of the group of people from Ewa.

Paul Stillwell: You had stayed ashore overnight?

---

* Clarence E. Dickinson, *The Flying Guns: Cockpit Record of a Naval Pilot from Pearl Harbor Through Midway* (New York: C. Scribner's Sons, 1942). Lieutenant (junior grade) Dickinson was a member of Scouting Squadron Six (VS-6) on board the aircraft carrier *Enterprise* CV-6). Shot down also was Ensign John R. McCarthy, USNR of the same squadron. They were flying SBD Dauntless scout bombers.

Admiral Erly: Yes. This little fellow really didn't want to head back, but he did, and dropped me at the main gate at Pearl. Then I went down to the ship, the *Cassin*. I was in civilian clothes. She'd been hit. There was fire in the bottom of the dock.

Paul Stillwell: Had the dock been flooded yet?

Admiral Erly: No, no. About this time some firefighting equipment arrived from the submarine base. I grabbed a bunch of people, and we went on the firefighting truck. We had been on the *Cassin*'s side of the dry dock. I took it around the other side and we hooked up the hose on the *Downes*'s side. The *Downes* had been hit, this time by a bomb, and it had hit on a torpedo tube, so she was really blazing. The fire was up around her depth charges. So we got the hose led out. I had it directed right on the *Downes*'s depth charges. It ended up there were two people from the sub base with me, a little Filipino and an electrician's mate, and then I was watching this thing. We were sitting right on top of the depth charges. I said, "Well, hell, there's no sense in three of us being blown up. Look, you two go back and get another hose. We need more up here. I'll keep this hose on the depth charges."

I weighed about 200. There was a lot of pressure on the hose, so I lay down on that hose, keeping the water aimed at the depth charges, keeping them cooled down so they wouldn't blow and blow the stern off the *Downes* and *Cassin* and blow the bow off of the *Pennsylvania*.

Paul Stillwell: You were still in civilian clothes at this time?

Admiral Erly: Oh, yes. About this phase, with the flame and the smoke, I took my coat and wet it, and sort of had it over my head. I stayed on that thing for—it was a real weird situation. You think, "Oh, Christ." You're looking at it and said, "Hell, it's going to go any minute." And it didn't go.

Paul Stillwell: Was anybody directing this effort, or was it individual effort?

Admiral Erly: No. I did this. No one came from the *Pennsylvania*. I could see that if those depth charges went, it was really going to wreak havoc, and that was my main concern. I must have stayed on that hose, it seemed like forever, and then was hoping the other hoses were going to come up. After a period of time, I found that I could lash it to an iron stanchion, went back, and they were struggling with another hose, got on the other hose and got another hose up there with them. I guess Dan Shea, the skipper, had been working from the other side, and about this time frame, also, they started flooding the dock, and, of course, then the *Cassin* toppled. And then about this time frame, also, some people from the *Pennsylvania* came out and gave us a hand. Before that, nothing.

Paul Stillwell: Was there any air attack still in progress at this time?

Admiral Erly: Yes, sporadic. Maybe that's why they didn't. Time frame I've lost. The time frame I don't remember, or even then.

Paul Stillwell: Your attention was pretty well focused on that hose.

Admiral Erly: Oh, yes, thinking it was going to be my last attention. Once you started flooding, that sort of took care of that situation.

Then I realized the *Shaw* was in trouble. There was a submarine down at the pier adjacent to Ten-Ten Dock.* I went and got an engineer. I forget the name of the submarine, but Otis Cole was the OOD.† I told him I needed an engineer who could operate a whaleboat, because then we had other hoses. I got in the motor whaleboat as coxswain with this engineer. We got a charged hose and towed it out to the *Shaw*. She was in a floating dry dock.

It's bugging me now, did I or did I not ever get that engineer recognized? I don't believe I did. There were basically two men who were with me on the hose that I kicked off, and I said, "Get out of here. There's no sense in three of us going. You get out and get some other hoses here, and maybe it'll help. Get another hose."

---

* Ten-Ten Dock, which was part of the Pearl Harbor Navy Yard, was so named because it was 1,010 feet long.
† Lieutenant Otis R. Cole Jr., USN, USS *Cachalot* (SS-170).

I did get them recognized for their actions. They were both advanced in rank at a meritorious mast for their actions. I did get that over to the sub base. They were submarine people. But I think I missed the engineer, come to think about it.

Paul Stillwell: Had she already exploded by the time you got there?

Admiral Erly: Yes, the bow had gone. She'd lost her bow at this point, and this is why the fire. About this time I was getting a little tired, I do believe.

Paul Stillwell: I'm not surprised.

Admiral Erly: After that, I guess we came back. Of course, by this time I pretty well looked like I'd been dragged through an oil field, and I went aboard the Pennsy. Someone said, "Oh, you can't come aboard."

I said, "Here," and showed them my ID. So they went below, got pants from somebody, a shirt from somebody, a cap from somebody, shoes, and got rid of what I was wearing. I got cleaned up somewhat, showered and scrubbed.

Paul Stillwell: Were your personal effects lost?

Admiral Erly: Yes, everything.

Paul Stillwell: What was the nature of the casualties on board the *Cassin*? Did the ship lose many people?

Admiral Erly: No, *Cassin* didn't lose any. *Downes* lost a group up in chiefs' quarters. When they got hit and the fire started, they moved forward, and that hatch on that *Mahan* type didn't have an escape scuttle that came up out of the chief's quarters. It had been dogged down. See, they dogged down anything, and they got in there and they were just roasted.

Paul Stillwell: Nowhere to go.

Admiral Erly: Nowhere to go. They couldn't come back out the other way. And so they took the casualties on that. The *Cassin*, evidently, had not that many people on board, and thank God, and the same thing on the *Downes*. *Cassin* people, we lost not a soul. Everybody got off. See, you had your liberty party and then you're right there.

What was really happening, if it hadn't, as I look at it, you can think the Japs were really under pressure, too, as you can imagine coming in there. If any one of those pilots had thought, "Hey, if I hit the dry dock caisson, I'll destroy or damage the battleship and smash the two destroyers."

They were really zeroing in on the battleship, and they only put one bomb in the battleship. And would you believe it, it had Jimmy Craig on it, who had been my last skipper in *Conyngham*. He had only been in "Pennsy" a short time as damage control officer, and it nailed him and part of his damage control crew in the *Pennsylvania*.* So they only put one bomb in the "Pennsy." All the rest, they were overshooting; where if they had undershot and got in the caisson, that rush of water in there would have caused more damage than really happened. You would have jammed everything in there. You would have probably never been able to salvage anything from the two destroyers, and the battlewagon would have been pretty well damaged. So you can see the Japanese were not so calm, cool, and collected, either.

Paul Stillwell: You were then a man without a job.

Admiral Erly: I was a man without a job. About this time, I got cleaned up and went out to regroup with Shea. What the hell did we do that night with Shea? I'm trying to think, did we go to the submarine base? Oh, no, the exec—I can't remember his name, because Rittenhouse was gone—who had been chief engineer on one of the other ships, the *Reid*, I think, and Shea, we went into town in the exec's car. We spent the night at the exec's house, and then came back to the ship in the morning. It was nothing.

---
* Lieutenant Commander Craig was killed that day.

I remember saying to Captain Shea, "What the hell? There isn't any damn thing I can do here?"

Oh, no, wait a minute. Yes, we did. Something else was worrying us now, and that was that we particularly wanted to get those depth charges off the *Cassin* and the *Downes*. That was done. I'm trying to remember the sequence of events. It's a little difficult. Did we end up on a tender, or did we go to the sub base to find a place to stay after that, maybe the second day? I ran into a skipper. There was a skipper who missed his ship. His ship was out, and something about his gunnery officer or something, and I was going to go with him.

Paul Stillwell: How does a skipper miss his ship in a situation like that?

Admiral Erly: Well, hell, the ships had emergency sortie, and he was in town.

Paul Stillwell: I know that that happened with the *Aylwin*.

Admiral Erly: Could be. Remember the skipper's name?

Paul Stillwell: No.

Admiral Erly: There was a sequence of events. I went to the destroyer tender with the intent of going with one skipper, and *Conyngham* had Chet Daniel as a skipper after he had relieved Jimmy Craig.* That's right. I finally ended up with him. His gunnery officer had been transferred on the day before Pearl. It all had to do with the move that went with the skipper of the four-piper that saw the Japanese midget submarine.

Paul Stillwell: The *Ward*.†

---

* Lieutenant Commander Henry Chesley Daniel commanded the *Conyngham* in 1941-42. In between Craig and Daniel in the ship was Lieutenant Commander Byron S. Anderson, USN.
† USS *Ward* (DD-139) was a *Wickes*-class destroyer commissioned 24 July 1918. On the morning of 7 December 1941, she fired on and sank a Japanese midget submarine near Pearl Harbor.

Admiral Erly: Yes. So I ended up going with Chet Daniel in *Conyngham*, and we put out to sea. No orders. I mean, I didn't have any, and no one was writing them at that point. I think we went out with a cruiser and met the *Saratoga*, which was coming from the States. Things were hairy at about this point, too, because I remember the exec, Cal Laning, calling me in and showing me a message addressed to the little task force we were in.[*] It said, "Combined Japanese fleet that's 100 miles south."

He said, "What do you think of that?"

"Well," I said, "this looks like it's it."

As it turned out, it wasn't. But we were out about seven or eight days, and I was really needed in that ship, I must say, because I told you about the ready service lockers, and they had gotten out, and *Conyngham* had fired and whatnot. I found all types of 5-inch/38 powder cans with no primer guard on them, live powder, and every safety precaution in the book had been sort of violated. Well, we got that squared away and got some drill.

Well, I'll never forget what Cal—there's one little thing that I can't help but grin about. Do you know that one of the inherent weaknesses in that *Mahan* class, for every gunnery exercise you had to crank down the windows in the pilothouse, or you would shatter them. Well, here I was sitting up there on the gun director as we were coming back in. We were making an approach off Diamond Head. Then I got a report coming to the gun director from number-one gun mount, "Periscope sighted, bearing so-and-so and so-and-so, from mount so-and-so."

So what did I do as gunnery officer? I said, "I cannot pick it up with the director range finder. You train out the mount on that bearing and fire where you think that periscope is."

We blew every goddamn window out of the pilothouse. [Laughter] This was Laning trying to check the alertness to see what was going to happen when he would give us something.

Paul Stillwell: Oh, this was just a drill?

---

[*] Lieutenant Commander Caleb B. Laning, USN. For an account of Laning's experiences as executive officer of the *Conyngham*, see his article titled "Why Don't We Do This More Often?" *Naval History* magazine, Winter 1991, pages 55-60.

Admiral Erly: That was a drill. I thought, "Oh, well, the exec should have learned something. When we arrived in port, I went up to the skipper, who was Chet Daniel, and said, "You know, Captain, I think I'd better go ashore and get a set of orders."

He said, "Oh, no. I don't want you to go."

I said, "Why?"

He said, "They won't let you come back."

I said, "Oh, you've got to be kidding. You need a gunnery officer."

He said, "I sure do, and that's why I want you here."

Paul Stillwell: That's why he didn't want you to go. [Laughter]

Admiral Erly: Well, I went ashore, and went up to the temporary quarters that Admiral Theobald had set up on the beach.* He had been the destroyer flotilla commander. His aide had been in *Clark*, and this particular aide was killed later on. Again, memory blank. Do you want to hit the book again? [Tape recorder turned off.]

Paul Stillwell: So D. M. Cummings is the name you've come up with?

Admiral Erly: Yes, D. M. Cummings.† I'm pretty sure that's the one who was sitting there and said, "Where have you been? We've been looking all over for you."

I said, "I have been in *Conyngham*, and they are in sad need of a gunnery officer, and I would like to get orders to *Conyngham* as gunnery officer."

He said, "I don't think the admiral will go for that."

I said, "Well, try it."

He came back and said, "No."

I said, "I would like to see the admiral."

I went in and stated my case, and he said, "No. If they don't have a gunnery officer, that's their own goddamn fault. I've told all COs that they should have trained reliefs for all department heads."

---

* Rear Admiral Robert A. Theobald, USN, Commander Destroyer Flotilla One.
† Lieutenant Damon M. Cummings, USN, was the radio officer of Destroyer Squadron Three on board the *Clark* (DD-361).

I said, "Admiral, but they don't have a trained relief, and we're at war."

Paul Stillwell: What had happened to the previous gunnery officer?

Admiral Erly: He fleeted up and became exec on the ship that Outerbridge had left.[*] Outerbridge was CO if the *Ward* that had sunk the midget submarine outside the Pearl Harbor entrance. So see, there was a progression of rapid changes, and they really didn't have a competent relief in the ship. I got not only told no; hell, no.

I might say that I should have had the guts to stand up and say to him what I said out of his presence, but I didn't. What I said out of his presence was, "If we don't get rid of some of these old fuddy-duddy admirals, we're going to lose this goddamn war."

Paul Stillwell: So the prediction was borne out that the skipper of the *Conyngham* made, that he'd lose you if you went ashore.

Admiral Erly: Right, sure did. Chet Daniel. Yep. And lo and behold, where do you think I ended up?

Paul Stillwell: I can't guess.

Admiral Erly: I was assigned to Admiral Bellinger's staff at Ford Island.[†] That was Patrick Bellinger, and he had all the patrol planes under him. So my life then became over to Ford Island, where I, among other survivors, stood watch in their command center. He had the patrol planes. He also was charged with the responsibility of air protection, sounding the air-raid signals, this type of thing.

Paul Stillwell: That sounds like a waste of your talent, on the one hand, and a disservice to the destroyer on the other.

---

[*] Lieutenant William W. Outerbridge, USN, was the executive officer of the modern destroyer *Cummings* (DD-365) before promotion to lieutenant commander and taking command of the old destroyer *Ward* (DD-139) on 5 December 1941.
[†] Rear Admiral Patrick N. L. Bellinger, USN, Commander Patrol Wing Two. Ford Island, which then had a naval air station, is in the middle of Pearl Harbor.

Admiral Erly: Yes, yes, obviously. Obviously. But you haven't heard the whole of it yet.

Paul Stillwell: All right.

Admiral Erly: Of confusion and where are you going to put people where they're going to best do what they can do. I guess I was there for maybe a couple of weeks, and I got a call from Captain Kitts, who was the fleet gunnery officer.* Somebody had finally done a little tracking down.

Paul Stillwell: He was on Kimmel's staff.

Admiral Erly: He was on Kimmel's staff. He called me over and said, "We are thinking about putting in some antiaircraft shore batteries on the beach, in particular 5-inch/38 batteries. Since you were gunnery officer and know the 5-inch/38 installation, I want you to take over and command this emplacement."

I said, "Yes, sir. That's something I would like to do and can do."

He was figuring on taking my gun director from *Cassin*, and we were going to take some guns from *Shaw* and *Downes* and set up a shore battery. Now, they were doing this also with some 3-inch AA guns from the battlewagons.

Paul Stillwell: Were these 5-inch guns dual purpose or single?

Admiral Erly: Oh, no, dual. It would have been an antiaircraft basic, but you could do them both.

I said, "Yes, sir, I'd like that. That's right down my line, because where I am is not."

So he said, "Well, we'll get your orders changed."

Well, let me digress for a moment. I had gone by the ship still in dry dock. You previously asked if I salvaged anything. No, but the enlisted men were there, and it was

---

* Captain Willard A. Kitts III, USN.

coming up around Christmastime, and I was getting ready to go back to Ford Island. I wasn't on watch at this particular time, but—and let me also add, one of the things you did while you were on a watch, you got in a boat, and this was, as I was saying, a week or ten days after the attack and everybody was still nervous, trigger-happy. I had a ride in a motor whaleboat at night across to go to the headquarters of the naval base. I went down into the intelligence center and got any enemy dispositions and other significant intelligence over high dope to carry it back to our plotting room center that we had over at Ford Island, and that used to be a hairy trip. [Laughter] You weren't sure whether or not somebody was going to open fire on you just by your moving in the harbor at night.

Paul Stillwell: You went to the Com 14 headquarters?[*]

Admiral Erly: Yes, yes, down.

Paul Stillwell: This is that basement code room?

Admiral Erly: Yes. In a little locked deal, and you got the information and so forth.

Well, that used to be part of keeping the update in everything we did and the plots and what air coverage we had and so forth and any reports. I know I've digressed a little from what we were talking about, but this was part of the function on Bellinger's staff.

Paul Stillwell: How had Kitts found out about you?

Admiral Erly: I don't know. Well, I imagine he had a roster of the ships that were out, and he wanted an officer with 5-inch/38 experience. Whom would you pick?

Paul Stillwell: You'd go somewhere there was an officer without a ship.

Admiral Erly: Yes, find somebody that was a gun boss in a ship that's knocked out, and I guess my name came to the top of the heap with him.

---

[*] Com 14 – Commandant of the 14th Naval District.

As I was saying, I had gone by the *Cassin*. Now, I went by the ship and, lo and behold, everything was practically gone, but at this phase, the crew was working, and somebody said, "Here, Mr. Erly, have an Orangeade," or something.

I said, "Sure. How are things going?" and so forth and so on.

Well, they had gotten down into the dispensary and, lo and behold, they'd gotten into the medicinal alcohol. [Laughter]

Paul Stillwell: So you had a screwdriver? [Laughter]

Admiral Erly: Oh, yes, I had several screwdrivers, and I had to go over and, frankly, about two sheets to the wind, I believe. I got there in time to go on watch. They had a very good chief there, and he sent down and got a turkey sandwich for this young, now senior lieutenant.

At about this time, God, they were getting all kinds of reports coming in and questions on whether we should go to GQ. I was listening to all this when Logan Ramsey came in; he was on Bellinger's staff. He was a big fellow.[*] He came in and said, "Do we press the button or not?"

I was feeling no pain, and I said, "Sir, from what I can see of this thing, I think we ought to wait another ten minutes and I think you're going to see it clarified, and I don't think we need to go."

Sure enough, that's what took place. It clarified and everything was fine. I then found that I had become indispensable to Admiral Bellinger's staff.

Paul Stillwell: If they could keep you supplied with liquor. [Laughter]

Admiral Erly: Oh, they weren't about to let me go. But finally, I think Kitts prevailed at the other end of the deal, and I ended up putting in naval shore battery number four at Ewa, which was quite an interesting experience.

Paul Stillwell: What sort of mounting did the equipment have in the ground?

---

[*] Commander Logan C. Ramsey, USN.

Admiral Erly: We documented this, and I'm sure that there is a report that I submitted that BuOrd should probably have in their file somewhere, because from the word go, of digging and pouring the concrete with steel reinforcement for the base that we put in to mount the guns and the revetments and the guniting that we did for the revetments and the ammunition magazines and how we installed them and all this I documented and made a quite lengthy report on this is how you do it, and I'm sure BuOrd's got a copy of that.*

Paul Stillwell: Did you have some help from the civil engineers?

Admiral Erly: Oh, absolutely. The civil engineers were in there from the word go. They did an outstanding job. Well, I was able to go and gather my gun crew captains and my fire control crew from *Cassin*. So I had the guts of the organization, and we even got a loading machine out there and we really set up a 5-inch/38 deal on the beach, with the whole bit that we needed to do the job.

Paul Stillwell: Did your installation essentially imitate a handling room and magazine from the ship?

Admiral Erly: No. No, you couldn't do it up from the handling room concept. We had to have ready ammunition lockers by the guns, and that's the way you had to do it. Then the magazines were all, for any protracted firing, I forget how many rounds that we had ready at each mount. There was backup in the magazines, which were down underground. For protracted firing it required manhandling ammo to the ready boxes. We also had an underground command post and even some machine guns. We had some of those mounted up in trees around the periphery. It was quite a setup.

Paul Stillwell: Did you set up some sort of watch bill organization?

---

* BuOrd – Bureau of Ordnance, which years ago was subsumed into the Naval Sea Systems Command.

Admiral Erly: Certainly. And we lived in tents. Then we had the Army. The 95th AACA group came in, and it was our job then to train the Army to take this over. Well, that was a help when they came in, because then they brought their mess, and we Navy file subsisted with them.

Paul Stillwell: How long were you there?

Admiral Erly: I guess till May of '42.

Paul Stillwell: Japanese seaplanes came over, I think, about March.*

Admiral Erly: Oh, yes. We went to GQ. We were up on that one. I remember that one.

Paul Stillwell: Did you get any shots off?

Admiral Erly: No, we didn't get any solution. We did not have radar.

Paul Stillwell: And they came at night.

Admiral Erly: That's right. So you needed a radar, and we didn't have it for that installation. Now, whether subsequently they ever put one in or if the Army came up with a portable one later on, I don't know. But, you know, the thought was that there was going to be an invasion of the island, and this is what they were looking forward to. We were antiaircraft shore battery number four, and Ken Dawson, who had been gunnery officer of *California*, was sort of the papa in charge of the Navy shore batteries that went in.†

---

* On 4 March 1942, in Operation K, the Japanese sent two Kawanishi H8K "Emily" flying boats on a long-range bombing mission from French Frigate Shoals to Oahu, Hawaii. This was a follow-up to the Japanese attack of 7 December 1941. However, clouds obscured the targets, and the planes' bombs did no damage. For details, see Edwin T. Layton, "Rendezvous in Reverse," *U.S. Naval Institute Proceedings*, May 1953, page 20.
† Lieutenant Commander Kenneth V. Dawson, USN.

Paul Stillwell: How many guns altogether were there set up for that purpose?

Admiral Erly: Well, I would say my battery was four and I think the other batteries were also four, so that would be 16 barrels. It was 5-inch. I also believe that there might have been some single-purpose coastal artillery installed. See, this was an antiaircraft shore battery. There were also, I think, some single-purpose batteries that went in, but I don't remember how many. The only ones that I was interested in to check their installation were the AA batteries. Mandelkorn had one, and I don't remember who had the others.[*] Mandelkorn was in the Naval Academy class of '35. That was an interesting facet as we phased out and phased the Army in and then finally turned over everything, lock, stock, and barrel, to them. That's when I was then released to go back to new construction.

Paul Stillwell: Well, the invasion never came, so you were obviously a very effective deterrent.

Admiral Erly: I would like that think that. But if the invasion had come, I don't think we would have done very well at repelling it at that. If it had come like the rumors, of course, that you were getting that they were a landing force, and as I told you once, a combined Japanese fleet is 100 miles south of you. The things that flew around really do not bespeak of a well-organized, analytical type of thing of what was actually taking place.

Paul Stillwell: They reflect human nature.

Admiral Erly: Yes.

Paul Stillwell: Well, why don't we get you to the new construction tomorrow, please?

Admiral Erly: All right.

---

[*] Lieutenant Robert S. Mandelkorn, USN.

Interview Number 3 with Admiral Robert B. Erly, U.S. Navy (Retired)
Place: U.S. Naval Institute, Annapolis, Maryland
Date: Thursday, 8 September 1988

Paul Stillwell: Admiral, we talked yesterday about the attack on Pearl Harbor, and today you want to provide me some of your reflections on that event and your reactions to it.

Admiral Erly: I talked about how I arrived at Pearl and then really got involved in what you would call the fire fighting, trying to save the ships and trying to prevent further damage. I really didn't have time until late that afternoon, around 3:00 or 4:00 o'clock, to even look around and to see the damage and the things that were taking place. It was an unholy sight, a devastating sight, really. It looked, at first glance, from the fires that were in progress and other things, with the ships careened aground and sunk, as if pretty well the whole fleet had been annihilated. You wondered what was coming next. There hadn't been any attacks for quite some hours at this time. It was a devastating feeling, almost that, here we are, the last outpost, and pretty well knocked out.

That also had brought to mind that I had been thinking that and reflecting as I had been talking with you yesterday. I left out an important part of what transpired, particularly when I was on that hose by myself directing it on the stern of the *Downes* to prevent her depth charges going up. I felt that I was in the ultimate moments of my life, that those charges were going to go, and when they went, I was going with them. It's amazing the way the human mind works. I accepted that. My whole life didn't flash in front of me. My only thought was, "Oh, hell." However, in retrospect, I think that was the moment that gave me another view of life, and perhaps of myself, that I could look the Grim Reaper in the face and not blanch and accept it. I feel that that incident has governed, and in some way helped, me throughout my Navy career and, actually, my life in general.

Paul Stillwell: The feeling that he'd had his chance at you and missed?

Admiral Erly: Well, not so much the chance, but that I had faced him, and he really didn't faze me; that's what I'm saying. Therefore, that I could go in harm's way and know that I could meet harm head on and not turn tail to it. That's the point, I think, the essential point.

Paul Stillwell: I wonder if part of that came from your conditioning—four years at the Naval Academy and another four years in the fleet after that—that you were in a profession that had risks and dangers to it, and you had accepted those.

Admiral Erly: Yes, possibly, possibly. I'm sure that that had a bearing on it. I guess people have certain characteristics; one is that I'm always ready to confront the problem, anyway, rather than turn away from it. Now, is that my naval training? I picked it up somewhere, and I guess the major influence in my life really was the Naval Academy. They do engender that type, that you are there, you are to lead, to demonstrate.

I was trying to think when I was getting volunteers to go in to do this back side of the dry dock as this fire truck came by with a driver, and I remember, "Come on you bastards. [You know, I'm taking it from something else.] Do you want to live forever? Let's get going and do something instead of sitting around cowering in a corner."

I wish I had been able to find that letter that I wrote, which was much more vivid. It was about a two-page letter. Maybe I'll come across it, but I doubt it.

But that was the essential story, I think, for the attack and what happened to me. As I mentioned to you, I put out to sea and there was a lieutenant who tried to contact me, but I was at sea, because he really didn't know what had transpired. So he wrote up something that I had been placed in charge of fire fighting at Ten-Ten Dock and the *Shaw* and so forth and so on, and I had received a letter of commendation from Admiral Nimitz.[*] I think that, again, it depends on how you're written up.

Paul Stillwell: Who was the fellow who did this?

---

[*] Admiral Chester W. Nimitz, USN, Commander in Chief Pacific Fleet and Pacific Ocean Areas, 1941-45. In December 1944 he was promoted to fleet admiral, a five-star rank.

Admiral Erly: He was a lieutenant, an old-timer. I don't know whether he was a reserve called to active duty or somewhere along the way. But he had come up with the fire truck, and then when I got the fire truck and the hose, he was gone. He just came up with a driver and whatnot, and I had gotten a group and was going. I continued on my own, really. He didn't place me in charge of the *Shaw* or anything else. Those were the things I did on my own. I want to say the name was Lieutenant Sparks, but I couldn't even recall that.

Paul Stillwell: Leadership sort of had to be spontaneous that day, because people hadn't gotten mentally prepared for this kind of a cataclysm.

Admiral Erly: True, true.

Paul Stillwell: Some probably reacted just the opposite way. They weren't willing to confront it that day.

Admiral Erly: Maybe some didn't. But, as I say, I couldn't see sitting in a corner waiting for the next wave of planes to come in. I felt something should be done and try to salvage something and prevent further damage. There was a wave that came in while we were in the process of firefighting, but at that point I don't recall any more bombs dropping in that general area.* I remember that to get where we connected the hose, we had to fight fire to get the hose over to the dry dock.

Paul Stillwell: Do you have any other impressions of that day? It's obviously such a vivid one for everybody involved.

Admiral Erly: Well, it's a vivid one, and I'm trying to crowd so much in. I remember finally things simmered down, and I don't know whether I had been cleaned up in the *Pennsylvania* or not. There's a hiatus in here somewhere. But I remember trying to get a glass of water or something, and the rumor was rife about this time that the water supply

---

* The second wave of Japanese planes hit targets on Oahu around 0900 and was over by about 0945.

had been contaminated and you weren't to drink any water. So I think there was a soft drink made available somewhere.

You know, it sort of becomes a jumble, and I haven't sorted it out. I'm trying to remember what happened that first night. As I think I mentioned, that Shea and the exec and myself, we went into Honolulu and stayed at the exec's house.[*] I was trying to get to the other side of the island, and I started out in the exec's car, and everything was darkened. I got a block away, and I figured I'd never get to the other side of the island. You know, there were patrols in the streets. So I turned and went back, and we spent the night and then back to the ship in the morning.

I think that is when I told Captain Shea, "Hey, look, I can't do any good sitting here looking at the good ship *Cassin*, because she isn't going anywhere."

Paul Stillwell: What was his attitude?

Admiral Erly: "Okay. Yeah, I agree with you."

Paul Stillwell: What sort of feeling did you have toward the Japanese at that point?

Admiral Erly: You can well imagine. I would say a fiery hatred, and it really stayed with me throughout the war. Even when I ended up in the Atlantic side and then against the Germans and the Axis, it didn't have the same feel as I had against the Japanese. It became really a personal vendetta, as far as I was concerned.

As a little aside, I did not lose quite everything in the *Cassin*. I did retrieve my sword. When they got into my cabin, the kids got my sword and gave it to me. But it was just a charred piece of steel, the sharkskin burned off, all the gold and the hasp was hanging, but the blade, and it still had my name on it. I kept that thing for a number of years, and when I had an amphibious squadron, which I took over in '61, in WestPac, I took that sword along, and I told my wife, "The first time one of these little Japanese

---

[*] Lieutenant Commander Daniel Francis Joseph Shea, USN, commanded the *Cassin*; Lieutenant Basil N. Rittenhouse Jr., USN, was executive officer.

guys wants to give me a doll or whatnot out there, I'm going to break this sword out and say, 'Fix it, you sons of bitches.'"

However, she's smarter than I am, and she said, "If you have that sword redone, it'll look just like any other Navy sword."

Of course, I have it mounted now. I had it mounted with a little plaque saying it was my sword and retrieved from the *Cassin* at Pearl. That gives you my feeling for the Japanese, and I do have a beautiful Japanese doll tendered to me by an admiral of the Japanese Self-Defense Force.

Paul Stillwell: There's a story, probably apocryphal, about the Japanese tourist who went to Pearl Harbor and asked where the *Arizona* was, and the tour guide said, "Right where you left it."[*]

Admiral Erly: Yes. Now the Japanese are our "closest ally." I guess now, as time and politics and war and whatever makes strange bedfellows, but I really for a number of years, even as you can see in the '60s, I was still not really convinced. I had been there during the Korean War also, in '52. When I saw their pitiful condition, even then, in '52, they were in a sorry state, as you'll recall. I think it eased off somewhat at that time, but even eight years later, I was—you heard my expression of what I was going to do with the sword. I guess we can really stay on that feeling that I was really upset when I was ordered to the other coast. That will come in when I was commissioning the *Frazier* (DD-607) at Bethlehem Steel in San Francisco. I guess that was in July of '42.[†]

Incidentally, after I left the shore battery, after turning it over to the 95th Antiaircraft Coast Artillery Unit, Army unit, I left, I think, in June and came back on the *Lurline* to the States.[‡] I had lost my uniforms, so I had been running around in khakis.

---

[*] The battleship *Arizona* (BB-39), commissioned in 1916, was heavily damaged on 7 December 1941 when a Japanese high-level bomber hit her with an armor-piercing projectile converted to a bomb. Her forward magazines exploded as a result, leading to a fire that burned for a few days afterward. Of the ship's crew of 1,514 at the time of the attack, 1,177 were killed.

[†] USS *Frazier*, a *Benson*-class all-gun destroyer was commissioned 30 July 1942 with Commander Frank Virden, USN, as the first commanding officer. She had a standard displacement of 1,620 tons, was 384 feet long, and 36 feet in the beam. Her top speed was 38 knots. She was armed with five 5-inch guns, ten 40-millimeter and seven 20-millimeter guns, four 1.1-inch guns, and five 21-inch torpedo tubes.

[‡] The *Lurline* was a Matson Lines commercial passenger ship that made regular runs between Hawaii and the West Coast of the United States.

Of course, I didn't have any clothes after that. The destroyers in those days didn't have laundries, and our laundry was done by the tender. There had been some of my clothes, washables, in the tender. So when I went to sea, I got a seabag, and underwear and stuff like that I bought from the small stores in the tender, so I did have some clean clothes to wear.

My first outfit, from shoes all the way up, came from the junior officers in the *Pennsylvania*. One gave me a cap; another, a shirt; another, pants; another, a pair of shoes; this type of thing, to outfit me. So when I went to sea, and really coming back to the States, a seabag was all I had. I had written ahead and had a set of blues waiting for me in San Francisco.

Paul Stillwell: Did the Navy reimburse you for your losses?

Admiral Erly: I said I threw away most of my records, but I did find something that I had forgotten. They reimbursed you, and it turned out to be about 40 cents on the dollar. But a number of items were disallowed, and I see where I submitted another claim in '48 because the law had been so changed, and I did receive an additional reimbursement. There were articles that were not claimable, like, a collection of pipes. But the law that was passed by Congress then permitted them to come up with others. So I guess I received, in the final run, about 50% of what I lost.

And then trying to make out an itemized list, like a Hudson's Manual, Marks Handbook, Bowditch.[*] Those are things that we had had as midshipmen and carried with us into the fleet, our professional books. You had to list each one specifically, and good Lord, when you're trying to list something, and if you didn't have a list to start with, it means that you're going to forget an awful lot. So the final reimbursement was almost seven years later.

---

[*] Nathaniel Bowditch (1773-1838) was an American mathematician and astronomer. He wrote *The American Practical Navigator* in 1802. The U.S. Navy bought the rights to it, and in revised editions it has been used since then as a guide to the principles of navigation.

Paul Stillwell: We talked about perhaps you could call it psychological preparation that got you ready for the war. What can you say about the professional preparation, the four years that you spent in the fleet before Pearl Harbor?

Admiral Erly: Again, we mentioned, what were some of the other indications? I'm thinking of the conditioning in the fleet, your battle problems, everything you were running through. The fleet used to have their fleet exercises. Remember, I told you the torpedo attack by the destroyers. I can also remember being in the *New Mexico*, we'd go out on the fleet exercise, and it was the battle line against battle line. In those days there was no radar. We did have the scouting planes you could send out. The whole scenario was to condition personnel to condition watches and wartime steaming, darkened ship, etc.

I was just thinking, the gunnery exercises conditioned you also to the actual gunfire with its related explosive noises and smoke and flame, particularly the younger officers. I was assistant turret officer in turret four of the *New Mexico*, and we would have observing parties. You didn't only fire your practices in the mount, but you would go to other ships and were safety observers on them, and you're used to shot and shell and gun firing and so forth and so on, and it definitely conditions you.

I started to tell you, and didn't get it on the tape, about boots and people's reaction to certain things, and as you mentioned, how the kids felt just going through the Strait of Hormuz in the Persian Gulf.* When you have a night battle practice, particularly in destroyers, and then I was thinking in *Conyngham* and *Cassin* both, you were not in an enclosed turret, so to speak. There was just a gun shield up forward, and the aft end was all open. Then you had your people and your ammunition train. And in addition, in those days those brass cartridge cases were expensive, and you didn't want them shooting over the side. So you always had a fellow that had a—I was trying to say it's not like a lacrosse racket, but the basic concept was that. He had a big oval, and it was meshed with rope. It was his job to deflect that powder case down onto the deck. Well, for night firing, it was rather eerie when those flashes went out. You got new members there.

---

* In January 1988, a few months before this interview, the interviewer had a tour of Naval Reserve duty on board Navy ships operating in the Persian Gulf.

Normally the chief gunner's mate would sort of roam around the guns, and his job was to make damn sure none of the crew took off. Well, once you got them through the first firing, there was no problem.

You were getting people conditioned from the various exercises you held. For instance, you called away the fire and rescue party, damage control exercises, saying you had taken a bomb hit, so forth and so on, in such and such an area. We were still doing that in those days. Then the damage control party was to go to the area and make proper repairs. This was before the war, and, of course, we were getting fed information from the British along the way of some of the things that they encountered, and they had some very good thoughts on damage control, which were coming to us. So I would say that the fleet and its personnel were really well trained for what was to come.

Paul Stillwell: And they proved quite adaptable, because things changed, what with radar and carrier task forces and underway replenishment.

Admiral Erly: I have wanted to tell you about when we lost *Cassin*. That was the big thing, and I should have mentioned it.

What the hell were we doing in the dry dock? I mentioned, the big item, which was that we were going to get an SC radar.[*] We were going to be one of the first destroyers to have it. We had unstepped the mast. I remember being there, and being superstitious enough, I grabbed the coins from under the mast, because we were going to put a new mast down.[†] The other item was incidental, a modification of the breechblocks on the 5-inch/38 and increasing some of the hull sheeting, which was off.

Paul Stillwell: Were those coins lost along with everything else?

Admiral Erly: Yes.

Paul Stillwell: How tight was the security on radar at that point?

---
[*] The SC was a surface-search radar.
[†] Navy tradition calls for putting coins under a new mast when it is stepped—that is, installed—aboard ship.

Admiral Erly: That I can't answer, because we didn't get it. All I had mentioned to you was that I had seen the bedsprings on the battlewagons. I was trying to remember if we had anybody off to school for this installation. We didn't have ETs at that point, but it would have been the radiomen who would have been responsible.[*]

Paul Stillwell: Was there any training or advanced work for you as officers in how you would use this new device?

Admiral Erly: At that time, no.

Paul Stillwell: What communication did you have with your family back in the States to reassure them on your safety?

Admiral Erly: None. I'm just trying to think of the first thing that—did I write them a letter? I can't remember. But I don't think that was really bothering me, if you follow what I mean. Bad news always gets there soon enough.

Paul Stillwell: It would probably bother them a lot more than you, the uncertainty, because you knew you were okay.

Admiral Erly: Yes.

Paul Stillwell: What do you recall about the attitude of people back in the United States and the atmosphere here once you got back to report to new construction?

Admiral Erly: I didn't really see much change, because my new construction was in San Francisco, and San Francisco had always been a most hospitable town to Navy. It was still as hospitable, if even more so, I guess, at that phase.

Paul Stillwell: Anything else to comment on before you get to the *Frazier*?

---

[*] ETs – electronics technicians, an enlisted rating.

Admiral Erly: No. I was just thinking of life at the shore battery. Of course, there was a whiskey embargo on. I had my troops out there, and they were being berthed with Marines, and we were trying to get what you would call a rec fund going. So some of the troops came to me and said, "Could they set up a little gambling casino and take an ante to provide for health, welfare, and recreation?"

So we set that up to get some funds and had our own little recreation command fund. The troops blended in well. As I said, I had taken a real cadre from the *Cassin*. My director crew, my gun captains, I got that pick. I got them through Captain Kitts.[*] He made sure I could get those personnel. We had my gun director and I think two guns from the *Shaw* and two from the *Downes*, because we had sort of rolled over. Of course, my gun director was okay.

Paul Stillwell: They were probably strictly optical directors at that point, weren't they?

Admiral Erly: Oh, yes, absolutely. No radar. No radar for them.

We had a good setup. We were down from the airfield. We had our own security guards, and I mentioned to you we had our own entrance. The Army then moved in, as I mentioned before, and we had a very good turnover. Plus, as I did mention, I submitted a report that must be an inch and a half thick. It showed every phase of the construction with photographs, because I was able to get the photographers from the shipyard, and we had to document and explain the process and the whole layout of it. If ever you wanted to put a 5-inch/38 antiaircraft mount down or set up one on the beach, that information would be available for somebody else to follow.

I guess that about covers the shore battery.

I came back on *Lurline* with orders to the pre-commissioning crew of the USS *Frazier* (DD-607).[†] The skipper was Frank Virden, out of the class of '27.[‡] The exec was Elliott Brown, out of the class of '31.[§] I was the senior watch officer and gunnery officer. I think there was a Lieutenant Stokes, out of about the class of '34, USNR, who

---

[*] Captain Willard A. Kitts III, USN, was on the staff of Commander in Chief Pacific Fleet.
[†] The *Frazier* was built at the San Francisco shipyard of the Bethlehem Steel Company.
[‡] Lieutenant Commander Frank Virden, USN, commanded the *Frazier* from commissioning on 30 July 1942 until 8 June 1943.
[§] Lieutenant Elliott M. Brown, USN.

was the communication officer. Then we had a full complement. I remember being back there, and we had the inspection by InSurv, the Board of Inspection and Survey, which came aboard to accept. I was gun boss, and I was pushing for additional ammo storage and to get some modifications so we could hold more ammo, because once you get into a fire fight, you would be amazed how fast the ammo goes, and the board went along with the recommendations that we had.

In the period that we were fitting out, they had done a beautiful job of painting all interior spaces. The ship was just great looking. No sooner did we commission than we started scraping all the paint off down to bare metal and put on nonflammable paint. The Brits had helped along this way in saying it. And, of course, that was reinforced by what happened at Pearl Harbor and in many of these things—that coat after coat after coat of paint just constituted a fire hazard. This was part of getting a ship ready for combat.

Paul Stillwell: When you talk about increasing the ammunition supply, was that a matter of increasing the magazine storage space?

Admiral Erly: There were some modifications where you could get extra rounds, and that's where we were trying to put 12 pounds in a 10-pound pack, if you could, and that's basically what it was. I think, also, I was after more ready-box storage.

Paul Stillwell: Were there adequate supplies of ammunition to fill that capacity?

Admiral Erly: At that time, yes. And the VT fuze, of course, was now coming along, I believe.* I'm trying to remember, when did we get the VT fuze?

Paul Stillwell: I sort of got the impression that it really got out to the Pacific in late '42 or early '43.

---

* Dr. Merle A. Tuve was instrumental in the development of the proximity fuze for 5-inch antiaircraft projectiles. It was also known as the VT, or variable time fuze. For a detailed account, see Buford Bowland and William R. Boyd, *U.S. Navy Bureau of Ordnance in World War II* (Washington, D.C.: U.S. Government Printing Office, 1953), pages 271-290.

Admiral Erly: Okay. Well, we're talking June of '42 now.

In some facets of the Pacific war at this time, after that initial attack on Pearl and, again, but the seaplane may be getting people all upset from the Japanese submarine, there was no other air activity there until you get into the big Pacific battles, which I missed, of course, because I was sent back with the *Frazier*. After we commissioned the ship, we had shakedown training. We escorted a battlewagon down from San Fran and started our underway training. We had pre-training. There was a 20-millimeter range and a 40-millimeter range up there outside of San Francisco, and I'd take my crews out there for shooting. So we were getting that training.

We had a surface radar, an SG and an SC, in this ship. I don't remember a CIC, as such.* We had a chemical recorder for ASW.† We were given sonarmen. I can remember that some of the sonarmen were musicians, because you were listening for change in tone, Doppler and so forth, and those people with that musical ear were very, very helpful in this.‡

We had not so many draftees at this phase. We had a lot of volunteers, and I saw a problem there. Here you had lads in this flush of patriotism, rushing to go into the service, to go out on a great white charger and fight the enemy and for love of God and country. They'd come aboard ship as young boots.§ What did they end up doing? They were mess cooking and so forth and so on, and that's a hell of an adjustment and a morale problem, really.** I could see that and tried to get them fit into the shipboard routine. Of course one of the worst jobs, I guess, for a lot of the youngsters is this mess cooking routine. If you've ever gone through with it, it seems so.

That was a challenge, to try to get them get into the shipboard routine and life and say, "This is just temporary. You're only going to be mess cooking for a while, and here's what'll happen. You can become a striker and you can be a signalman and so forth

---

* CIC – combat information center.
† ASW – antisubmarine warfare.
‡ Doppler is an apparent change in the pitch—that is, frequency—of sound or a radio wave caused by relative motion between the source and the listener.
§ "Boot" is Navy slang for a new recruit. Typically the young men had been through recruit training but not much else before reporting to their first ship.
** A mess cook does the extra chores involved with feeding the crew but not the cooking itself. Mess cooks serve the food, wash mess trays, and clean up the mess deck.

and so on, but you've got to go through the steps. This is the layered way it is, and this you must accept."[*]

I think that was more devastating for the volunteers than later for the draftees. I sensed that and felt for them and tried to ease our patriotic youngsters over that first reality. It was a definite problem. I'm sure if my ship had it, I'm sure it must have been prevalent for that first flush of volunteers that came in.

Paul Stillwell: What were the challenges that went with putting together a new ship as opposed to stepping into one that's been a going concern for years?

Admiral Erly: I've always felt that it's much easier to put a new ship in commission, because then you can direct which way it's going. You can build its morale, you can build its being, because I think a ship takes on an aura of the people that man it, and the attitude of the people that man it permeates through the ship, and the ship really becomes a being. I would much rather put a ship in commission than go aboard a ship and inherit, maybe, its problems; or if it is at the top of the pole, then how do you keep it there? I would rather take a ship, commission it, and then gauge what it's done, and that tells you personally how she stands.

Paul Stillwell: Another advantage of a new ship is you don't have to counter that syndrome, "Well, we've always done it that way."

Admiral Erly: Yes.

Paul Stillwell: What do you remember about operating the *Frazier*—this new radar device you had, how she handled, the training of the crew, and so forth?

Admiral Erly: Well, again, it was drill, drill, drill, shakedown training, get to know your ship, run through all the drills, repetition. The various department heads organized

---

[*] A striker is a non-rated enlisted man or woman officially designated as being in training for a specific petty officer rating.

things. I was gunnery. I wrote my section for the ship's organization book, and, of course, the exec was charged with coming up with the complete ship's organization book. You get those things down. You've got your condition watches; you had to make out your watch quarter and station bill; how you were going to cruise; if you were, were you going to cruise standing one and three watches, which was basically what we did.

We started that with Frank Virden, and I recommended we do it, that our basic wartime cruising situation be a condition cruising situation, because that's the way we were going to end up, and it basically came down to one in three. I would demand and ensure that so many minutes of each hour were devoted to training, either going through casualty control procedures or pointer training, sending the loading crew from the gun mount back to the loading machine to run through several strings on the loading machine, keeping them busy. Don't have them just sit in place and do nothing on watch; have them gain something from it. I felt that that was particularly necessary during the night hours on the midwatch and the morning watch and the other, where everybody has a tendency to go off, and the answer was, keep them moving, that'll keep them alert, and sort of rotate them. If you had them on the mount, rotate people up in the pointer trainer seat and this type of thing. Again, keep your training cycle going so that every man in that particular team could do every job that was required. So utilize the time instead of just putting in hours and to be ready and to be alert. Be alert.

The shakedown, we worked out of San Diego. We got gunnery shoots in, radar CIC. There was no such thing as a combat information center. If you'll recall, what happened later on, we got the DRT and put it flat and made a table, and then you could have a surface plot.* Well, the DRT in this particular case in *Frazier* was vertical, and the DRT, where else would you expect it to be? It would be up in the navigator's space, up behind the bridge. It was vertical, which made plotting cumbersome. The exec normally took over that position and would be doing the plotting and then calling in to the captain in the pilothouse—ranges and bearings and so forth.

---

* DRT – dead reckoning tracer, a mechanical device used in the combat information center to maintain a plot of the ship's movements.

I'm trying to remember. We were out escorting a jeep carrier.* I must say this. I think that we probably decimated more blackfish or dolphin or something out there on the West Coast. We dumped more damn depth charges on fish contacts, I am convinced, than any other destroyer. Old Frank Virden, boy, he would flip them at the top of a hat. We were with this carrier. We'd get a sonar contact, and then we'd go out and we'd drop charges.

In this incident we were coming back to join up, and I had the deck watch. Old Elliott was in there working on the DRT plot, and Frank had been conning the ship all over the ocean.† We were coming up astern of a carrier and we're really making it. All of a sudden, I looked, and goddamn, it wasn't the stern. I said, "Captain, that's the bow." We just got disoriented. I hit the engine order, telegraph, frantically, wham, wham—emergency flank speed—and I yelled, "Give me everything you got." Well, we just got across, or we'd have been cut in two. We kicked hard left rudder and went right down the side of the jeep carrier. I'll never forget that one. That was one of the close ones.

Paul Stillwell: Was this at night?

Admiral Erly: Yes. Oh, definitely at night, darkened ship. Certainly. This was wartime, but, again, we didn't have CIC. The surface plot wasn't keeping up it. Elliott didn't have the plotters and other help. He was doing most of it himself, with a talker relaying it. Instead of being an evaluator, he was a plotter, and therefore his information, by the time he realized it, it was too late. It was a Mark II, Mod II eyeball that saved us.

Paul Stillwell: This was part of that conditioning process for the way of war. What else do you recall about Commander Virden?

Admiral Erly: He was a good skipper. Frank was a good skipper.

Paul Stillwell: Later made admiral.

---

* "Jeep" carriers was the nickname for the escort carriers, CVEs, which were considerably smaller than the large attack-type aircraft carriers.
† The individual with the conn—normally an officer—directs the ship's movements in course and speed.

Admiral Erly: Yes. I consider him a good friend of mine. I remember when we got into the South Pacific. You know, our sailors are the most innovative guys, God love them. I was called to the bridge by Frank. He said, "Look at that. Look at that."

"Yes, sir."

He said, "That's awful."

I said, "No, sir. That's keeping salt spray out of those 20-millimeter gun barrels, sir, and I think the gunner's mate should be commended."

They'd gotten condoms. And later, you know what came out from BuOrd? They had a little rubber cap to fit on there to prevent that. Well, here was a good old American sailor came up with a good logical solution. Frank was a little upset, but I convinced him that it was not obscene, that it was really doing a job, and that the gunner's mate should be commended, not reprimanded.

Paul Stillwell: There probably wasn't much opportunity to use them for their intended purpose, either.

Admiral Erly: That's right, absolutely not. He was always just looking for a fight, and I was with him all the way if we could—really. He was just looking for it, and we just didn't run into it.

Paul Stillwell: In what sense do you mean "looking for a fight"?

Admiral Erly: Oh, he was just hoping to tangle with the enemy. Someone else might turn tail and run. Hell, no. Frank would put bow to and, "Let's go, boys," and I was all with him for that. He was really, as I say, very eager. He wanted to knock off a Jap sub, and so did I, and he would have loved to engage in a gun duel with Japanese destroyers.

We're getting a little ahead of ourselves to get out there. We had our shakedown training and then left the States and went into Pearl, and at that phase. Serpell Patrick was the destroyer gunnery guy out there in that time phase.[*] As you came into Pearl, you

---

[*] Lieutenant Commander Goldsborough Serpell Patrick, USN, was on the staff of Commander Destroyers Pacific Fleet.

were greeted by a high-speed surface target, and you went through the routine. So I remember that one.

We opened up right on it, went to rapid continuous fire, and got a mighty, "Well done and welcome to Pearl," from the gunnery officer, Patrick, who also, as you recall, later made admiral. I don't know whether you've had his debrief or not.

Paul Stillwell: No. I had a little correspondence with him. I think he was the CO of the *Wisconsin* in the mid-'50s.

Admiral Erly: Well, he was an old gunnery expert.

From Pearl, then we started to wend our way on out, ending up in Guadalcanal, and doing that run from Tulagi back and forth.*

I told you Frank was always looking for a fight. I had fire control radar, and we got out there one night, we got a contact, and I was on it. And all of a sudden, I realized it's one of ours, and I had a solution. And I got an order: "Commence firing." I didn't fire.

Paul Stillwell: What kind of contact? An airplane?

Admiral Erly: No, it was surface.

Then another "Commence firing." I didn't commence firing.

Then finally somebody came blaring over the voice TBS: "I am bearing so-and-so from you, and if you shoot, I'll shoot back."† It was friendly. I forget which destroyer it was, but I had it pegged as such.

The difference, I think, between Frank and myself would have been that I would have had my gun boss down and racked him up on the corner and said, "You son of a

---

* On 7 August 1942, U.S. Marines invaded the islands of Guadalcanal and Tulagi in the Solomons chain as part of the first U.S. counteroffensive in the Pacific War. The primary purpose was to gain control of an airstrip on Guadalcanal and thus to prevent the Japanese from achieving control of the surrounding air and sea regions. The campaign was long and difficult before organized Japanese resistance finally ended on 9 February 1943.
† TBS was a device for short-range voice communication at sea. It got a nickname, "talk between ships" because of its designation.

bitch, when I tell you commence firing, you better commence firing. I don't care right or wrong."

Frank and I never discussed it. He never said a word to me.

Paul Stillwell: I take it he found out pretty soon that it was friendly.

Admiral Erly: Oh, yes. Not a word was said.

Paul Stillwell: Well, the CO's in a real dilemma there, of course.

Admiral Erly: Yes, he is. Yes, he is.

Paul Stillwell: Do you chew out your gun boss for not making the same mistake you did?

Admiral Erly: Yes, I'll a similar situation while I was CO of the *J. C. Owens* in the Korean War.

Paul Stillwell: Well, did you provide feedback to Commander Virden at the time, or were the circumstances—?

Admiral Erly: I was trying to say no. Things were happening awful fast. I'm trying to remember. As I said, we killed about all the blackfish in the Pacific Ocean with depth charge attacks before we got out there.

Paul Stillwell: Well, that may explain his reaction. He may have been overeager in this case.

Admiral Erly: Oh, I'm sure. Yes, he was. He was always looking for it, and I condoned that. I liked that. I liked that.

Paul Stillwell: Well, how soon did you find a real fight?

Admiral Erly: Not while I was aboard. I'm trying to remember this time frame. It was in this time frame that, while we were in that Tulagi area, that I got orders, "Detach. Proceed immediately." I was sitting up on the gun director, and I think I've told you the doctor who was on coding board duty—[telephone interruption.]

You know, you try to—what sticks in your mind. The thing that stuck in my mind, what would I have said to my gun boss, right or wrong?

Paul Stillwell: You think now, in reflecting a little more, that you did tell the bridge that it was a friendly ship?

Admiral Erly: Yes, yes. "That's a friendly. That's a friendly."

I also was thinking of a cute one when I went to the head. We were going out, and we really thought we were going into our first firefight. You know, I could talk with a voice amplifier to all gun mounts. And knowing everybody was charged up, I said, "Hey, guys, this reminds me of the story of the June bride. She knows she's going to get it, but she doesn't know how long it's going to be," to relax them.

Paul Stillwell: This eagerness is reminiscent of the experience the *Vincennes* had a few months ago, where people were untested in combat and overreacted.[*]

Admiral Erly: Oh, sure. When you draw that, I think you also can say perhaps the *Vincennes* would not have been so edgy if it hadn't been for *Stark*.[†]

Paul Stillwell: That's true too.

---

[*] On 3 July 1988, Iran Air flight 655, an A300 airbus en route from Bandar Abbas Airport to Dubai, United Arab Emirates, was destroyed by two SM-2 Standard missiles launched at a range of nine miles by the Aegis cruiser *Vincennes* (CG-49). All 290 persons on board the civilian airliner died.

[†] On 17 May 1987, while she was operating in the Persian Gulf, the guided missile frigate *Stark* (FFG-31) was hit by two Exocet air-to-surface missiles fired by an Iraqi Mirage F1 fighter. One of the two missiles exploded, resulting in heavy damage and fires. Of the *Stark*'s crew, 37 men were killed and 21 injured. For details, see Jeffrey L. Levinson and Randy L. Edwards, *Missile Inbound* (Annapolis: Naval Institute Press, 1997).

Admiral Erly: You remember the skipper of the *Stark* got relieved.* If I were the skipper of the *Vincennes*, I'm sure I would have taken the same action he took; whereas I really fault the skipper of *Stark*.† I haven't read any of the inquiries of the investigations, but you know how you sit and be the supreme judge when you're not involved.

Paul Stillwell: And with the benefit of hindsight too.

Admiral Erly: Oh, sure. Well, I could give you a little philosophy, or maybe it would become a little long. I can't understand why the *Pueblo* was not sunk.‡ I think there should have been a strike called in and *Pueblo* taken out, if the damage to be done was that inimical to our national interest. The crew there, I'm sure, would have been willing to have been sacrificed if they thought they were helping their country, and that's what they were being paid to do.

I think Bucher erred, and I guess his fighting spirit was dimmed by a little blood and guts that got spilled on the deck that shouldn't have. I think that warrant that rang up stop on the ship probably is the one that swayed Bucher more than anything else to turn belly up. He should have kept that ship going until it was sunk. That's my humble opinion.

Back to the good ship *Frazier*. It was about shortly after this incident that—and this has to be now in December of '42. I was sitting on the gun director, and the good doctor came running up waving these orders. "Hey, Bob, orders, orders, orders."

I looked at it: "Detach. Proceed immediately." I knew that was a hoax, and the next line convinced me that it was. It said, "Detach. Proceed immediately. Report to

---

* The commanding officer of the *Stark* at the time of the 1987 incident was Captain Glenn R. Brindel, USN. He received a letter of reprimand and soon after agreed to take early retirement with a reduction in rank to commander.
† Captain William C. Rogers III, USN, commanded the Aegis cruiser *Vincennes* (CG-49) from 11 April 1987 to 27 May 1989. He and his wife Sharon wrote a book titled *Storm Center: A Personal Account of Tragedy & Terrorism* (Annapolis: Naval Institute Press, 1992).
‡ USS *Pueblo* (AGER-2), an electronic intelligence ship, was seized on 23 January 1968 in the Sea of Japan by North Korean naval forces. The ship's crew members were held as prisoners until 23 December of that year. Of the 83 officers and men on board, 28 were intelligence specialists. Her commanding officer was Commander Lloyd R. Bucher, USN.

Gulf Sea Frontier [never heard of it] for duty in connection Cuban Navy," and that did it.[*] Who ever heard of the Cuban Navy?

So I ripped it, threw it up in the air, and poor old Doc Jackson looked at me and his face dropped and he said, "Bob, I've got to go back and decode that all over."

At this time, anything, orders or anything else, came in encoded. And, sure enough, it was a legitimate set of orders. Frank Virden sent off a message requesting that they not be executed, and he got turned down by BuPers.[†] "Negative. Carry out those orders."

Paul Stillwell: Did you find out how BuPers, in its wisdom, reached into this destroyer to pluck you out?

Admiral Erly: Later. That becomes part of another story. Yes, the reason I was plucked out was on account of Rittenhouse. Basil Rittenhouse was the destroyer detailer. See, he had been my exec in *Cassin* and had been transferred just before Pearl. That's amusing in itself, because I finally ended up in the Med, and where did I run into Rittenhouse? I was exec in this time in the *Laub*, and Rit was skipper of one of the cans over there.[‡]

I ran into him, and Rit said, "Don't hit me, Bob. Don't hit me. I want you to know that I didn't want to take you, and I knew you didn't want to leave that ship."

In those days, they had a cardex system. He said, "I kept punching the file, and every damn time your name would come out. What we needed was a destroyer sailor. We needed someone experienced in gunnery, ASW, depth charges, this type of thing, and to have some knowledge of Spanish. Your card kept popping out. I had no alternative. I had no one else to do it. I knew you didn't want it."

Paul Stillwell: That was two straight Decembers that you were pulled out of destroyers on the verge of dealing with the Japanese.

---

[*] The Gulf Sea Frontier was established 6 February 1942 at Key West, Florida. It moved to Miami in June 1942.
[†] BuPers – Bureau of Naval Personnel.
[‡] Commander Rittenhouse served as commanding officer of the destroyer *McKenzie* (DD-614) from 1 October 1942 to 12 November 1944. He was awarded the Bronze Star for his performance during the Allied invasions of Italy and Southern France.

Admiral Erly: Yes. But that was why. That damn Spanish qualification, I think, was what did me in, and my Spanish really wasn't that good. I had tried to keep my hand at it. I damn near failed it at the Naval Academy. I don't know what my final grade was. But I kept after it, and through the years, I passed the ultimate test in my languages. I feel if you can pick up a telephone and do business over the phone in that language, you're qualified. I feel in my Spanish, as in my Portuguese, I probably have a great big gringo accent, but I find that my great big gringo accent, and my being able to comprehend and also to communicate, is probably a bigger plus in many situations with the Latinos than it would be if I were perfectly fluent. And the fact that I'm a blue-eyed gringo, again, speaking their language, or attempting, even though I may not be as erudite and as polished and my pronunciation not as clear as a real polished linguist, that sometimes it becomes more effective.

Paul Stillwell: It shows you're making an effort.

Admiral Erly: Oh, yes. I found that in some of my mission duties that my people who had a name of Hernandez or so forth and so on couldn't be nearly as effective as a good old Irish-American, if you follow the reason. It's been to my advantage, except I felt that that was to my disadvantage.

To go back to your question again, I was very truculent on this bit of being ordered out of the Pacific theater. It really got to me. I was mad. What the hell could I do? BuPers, in its infinite wisdom, forgot to put air travel in these "detach, proceed immediately" orders, and here I ended up in New Caledonia, and Halsey was in the same camp out there.* I forget the name of the camp. I happened to leaf through my orders and found it. I finally left on a Matson Line freighter, got back to San Francisco. That was an uneventful cruise. We came alone, but she was a fast ship. She made about 18 knots.

I'm trying to remember the little kid from Smackover, Arkansas. That was a little aviator that came back with us. I became very fond of him on the trip back. We chatted

---

* Vice Admiral/Admiral William F. Halsey Jr., USN, served as Commander South Pacific Area from 18 October 1942 to 15 June 1944. He was promoted to four-star rank in November 1942.

a lot. He'd been shot down. He was small. He had very black eyes and sort of an olive complexion, and he was afloat in his life raft for I don't know how long, and his eyes had swollen sort of shut. So he washed up on the beach somewhere, and the natives thought he was a Japanese. I ran into him later. I think I had him at line school later. His name—it's one of those things. But I remember that one tale.

The reason we got into it—of course, what do you do? There were some other people there. He and I sort of teamed up, and there was a loud-talking type there, and then there was, of course, the inevitable crap game, as you would expect, that was going to take place, and this guy had just been cleaning all the money out. So we pooled our resources the night before we were getting into San Francisco, and we got on a lucky roll and we really cleaned that guy. So I always have fond memories of my little friend from Smackover, Arkansas.*

Paul Stillwell: Was he a carrier pilot?

Admiral Erly: Yes.

Paul Stillwell: Do you remember the ship that you rode?

Admiral Erly: Well, we came back on the *Hawaiian Merchant*, and we were in a temporary structure topside. There were about eight of us on this spot. I remember I used to just take a blanket and go out and lie on deck.

Paul Stillwell: Did you get any training en route to your assignment in Cuba?

Admiral Erly: No, I didn't. I thumbed my way, really, across the country on troop trains. I traveled with a lot of Army. I finally ended up in Miami, where ComGulf Sea Frontier

---

* The description of the aviator fits Lieutenant (junior grade) Jefferson H. Carroum, USNR, of Bombing Ten (VB-10) from the carrier *Enterprise* (CV-6). He was from Smackover, Arkansas. For details see Edward P. Stafford, *The Big E: the Story of the USS Enterprise* (New York: Random House, 1962). Carroum's plane went down in the Solomons on 14 November 1943, which was a year after Erly left the South Pacific.

was headquartered. There I met my boss, who was Captain Jerry Galpin, out of the class of '20, which graduated in '19.*

I was a senior lieutenant. I walked in to meet Captain Galpin and said, words to this order, "I don't want this job. I want to be back in the Pacific, and I don't want any goddamn part of the Cuban Navy."

Jerry was a very direct guy. He said, "Get your ass to Galveston. There are two Cuban ships there that are having sonar gear, depth charges, and some 3-inch or 5-inch guns being installed. I want you to get over there, get them out of that Todd Shipyard, and get them back to Cuba, and we're going to use them in convoy operations."

Paul Stillwell: He probably wasn't any more eager to be there than you were.

Admiral Erly: Yes. Jerry was a surface sailor who had been on a staff somewhere.† He'd been out in PacFlt. So I again troop-trained it in any way I could and got over to Galveston, and stayed up all night, even though I had a bunk, because I ran into some gal who was pretty good at Spanish, and we worked on my Spanish all the way from New Orleans to Galveston.

I got in there early in the morning, went immediately to Todd Shipyard, and got our rep. He was a man out of '35, had been in, gotten out, was in the reserve, and was there as a Navy EDO type.‡ I told him what my orders were, and I went through the *Cuba* in the yard, and the crew was all off, and the *Patria*.§ I went through those and then I said, "I want to meet the skippers of the two ships."

The crews were living in a house on the beach, and a lot of the officers were living in the Buccaneer Hotel in Galveston. I hadn't had anything to eat. After I had gone through the inspection, all of a sudden we were headed out to the house. This was now about 3:00 in the afternoon. As we went by a little store, something went off.

---
* Captain Gerard F. Galpin, USN.
† As a commander, Galpin had been on the staff of Rear Admiral Frank Jack Fletcher, USN, Commander Cruisers Scouting Force.
‡ EDO – engineering duty only.
§ The *Cuba* was a 2,055-ton sloop, and the *Patria* was a 1,200-ton training ship. Both were built by the Cramp shipyard in Philadelphia, and both were launched on 10 August 1911.

Clang, clang, clang, went the alarm bell. I said, "Hey, stop." I went in and got a quart of buttermilk and drank it.

We then went and called on the skippers. Now it was about 4:00. Well, there was nothing to do, but they broke out their Cuban rum. Then they had some other officers in. They had had their wives over, and the wives had left. Evidently there was this one skipper of the *Patria* who just didn't see any sense of going back to Cuba. He was enjoying life.

I remember that night well. There was quite a lot of rum consumed, and by the time I left the two skippers, we had sort of reached a rapport. No one told them I was coming. I had to explain what my job was, that I was going to be part of the naval mission to Cuba, and I was there to help them to get their ships equipped and ready to sail. I explained that I had inspected their ships, and I realized there were some problems to be resolved.

Paul Stillwell: After this rum, you were all on the same team—united to win the war.

Admiral Erly: Oh, yes. Well, actually, I found that one, who is still a good friend of mine, is Braulio Fernández Hernandez. He was the skipper of the *Cuba*. I still correspond with him at Christmastime. He came out of Cuba and is in Miami now.

Paul Stillwell: Were these ships built in Cuba?

Admiral Erly: No. They were built by Cramp Shipbuilding of Philadelphia. The *Cuba* had reciprocating engines, and she used loofa sponges for boiler feedwater, this type of thing. We were installing sonar gear, including the chemical recorders, in addition to depth charge racks and K-guns, so I had a sonarman sent to help.*

The ship got a 3-inch surface gun, and I think we put a 5-inch gun up forward on the bow. While I was there, we had to test-fire. Again, I got that done for them. They had the same damn windows that the *Mahan*-class destroyers had, and I said, "No way.

---

* The Mark 6 depth-charge projector, known as the K-gun, was used for hurling depth charges at submarines.

The first time that gun goes, you're going to blow every window out," and I convinced our EDO type.* So they then replaced those big windows with portholes for their bridge.

Paul Stillwell: How long did the period last in Galveston, getting these ships ready?

Admiral Erly: I would say that I was probably in Galveston a good two months. I had to get the crews back on board, had to get the ships restowed, we had to get ammo, had to check out all the gear, get them provisions, do all of those things. A lot of these things were being done with working through OPs, which I didn't have to work. They had to work through their naval attaché, in Washington, and some of this was Lend-Lease type of stuff.†

Paul Stillwell: Did they get radar?

Admiral Erly: No, they did not get radar. They had a sort of an antiquated range finder. They had no fire control system. They just had the guns cornered.

Paul Stillwell: Did you have some training for them as part of this package for the crew?

Admiral Erly: We got to test-fire the guns. We had to go out and do that, and I remember we had a hang fire, which I cleared. The training came later. The main thing was to get them back to Cuba. We helped with the watch, quarter, and station bill, this type of thing. They were getting organized. They had some thoughts there.

They had an exec who was pretty good. His name was Jorge Augustino. He had been over and been with the Spanish Navy in the Spanish Revolution side of the picture and then come back and was the exec in the *Cuba*.

The *Patria* was a smaller ship, and she was really their midshipman training ship. I think she was faster than the *Cuba* and had better lines.

---

* The *Conyngham* (DD-371) and *Cassin* (DD-372), in which Erly served, were in the *Mahan* class.
† The Lend-Lease Act, passed by the U.S. Congress on 11 March 1941, was a device that enabled the United States to provide military aid to Great Britain without intervening directly in the European war then in progress. The program was later expanded to include aid to other Allied nations as well.

As I say, my mission was to get them seaworthy and back to Cuba. At this point I was joined by a Lieutenant Ned Bent, class of '40, who became the liaison officer with the *Patria*, but I kept track of both.*

Paul Stillwell: Was he also a Spanish speaker?

Admiral Erly: Yes, but Ned ran into a booby trap, in that we were given certain ship identification codes, U.S., but to be used by the Cubans. I felt that it should be turned over to the skipper, to be kept in his safe, because there was no security otherwise, and Ned did not consult with me. He opted to keep it himself, and you can see what that bred. So he and the skipper of the *Patria* were at loggerheads. The captain felt that Ned didn't trust him, you see. That was just too bad, because Ned was really gung-ho. By the time I got hold of it, it was too late, so we had to move Ned off that ship and later put him with the casos submarinos, the 83-foot coast guard cutters.

I said, "Look, if you're going to work with these guys, you've got to sort of accept them as is, as equals, as peers, and so forth. If you're going to have any confidential pubs, unless you're going to sleep with them next to your chest, there's no way you could protect them. If they wanted to get them, they'd have them anyway. You've got to be logical about these things and analyze the situation."

But Ned had a problem anyway. His skipper was noted as being bullheaded and sometimes—and this is what Braulio, the skipper of the *Cuba*, said, "He's a little touched. He boxed at the Naval Academy. Maybe his brains are scrambled a little."

I said, "Yeah, I boxed at my Naval Academy, too," and we let that one go.

Paul Stillwell: Did you then get into an operational phase with these ships?

Admiral Erly: Not right away. First we wanted to get them trained. So when we got them back to Cuba, we got them down to really go through the training cycle at Guantánamo Bay—ASW, gunnery shoots, damage control, this type of thing. I went down there, and we put them through that. We then sent them over, and I went with

---

* Lieutenant Horace E. Bent, USN.

them, to Miami to the Sub Chaser School, and they went through that.* They went through the convoy school, drawing up positioning of ships and how you would make the convoys, this type of thing. They went through all that routine. They went through the school of ship's officers. We sent the crews off to fire fighting, damage control—everything that was available. So they got really worked up well.

Paul Stillwell: Did you encounter that fellow McDaniel who ran that school at Miami?

Admiral Erly: Yes.

Paul Stillwell: Any impressions of him?

Admiral Erly: He certainly tried to get people's attention. Of course, he was really painting the cruelty of the Germans and their machine-gunning of people and lifeboats and so forth, trying to really drum up the hatred for the Germans. I sat in on some of the classes, just to see how they were going. I didn't take the complete course with them at all. I just sort of monitored, because at the same time we were getting further things done in *Cuba*.

We had some ventilation systems put in, we had bunks put in in the crew's quarters, we modernized the galley, we modernized their head system, so forth and so on. While they were off being trained, we were also getting a lot of work done in the ship and really getting her topped up, making her more habitable, particularly for the crew.

Paul Stillwell: What language was the instruction in when they were trained in Miami?

Admiral Erly: English. English.

Paul Stillwell: How well could they comprehend that?

---

* Officially the school at Miami was the Sub Chaser Training Center, commissioned on 8 April 1942. The commanding officer was Lieutenant Commander Eugene F. McDaniel, USN, who had been executive officer of the destroyer *Livermore* (DD-429) on North Atlantic duty.

Admiral Erly: Most of the officers spoke English. Then when you sent your crew to training, some spoke English enough. Other times they would send the younger English-speaking officers along, as they went through the gas mask chamber to do the interpreting. I don't recall any Spanish instructors at the school at that phase. We were too busy training our own people at that point.

In July of '43 I made lieutenant commander, and that's what the skipper of the ship was. So immediately I jumped in prestige.

Somewhere along the line I'm remembering somebody was saying—and I don't know how it got back up to OpNav or OP-17—that I could have taken over the ship, that the crew would have followed me. I had done a great deal for the crew. We got mess trays. We got the business up of sterilizing the trays. Normally they would come with a spoon and their own plate they kept in their locker before. And the old heads, God, were terrible. The old heads and their showers and the crew's living quarters, instead of swinging hammocks they now had bunks. I guess they figured, gee, we ought to go that way. That came out of it somewhere and got back to me later, after I had left really, that, "Did you realize that that crew would have gone with you at the drop of a hat?"

Paul Stillwell: How effective were those ships after the materiel fixes and the training?

Admiral Erly: They never nailed a submarine. But they were out there. They did convoy duty. And they really wanted to. What I'm really saying is, what I was impressed by was the general gung-ho attitude, particularly of the officers. They were so proud that they were one of the first to declare war on the Axis and had joined in with the United States the day after we did. They were very, very proud of that. And from being shipmates—I lived aboard, I was with them—I get really to know them, and I was quite impressed with their knowledge. They took their duties very seriously, and they were competent.

They wanted, more than anything, to nail a sub—even, I think, as much as Frank Virden and I did. I wanted them to nail one. I remember we were running up en route to Miami. First we ran on across to Key West and got some ping time on a sub there before we went on up. I remember staying up all night up in their spotting tower, hoping we would spot something going up the coast to Miami. Everybody just really wanted to knock off a German submarine. That would have been their frosting on the cake. It was there. They wanted it, and wanted it bad.

Paul Stillwell: By that time the U-boat force was beginning its decline, so you probably didn't have as many potential targets.

Admiral Erly: True. Now we're talking the summer of '43. I guess you didn't see the burning ships off the coast, but the subs were still around. As I say, they had the desire. They had the desire.

Paul Stillwell: Well, they probably got part of that from you.

Admiral Erly: No. I really think that they had it within themselves. As I tell you again, the point that they were so proud that they had joined and declared war against the Axis and they were there and ready, willing, and able to go now. I feel they felt that the U.S. had given them the wherewithal to do the job, see, with the depth charges and the K-guns, plus the surface armament, not to mention the essential deal was the sonar with a chemical recorder. So they had all that they needed.

Paul Stillwell: So the skipper got over being used to the creature comforts at Galveston?

Admiral Erly: Well, the skipper of the *Cuba*, which I spent most of my time with. Later I did go to the *Patria* to put her through some of her training paces and ride her, and had a lot of fun, but the skipper had changed then. I remember we were sitting there getting under way from—I don't know whether it was Cienfuegos or one other port. I said to him, "How long do you think it would take for you to get your ship to general quarters?" "Zafarocha de combate? [phonetic]"

Oh, I think he mentioned something.

I said, "No way."

We were sitting up on the open bridge having our snack, so he went and pulled the general alarm. He didn't make it. He wasn't too far off. He was about 30 seconds off.

I said, "See, you've got to do it more often."

But this was a way of getting things done. I really wanted to run him through some drills, so you say, "Well, what do you think? What do you think you could do it in?" and not saying I was really an official liaison. I had no command in the ship. But, "How do you work them? How do you get them to do what you really want them to do?"

Paul Stillwell: Well, it sounds as if even though you had the initial reluctance, you got into it with both feet once you got there.

Admiral Erly: Well, hell, yes. That's the only way to go, isn't it? If you're going to do it, do it, and it paid off for me. We're moving along now. I had shifted around the *Patria*. I put her through her paces. I then went with the casos submarinos and took them to Gitmo, also, and ran them through the training—basic ASW deals that we'd done the others. I developed a visual signal, flag hoist general signal book for them and a tactical book for them to make a coordinated attack and this type of thing.

After that, I guess I had been down there about seven or eight months, so I went in to see Captain Galpin and said, "You know, I'm missing out on what's going on in my own Navy. I've done my best that I think I can do for you and what I've done for the Cuban Navy, and I very respectfully request that you consider letting me get out of here."

He said, "Okay, go ahead and write your letter."

We checked with the commodore, too, of the Cuban Navy, and I sat down and wrote a letter requesting to be returned to more active theaters of war. I was willing to take anything just to get back in my own milieu, my own Navy, although I enjoyed the friendships that I made, and as I say, I still have them.

I'm a member of the Cuban Naval League. I went to a big reunion that they had down there. This is an active organization in Miami of former Cuban naval officers. I guess I went down there in '76, or '75. Braulio, the skipper of the *Cuba*, was there with his family. His daughter is the principal of a high school in Miami, which I remember when she was that high in Cuba. So I have maintained my contact with them. the skipper. He was class of '33 from their naval academy. Braulio's got to be about three, four years older than I am. They're a very staunch people, very staunch. As you will see, this influenced me later on in my life when I was at the National War College.

Back again to my friend Braulio, as he pointed to me and said, "Hey, here's my grandson." The grandson was lifting weights and a typical American high school student. He is as completely Americanized as anybody, and Braulio said, "You know damn well he's never going to go back to Cuba. No way."

He sort of feels it's a forlorn dream for a lot of them. It's a wish that the elders have. But their children, of course, as you know, and that's what the U.S.A. is, a melting pot. When people come in, it takes one generation and they're practically completely Americanized. So you don't have that carry-on of people that want to go to Cuba. It's the oldsters that are maintaining the thought that they want to see that free Cuba. Every once in a while you get a Cuban out, and he'll tell you what's happening down there.

Paul Stillwell: Well, after you got Captain Galpin's okay, how did BuPers react to your request?

Admiral Erly: Oh, BuPers hopped right on it. I could have been exec in commissioning a new ship. In fact, Frank Johnson wanted me to be his exec.[*] I had at that point been away, and what I wanted was to go to sea. This was my communication with BuPers: "No, I really have been away now, it'll be just about a year, and I feel that I don't want to spend another six months on the beach. I want back at sea. Wherever you need an exec, plug me in. They plugged me in, and it turned out to be an Atlantic ship.

Paul Stillwell: What ship was that?

---

[*] Commander Frank L. Johnson, USN, was the first commanding officer of the destroyer *Purdy* (DD-734), built at Bath Iron Works and commissioned on 18 July 1944.

Admiral Erly: That was the *Laub*, which was a sister ship of *Frazier*.*

Paul Stillwell: Where did she operate from?

Admiral Erly: She was running fast convoys to Europe. Alex Hay was the skipper.† Evidently they'd been having trouble. They'd been flopping through execs, the doctor was a lush, there was drinking on board.

Paul Stillwell: Well, this was a made-to-order challenge for the new exec.

Admiral Erly: Yes. It didn't take long until I called the officers in the wardroom and said, "If I catch any of you drinking in the ship, anytime, I'm going to get you a court-martial." I should have had the captain there.

Paul Stillwell: Was he part of the problem?

Admiral Erly: I think things had gotten slack. Some of the officers had started nipping and going up on watch. That can permeate when you've got the odor of booze on your breath or something of that nature. I gather there had been as much as the previous exec had been goosed on the bridge and then all that type of crap. So I started to take a real hard-nosed approach, as soon as I sensed what the problem was and that they really needed a son of a bitch—and they got one.

Paul Stillwell: Why had there been so much turnover in execs previously?

---

* USS *Laub* (DD-613), a *Benson*-class destroyer was commissioned 24 October 1942. She had a standard displacement of 1,620 tons, was 348 feet long, and 36 feet in the beam. Her top speed was 37.5 knots. She was armed with five 5-inch guns, ten 40-millimeter and seven 20-millimeter guns, and five 21-inch torpedo tubes. She fought through the remainder of the war. She was decommissioned and placed in reserve 2 February 1946.
† Lieutenant Commander Alexander G. Hay, USN, commanded the *Laub* from 9 August 1943 to 17 March 1944.

Admiral Erly: I guess the same thing that was probably happening in the Pacific. You know, they'd get somebody in there, and then there were new ships coming on line, they were pulling people out, and this type of thing.

Alex was the class of '34. Hell of a nice guy, actually. I had him for maybe four or five months, something like that. Then I forget where he went. We started out with a fast convoy, and there were four fast escorts. One was having trouble and lagged behind, so we ended up with three, and I'm trying to remember who the hell the screen commander was. I don't think it was us.

But then we had this one ammo ship that kept breaking down, and we got out there on about the third day, pretty rough, and they threw a rotating asymmetrical screen around this ship that was stopped dead in the water. We took one hell of a roll. I swear, she must have gone about 72 degrees. What does that get you? That gets you water down the intake ducts, which in those days, in that type ship, would you believe it, the blowers came right out on the electrical distribution board. It took off the bulwark from the break of the deck as it came aft on the starboard side. That bulwark hit the starboard screw, and so then you only really had one screw because then you had to secure that shaft, because then you were going to wipe the bearings if you didn't.

So we then had to radio on off and came back into New York on one screw. Of course, the switchboard needed rewiring, and then there needed to be some deflectors put in so it wouldn't happen again and the bulwark reinstalled and the prop repaired.

I'm trying to remember. We went to GQ to get a muster. We lost one man over the side on that one. Something sticks in my mind, did we have a bad muster or did we know it at the time? It was blowing like hell. We lost one man over the side; I'm sure on that. So it was a combination of wind, sea, and rudder that did it. I was down below when this happened, but when she went over there, and you could still feel it, you wonder, "Is she going to come back upright?"

Paul Stillwell: It was a legitimate concern.

Admiral Erly: She did.

Paul Stillwell: What do you remember about the operational nature of your duties as exec?

Admiral Erly: Oh, that's easy. The exec is everywhere. He's got his nose in everybody's business. Has to. Get around the ship, see what's going on, make sure everybody's there. Being the navigator was part of the exec's function in those days. You didn't have an exec plus a navigator. That meant morning stars, evening stars, trying to get a fix, and then that was helpful to me in some cases out there it was a problem when you couldn't see the horizon because it was bad visibility. You know that the fire control radar has a stable element, so if you get up on the range finder and get your star sight there, you've got an approximation. So you could still get your navigation that way. When the hell did Loran come in?*

Paul Stillwell: That I don't know.

Admiral Erly: We didn't have it at that point, I'm sure. But, as I say, the exec's job was all-encompassing, whether or not you were recommending to the skipper the qualification of officers of the deck, etc. I'm trying to think if we had the seasick cases on. I don't believe we did. Every time you came into port you got some new junior officers and new crew members. That meant the period of training had to continue. Inspections. Things just had to continue going, and that was, of course, the plan of the day, the drills, what was to be accomplished that particular day, and that all fell on the exec. You tried to get your inputs from the captain, see what he wanted done, and this type of thing. I'll tell you, the exec, of course, particularly in the destroyer in those days, was probably the most demanding job of any billet in the ship, saddled with the safe navigation, period, period, period, exclamation mark.

Paul Stillwell: Well, this time you had gotten what you asked for. Were you satisfied when you got it?

---

* Loran (long-range aid to navigation) is a system of electronic navigation that involves the reception of pulse signals transmitted simultaneously by paired stations ashore.

Admiral Erly: Oh, yes, I was back at sea, sure. Hell, that was a great part of it. I was just thinking, the only good fallout from an otherwise bad time for the ship is we returned to port for repairs. In that time frame I was married to my wife Lois, whom I had met in Cuba, and that was fate.* So something good comes out of everything.

Paul Stillwell: How had she happened to be in Cuba?

Admiral Erly: Her company was Plymouth Cordage Company, and as you know, once Manila fell, everything went, including the hemp. There was a substitute called sisal, and Cuba had quite a harvest of sisal. So the War Production Board needed all the sisal they could get. She was their representative down there buying up sisal for the Plymouth Cordage Company.

Paul Stillwell: How had you specifically encountered her?

Admiral Erly: When the ships were in, and if I was on the beach, I stayed at the Hotel Nacionale. That's where she stayed, and that's where we met.

Paul Stillwell: Well, then, you have your good buddy Rittenhouse to thank for your wife.

Admiral Erly: Yes, we got together with Rit and Vi years later. He's dead now. He made admiral when he was over there in MAAG Spain.† Rit was quite a guy. In fact, we became friends later on.

Paul Stillwell: Back to the *Laub*. What operational highlights do you remember from those convoys, other than your nearly capsizing?

Admiral Erly: Well, we then cycled back into going from New York up to Casco Bay, Maine, underway training, doing the various gunnery drills, doing your ASW bit, also

---

* Erly married Lois Richards on 14 April 1944.
† MAAG – military assistance advisory group.

doing the "assist ship" bit. Research and development had gotten this point of how to kill the deep-diving U-boat. The standard procedure was for the U-boats to go deep once they were under depth-charge attack. The only way to get them, really, was to have another ship pinging on it and coaching the attacking ship in over the U-boat and giving the order to fire the depth-charge pattern.

That's what they called the assist-ship ASW doctrine. We practiced those types of things. Of course, the gunnery shoots, other exercises were just anytime, really. When you returned from a convoy mission, you transferred some crew members and got new ones. You got both enlisted and officers. So again it was that process of getting them to become a part of the team organization.

Paul Stillwell: A mini-shakedown?

Admiral Erly: Yes, yes. You need it. There's another little old axiom. I say the most dangerous time for a ship is anytime she leaves the shipyard, if she's been in a shipyard for a while. That first time under way, be careful. Be extra careful. You can't emphasize that enough, because the most classic example is the *Missouri*, and I could cite lots of others.*

Paul Stillwell: With a new skipper.

Admiral Erly: Yes. They had a new skipper. Even with an old skipper. That could well have happened on the *Missouri* after being in the shipyard.

Paul Stillwell: Did you have contacts with German submarines during these convoys?

Admiral Erly: Nope, not one. Worst luck.

---

* The battleship *Missouri* (BB-63) ran aground near Norfolk, Virginia, on 17 January 1950. Her new commanding officer, Captain William D. Brown, USN, was relieved on 3 February 1950 by Captain Harold Page Smith, USN, a previous skipper. For Smith's recollections of the event, see "The Value of Confidence," *Naval History*, Fall 1991, page 36.

Paul Stillwell: Was yours mainly the sheepdog role, keeping the convoy rounded up?

Admiral Erly: Yes, and particularly if you had a storm. That became more evident to me later when I was commanding officer of the *Phelps*, the escort commodore's flagship for GUS convoys.* Normally the sheep-dogging came with the GUS. See, the fast convoys that the *Laub* escorted, you didn't have that many ships, and normally they were special cargo, like special ammo or things of that nature, and you were moving at a good clip. They weren't straggling all over the ocean. When you got to the GUS convoys and you got 72 ships to 100 ships at eight knots, that was something else again.

For the fast convoys, you moved out. You'd normally try to set the speed at 15 knots and not change one rpm. You'd try to get your plant and get it leaned down just to hold that speed and try to get your optimum efficiency, because sometimes the refueling opportunities became few and far between. Normally in the slow convoy, you'd get oil from somebody. You could replenish en route, so that wasn't as bad. You always had an oiler or something along. In the fast ones you didn't, and that was stretching it on your fuel capacity.

Paul Stillwell: What destinations did you go to at the other end?

Admiral Erly: Actually, the ones that we went to were in the Mediterranean. We'd end up in Mers-El-Kébir—Oran, if you will.

Paul Stillwell: Where the British had done a number on the French in 1940.†

Admiral Erly: Yes.

Paul Stillwell: Were there still remnants of that?

---

* GUS signified slow westbound convoys from Europe, the initials standing for Gibraltar to the United States.
† On 3 July 1940, shortly after Germany invaded and conquered France, the Royal Navy bombarded ships of the French Navy—until then an ally—in the port of Mers-El-Kébir to keep them from falling into German hands. The action, which killed 1,297 French sailors, demonstrated Britain's resolve to remain in the fight.

Admiral Erly: Oh, hell, yes. An oil tanker was firmly there because it couldn't move, but it could still hold oil. That was where we refueled. It was manned by Frenchmen. There were still sunken ships in the harbor that you had to avoid, but that's where you moored.

Paul Stillwell: What memories do you have of being ashore in North Africa?

Admiral Erly: Hot, dusty. We got a little bit more going when we got over there, reporting in. I'm just trying to remember. With *Laub*, during this period that we were back getting repaired or shortly thereafter or in Casco Bay Tony Roessler came aboard and relieved Alex Hay.* The next time we took off, I think we had another fast convoy.

Being in Naples—and, again, you were mentioning the VT fuze, because you could spot the German aircraft way up. Boy, he was climbing over there. He could come zinging across way up in the sky. They would come in and drop mines that then became floaters. I remember we were anchored just outside the harbor off Naples, and, lo and behold, here came this floating mine. We had enough time to man fire hoses and keep it away from hitting the ship. You didn't dare try to explode it with a rifle at this point; it was too damn close aboard.

I guess we should get into the *Laub* being almost been cut in two off Anzio.†

Paul Stillwell: It sounds interesting.

Admiral Erly: Well, I mentioned gunfire support missions, and the Anzio bit was going on. We'd been up there before with various cruisers and normally with a couple of other destroyers, and what you do would be to be out in front as ASW escorts. We were clocking along at about 25 knots. Our sonar gear is no damn good at that speed. We were just out there, two horns before the main body. We went in and had gunfire support missions off Anzio and then ended up back in Naples. We were in a gunfire support element group.

---

* Commander Anthony C. Roessler, USN, commanded the *Laub* from 17 March 1944 to 1 July 1945.
† The Allies invaded Anzio, a city on the Italian coast about 35 miles south of Rome, on 22 January 1944.

This one deal, we were with the "Philly," getting ready to go into Anzio, and it had been a pretty rough schedule. I'm trying to remember what had happened. Tony Roesser was the skipper. I was trying to protect him, and I spent long hours on the bridge to allow him to rest. I guess I turned in about 3:00 or 4:00 o'clock. We were making 25 knots. We were on the port bow of the *Philadelphia*. The officer of the deck, Lieutenant Hunley, was the first lieutenant and also the senior watch officer. We got an order to form 18. He said he informed the captain. I was down below at this point, crapped out. It was executed, and from what I gather happened, instead of turning outboard, he turned inboard, and all of a sudden, the first thing you knew you were starting the clock. You've got a 30-, 35-, 40-, 45-knot closing situation. It didn't take very long to eat up 1,500 yards. The end result was that the *Philadelphia* hit the *Laub* at the juncture of the after engine room and put 70 feet of her bow through the other side.[*]

Paul Stillwell: That's from the high relative speed you're talking of.

Admiral Erly: Oh, yes, sure. I think that the board of investigation inquiry, the *Philadelphia* had backed, and the hell of it was, I think she backed out too soon, because we could have damn near sunk.

This is all conjecture on my part. I was in my bunk, fully clothed. I was feeling these concussions go off as my head was bouncing on a steel deck. I thought I was having a nightmare. I was catapulted from the bunk out on the deck and knocked out. So I came to, feeling this, and I realized I was in a dead ship, but with these explosions going off. I got up and staggered out, wondering what the hell was going on, still a little groggy. We were listing. The exec's stateroom was up here on this level, and was looking down almost at the hatch of the forward fireroom. There was a lot of activity, and I heard somebody yell, "Abandon ship!"

---

[*] In the early morning of 23 May 1944 the light cruiser *Philadelphia* (CL-41) was steaming on the way to the fire support area off Anzio, Italy. The destroyer *Laub* (DD-613) was off the port bow and destroyer *Kendrick* (DD-612) to starboard. At 0427 the *Laub* received orders to take station astern, and at 0433 a signal was sent to change base course. When the signal was executed a 0434 the *Laub* turned the wrong way and into the path of the *Philadelphia*. The bow of the *Philadelphia* hit the *Laub*'s starboard side abreast of the after stack. Two of the destroyer's men were killed and four injured. The commanding officer of the cruiser was Captain Walter C. W. Ansel, USN. Ansel's Naval Institute oral history covers the collision.

I jumped down, and said, "Hey, what's this abandon ship?" I looked up at the bridge. It was jettison ship. So I said, "Back down in that fireroom."

So we got that stemmed.

Paul Stillwell: Had the keel been broken?

Admiral Erly: It only remained about two inches from being severed. The only thing that saved the ship from really buckling was the port propeller shaft. Otherwise, she would have gone. When we got her in dry dock, she was damn near severed. Yes. It was really fortunate the ship hadn't gone down, say, basically like the *Wasp* and the *Hobson*.[*]

I guess it was sort of a nightmare what happened next—the question of trying to save the ship. As I told you, I learned a very valuable lesson here on this damage control, and the words "abandon ship." From that day forward, in any ship I was ever in, the words "abandon ship" were never used. The abandon ship bill required to be in the ship's organization book was called disembarking drill. Under that in the ship's organization book, it stated, "The words 'abandon ship' will never be used in this ship except by the surviving senior." This business "abandon ship and provide" never was used in any ship under my command. Never.

The other thing was that your shoring timbers and your emergency acetylene cutting equipment and that type of thing were emblazoned with great big red letters, "Do Not Jettison," because in this flurry of what was going on, they even threw over the damn shoring timbers, and later I had to have another destroyer come alongside to pass them to us in order to shore up the after bulkhead of the engine room.

Immediately, here you were in the war zone, and we were worried again about air attack. Here we were a cripple out there, and the 40-millimeter mounts that were back there were wiped out. We lost, really, that 5-inch mount that was in that local area. We were having progressive flooding. We were just fortunate that the *Philadelphia*'s bow

---

[*] On the night of 26 April 1952, during an eastward crossing of the Atlantic, the destroyer minesweeper *Hobson* (DMS-26) turned in front of the aircraft carrier *Wasp* (CV-18), collided with her, and sank. Of the *Hobson*'s crew, 176 men were lost, including the commanding officer, Lieutenant Commander W. J. Tierney, USN; 52 were rescued. See Winston Jordan, "Flank Speed to Eternity," *Naval History*, Spring 1988, pages 12-17.

penetrated where it did. If it had been even another five feet aft, we'd have lost that after sleeping compartment, which flooded out later, but we would have lost the crew there. As it was, we were fortunate in that we only lost two people out of the engine room. The after engine room took the main brunt, but the fireroom just forward of it flooded. But it was evacuated safely.

Some of the crew in that after engine room swam out the side and were pulled aboard around the stern. See, all this came out later. Thank God, they got them on board before young Cramer got rid of the depth charges.[*] Hell of a nice kid, later made vice admiral. I remember when he made admiral, I wrote him then, and he replied, "I've always remembered what you said to me when you were exec of the *Laub*." He recalled that I came to my stateroom one morning and, "You looked up and you said, 'Mr. Cramer, what have you done for the Navy today?'" He had gone aft, and he was the one who was jettisoning the depth charges.

Paul Stillwell: Certainly something that needed to be done.

Admiral Erly: Yes, if we were going to sink, get rid of them. I later said to him, "Shannon, did you make damn sure that the safety forks were in?"

"Well, the safety forks were in."

What I gathered, and I found this out, with ultra-deep water, the pressure will activate the exploder mechanisms, even with the safety forks in. And I believed Shannon, because he wouldn't lie. We were getting that deep-water explosion, and it was those depth charges going off way deep that woke me, that brought me to. The explosions could have sunk us if it hadn't been for those shafts. It's a damn wonder that the explosions didn't complete the job on the shafts. In retrospect, as you look back, it would have been smarter not to have jettisoned everything, but there you go. I didn't give the jettison order; the CO did.

We finally got the shoring done. We even got a collision mat over on that one side. They reported to me that the damage control party had done their bit. So I went aft,

---

[*] Ensign Shannon D. Cramer Jr., USN, reported to the *Laub* after graduating from the Naval Academy in 1943. He later went into submarines.

went down below by myself, opened the watertight doors and closed them behind me. I went forward, and when I got to this one bulkhead, all the shoring had fallen on the deck, and the old bulkhead was surging toward me. So I went out carefully, closing the watertight closures behind me. I got Hunley, and I said, "Look, you get that shoring, get it back up there, and put a watch down there to make sure it stays in place."

Then I said, "Well, Jesus, what's going on here?" I looked over the side and, man, we were making a good way through the water.

I got to the bridge. I'll never forget him, Sam Warren, a little communications officer, was there. I said, "What's going on, Sam? What the hell speed are we making?"

He said, "I told the tug to make maximum speed."

"Tell him to slow to five knots right now."

Sam had thought that the faster we got to port, the safer we would be. Well, what he was about to do was to really flood the whole damn ship, and we were going to sink. If the CO had been on the bridge, this would not have happened. However, he was so despondent about the collision that he went to the sea cabin and did not reappear until we got to Naples.

So we got slowed down. It took us measurably longer to get there, but we got there. We got back into Naples and went into dry dock.

Paul Stillwell: How much in the way of repairs was the facility there able to do?

Admiral Erly: They did some welding, and, of course, you were going to have to do that whole engine room. You were going to have to do the whole fireroom. They built sort of a box structure, a caisson, just for strength, over the starboard side. They also reinforced the keel.

I got a good impression of our British friends there. The British had control of the shipyard. They recommended, when we came in for the work, if we could have a soup kettle for the Italian workmen. So we did this. But then, I think about the second or third day we were there, they went on strike.

Paul Stillwell: One problem after another.

Admiral Erly: Yes. Well, it didn't last very long, because the British lined all these workmen up. I watched with interest what was taking place. I said, "Secure the soup kettle." If they were going to strike, they don't get any more chow from us.

This little limey commander got up there and said, "Either you go back to work or we're going to shoot you. We're going to start at this end of the line and we're going to shoot you three at a time unless you go back to work." They went back to work.

About this time, I had become the subject of traffic between Jimmy Clay, who considered himself to be ComDesLant a la Europe, to report to his staff in Oran.*

Roessler sent a dispatch that said I was going to have to go off for the investigation that has been formed and that I was needed with the ship.

The staff in Oran came back with a message, "Sending a qualified relief, but get Erly on the way. We need him."

Bradley was the name of the fellow from Boston, who reported on board; I forget what ship he came from. He relieved me while I went on temporary duty with Clay's staff. George Wright was sort of acting as Jimmy Clay's chief of staff.†

Who was on that staff with me? What they wanted me there for was to be sort of their senior staff watch officer under way, and we were rehearsing for the Normandy invasion.‡ Les Sell was there as a young lieutenant.§ He came also, was one of my watch standers that I was training. I forget who else. That's what we basically were doing, working on those plans and had our rehearsal. We did go through rehearsal. After we had gone through the rehearsal, I went back to the States in *Laub* on the end of a tether line.

[Tape recorder turned off.]

Paul Stillwell: We were talking before about the *Laub* problems. I was interested in the story you told me during the break about recovering the bodies of the two dead sailors.

---

* Captain James P. Clay, USN. ComDesLant – Commander Destroyer Force Atlantic Fleet, the type commander.
† Commander George C. Wright, USN.
‡ D-Day for the Allied invasion of France at Normandy was 6 June 1944, about two weeks after the *Laub*'s collision. Perhaps Erly meant the upcoming invasion of Southern France in August 1944.
§ Lieutenant (junior grade) Leslie H. Sell, USN, later a flag officer.

Admiral Erly: Well, as I explained to you previously, that we had lost two personnel, and they were in that after engine room. It wasn't until we got in the Italian Navy shipyard in Naples, and de-watered the space, which was a crushed mangle of machinery and electrical distribution boards and so forth, we found one cadaver and extracted it with no problems.

Some engine room personnel came to my cabin and informed me that they had located the second body, but couldn't get it out because the right foot and leg were enmeshed in the wreckage. It was essential to get the corpse out, both for morale and sanitary reasons. I looked for the ship's doctor, and he wasn't available. So I made myself available and crawled in on my stomach to the area. I couldn't reach any farther in to the cadaver, but I saw that a crowbar or extension could be used to free the ankle and limb, and with a crowbar I was able to get the corpse free.

Paul Stillwell: Essentially an amputation.

Admiral Erly: Yes, by an amputation at the ankle.

I was just thinking that at about this phase—this was in May, because I received a letter from my wife mentioning the holiday Memorial Day, and that day, of course, I'd attended the funeral in the cemetery close by Naples, where we buried two of our shipmates. So I wrote her back and said that Memorial Day was not a holiday, that it was a day of recognition for those who had given their lives for their country, and that I had just attended a ceremony for two such, so please don't call Memorial Day a holiday.

Paul Stillwell: How did the rest of the crew react to that experience, not only the collision, but the loss of shipmates?

Admiral Erly: As I say, the American sailor takes the hard ones and bounces back. Their main aim was to get the ship back on the line, and they went at it wholeheartedly, as they did after the collision to save the ship, because we could have lost that ship.

Paul Stillwell: Was there any threat of air attack in the shipyard?

Admiral Erly: Oh, yes. Yes, that was something else that, of the horribleness of war, of what it means to people. We were there for a bit, and we were able to get an apartment out in town as a recreation center. I remember one evening being there, and I guess it was about 1:00 in the morning. A bombing raid came in, and I could hear the city of Naples come alive with the pitiless cries of fright—and that'll always be with me—as the Italian people awakened and were running for the tunnels and the shelters. It's a very horrible sound. You could just hear the wailing. It brings home just how awful war is. And this was not against military targets; this was against the city.

Paul Stillwell: Did you develop sort of a fatalistic attitude yourself?

Admiral Erly: Well, certainly. I just stood out there and watched the bombs fall. I had a ringside seat.

Paul Stillwell: Almost like a spectator sport.

Admiral Erly: Yes. I wasn't about to run for cover.

Paul Stillwell: Were you involved in any of the investigation or court of inquiry following the collision?

Admiral Erly: No. No, I forget where it was held, because the officer of the deck and the captain—I'm trying to remember who else went off. They went somewhere for the investigation.

Paul Stillwell: Do you remember any of the substance of the work you did when you were on Commodore Clay's staff?

Admiral Erly: No. Remembering the planning, my main job was to whip the staff watch officers into shape so they would be able to be on the TBS, the voice radio, putting out the tactical signals, that type of thing. I was actually the commodore's signal and tactical officer.

Paul Stillwell: Well, it sounds like that was an operational role instead of just planning.

Admiral Erly: Oh, yes, it was basically.

Paul Stillwell: Where did you operate from?

Admiral Erly: We actually operated from the bridge of a destroyer, in one corner.

Paul Stillwell: Where was the destroyer?

Admiral Erly: We did some maneuvering. We were home based in Oran. The staff was in a destroyer tender in Oran, but then they wanted to be more of a shore-side kind of schedule. As I said, Jimmy Clay was operating as a Mediterranean DesLant, so to speak, which made it a little embarrassing at times, because my desron commander was Charlie Cater, and he happened to be senior.[*] But the way it was set up was Jimmy Clay had set himself up with his little empire. He sort of maintained being DesLant's rep there for the destroyer force.

Paul Stillwell: Clay later went up to Casco Bay, and he was there at the end of the war.

Admiral Erly: He actually was DesLant's chief of staff at the end of the war with—who was the admiral?[†] I don't think he got along, because, with a little more on that, which I got firsthand because I later ended up as exec of the *Yosemite*, which was DesLant's flagship. Well, Jimmy Clay had gone, but the skipper was a Captain Jimmy Benson

---

[*] Captain Charles J. Cater, USN, Commander Destroyer Squadron 16.
[†] Rear Admiral O. M. Read, USN, commanded Destroyer Force Atlantic Fleet from 20 September 1944 to 6 October 1945.

when I got there.* He had been skipper, and he hated Clay with a vengeance for some reason or other.

Clay had been kicked out of the admiral's mess, came over to Jimmy's mess and tried to run Jimmy's mess, and I think Jimmy kicked him out of his mess, so there was no love lost. Now, I'm giving you hearsay, which I got from Jimmy Benson, and I was with him roughly six months as his exec in the *Yosemite*.

Paul Stillwell: What observations do you have of Clay from that time in the Mediterranean?

Admiral Erly: I wasn't vividly impressed, really wasn't. I thought that he didn't set a very good example for his juniors. He had a French babe on the beach. I don't know really, because I wasn't there for the invasion, if he did make a valuable contribution or if he functioned as the overall coordinator of destroyers or not. I don't know what history says, do you?

Paul Stillwell: No, I don't.

Admiral Erly: I don't know. I felt that I'd sort of been shanghaied down there, anyway. Maybe my opinions are biased.

Paul Stillwell: Well, you'd been shanghaied to the Cuban thing, and you've got a more favorable memory of that.

Well, any other observations on that tour of duty with Clay?

Admiral Erly: It becomes sort of hazy. I have no idea. Was I there one month, two months, three months? I don't even know whether I had a letter of fitness report or anything else. The one that seemed to be the steady one was George Wright, really, and he was sort of waiting in the wings, I think, to get a desron or something of that nature at

---

* Captain James F. Benson, USN, commanded the destroyer tender *Yosemite* (AD-19) from 8 December 1946 to 12 November 1948.

that point in time. He sort of functioned as a chief of staff to Clay, so I really saw more of George Wright than I did of Clay.

As soon as we came back to the States with *Laub*, I took leave and went to Washington to get a command. I went to BuPers. And, like ships passing in the dark, there was this one officer talking to the destroyer detailer. It was little Dave Martineau.* When it was my turn, I said, "I'm so-and-so, and I want a destroyer command."

Dave was going to go to new construction after commanding the *Phelps*. He had brought her around to Charleston, and she was in there for an ultimate armament conversion. Martineau needed a relief, and I was it. Even after being in the Pacific campaign, she still had those single-purpose 5-inch/38 guns.† Hard to believe, but true.

As I stepped up to bat, the detailer threw the ball and said "*Phelps*."

I said, "Fine. When, where, and how?"

So I went back to Boston, and my orders were in the mail. Montgomery Bradley, the temp that Clay had put aboard, was still on board, so my relief as exec was already there.‡ So we packed up what little of our few possessions and headed for Charleston, South Carolina.§

I relieved a ship that was a mess.** The ship's company had moved off the ship because of the ultimate armament conversion. Because of the disruption from the yard work, the ship was not habitable.

So I relieved Dave. I hadn't been there very long, and I was walking through the ship. As I walked through one of the officer's stateroom, I noticed a yard workman dropping something, and I picked it up. It was a personal diary, and you're not supposed to keep personal diaries in wartime. Then I started looking around, and I found some confidential pubs. Well, what did that mean?

---

* Lieutenant Commander David L. Martineau, USN, commanded the destroyer *Phelps* (DD-360) from 14 December 1943 to 26 August 1944.
† The single-purpose guns were only for surface firing, not antiair as well.
‡ Lieutenant Montgomery S. Bradley, USNR.
§ Lieutenant Commander Erly commanded the *Phelps* from 26 August 1944 to 6 November 1945.
** USS *Phelps* (DD-360) was a *Porter*-class destroyer, commissioned 26 February 1936. She had a standard displacement of 1,805 tons, was 380 feet long, and 36 feet in the beam. Her design speed was 37 knots. She was originally armed with eight 5-inch guns and eight 21-inch torpedo tubes. During World War II her armament was altered several times by the removal of 5-inch dual mounts and the addition of antiaircraft guns. The *Phelps* served throughout the war and was eventually decommissioned on 6 November 1945.

Paul Stillwell: Well, you had two violations right there.

Admiral Erly: Yes. So I called all the officers together. I said, "Okay, I found these things. All your registered pubs are supposed to be accounted for." I got the exec, Willie Hartz, and said, "You get the officers, you go down, you fine-tooth comb that ship, and you get every bit of classified material out of that ship."*

Well, after about three days of concentrated effort, they reported they had everything, and I had to make a considered decision.

I had to sit and say, "Have we really caused a security leak? Could anything that any yard workman has seen be inimical to the war effort?" I made the assumption then that, "Okay, we've covered all bases. I don't think that there has been anything inimical to our war effort." So I put that incident in my back pocket.

Now I'll skip to—oh, God, I guess, about a week before we were getting ready to get under way. They eliminated the spacious commodore's quarters and the captain's nice quarters. The *Phelps* and her sisters were designed as destroyer squadron flagships. The shipyard cut everything off, and we went with a new superstructure all the way up. We ended with a DE-type bridge and a CIC, the whole schmear.† The big after mast came off, and the forward mast came down. We were a lower silhouette throughout.

In the process, they had taken the safe out of the captain's cabin. We were ready to get under way, and I'd been assured that everything had been accounted for. A DE skipper came aboard and requested to see me and came up to my cabin, threw this thing down on my desk, and said, "This came out of a safe that we picked up on the pile over there to have an additional safe in our ship."

I said, "What about it?"

He says, "It's confidential."

I said, "Thank you very much."

He handed me documents that were for COs' eyes only, confidential. These were DesLant letters, and what they were saying was, "For those officers and so forth who are not really up to DesLant's standards, send them to the DE." [Laughter]

---

* Lieutenant William H. Hartz Jr., USNR.
† DE – destroyer escort.

Well, what do you do? I called in Willie Hartz, my exec, and I said, "Willie, look at this. You told me that everything was accounted for."

He said, "Well, that came directly to the captain."

So I knew he had an out, but I'm just saying, "Look."

Well, that was my starting episode.

Paul Stillwell: Did things get better from there?

Admiral Erly: Oh, yes, they got better. They got better. It was blood, sweat, and tears, but it got better. I was just thinking, for an inspection, what I added to my inspection party was a couple of people from our R division.* They had a hacksaw and they had the biggest pair of bolt cutters you ever saw, and we went through the ship. The shipyard had done a lot of rewiring, but there was old cable hanging still left. I guess we must have gotten rid of tons of extra stuff that was just left in there, in our inspections, by doing it that way.

We had to do all the degaussing bit and all that type of stuff, test firings, so forth.† We then left Charleston and went to Norfolk to pick up the convoy, our escort commander and his staff. The staff, I guess, consisted of a lieutenant communicator, chief radioman, and a yeoman and a four-striper. In this case, was a guy out of the class of '25 by the name of Red Markham.‡

So we went off on our first convoy, which was a USG—United States to Gibraltar. We started with it from Norfolk, and I don't know how many ships, maybe 30. Went down and joined up with another element of it from New York, and by the time we got through, I guess that first convoy was pushing 100. The first night was always really a melee, and if you had only one or two collisions among the merchantmen, you were doing well.

You tried to keep it simple, no complicated maneuvers and so forth, and you were not moving at more than about seven or eight knots. You had the old Liberty ships and

---

* R division – repair.
† Degaussing is the practice of wrapping electrical cables around the hull of a ship to reduce its magnetic tendencies. Ships run a degaussing range to check the effectiveness of the equipment.
‡ Captain Lewis M. Markham Jr., USN, Commander Escort Division 21.

so forth and so on.* You tried to get them in, and then by daybreak, we'd peel off and go down and start counting noses—up and down the columns, up and down the columns. After we got a nose count, then we would then go alongside the convoy commodore's ship and yak at him. We had some sound-powered phones, so the escort commander and the convoy commodore could talk. That used to be the routine procedure.

We also had a doctor on board, which meant, in many cases, for some of the armed guard crews and whatnot, we were their hospital source. If there was an appendectomy or whatever, we would normally get it.

Paul Stillwell: Did you tell me before that you refueled from one of the merchant ships during this type of an operation?

Admiral Erly: Yes. Normally we would schedule about halfway over and, weather permitting, if there was oil, you'd go alongside and get a drink.

Paul Stillwell: Was this the alongside method or did you trail a hose?

Admiral Erly: Oh, alongside. We'd go alongside.

Paul Stillwell: So it was a normal Navy-type fleet oiler?

Admiral Erly: Yes, in some cases, but in others it was a civilian oiler. You'd go alongside and maintain position out there. The only connection was your hose.

It was humdrum. There were exercises. You'd fire a burst, and then the escorts were supposed to get on it. You would rotate some of the screening units. You always had somebody bringing up the tail end also. But since I was a flagship, I normally was in the van, except when we went checking back through the convoy on what was going on and so forth. We'd go back through and up alongside to confer with the convoy

---

* The Liberty ship was a mass-produced cargo ship designed by the U.S. Maritime Commission for use by the Allies in World War II. All told, American shipyards built 2,770 Liberties. The standard Liberty was 442 feet long, 57 feet in the beam, and had a light displacement of 3,337 tons. It had a cargo capacity of 10,920 deadweight tons. Maximum speed for a Liberty was about 12 knots.

commodore. The convoy commodore and the escort commander were getting the daily enemy submarine summaries that were coming out of OpNav. So you might have to alter course if there was a possible submarine contact up ahead. Actually, in all of our convoys we never made a contact, but we altered course several times to avoid U-boats.

Paul Stillwell: Did you deliberately avoid some contacts?

Admiral Erly: Oh, yes. You wouldn't take that wandering herd into a known submarine threat. [Tape recorder turned off.]

I pointed out to you, we'd get the daily summary of submarine activities from CominCh.[*] They had this special shop set up in CNO to analyze all the intercept traffic or anything and put it down, and they would definitely come out and tell you where any submarine concentration was. They knew the convoy's routing, and I'm sure they were tracking us.

Paul Stillwell: Do you know that you got inputs from the decoded German radio traffic?

Admiral Erly: Decoded, that I don't know. But I'm sure that they were DFing everything they could get.[†]

Paul Stillwell: What were the satisfactions of taking command after this period of preparation that you'd been through?

Admiral Erly: Well, I think there's a satisfaction. The *Phelps* has a reunion every two years, and the last reunion, which I could not attend, was at Charleston. Every time they have one, they ask for an input from me, a letter or something. I wrote them this time what I thought was a great place for the reunion for me personally, because, again, that had been the assumption of my first command. It was the awesome responsibility that I

---

[*] CominCh was the abbreviation used for Commander in Chief U.S. Fleet when Admiral Ernest J. King, USN, held that title from 1941 to 1945. He was promoted to the five-star rank of fleet admiral in December 1944.
[†] DF – radio direction finding.

felt to go in harm's way with my main responsibility to lose no man heedlessly or needlessly. And, of course, I took to that command a lot of practical experience that I had gone through. As I mentioned before, in the ship's organization book things that we would do, and I set my ship up and had it run where I thought it would be most efficient.

Also, a ship of this type had foundered in a hurricane off of Bermuda.* I was fortunate that the skipper of that ship survived, and he came aboard the *Phelps* with members of the court of inquiry.† I had a chance to discuss with him, what would you do if you had it to do over again? If you ran into that situation to save your ship, what would you do? And his answer was, "Put that sea and wind on the quarter and go with it."

However, I even did more than that. I had manufactured a mammoth sea anchor, with a heavy line. If the ship lost all power, I would have been able to deploy this sea anchor to sort of hold us up into the sea, if worst had ever come to worst. Thank goodness, I never had to use that, but I thought ahead far enough, what would happen if I lost all power, and I had devised this device.

Paul Stillwell: What was it made of?

Admiral Erly: Basically, canvas and heavy manila line.

Paul Stillwell: Where did you stow it?

Admiral Erly: Actually, under way we would stow that in the waist of the ship—the break of the foredeck and the main deck.

Paul Stillwell: Had the ship's handling been affected by these operations you'd been through?

---

* USS *Warrington* (DD-383) encountered a hurricane off the Florida coast and attempted to ride out the storm. Water entered into her vents, leading to a loss of electrical power and propulsion. On the afternoon of 13 September 1944 her crew abandoned the ship shortly before she sank. Only five officers and 68 enlisted men survived. For details, see Robert A. Dawes, Jr., *The Dragon's Breath: Hurricane at Sea* (Annapolis: Naval Institute Press, 1996).
† Commander Samuel F. Quarles, USN, was commanding officer of the *Warrington* from 15 August 1944 to 13 September.

Admiral Erly: Never having handled that before, I really can't answer. However, I did find out that, with the high bow that she had, you had to maintain a fairly good way to maintain control, because if you had any wind, it was going to push that bow. I learned early on, you just had to keep way on. Now, she did not have twin rudders. It was a single rudder. So that meant she was going to handle differently than the *Sumner* class with the twin rudders, and she did handle differently.* Mainly, you had to maintain more way so she wouldn't fall off on you. I have felt that she did not handle as well, say, as, or respond as well or as fast as the *Mahan* class or *Frazier* or *Laub*.

Paul Stillwell: Do you think the rudder was part of that?

Admiral Erly: Possibly that, and that high bow sail area, extremely high bow.† But the extremely high bow was good in one aspect, that you had a dry deck, where a lot of the other cans had a wet deck. So you get some of the good with the other.

Paul Stillwell: I think that was the purpose of it.

Admiral Erly: Well, of course, you've got to remember, she was a bigger ship than the others when she was designed. I would say this, that after cutting my teeth on ship handling really basically with her. When I took command of the *Owens*, which was a *Sumner* class, I felt like I had two tugs available one on either quarter.‡ I could make no ship-handling error, particularly on docking or anything of that nature. It was so easy after having struggled with the *Phelps*.

Paul Stillwell: What do you remember about your wardroom officers? Were they nearly all reservists at that point?

---

* The 2,200-ton destroyers were those of the short-hull *Allen M. Sumner* (DD-692) and long-hull *Gearing* (DD-710) classes, both built during World War II. The ships of the former class were 376 feet long, versus 390 for the latter. The extra length provided added fuel capacity.
† "Sail area" is a term for a ship's vertical surfaces on which the wind exerts force.
‡ Commander Erly was commanded the destroyer *James C. Owens* (DD-776) in the Korean War.

Admiral Erly: I would say the large percentage was reserve. The exec was a reserve. The gunnery officer, reserve. I think it was at least 80%. I had one young ensign, Hal Castle, on board.* The communicator was a reserve, also, Tom Harrison, who was a young lawyer and, I guess, is probably retired now in Washington, D.C. I think what you saw in my ship was probably indicative throughout, because you've got to remember, without the reserves and with the ships coming on line, we never would have been able to man the ships. They were essential.

As I say, a fair chunk of those reserves—I have no idea the percentage—went on and made a regular Navy career. As an aside, starting with the class of '30 through about the class of '40, that resulted in sending home of captains with 25 years of service. One-third of captains in your regular Naval Academy classes were sent home early, with 25 years' service. This was what we called the hump, caused by these real competent reserves coming in and taking regular commissions. Evidently BuPers or somebody in the numbers personnel racket got screwed up. But to keep promotion from stagnating, they had to make a special cut.

Back from our digression. We were still in *Phelps*, were we not?

Paul Stillwell: Talking about your officers, I wonder about your enlisted men also.

Admiral Erly: Oh, a high percentage were reserve, a high percentage.

Paul Stillwell: How capable were these two groups of men?

Admiral Erly: Extremely so. I had a fire controlman who I just thought was the greatest. He was so conscientious, he worked himself into a nervous breakdown. I had to land him in Mers-El-Kébir. Again, it was this business where it used to take, good Lord, 15-16 years to make chief. We had some of these bright young fellows come in, and they were pulling the load, doing the work. They were making chief in four and five years. And, of course, you know where our chiefs went. The chiefs fleeted up and put on gold stripes and became also part of the backbone of your amphibious Navy, in particular. A lot of

---
* Ensign Hal C. Castle, USNR, later augmented to the regular Navy and retired as a captain in 1973.

the LST skippers and the LSMRs and all those were people that had come up through the ranks.* So you siphoned off these people that had taken quite a few years to become your leading petty officers, and then you were replacing them, and I'm sure the responsibilities upon these youngsters took their toll. This is what this young lad was. He was a young first class. Terrific lad, but he just worked himself into a nervous breakdown, and I think it was the responsibilities of the job. He took them seriously.

I really can't praise enough, really, our young sailors and officers. They came in, they saw the job, they grabbed hold, and they did it. I'm sure that's true today, too, in the same bit. Of course, you've got a volunteer force now. In some of these cases, these were inductees rather than volunteers, and I told you earlier on that probably some of the inductees were better adjusted to assume the role that had to be assumed as they came in, rather than the young volunteer who dashed off to win the war single-handedly.

Paul Stillwell: The guy who was inducted figured it was going to be bad, and he wasn't disappointed.

Admiral Erly: That's right, exactly. He didn't have this high vision of being on a great white charger and going in single-handed and defeating the enemy. Yes, yes.

Paul Stillwell: You described earlier how you had to become an SOB taking over as exec of the *Laub*. How would you characterize yourself as the skipper of the *Phelps*?

Admiral Erly: With the start that I had, I would say that the SOB mantle still reigned. I felt that I had been let down. I had seen the situation, and I thought I had it pretty well corrected. I felt that things had been lax and laissez faire, and I set certain standards and maintained them. I would think that probably I would be considered the hard-nosed skipper in *Phelps*. In *Owens*, I would be considered not in that category.

Paul Stillwell: More of a father figure type?

---

* LST–tank landing ship, an amphibious warfare ship capable of putting her bow directly onto a beach, opening bow doors, and lowering a bow ramp to permit vehicles to exit. LSMR – rocket-equipped medium landing ship.

Admiral Erly: Yes, and protector and so forth and so on.

Paul Stillwell: What else do you remember from the convoy operations in the *Phelps*?

Admiral Erly: We were on the high seas when the Germans surrendered.* As we ended up, we really thought we were going to have some fun when we came back from Europe. We came back and went into the shipyard and had what we called an ultimate armament conversion, in which we really became a floating automatic weapons platform. My God, you never saw so many 40-millimeter mounts and 20-millimeter mounts. We were getting ready for the invasion in Japan. That went on in the shipyard when we came back from our last deployment. We had taken our last convoy over, and we came back independently.

Paul Stillwell: Did this give you any concern about the ship's stability, putting on all those new guns?

Admiral Erly: Oh, for metacentric heights?† No, no. She had a lot of reserve stability. I'm very sensitive in timing that, and as I told you before, remember, she had really been, really cut almost down to the main deck and then came back up again. So she was more like a greyhound of the sea. As I say, the silhouette almost looked like some of those DEs, because we ended up with that little open bridge above the pilothouse.

As I was talking about the *Phelps* crew, I remember saying that it was the awesome responsibility for the safety of the ship and the men in it. That's what really comes down to it, whose ultimate responsibility, and it turns out to be you. You don't have anybody to turn to. So it's awesome. As I look at my night order book and I continually would stress, particularly as we were getting ready to come into a port or anything else, and I'd say, "Hey, now's the time to stay sharp. Caution, caution, caution. Don't slip into and get caught unaware. Be alert. Be alert."

---

* Victory in Europe Day, 8 May 1945, when the German surrender was ratified in Berlin.
† Metacentric height is the distance between a ship's center of gravity and her metacenter; the greater the metacentric height, the greater the ship's stability.

You continually have to preach it. You sound like a broken record. Ultimate aim is the same thing. Don't lose any man needlessly or heedlessly. In '68, I guess, I happened to look at a *Navy Times* or something like that and I saw something in there from a *Phelps* reunion. Anyone interested contact Harold Placette, who was a radarman first class in the *Phelps*. Being the last skipper, and I was the only one on active duty, I'm sure, at that time, I sat down and wrote Harold a letter and said, "Well, Harold, congratulations. I'm glad to see you're doing this." I pointed out that the *Phelps* would always have a special niche in my heart because it was my first command and one I'd never forget, and if I could help him in any way, just to write me.

So we started a deal, and I gave him some hints of where to go and naval history and we could get a roster and so forth. Now they have a reunion every other year. Normally Harold comes at me. I only made one reunion; it was in North Carolina somewhere. And just as an aside, I went from that reunion down to the Cuban Naval League reunion in Miami. This was back in about, I guess, '76 or so, somewhere in that time frame.

Paul Stillwell: What kind of reaction did you get from former crew members when you went to the reunion?

Admiral Erly: Oh, great. There were some that come up, "Oh, do you remember when?" and my telephone talker on the bridge, "Oh, yeah, remember?" and so forth. It was great. But they hold it now in out-of-the way places, and my wife doesn't really look forward to that type of deal. So unless I'm the principal speaker, I normally don't go.

The same thing happened in the *J.C. Owens*. I was a principal speaker, and, again, it's normally a good crew member to do it. You don't want an officer to do it. You want a crew member to get this thing started. This was a chief fire controlman by the name of Warren that got the *J.C. Owens* going. They had it last June out there in Mission Valley in San Diego. I was the principal speaker, and I went over and talked. I located the original skipper for them, but he couldn't come.

There were a lot of people there but not so much from my tour. I'd say there were only about four or five from my tenure of two years. See, the ship commissioned in '45.

The ship was given to the Brazilian Navy.* They've got a reunion in Orlando coming up in October, which I don't think I'm going to make. They got my exec as the principal speaker, but I think I'll either pass to Sam, my exec, or to Warren.† I gave him some good info about what the Navy was doing and whatnot in the Persian Gulf and a few other things. I've got some material, about maybe four or five minutes, which I will ask either one or the other, to read from me to the crew as a follow-up on what I told them last June.

Back to the *Phelps*. As I say, we finished up coming into port. I would try to tell you, at times I had a little heartburn in that ship, as being a flagship, and lessons learned, I told my officers, actually, not so much the crew—"Look, we've got a flag on board. That's to be our mission. Our mission, then, is to support that flag. Let's make sure we make everything fine. Make sure that we cooperate. Make sure they get everything they need and so forth and so on."

Well, I got a little commodore on board, and he liked the frontal assault. Then before too long he was saying, "You people aren't cooperating."

I said, "Well, what do you mean?"

"Oh, your communication division."

I said, "Just a moment."

I sent for Lieutenant May, the commodore's communicator, and my communicator, Lieutenant Harrison. I said, "The commodore says that we are not cooperating and so forth and so on."

His communicator said, "Oh, no, no, everything's fine."

My communicator said, "Everything's fine."

The commodore hemmed and hawed, "Oh, Christ I've made a boo-boo."

So it went this way. He'd get on the bridge, and I didn't like the way he conducted himself on my bridge, and I had it. This went on and other things went on. At that time, the commodore would come on board—talk about setting an example. He'd be so goddamn dead drunk he couldn't come out of that cabin for two days. We sailed. I

---

* The *James C. Owens* was decommissioned as a U.S. Navy ship on 15 July 1973 and transferred to the Brazilian Navy that same day. She served for Brazil until 1995 and then was scrapped.
† Lieutenant Commander Samuel L. Collins, USN, was executive officer of the *James C. Owens* in the early 1950s.

had formed the convoy, I had checked it, I knew where the ships were. Then he came out of his cabin, and he wanted to stalk around the bridge like a little goddamn bantam rooster.

I took enough of this until I decided it couldn't go on. I went down in his cabin, where it was just the two of us, eyeball to eyeball. He was sitting in the chair, and I walked in the room and I stuck my finger in his eye. I said, "Hey, look, unless you can conduct yourself like an officer and a gentlemen, don't you come on my bridge. You got it, Commodore?"

I turned and stalked out.

Paul Stillwell: I bet that was not too welcome, either.

Admiral Erly: Well, now, just a minute. I figured I'd had it up to here. I wasn't going to take any more of covering his number and doing all this other business. I just figured, hell, if he had any guts, which I didn't think he had, he should relieve me. He didn't. He didn't have any guts.

Paul Stillwell: Was this Markham?

Admiral Erly: Yes. We got into Mers-El-Kébir. I'll never forget this one. There was an officers' club up the way. He really would slop it up. Thank God, the bartender was alert that night. I was standing at the bar, and the commodore sucker-punched me. He really did. It drove me back in the bar, and I had this fist. The bartender locked me, and the commodore ran.

Paul Stillwell: The bartender prevented you from retaliating?

Admiral Erly: Yes. I'd have killed him. Oh, Lord.

Paul Stillwell: Did things go downhill from that high plateau?

Admiral Erly: No. Things got better, because I figured I'd about had enough of this. It's a good thing he didn't come back to the ship that night, because I went aboard and said, "As soon as the commodore comes on board, I want to know it. You wake me up." He didn't come back. He didn't show.

Now, the next day, *Laub* was in port and old Roessler was aboard. I went over and I said, "Hey, Tony, come on with me. I want to tell you what happened last night. What do you think?"

He said, "Hmmm. What do you want to do? Do you want to prefer charges? You got witnesses?"

I said, "Sure, we got witnesses."

We went to the officer's club. and the commodore came in, all sheepish, "Oh, I want to apologize".

So I said, "Okay, apology accepted."

Of course, things were better. But he was something else. But I'd really had it, you know, to confront him. Things had gone from bad to worse. I found out later that he was afraid to conn his own ship, but he would criticize everybody. I had a little fun with him too.

I'd say, "Hey, Commodore, would you like to make this approach on the convoy commodore's ship?"

I'd take it away from him. Goofing it. It wasn't the happiest of times.

Paul Stillwell: No.

Admiral Erly: But I survived.

Paul Stillwell: Was this a desron commander, desdiv?

Admiral Erly: I don't think he ever had a desron. What they did was take some of the skippers that had made the convoy runs, and then they ran them through a little course and made them what they called escort commanders. They were fresh-caught captains, as a general rule. They were comparable, really, to some of the desdiv commanders. But he had quite a few ships when you get out there on the screen. We had a lot of U.S. Coast Guard DEs. That's basically what we had in the convoys. Very few destroyers. We were the number-one destroyer type. The *Georgetown Victory* had a sister ship, and I'm trying to remember what. She ran convoys too. We had a squadron commander, but I never saw him, never saw him—nor he me.

Well, we came back, and Markham and I spoke. As I say, things got along. He went back to the Board of Inspection and Survey and clued me. I got a letter from him saying, "Hey, I want you to know it first. It looks like they're going to scrap your ship."

Well, when we came into New York, we had a team come on board, and they went through the ship. I read their statement. We couldn't split our engineering plant. That's a black mark definitely for damage control, can't split your plant. By that I mean, you can't take the steam from the forward engine room and put it to the after engine room. They said, "Structurally and everything else, but the ship's hull and all fittings and whatnot were far superior to a lot of the new construction."

Paul Stillwell: What would you attribute that to?

Admiral Erly: I would probably attribute it to the calculated, experienced work force that was available and measured turnout of a product prior to the war, instead of that assembly line bit, with a spot weld here and a spot weld there and good old Rosie's pants in between, which took place on some of the other ones. I think it was the seasoned workers that were producing these ships at a measured pace.

But she finally became razor blades somewhere along the line. We decommissioned her in early November.* It was pretty hard to order to bring down the colors and the commission pennant. My first command. We had, of course, to lay her up and go through the steps. I was detached in December.

Paul Stillwell: When did that process of mothballing start? Was it right after you got back from Europe?

---

* The *Phelps* was decommissioned on 6 November 1945, struck from the Navy List on 28 January, and scrapped shortly after by Northern Metals Company of Philadelphia.

Admiral Erly: No, no. No, no. Remember I told you, we went to the ultimate armament conversion. After we came back and had the ultimate armament conversion, we had shakedown training. We went up to Newport, Rhode Island, where we took the 5-inch/38 crews and the 40-millimeter crews. I think it was the *Franklin Delano Roosevelt* crew that was getting ready for commissioning.* They had also some young ensigns and crewmen. We acted as a training ship, running in and out of Newport, and having antiaircraft drills—firings—off Newport for, oh, six weeks, seven weeks, somewhere in that time frame. When did the war end in the Pacific?

Paul Stillwell: I was August 14th in this country, 15th over there, when they ceased hostilities.

Admiral Erly: Okay, we probably went up there in June and stayed there probably for about another two weeks after the armistice was signed. Then we were sent on down to New York for the pre-decommissioning. We started releasing personnel, off-loading ammo, and then trying to keep the kids honest up to the last. All of a sudden .45 automatics would try to disappear, and you would have to say they are accountable, they're a Title B. "I'm sorry, friends. Cough up or nobody gets off the ship." It worked. They coughed up.

So she went out of commission, and knowing that she was going out of commission, I had talked to my wife and said, "Hey, you know what? I probably should go to Washington and get a Washington job and be a bright young boy in Washington, or maybe we should go and have our honeymoon in South America on a naval mission. What do you want to do?"

Well, of course, you know what she opted for.

Paul Stillwell: South America.

---

* USS *Franklin D. Roosevelt* (CVB-42), a *Midway*-class aircraft carrier, was commissioned 27 October 1945. She had a standard displacement of 45,000 tons, was 968 feet long, 113 feet in the beam, and had an extreme width of 136 feet. Her top speed was 33 knots. She had 18 5-inch mounts and could accommodate more than 100 aircraft.

Admiral Erly: Yes. So I went down to OpNav and I got into—I guess it was old OP-27. It was an Admiral Spears who was heading it up, but I talked to his exec.[*] The number-two guy was a retired officer by the name of Metz.[†] They called him Egg Metz.

I said, "Gee, I really am interested in going on a naval mission."

He said, "Why?"

I said, "Well, I was on one for a short time; I was on a naval mission in Cuba."

"Oh," he said, "we need somebody who's had mission experience in this office. You're just what we need."

I said, "Captain, please forget I ever walked through the door," and I left.

I got back to the ship. Two days later there were orders for me to OP-27, OpNav.

Well, I had 30 days' leave and I went on leave, and "Oh, well, guess I better make the best of a bad thing, which I really don't want. But I'll go ahead. It's still Washington duty, and it could be worse."

So I reported in, and this Captain Metz said to me, "Well, where are you going?"

I said, "Sir, I'm going to Venezuela."

"Oh, good. Well, go ahead and get yourself squared away," and so forth.

Paul Stillwell: He didn't remember the previous meeting?

Admiral Erly: No, and I wasn't about to tell him, either. I had permanent orders to OP-27. All the rest of the people going on mission duty were on TAD to OP-27—temporary additional duty and drawing per diem. Since I had permanent orders, there was no per diem.

But he said, "Go ahead," and I went. I went and got a set of orders. I got permission for Lois to travel out of the country. We got passports, we got shots, we got everything. About this same time frame, they had gotten rid of President Gomez down there.[‡] They had changed with the revolution, and the young Turks had taken over, and

---

[*] Rear Admiral William O. Spears, USN (Ret.).
[†] Captain Earle C. Metz, USN (Ret.).
[‡] Eleazar Lopez Contreras was President of Venezuela from 30 June 1936 to 5 May 1941. He was succeeded by Isaias Medina Angarita, 5 May 1941 to 18 October 1945. Rómulo Ernesto Betancourt Bello took over on 19 October 1945 as the result of a coup d'etat and served until 17 February 1948.

so they sent up a lieutenant and an ensign to be the new naval attachés. The senior man was Larasalvo, and he later got to be their CNO.

So I took Larasalvo by the hand. He said, "Now, I'm a lieutenant commander." So I took him down to Jake the tailor's, or wherever it is, to get him properly striped. I was taking him up to OP-27 to call on the admiral, and I sort of took him under my wing. In fact, I had an old beat-up Studebaker which I had bought right in Newport, Rhode Island, when I was up there at the end of the war. They took that car, and I said, "Okay, that means then I can ship a car in later," and so I had all this agreement with them.

Then I got my clearance, and Lois and I grabbed a train to Miami. Then we got a plane out of Miami to Venezuela, where I was acting chief of mission for about six or seven months, until a commander out of '32 showed up, Ray Pitts.[*]

Then, about a year later, BuPers modified my orders, so I was legitimate. I never did get to collect per diem. But I thought it was a small price to pay for getting to Venezuela.

Boy, you talk about prices. A loaf of bread was a buck, you got ten eggs for a dollar and a quarter, a bottle of scotch was equivalent to about 50 bucks. Things were high down there, as you could see. But things got better later on, because we got established, and we could get a food shipment in from Bayonne.[†] We survived a lot off of canned stuff.

I was acting chief there and then coordinator of training for them. We had a house right on about the 12th hole of the golf course in the country club, which I had taken from a reserve officer who was going to inactive duty, Chester Wine. Amazingly enough, when we got the ships, the *Patria* and the *Cuba*, we went into New Orleans to be degaussed on the degaussing range there, and Chester was at that point on the staff of the commandant in New Orleans, and later he went on down to Venezuela. He spoke Spanish. He was from Texas. Nice guy. Nice guy. So we went down there, with the help of the Salvation Army.

Paul Stillwell: What do you mean by that?

---

[*] Commander Ray M. Pitts, USN.
[†] Bayonne, New Jersey, Naval Supply Depot.

Admiral Erly: Good Lord. You had to go down with full furniture, and we didn't have that, living from pillar to post. We got married in April of '44 and had rented apartments. So we had to buy furniture and appliances for a four-bedroom house. The Salvation Army came in very handy. Really, we had a hell of an outlay. We had to buy kerosene heaters for our hot water at Sears. Now, Chester was feeding me all of this stuff that you needed to have down there. You used kerosene for your cooking. We were going to have to entertain. We had to buy beds.

What we did find was that there was a place out in Virginia, over there on that side where a lot were apartments were. We saw an advertisement where somebody had some living room furniture for sale, and we went. It was a reserve officer going back, and the rent was paid up. We just lucked on this. So he said, "Hey, you can have this apartment." We used that as a central place to shove everything in, so the packers could come in, and we could pack out from one spot. So it worked like a charm. But this was also, even with all the shortcuts we were taking, for us to go down there, this was an expenditure. In those days the expenditure was about 3,000 bucks.

Paul Stillwell: That's a lot for those days.

Admiral Erly: You better believe it. We're talking 1945. Yes. Well, it was a very interesting tour of duty down there, because we became very friendly with Delgado Chalbaud, who was the Minister of Defense, and Rómulo Betancourt, who was the President, and, of course, then some of the wealthy families.* The Herrera family was one.

We had the pleasure, I think, of entertaining the President of Venezuela in our quarters—I would say to the envy of all the attaché group. This came about because I was there for six months and then went to the States. They had opted to buy a LST from us. A Venezuelan naval commission had looked at this LST, which was up the James River from Norfolk. This was before I had ever entered the picture. I came up with a

---

* Carlos Delgado Chalbaud was Venezuela's Minister of Defense from 1945 to 1948, then was part of a military coup that resulted in his being the nation's President from 1948 to 1950.

group of officers and enlisted men to go through training at Little Creek for the amphibious side of it and to sort of act as their liaison, steer them around problems.*

Well, the first thing I scheduled was to go up the river to look at this LST, and, lo and behold, what did I find. It had been demilitarized. The cables to the 40-millimeters had been cut, the radar cables cut, everything. All that stuff was off. The Venezuelans were going to be getting amphibious training. I called on Vice Admiral Barbey who was ComPhibLant.† I explained the setup to him. He wanted to know if he could help in any way. So when I found that the LST had been demilitarized, I went back to him. I also called Washington, and they said, "Oops. Tilt. See if you can find another one that will meet their specifications."

Admiral Barbey made all his LSTs available. I looked at so many LSTs, I was getting blind. I finally stumbled on one that was beached at Solomons Island, just below Patuxent, and, boy, was she spic and span. I had been in so many of them where they were rundown and neglected. I finally got to say, "Hey, how much time have you got left before you're getting out?"

They'd say, "Two weeks."

I said, "That's two weeks too long. You've got a garbage scow here, and you really should be drummed out of the service, not getting out."

I found this LST, and it was impeccable. I congratulated this jaygee, and he said, "Oh, I didn't have anything to do with it. The commanding officer really did all this."

I said, "Well, where is the commanding officer?"

He said, "Oh, he's waiting general court-martial in Norfolk, because coming out of New York with a cargo, we had a collision."

So I went back to Admiral Barbey, and I said, "Boy, did I find a beautiful LST. Just beautiful," and so forth. I said, "That commanding officer really should be commended, and I sure would like to see him in command when these Venezuelans go aboard and they take over the ship."

He said, "Oh, well, why not?"

I said, "Yes, sir, but you've got him awaiting trial by general court-martial."

---

* Naval amphibious base, Little Creek, Virginia, near Norfolk.
† Vice Admiral Daniel E. Barbey, USN, served from March to September 1946 as Commander Amphibious Forces Atlantic Fleet.

He said, "What? Get my legal officer."

Well, the end of it was that, I think that this was Lieutenant Cantwell, who was, I guess, an old chief boatswain's mate, and I think he got a gentle letter of reprimand, tap on the wrist. He was immediately taken back, put in command of the ship, and then he saw the Venezuelans all through their training, and then finally turned the ship over to them. The moral of the story is, do what you're supposed to do, and once in a great while luck will prevail, and you will be rewarded. And in this case, he was rewarded for keeping a taut, clean ship.[*]

Really, Admiral Barbey was a great help. He left ComPhibLant and went on down to the Caribbean and was in San Juan. The Venezuelans, when I told them what a great help they had been, he also entertained them in the flagship. He would have this Lieutenant Commander Gershey [phonetic], who was the senior Venezuelan, and his wife, whom we had brought with us. We were staying at the old Chamberlin Hotel and took them to dinner and entertained them.[†] So when we got back to Venezuela, we got Uncle Dan the Order of the Liberador and had him come down. We got him decorated down there for his help.

Which brings the reason I've gone to such tales on this. About this time, because when the LST came in, they had a big reception down there. I, at this time, did not really know President Rómulo Betancourt very well. But there was a lot of booze flowing, and all of a sudden I noticed this guy was draping himself all over the President, was drunk and disorderly. I thought, "God, he's the President of the country. Why don't some of his aides or somebody step in?"

No one stepped in, so old dumb Erly, he just went up, got this guy, put his arm behind his back, and got him to one side, got him away from Rómulo.

Well, would you believe, as we get ready to leave the ship, then the President's aide came over and said, "The President wants to know would you and Mrs. Erly ride with him, and we thought we would stop for a bite of supper."

---

[*] The *LST-907* was transferred from the U.S. Navy to the Bolivarian Navy of Venezuela on 25 November 1946. She became the training ship *Capana* while in Venezuelan service.
[†] The Chamberlin Hotel, since converted to a retirement community, was a posh establishment near Old Point Comfort in Hampton, Virginia—across Hampton Roads from Norfolk.

So we went with the pres, with our feet up like this on top of the machine guns, in the back seat of the presidential limousine. He found that we were going to have a reception for the officers. So he said, "I'm coming."

Paul Stillwell: Nice engaging chap.

Admiral Erly: So he came with his wife, and we had a reception for the officers. And when we had Admiral Barbey come down, and he and Katie, his wife, stayed with us, we had a big reception in honor of Admiral Barbey.

We said to Rómulo, "Hey, can't you come?"

He said, "Well, you know I can't come, because it's in honor of somebody else. But however, since it's at your house, I'll come anyway." So they showed up there.

Paul Stillwell: Did you have some consultation with them on how to formulate a Navy or to build one?

Admiral Erly: They had their own concept of really what they wanted, and our State Department had a concept on what they thought they should have.

Paul Stillwell: And you were in the middle.

Admiral Erly: Oh, yes, definitely in the middle. But the LST—evidently the State Department, of course, had to go along with every one of these things.

In this same time frame, yes, they wanted to buy some pistols, automatic weapons, and whatnot, and Dr. Corrigan was our ambassador.* He also happened to be in the States at this particular time. So I went over to the State Department to talk to Dr. Corrigan and said, "Hey, look. This is for the Venezuelan Marines, and they want these arms, and they want certain ammo."

He said, "Oh, well, let me see what I can do."

He went and he came back and he said, "No, they can't have it."

---

* Frank P. Corrigan was U.S. Ambassador to Venezuela from August 1939 to September 1947.

I said, "Well, Mr. Ambassador, I can tell you this. I've been shooting with Delgado Chalbaud, and he assures me that if we won't sell it to him, they're going to get it from Belgium or some other spot. And they'll have it, because they've got the money." At this point, Venezuela was on the plus side of their budget. They didn't have a national debt, and they had money.

The ambassador said, "Oh, well, I don't think they'll do that."

I said, "Yes, sir, I guarantee they'll do it."

They got turned down. So the Venezuelans turned right around and bought what they wanted.

I had said to the ambassador, "Here we are, the main thing we're trying to talk throughout South and Latin America in this time frame, standardization of arms. For ammunition, the whole bit, if we're going to, let's carry through."

At this time, of course, I was becoming a staunch believer that we should look after our own back yard, and this is what I told Admiral Barbey. I said, "We should be looking there for standardization of arms. We're preaching all of this, but when we've got to carry through on it, the State Department turned right around where they wanted to buy U.S. arms and wouldn't permit them to have it."

He said, "Oh, no, this will throw the balance, and then Colombia will think we're giving arms here and so forth."

Well, they were not giving; they were selling. This, I think, has been part of our whole problem.

Again, to what we were talking about naval missions, I cautioned my Cuban friends at about this time frame, who were saying, "Well, it costs them too much for a naval mission, and we are going to abolish it."

I said, "Particularly in this time frame and the step-down, with a lot of surplus shipping and other things that you possibly need, I think you should maintain your naval mission, because it can be most helpful to you in that regard of obtaining things that you need." And they kept their naval mission.

They had indicated they were going to get rid of it. Actually we stopped in Havana, of all places, with our plane. I called Braulio Fernández and said, "Hey, I'm passing through. I want an update on what's going on." I talked with him and said, "Hey you better relay this is the thing to do." And they did. They maintained that mission for some years after that.

But here was the very thing that we were trying to do, standardization of arms in the hemisphere. Our biggest opponent was the State Department. Dr. Corrigan was a fine little man. I told him later, "I don't know how more positive I could have been to you, Mr. Ambassador, in telling you what was going to happen. I really couldn't push it home any more than I did. But I can't understand the State Department."

He wasn't really a career diplomat; he was a political appointee. He had been first Panama, and then he came over to Venezuela. He didn't come up through the ranks.

Paul Stillwell: Did you get involved with training Venezuelan Navy personnel?

Admiral Erly: Overall coordination, nothing more. We also had another officer, actually a classmate of mine there, Tex Lander.[*] He ended up in residence at their naval academy and helped prepare their curriculum and this type of thing. Mine was a general overall view of training, trying to line up training for them in U.S. or in other spots where we could get them in, trying to get vacancies for them at the General Line School and things of those natures for their officers and enlisted.

Paul Stillwell: How would your role best be described? Liaison?

Admiral Erly: Yes, basically.

Paul Stillwell: And something of a consultant, it sounds like, also?

Admiral Erly: Yes.

Paul Stillwell: Any other interesting events you remember from that time, any accomplishments you could cite beyond the LST for working with them?

---

[*] Lieutenant Commander Robert B. Lander, USN.

Admiral Erly: Oh, well, no, except for the direct pipeline of knowing what was going on. It would seem about once a quarter there would be an abortive revolution. Then all the troops were kept ready in their barracks. After about the first day or two, Delgado Chalbaud, the Minister of Defense, would get bored with this and come out to our house and sit down and tell us everything that was going on and what had happened.

Paul Stillwell: It sounds like you had a great position to be an intelligence officer.

Admiral Erly: Yes, more so than being a naval mission type. And this irked the hell out of the attaché, because he didn't have this access.

Paul Stillwell: So did you feed it to him or send it straight in?

Admiral Erly: Oh, some of it I just sat on and some I fed to him. I figured I was being a conduit, anyway. That's what Delgado was using me for.

Paul Stillwell: Well, evidently he trusted you to use you in that role.

Admiral Erly: Yes, sure. That was interesting.

Paul Stillwell: How did your wife wind up enjoying this South American honeymoon?

Admiral Erly: Oh, she enjoyed it. She enjoyed it. We had this gorgeous home. She had a cook, a housemaid, a laundress, and we had a gardener. We had a staff of four. Plus, the Venezuela Navy provided a chauffeur for me.

Paul Stillwell: It sounds pretty nice.

Admiral Erly: Well, as I say, it was a hell of a outlay, and, of course, the entertainment. I found they had one cute little trick. If you invited them to your house, you'd better count your silver and your spoons, because it was the thing that you would take as a memento of the occasion. You took something from the host. [Laughter.]

No, we went down. As I told Lois when we went down there, "We're not being sent down there to fraternize with the American colony. That's not our job. Our job is to go down there and to make friends with the Venezuelans," and that's what we did. That's what we did.

Paul Stillwell: Did any of those contacts prove useful to you in later years?

Admiral Erly: Useful? Oh, yes, many years later, as an admiral I went back with Dave McDonald when he was CNO, and we had the South American CNOs' conference.* It was hosted in Venezuela, and all of my little ensign kids and jaygees from the time when I was down there, a lot of them had attained flag rank. There were all of them in that receiving line. Old Dave McDonald didn't know what was happening. We got off the plane and all of them were there, giving me the bear hug, like old home week. They were very helpful.

I was Admiral McDonald's number-one adviser at the conference, and then, of course, when there would become a meaty question that needed resolving where the U.S. rep—I was the U.S. rep and would have to get together with—there would always be a Venezuelan there who would be my sidekick, so to speak, as we were working out specific problems. Many problems involved all the South American navies and required their concurrence.

Paul Stillwell: This was all very much in contrast to how you'd been spending your time previously in the Navy.

Admiral Erly: Well, I found that I became a semi-diplomat. I really found that the best tactic in working, particularly with the South and Latin Americans, was just to be absolutely candid and honest and forthright, and you had no problem. Don't try to

---

* Admiral David L. McDonald, USN, served as Chief of Naval Operations from 1 August 1963 to 1 August 1967. His oral history is in the Naval Institute collection.

double-talk it or anything else, and, of course, never be patronizing, because a lot of them have a basic inferiority complex, and you don't want to get that bit going.

Paul Stillwell: Well, where next after that?

Admiral Erly: I came back to the States and out to Newport, Rhode Island. From sunny Venezuela, we arrived in Newport in, I guess, January or February 1948. I was en route to be exec in the *Yosemite*. We had rented a house sight unseen. It was J. T. O'Connell's old place on the Point. Castle Hill was the name of the area, and it sounded great—gardeners, cottage. We paid a couple of months' rent on it. We arrived there this cold night, checked in the Muenchinger-King Hotel, and then went charging out to see what we had. The place was locked. This was late in the afternoon. We knocked on the door and said, "Hey, do you have the key?"

"Oh, yeah, we got the key."

"Well, let's go look."

"Oh, no, come in. You look cold. Come in, have a drink."

Well, we sat and had two drinks, and then we went over looked, and we knew why they wanted us to have a drink first. They had said this place was supposed to be completely furnished. It was a mess.

It was owned by J. T. O'Connell, who had an old hardware store and was one of the richest guys in Newport, really. He was in Fortune 500 later. I had paid him two months' rent. That put a gleam in my eye. He had a handyman. Finally, we went out the next day, and he sent his handyman around. I let the handyman know that I had been paying rent and this was what I was getting. He said, "Come on out. We'll go up to the big house, and you can select anything you want."

So we went up to the big house, selected all the good pieces of furniture. Then I saw other things that were needed. J. T. had a hardware store, so I started just going to his hardware store and getting anything I needed for the house, and I'd sign R. B. Erly for J. T. O'Connell. I'd never met the man.

First thing you know, here came old J. T. out one Saturday. "Oh, won't you come in Mr. O'Connell? Here, have a cup of coffee. I'll give you a sandwich."

He was looking around, looking at this. I had made canopies; I had put in a built-in bookcase; I had painted the stairs, which were a disaster; I had closed off the other apartment and painted it out. Anything I ever needed for that house, I just kept right on, R. B. Erly for J. T. O'Connell. He never said a word.

Paul Stillwell: Now, who was this man?

Admiral Erly: He was a self-made millionaire. Had the biggest hardware store in town, had a lot of contracts with the Navy. His dad had been a saloonkeeper at one time there in Newport. The guy knew everything about it. We stayed there, oh, I guess, until the ship had to move and was going for an overhaul up in Boston, and we wanted to be closer in town. I didn't know where we were going to go. But then all of a sudden from the ship I found that I was going to go to the staff of the General Line School.* We thought at this point, "Well, hell, let's buy a house rather than paying rent."

So we found a house that we liked, and I wanted to really close down on that house. So I went down to J. T. and said, "Hey, I need a check now for 4,500 bucks."

He said, "What for?"

Paul Stillwell: Obvious question.

Admiral Erly: Yes. I said, "Well, I'm buying a house."

He said, "I know every piece of property in Newport. Let's go look."

We went and looked, and he says, "What are you paying for it?"

I said, "Eleven-five."

He said, "That's a good buy."

Paul Stillwell: Why would he do that for you?

Admiral Erly: Well, he liked what I had done for his property.

---

* The General Line School was intended to provide officers with a broad range of naval knowledge. It was particularly useful for those who had been in a particular specialty, such as aviation, and not exposed to the Navy as a whole.

Paul Stillwell: Oh, I see.

Admiral Erly: Sure. He used to drop by. He wanted me to go crabbing with him and a few other things. We sort of hit it off, and he knew what was bugging me.

Paul Stillwell: So he was your banker?

Admiral Erly: Yes, he was my banker, and he smoked cigars. I went to him and said, "I'll pay you back Monday." This was the weekend coming up, and I wanted to cinch it. I had money down in Mississippi, which I had to get out. So as soon as that came out, I wrote him a check and gave him a box of the biggest, best cigars I could get.

Years later we were in Norfolk. He went on one of those Navy guest cruises, and they particularly asked to see us when they came back in. When I went up there, the old man was getting a little feeble. I also went up there when I was an admiral in about '69, maybe, and took him out to lunch and we chatted. That was just one of those things that developed.

Paul Stillwell: It certainly had an odd beginning.

Admiral Erly: Yes. I was madder than hell. I'd been paying that rent, and then to find what I found. But as I say, it all turned out okay.

Paul Stillwell: What do you recall of your job in the ship?

Admiral Erly: Well, that was interesting.* I walked in the exec's stateroom, name of Henry Dusinberre.† He was about the class of '20-some-odd, but had been a reserve, had gotten out, and then he was back on duty. I saw a piece of wallpaper he had stuck up in his cabin.

---

* USS *Yosemite* (AD-19), a *Dixie*-class destroyer tender, was commissioned 25 March 1944. She displaced 14,037 tons, was 530 feet long, 73 feet in the beam, and had a maximum draft of 26 feet. Her top speed was 20 knots. She was originally armed with four 5-inch guns. She remained in service until decommissioned on 27 January 1994.
† Commander Henry W. Dusinberre, USN, Naval Academy class of 1923.

"God, what are you thinking of doing, papering your cabin?"

"Oh, no," he said, "That's going to be wallpaper for the girls' room, and I'm just trying to see how it's going to look."

I had a lot of fun there. The repair department was running the ship, not the exec, and that took a little reorientation.

Paul Stillwell: How was that manifested? What sorts of things did the repair department do?

Admiral Erly: The repair department was prescribing the liberty. The repair department was practically doing any damn thing they wanted to do. The ship, as far as I was concerned, wasn't being properly maintained. Granted, the mission of the ship was to render service to destroyers alongside. I had to keep telling myself that when a destroyer wasn't alongside, we were not doing our mission.

But at the same time, there came a period of time when you needed to be able to move. You need to be mobile. You needed to be sure that your engineering plant was functioning. You need to be sure your radar is functioning. We had a 5-inch/38 gun system on board. You wanted to be damn sure your guns could shoot. You had all the components that any other ship had, but it had become just moored in its own coffee grounds. The damn thing hadn't moved in months, and it showed it. The attitude in the ship's company, of course, what you were having in ship's company—also, we were still change, change. We had so damn many chiefs you couldn't move without running into one. There were too many chiefs.

Paul Stillwell: That was a problem throughout the Navy, that and demobilization.

Admiral Erly: Yes. Well, and a lot of these chiefs had been officers and had opted to revert back to chief rather than stay as officers. See, now we're talking '48. In other words, there were too many chiefs and not enough Indians. The repair spaces were not well maintained, were dirty. I started also sitting in as the exec on the arrival conference of ships with their orders, so it just wasn't the repair officer saying yes, aye, or no on what was going to be done or not to be done.

The skipper was little Jimmy Benson, and he was the one that gave me some of the stories about Jimmy Clay.* The admiral threw him out of the flag mess, and Jimmy ended up throwing him out of his mess.† I'm saying Jimmy Benson, who was an ordnance PG, who was my first skipper for about six months.

But getting in there, Dusinberre had sort of, I felt, let some of his responsibilities devolve upon the repair officer, and we had to get that back in perspective, which we did. I think things went along better and smoother. We got away from a "we" and "they" complex, "we" being the repair department and "they" being the other part of the ship's company, and we were trying to weld it into "us." This is what had had happened, and we succeeded in that.

We got mobile; we got under way. We got in the program time to be able to go out and do some of the exercises that we were required to do and to do our gunnery shoots and to maintain our proficiency and our radar navigation and all the rest of this stuff.

Paul Stillwell: Did you get some feedback from the customer destroyers that they were becoming pleased with the product?

Admiral Erly: Yes, with their treatment, and also the fact that they were coming through a cleaner ship when they were coming and going back and forth. It was a crap house.

Also, at the same time, mind you, we were a flagship, and we had to keep the flag happy too. You were juggling many, many things. You had to take care of the embarked flag, not only the enlisted personnel, but the staff. DesLant's staff was sizable. So all those functions, when you stop and look at them, you're a juggler trying to keep everything in perspective, making sure if you concentrate on just trying to please the staff, what the hell's going to happen to the other two functions? You had to keep everything in balance and everybody happy.

---

* Captain James F. Benson, USN, commanded the *Yosemite* from 8 December 1946 to 12 November 1948.
† The *Yosemite* was the flagship for Commander Destroyer Force Atlantic Fleet.

Paul Stillwell: Who was the admiral on board?

Admiral Erly: I had two of them. Sol Phillips was an admiral from Texas and had a great sense of humor.* He had more damn jokes, and he had people from all over the world sending him jokes, and when he'd get a good one, he'd come stand in the door of his quarters and guffaw and guffaw. Everybody would come running, while he'd give them the latest joke. His chief of staff was Henry Crommelin.†

Sol was relieved by Felix Johnson, and in turn Felix was relieved by Slim Wooldridge. Felix left there and went back to become head of ONI. I think Sol Phillips went to OpNav somewhere. He was an old destroyer type. Then Slim Wooldridge came; I don't think his heritage in destroyers was that strong. He had been in submarines and so forth.‡ But Tiny McCorkle, who, as I found out last night, has just moved into this retirement home out here.

Paul Stillwell: I knew he was coming here. I didn't know he had made it.

Admiral Erly: Yes, he made it. He made it. He's there; he's settled in.

I would say the tour in the *Yosemite* was a definite challenge, and it turned out being fun and making some very good contacts, very good contacts.

Paul Stillwell: Such as whom?

Admiral Erly: Well, I was thinking Felix Johnson and Tiny McCorkle.§ McCorkle particularly, I feel, had probably the greatest impact on my Navy career. You know, trying to look back and second-guess, if he hadn't pulled me, literally, into Washington,

---

* Rear Admiral William K. Phillips, USN, commanded Destroyer Force Atlantic Fleet from 29 March 1947 to 21 April 1948.
† Captain Henry Crommelin, USN.
‡ Rear Admiral Felix L. Johnson, USN, commanded Destroyer Force Atlantic Fleet from 21 April 1948 to 25 August 1949. His oral history is in the Naval Institute collection. Rear Admiral Edmund T. Wooldridge, USN, commanded Destroyer Force Atlantic Fleet from 25 August 1949 to 27 July 1950.
§ Captain Francis D. McCorkle, USN, was DesLant chief of staff from 1948 to 1950.

then what? Who knows? Once he got me into Washington, and then I went from several jobs that were enhancing career and exposure-wise.*

Paul Stillwell: From that tour of duty in the *Yosemite*, then you went to the General Line school. What was the purpose of that school?

Admiral Erly: Actually, the line school was particularly designed to take in those World War II reserve officers who had accepted regular USN commissions. Normally we had them from lieutenant, lieutenant commander, and commander. I don't think it was an over preponderance of aviators, but there was a good percentage of aviators, I'd say about 50%, maybe more, maybe 60%.

They were given a year, which was the basic old bit of seamanship and navigation, antisubmarine warfare, and the combat information center setup, engineering, electrical engineering, steam engineering. They really covered all aspects, really, of what one would be required to do under the old examination for promotion concept. I would say basically that they would have been qualified, after going through line school, to take the promotion exam for the next higher rank. It was a great equalizer for them, and also to bring them up to speed, particularly the young aviators that I encountered there, which Kent Lee was one, among many.†

Some of the discussions I had with them, they would say, "Well, I don't see why we need all this ship's engineering bit and electrical engineering bit. We should be studying aircraft electronics and aircraft construction, and we can't see any need. Of course, we buy what you're teaching at CIC and what you do and your lecture in control of aircraft and intercepts and all this and antisubmarine warfare. Yeah, we can buy you, but we can't buy some of the others."

I'd say, "Oh, yeah? Well, you're just missing the point, because one of these days—if you're going to stay in, and we trust that that's what you are—you're going to be more than just a plane jockey. You're going to be a ship skipper, and then you're going to have to know that engineering plant, because you're going to have to go down

---

* This tour in OpNav was from 1955 to 1958.
† Lieutenant Kent L. Lee, USN. The oral history of Lee, who retired as a vice admiral, is in the Naval Institute collection.

below and see what's going on and be knowledgeable in that plant. You just can't sit and push buttons and expect things to happen, because they well may not happen."

Some of them had a little difficulty in taking that aboard. They thought that their time was being wasted. However, I would say later, I did see some of that same group that I taught at line school who would come through. And everyone that came, of course, cycled through my office, because they had to get my words of wisdom and things to be careful of as a CO, which I talked to every PCO that ever came through what to look out for and the pitfalls to avoid.[*]

Paul Stillwell: What job were you in then?

Admiral Erly: Well, I was chief of staff of the Amphibious Force Pacific Fleet.[†] Particularly when these lads were coming in for their deep-draft command. It was a requirement that they have a deep-draft command before they got a carrier. The amphibious force was open as one way. Before that, they had the oilers and the ammo ships and some of that, but they were having such a backlog that they opened up the amphibious ships, also, to them. They at that point were glad that they had had that basic engineering.

Paul Stillwell: What was your job at the line school?

Admiral Erly: I was the senior instructor in CIC and ASW, which was interesting. We would rotate. We had a whole year to get through the class, and I'm trying to remember. The length of my course, I would imagine, was about two months to get through both CIC and ASW.

Paul Stillwell: Was it a pretty demanding pace for the students?

---

[*] PCO – prospective commanding officer.
[†] From 1963 to 1965, as a captain, Erly was chief of staff to Commander Amphibious Force Pacific Fleet.

Admiral Erly: Yes, they were kept busy. But there was still time for relaxation on the weekends. It was a school from Monday through Friday. I think there were some engineering P-works on Saturday in some cases. But they had navigation. They had the things that they needed to get, including leadership. We didn't get too technical when we got into radar. We provided some of the basic explanation of radar, but my course was basically the actual plotting drill. In ASW we put them in with the consoles with the chemical recorder. They were getting a range rate, doppler up, this. And then afterwards we could show them exactly what happened on the tactical trainer. So they really had a hands-on experience. Also, for the plotting for CIC, we had mock-up CICs, they had not only the theory, but the practical side of it. I think it was a good course.

Paul Stillwell: Did you enjoy instructing?

Admiral Erly: Oh, I found it a challenge, because you want to be letter perfect, and I found that I really wanted to know all that I could about it, instead of just the brief outline of each lesson to be covered. To prepare myself for each one, I would write out in longhand the exact words that I was going to use, not that I would use it, but I would prepare myself that way, to go to that trouble to do it. I found it a challenge. I would say for about every hour of classroom instruction, I put in perhaps four or five hours in preparation.

Paul Stillwell: That's impressive.

Admiral Erly: Well, if you're going to do it, you want to be able to do it right. I felt I grew with the job. I also had a lot of fun.

They had a Professor Maxwell who was a civilian educator. He was part of our staff at the line school, and I found out that he was teaching a class, public speaking, at the war college. I thought, "What the hell, here we've got one of our own professors."

So I formed a public speaking group among our instructors, and, hell, we turned out about 20. With a little pressure, Professor Maxwell became our instructor after hours so we'd be more effective in making our presentations.

Paul Stillwell: What did you have in the way of simulators and training aids?

Admiral Erly: Well, we had that ASW trainer. For the combat information centers you could just—you had things to read off, blips, range, bearings, this type of things, and then the plotting, and the various station that you would have and the mock-up CIC. Nothing comparable.

You've got to remember, a lot of some of this stuff that we were using in those days was actually handmade in some cases, your own training aids and whatnot. It's not like it is today, where with the computer you can practically duplicate anything. It was real rough.

There was in Washington, D.C., out on East Capitol Street, at the end of the war and during the war, they had this training-aids setup. They were the ones that came up with the mock-up of the training for the 20-millimeter where you could electronically simulate the firing. Things like that at the end of the war sort of went down the drain for a bit. I gather now, however, that with their setups in combat information centers in ships, that they can now crank in problems and duplicate just about anything you want and run through drills, much, much more sophisticated and, I would say, much more practical and productive, and economical of training funds.

Paul Stillwell: Did you get a chance to get out on board real ships to instruct and practice?

Admiral Erly: No. The most they got from navigation, they had some small yard craft. They'd get out and be able to do some bumper drill, and that was about it. But we did not schedule cruises, as such.

Paul Stillwell: You mentioned their reluctance about engineering. How would you describe the motivation level for the overall course?

Admiral Erly: Well, they needed to pass the course.

Paul Stillwell: So they did what they needed to do.

Admiral Erly: Yes. They had to pass the course or be passed over for promotion. Why stay regular Navy unless you were going to pass the course? At that time, they were talking again, if you will recall, of putting back in promotion exams, which had been terminated during the war.

Actually, the last exam I took was for captain, but I had already qualified for most of it. I did the reading; I did the correspondence courses. The only full one I took, where you went from the A to N in seamanship and navigation and international law and steam engineering, ordnance, was from ensign to jaygee. Hell, I think that navigation, working out star sights, plotting positions, the whole bit, was from ensign to jaygee, and that was back in 1940. Did you in your career ever take a promotion exam?

Paul Stillwell: No. Those were long gone.

Admiral Erly: Perhaps they should come back, I don't know. I really felt from taking that jaygee's exam, by the time you got through cramming, you really felt you had been brought up to speed again. It's not all bad. Not all bad. Because perhaps all of us are not a born Rickover that says, "Oh, I'm going to master this or master that."* As he said, "Don't be lazy. Always do something." Now whether he himself did that, I don't know, but he professed to.

So I found line school a challenge just to be an instructor and prepare yourself to make an adequate presentation and not to let your students down by being sloppy.

Paul Stillwell: Are there any of the other students besides Lee whom you remember?

Admiral Erly: Yes, my little pilot friend from Smackover. Hank Suerstedt was one.† Oh, if I could look at the list I could probably pick a lot of them out, because in my time I

---

* Rear Hyman G. Rickover, USN, was considered the father of the nuclear Navy. He ran the U.S. Navy's nuclear-power program for many years, from 1948 until he eventually left active duty in 1982 with the rank of four-star admiral on the retired list.
† Lieutenant Commander Henry Suerstedt Jr., USN, a naval aviator.

would say at least 10 or 20 of them marched by me or through my office when I was chief of staff at PhibPac. And you better believe, in each and every one of them, if I remembered it well, I reminded them of discussions about why engineering. [Laughter]

Paul Stillwell: I imagine you did remind them.

Admiral Erly: Although I didn't teach that, you see, but I did think it was a necessary adjunct, because I'd seen too much of what happened in the engineering plants when skippers sat on the bridge and just rang the engine order annunciator and thought that's all they had to do and paid no attention to the plant down below. The plant went to hell in most cases.

Paul Stillwell: Well, how had you learned that in your own case?

Admiral Erly: Well, you've got to remember, when I graduated as a young ensign, we were force-fed through a system. Basically, young ensigns are supposed to be trained—and possibly they still are—and I see that in the surface warfare school and things that are going on.

Well, I think I've about exhausted line school. I did set up a visual arts program. I found a young enlisted man who was good with the spray gun. I was able to get the school to buy the equipment. We were able to turn out all kinds of training aids and posters and this kind of thing. I felt that was fun doing that. That was something innovative, really. And as I say, that public speaking course which I got started, I felt benefited a lot of people, including myself. I enjoyed line school, and I felt it was a challenge. I felt I came out of there better prepared to think on my feet and make an adequate presentation.

Paul Stillwell: Anything else on the line school?

Admiral Erly: No, except they have a line school now, of course. It's changed from the concept of what we were doing. What we were doing was bringing people up to speed with their other contemporaries who had gone to the Naval Academy, who'd been in NROTC units for four years and so forth. What you tried to do was give them a year out and compress into that and inject into them enough to bring them up to be contemporary with their peers, really. And it did that.

But now the Naval Postgraduate School really is where they go and get master's degrees and this type of things, and if they don't have a college degree—I'm thinking of some of our enlisted types now, that some of the programs that they can go there and then end up with a degree. And they're accredited, which is a good thing. It's in Monterey now. Of course, what the old line school was where I taught in Newport, is now OCS, Officer Candidate School.

Paul Stillwell: Was that OCS being formed about that time? How did the time work out?

Admiral Erly: At the start of the Korean War, we closed line school.* They kept some of the staff there, and that staff finally came up and set up the OCS system, but using the basic plan that line school had had.† I think about two years before that they had split. They had two line schools. There was the line school in Monterey and the line school on the East Coast at Newport.

But once you got through that deal, I can see where the need for the line school in Newport vanished. And of course, as I say, the whole concept of line school is now changed. It's really a center of advanced learning, not a center to pump people up to a certain level.

Paul Stillwell: Well, thank you very much, Admiral. I look forward to our next meeting.

Admiral Erly: When is that going to be?

Paul Stillwell: Whenever and wherever.

---

* The Korean War began in June 1950.
† The Navy's Officer Candidate School began operation at Newport in 1951.

Interview Number 4 with Admiral Robert B. Erly, U.S. Navy (Retired)
Place: U.S. Naval Institute, Annapolis, Maryland
Date: Thursday, 21 September 1989

Paul Stillwell: Admiral, it's a pleasure to see you again back here in Annapolis after more than a year. We were talking last time about your tour at the General Line School in Newport, and now you're ready to recommission the destroyer *James C. Owens*. So if you could pick it up at that point, please.

Admiral Erly: As you know, at the outbreak of the Korean War, the line school was closed and terminated, and all the students and staff were sent back to sea. I was fortunate enough to obtain another destroyer command, and it was USS *James C. Owens* (DD-776).* She had been laid up in the reserve fleet in Charleston, South Carolina.

    I arrived in Charleston to take this new command on a Sunday. I was the first one there of my crew, and the first thing I did Monday morning was go to the shipyard and get permission to go in and take a look at the *J. C. Owens*. It was a very disheartening day for me as I went through the ship. I walked through the compartments and just looked at the general maintenance. I thought, "My God, I've inherited an eight ball."

    You could see when the paint job was done that they had painted over matchsticks and rust. The whole general tenor of the ship's upkeep reflected utter disregard of basic tenets of keeping it shipshape and ready.

Paul Stillwell: How long had she been out of service?

Admiral Erly: She had been out of service only about six months. As things evolved and I found out more about her condition, I became more and more alarmed. She and the

---

* USS *James C. Owens* (DD-776), an *Allen M. Sumner*-class destroyer, was commissioned 17 February 1945. She had a standard displacement of 2,200 tons, was 376 feet long, 41 feet in the beam, and had a draft of 16 feet. Her design speed was 34 knots. She was armed with six 5-inch guns and ten 21-inch torpedo tubes. She was decommissioned 3 April 1950 at Charleston and recommissioned there on 20 September 1950. She remained in U.S. service until 15 July 1973, when she was transferred to Brazil and renamed *Sergipe*.

other ships in her squadron had been laid up, and they had not had an overhaul in years. They were due for an overhaul, and rather than overhaul them, they were decommissioned and put in the reserve fleet. So they were in horrible shape mechanically, in housekeeping, in spare parts, hand tools, etc.

Paul Stillwell: Had she gotten a standard mothballing package with dehumidification and so forth?

Admiral Erly: Oh, yes, she had all that. But I think her general state and general cleanliness, her general maintenance, the whole damn bit had been well below par.

As I remember going home and telling my wife, "Oh, boy, I have really inherited a challenge. I'm sure I've gotten the eight ball of the squadron. I haven't gotten in the ship's files, but I'm going to find that out soon enough."

Paul Stillwell: Was there, because of the Korean War, a sense of urgency about getting her back into commission?

Admiral Erly: Oh, yes. We were the first wave coming back, and, boy, were they pushing to get us on line. We were to set the example of a fast recommissioning. So it became a bloody fight from the very word go. Spare parts were lacking. She had been stripped. There wasn't a single hand tool on board. As time went on, my first impression proved to be correct. As I got farther into the ship and as I started having officers reporting and crew reporting, we found more and more deficiencies. Then it was trying to fight with the reserve group commander and his material officer to get essential repairs made that were needed. I was very, very frustrated.

Paul Stillwell: How much support did you get from the shipyard at Charleston?

Admiral Erly: The assistant EDO down there was Commander Willie Price, USNA, '36, who had been on the boxing team with me.* So I took my woes to him. I had a hell of a

---
* Commander William N. Price, USN.

time. I can't remember the captain's name, but a captain was the material officer in the reserve fleet, and he didn't want to approve anything to get jobs done. I would go to Price, and we'd get things started, and the work was being done. Then I would go up to the captain and say, "Sir, I need a job order to cover this, because it's being done." This was the way I got a lot accomplished. You can imagine that I was not his favorite commissioning skipper. I just had to fight for everything I got for the ship.

Paul Stillwell: What about getting the crew? Were they recalled reservists?

Admiral Erly: When you want to get into that, there's another heartbreaker.

Paul Stillwell: Well, here I am. Please tell me.

Admiral Erly: About this time, the *Missouri* was tagged to deploy.[*] Therefore, she had to be combat manned. Therefore, the qualified reserves, particularly the engineering types that were designated for our destroyer division, went to the USS *Missouri*. When we got the boilers fired up and were going to stand a boiler watch, our lack of experienced BTs became a major problem.[†] I had BTs second class and first. The only type of boiler that they had ever seen was an old donkey boiler. They had been with Seabees or in LSTs of the amphibious force.[‡] I had no qualified boiler technicians. It was horrifying.

Immediately after recommissioning, we went to a steaming watch.[§] The next morning I was informed that we had a low-water incident. Luckily, there was no damage. I assembled all of the B division and said, "Of all your group, now, I want you to be very, very honest with me. The safety of the ship depends on it. For those of you that feel that you can adequately stand a safe steaming watch, step forward." I had one fireman apprentice that stepped forward out of the whole damn group.

---

[*] In mid-August 1950, the *Missouri* (BB-63), then the Navy's only active battleship, was hurriedly prepared to deploy to Korea. On 19 August she left her homeport of Norfolk to head for the Western Pacific. Her first firing mission in Korea was on 15 September.
[†] BT, boilerman, was an enlisted rating at the time. The title was changed to boiler technician in 1976.
[‡] Seabees is the nickname applied to members of the Navy's mobile construction battalions (CBs), who did their work ashore. LSTs, tank landing ships, were powered by diesel engines rather than steam.
[§] The recommissioning was on 20 September 1950.

Paul Stillwell: Was he your leading BT?

Admiral Erly: Yes, in knowledge but not in rate. He had come from the reserve group and learned to stand a steaming watch in port.

Paul Stillwell: So he probably hadn't had a lot of experience under way.

Admiral Erly: None. You can see we had to set up an intense training program. We went to ComDesLant for qualified BTs.* Thankfully, they provided a nucleus of talent. But this is what you ended up with in this gamble. So you had training to do. Oh, well, we had lots of fun and lots of intensive dockside and underway training. Thank God I was an ex-gun boss, because we made an underway trip to test-fire our 5-inch/38 guns. We test-fired mount 51. Then we were ready for mount 52.

I said, "Commence firing."

Nothing happened.

The gunnery officer reported that the right gun was loaded but would not fire, that it was a hang fire.

I said, "Try our auxiliary battery." Still no action or reports from the mount. Finally, I told the exec, "Hey, I'm going to the gun mount." So I went down, walked into the gun mount, and took a look at the gun. I could see the breech plug was just about that far from closing.

Paul Stillwell: Quarter of an inch.

Admiral Erly: Yes. So I turned to the gunner's mate, and I said, "Get a rawhide maul for me." I got the maul, came up under the breech plug and banged it, and it came up. I said, "All right, now depress the firing key," and it fired. I had encountered this problem when I was gunnery officer of the USS *Cassin*.

I then told the gunnery officer, "Okay, you're going to get all the gun crews and all the gunner's mates to witness the bleeding and recharging of the recoil cylinders. This

---

* ComDesLant – Commander Destroyers Atlantic Fleet, the ship's type commander.

will demonstrate in slow motion the firing sequence and powder case ejection. And then on recharging, you can see how the breech plug moves up and the whole cycle operates in the gun mount." You can be assured that from that time there was a rawhide maul in each gun mount and personnel trained to use it. So these were part of the things. Not only did you engineer it. Every drill on the ship, it was just school ship, school ship, school ship. Of course, I went back to the BT situation. You didn't think that I was going to go with just a fireman.

We had a rep from DesLant down there, and I went to him and said, "You just can't send this ship to sea with these inexperienced people. We can't get them trained in the scheduled time frame. You're going to have to get me some competent boilermen."

I was pretty well off in the other engineering ratings.

Paul Stillwell: Did DesLant have the clout to get these people from BuPers?

Admiral Erly: Well, DesLant had its own personnel pool and could transfer their personnel around. I'm just saying, for these ships you had to get some know-how.

Paul Stillwell: Was that the solution to it?

Admiral Erly: They sent me a qualified chief and first class BTs. That and a lot of training. But I'm just saying, you could not have gotten the ship under way with the initial complement because of their lack of qualifications. Particularly those from the reserve side of the picture didn't meet it. Oh, Lord, when it finally ended up, I'd say it was still about 75% reserves called to active duty. Basically, my officers, I'd say, were at least 75 to 80% reserves called to active duty.

Paul Stillwell: Were the people willing to learn and participate?

Admiral Erly: Oh, yes, yes, yes. But I think of those who were so hopelessly outclassed. Here you were a petty officer second and first class, and I was thinking back to my boilermen and some of those other ratings that are so essential in the engineering department. They just didn't have the background, and they shouldn't have had the rate.

Paul Stillwell: Some of those people who were recalled for Korea had gotten out after World War II and got themselves set up in civilian life and didn't really want to go back. So there was another motivation challenge.

Admiral Erly: Well, I don't think these people were using it as an excuse, because I basically found that they had been donkey boiler people. I'd say, "How did you end up like this?"

"Well, when I went in the reserve unit—"

Paul Stillwell: They had to put them somewhere.

Admiral Erly: Yes, and, of course, the reserve unit was completely voluntary.

Paul Stillwell: It sounds like a real challenge.

Admiral Erly: Yes, it was, all the way. It was fight, fight, fight all the way, even to the question of essential equipment. I remember they delivered a bunch of beat-up life preservers. Charlie Marinke out of '38 was the reserve fleet commander's chief of staff.[*] We got there, and we'd have a weekly meeting, and normally it was old Erly getting up there bitching about this or bitching about this, and I said something about the life jackets. I said, "I don't think that they're buoyant enough. I think they've been compressed and slept on and whatnot. They're dirty and splattered with paint and all the rest. I think somebody's going to have to come up with some proper jackets."

See, we were the test model, and they were trying to do it fast and as cheap as they could do it. They should never have picked this particular group, I guess, to do it with, because they had been stripped of spare parts and were in need of a major overhaul.

---

[*] Commander Charles A. Marinke, USN.

We got new life jackets because after he made some comment I said, "Well, goddamn it, you're not going to sea, but I'm going to sea and my people are, and I want them properly taken care of."

Paul Stillwell: Did you get the engineering plant into a shape you were satisfied with?

Admiral Erly: After a time. After a time. We had to go up to Norfolk and did some work there. Then we went to Gitmo for underway training. From Gitmo, then we came back and got an overhaul, which was sadly needed. We got through Guantánamo and did well.

Paul Stillwell: Did that bring the crew together as a team?

Admiral Erly: Oh, yes. That's the only way you can do it; I really believe that. I can digress a little about the training on the East Coast versus training on the West Coast. That cutting the umbilical cord, get away from continental U.S., get away from family, get away from it, that's what makes the ship. And when you go to Guantánamo, then you start to really get people thinking in terms of the ship, and they're not thinking of the family on the beach. There's not a hell of a lot to do in Guantánamo, anyway, but to think and get prepared for the next ship exercises, go up and play softball and have some beer and keep your crew happy that way. But they're really thinking in terms of the ship.

On the West Coast, you keep coming back into port, because you drop off the fleet training group, because they have to go home, you see. Then you swing around the buoy, maybe overnight, and there's the beach and home. It's an allure, a distraction. So if you're going to shake down a ship and really go to under way training and do all this, then you want to get as far away from your home port as you possibly can.

Paul Stillwell: Back in that era, the Navy didn't make the conscious effort to take care of the families back home that it does now. Did you have a program for that?

Admiral Erly: Oh, certainly. You set up your own organization, so to speak. I know that when we were out and the ship was out that my wife Lois personally had driven women to the hospital to have children and things of that nature. You take care of your own. You set up your own bit. I have given away brides at ship's weddings.

I would also say in another point that I thought that the Navy Relief was a big source of help along that way. In addition, the American Red Cross, and I strongly endorse both of those organizations. We are a little more formalized now, an ombudsman and all this, but it always had been, you know, you take care of your own, and that's what we were doing.

Paul Stillwell: Apparently it was done better in your ship than some, because I talked to a man who was a chief petty officer in the *Trathen*.[*] His ship deployed to Korea. He said his wife and he didn't even know about the commissary services, the health care, and what have you. She went to a civilian doctor. And he said it's certainly much more institutionalized now.

Admiral Erly: I can't believe a CPO would be that ignorant. He should have hit the red button and gotten points of contact. The first one she should have been told about was Navy Relief, and then they've got volunteers there that will send them in the right direction and tell them what they can expect. During my time in the Navy, I thought Navy Relief made quite a contribution. I know my wife spent a lot of time with it. In fact, she put in untold hours during all my commands.

Paul Stillwell: Your exec had an important role in molding that crew together from those circumstances. How did he accomplish that?

Admiral Erly: Well, I had Sam Collins, who was out of the class of '39.[†] Sam was a good old southern boy, very deliberate, going to pin everything. Very much a detailist. He and I became, I think, a very good team. I would be the prodder, and he would be the

---

[*] See the Naval Institute oral history of Rear Admiral Jackson K. Parker, USN (Ret.).
[†] Lieutenant Commander Samuel L. Collins, USN.

implementer, and it worked well. He'd been in destroyers before and, in fact, was way behind his class, actually. He was out of the class of '39 and had had the misfortune to somewhere in the early part of World War II, when one of the mass promotions came out, and his was held up by his skipper.

But he was a plugger. He stayed right in there, and he did a great job. Later he came to PhibRon 5 as chief staff officer. I had gone by that time, but I approved his coming. He made commander, and then he finally made captain. But he just hung right in there. He had lost hundreds of numbers, but he hung in there and had a very successful career.[*] We're still close. He lives in Virginia Beach now. We've stayed in contact through the years.

Incidentally, for crew morale I ensured that any crew member on his birthday got a signed birthday card from me, a birthday cake, a gallon of ice cream, and head of the chow line privileges with seven of his friends.

Paul Stillwell: Do you have any other recollections about that pre-deployment period?

Admiral Erly: Yes. Spike Fahrion was ComDesLant.[†] We left Charleston and came to Norfolk and reported to the flotilla commander. En route I had the *Haynsworth* with me. Herb Rommel was the skipper, and had been in DEs before.[‡] As the senior I received his daily fuel and water report. I saw that his feedwater was being used at an exorbitant rate. I questioned his reports.

Finally, I got him on the TBS and said, "Herb, do you realize what's happening? You're losing feedwater. There's an open drain. Now, if you want to end up arriving in Norfolk on the end of my towline, fine. But if you don't want to do that, you'd better damn sight find out where you're feedwater's going and do something about it."[§]

Paul Stillwell: Was this a matter of inexperience on his part?

---

[*] This refers to numbers on the precedence list for naval officers.
[†] Rear Admiral Frank G. Fahrion, USN, commanded Destroyer Force Atlantic Fleet from 27 July 1950 to 2 January 1952.
[‡] Commander Herbert F. Rommel Jr., USN, commanded the USS *Haynsworth* (DD-700) from 1950 to 1952. DEs – destroyer escorts.
[§] TBS – voice radio. The feedwater was used in the ship's boilers.

Admiral Erly: Well, I think we were talking back in a time frame when some COs stayed on the bridge, and as long as the bells got answered, they didn't go near the engine room.* This attitude developed toward the end of World War II. He really didn't realize that he had a problem. He should have been on water hours. I used to always look at the reports, and all of a sudden, I'd call the chief engineer up and say, "Okay, start checking. Something's going haywire here, and if you don't look out, we're going to be on water hours and you're going to be mighty unpopular. Find out where that feed water's going, because we're sure as hell not using it."

Paul Stillwell: Something his engineer should have told him.

Admiral Erly: Right. Well, that's why you get that report. But Herb wasn't even learning. You're required to send those reports to the senior officer in tactical command. I was that senior in charge of the safety of both ships. Again, it was that mentality that came to us in World War II and was still prevalent even in the Korean War in some cases. Some COs just rang up the RPM, and as long as the engine room answered, fine. They didn't deem it necessary to include the engineering spaces on their daily or weekly inspections

Paul Stillwell: You mentioned Fahrion's name. Was he taking a personal interest in this project?

Admiral Erly: Yes, because we were joining Destroyer Force, and he was ComDesLant. I'm trying to remember. I was chuckling a little, because—it had to be the first go-round of the shakedown training, because they had this preservative on the decks. They had coated all exterior decks with a tar-based substance. We hadn't gotten that off the decks yet when we were sent to Guantánamo for shakedown training.

But, lo and behold, as we entered Guantánamo Harbor, we received a message from ComDesLant that we would be inspected at 0900 the following morning. This was

---

* Bells accompanied orders to the engine room, so in this case "bells" refers to orders to change speed and/or direction, i.e., ahead or astern.

a jolt, for we were not prepared for an inspection, mainly because we had taken on many spare parts and stores just prior to our departure. They had yet to be cataloged and placed in proper storage. So we just weren't shipshape, although we had adequately secured all gear for sea.

Immediately on mooring, we had all hands and the ship's cook turn to, preparing for inspection. We obtained a 50-foot motor launch from the base boat pool and loaded it with all non-stowed gear. Early the next morning we moved the launch out of sight at a base pier.

Paul Stillwell: Just hide it for the time being.

Admiral Erly: Yes, hide it for the time being. So that's what we did.

Old Spike came aboard with his chief of staff. We had made many habitability improvements. The wardroom furniture, which was worn out and paint spattered had been slipcovered at our expense. We had all chipped in. I paid for my cabin decorations. All of this was necessitated by the lack of proper care by the previous crew or crews. We had taken care of a lot of that. A lot of it was done where I got the material from the shipyard, and my crew effected repairs. So we had come a long way. Old Spike was quite pleased with the way we looked.

I also had been exec of the *Yosemite*. I kept contact with the ship when I was an instructor in ASW and CIC at the Newport General Line School. I still had contact with the *Yosemite* off and on, because it was up there in Melville with the DesLant staff. Since I was teaching CIC and ASW, the DesLant staff had an interest, particularly from the ASW aspects. So I went to the *Yosemite* and got new laundry bags that we put in the crew's living compartment of the *J. C. Owens*. You know, you react and do what you have to do. So we looked pretty good for the surprise inspection.

Paul Stillwell: Did you use any gimmicks to fire up the crew?

Admiral Erly: Oh, well, from the very start when we recommissioned the ship, I'd call all hands together. I'd go back and stand on the blower aft and say, "Hey, gather round and—" I told them early on, "If ever there's an all-hands evolution and if something isn't going right and we all have to be here, you better be damn sure I'm going to be here with you."

I'd keep them briefed eyeball to eyeball, and if I couldn't do that under way, I'd come up on the PA system and give them the skinny of what was going on, tell them, "This is this and so forth."

So the crew was always well cut in, and I remember that I'd try to throw in a joke or two. I remember this one, "Why are we doing this?"

I would say, "Do you ever think of why the good Lord put nipples on a man? It ain't because; it's maybe just in case," or something of that nature. The crew members were cut in.

Also, I had something else going with the chiefs I had. The chief boatswain's mate was a senior member of the CPO mess. I had a talk with him. I said, "I expect you to run the CPO mess, and I expect you to keep the chiefs up on the step. You take care of the chiefs, I'm going take care of the wardroom, you got it?"

So that was the way, and we worked the ball game.

Paul Stillwell: That was music to his ears, I'm sure.

Admiral Erly: Oh, sure, sure.

Paul Stillwell: What kind of shape was your electronic suit in?

Admiral Erly: Not too bad. It was a question of the personnel in it. Actually, the electronic suit, I thought, was an improvement over my electronic suit I had in the *Phelps*, which I had during World War II and put out of commission in '45. The CIC setup was better—SG, SC, fire control radar system. We got the bugs worked out, except for the 40-millimeter automatic gun control. We continually had trouble with that, even when we were in Korea.

I really can't quarrel with that or with the sonar. The sonar was better than what I had in the *Phelps*. We ended up with going through and doing well in our Guantánamo training. Did damage control, engineering casualty control. You know, by the time we had gotten through our second tour of Gitmo, we were pretty well peaked.

Paul Stillwell: Did you have any submarine services for ASW training?

Admiral Erly: Oh, yes, definitely. See, that's another good thing around at Guantánamo. We got lots of ping time, lots of ping time. And this again, as I thought I was mentioning, that it's amazing how some of your duties help you. In this case, it was my tour as head of ASW/CIC at the General Line School. I ran so damn many runs on the ASW trainer, pretty soon I just had a sensing, from what was going on and what the chemical recorder was saying and what else was saying, whenever we'd get a sub to practice with, I had him pegged all along. A lot of times the combat information center had no idea which way to tell me to turn. But I was with him and anticipating what was going on, because it was just a mental imaging of what the submarine was doing from the information being fed to me. So that was a great big dividend.

I might say, "Fire ten seconds early. Fire late," figuring, okay, he's going into a tight turn, this type of thing. So, yes, it paid in more ways than one. It paid off for me professionally, yes, including this business of the maneuvering board.[*] Normally I had the ship within five degrees of the course, and by the time combat would come up with a recommendation, I was already there—you know, your mental maneuvering board. A lot of that, I think, came from the year of just running those with class after class. Rote and repetition. Yes, I think that helped a great deal. Besides, I had Hedgehogs, which we didn't have in *Phelps*. I felt they made the ship a much more effective antisubmarine unit than we were in *Phelps*.[†] The Hedgehogs alone were one hell of a good weapon.

Paul Stillwell: Where did you get your shore bombardment workup?

---

[*] A maneuvering board is a sheet of paper containing a compass rose, concentric circles, and logarithmic scales. It is used for working out relative motion problems for ships that are maneuvering. In years past it was known as a "mooring board."

[†] Hedgehog, developed in World War II, was a British-designed spigot mortar that fired its weapons out ahead of the attacking ship. It was the first ASW weapon that could be fired while the surface ship remained in sonar contact with the target. Its name came from the collection of spigots in the launcher; they stuck up like porcupine quills.

Admiral Erly: Oh, Vieques.* We did that. We did very well on that. And stayed away from *Moale* Shoal. You know about *Moale* Shoal?

Paul Stillwell: No.

Admiral Erly: Well, the USS *Moale* struck a shallow spot and suffered hull damage.† Thus it was named *Moale* Shoal, and all of us steered well clear of it.

Paul Stillwell: It sounds like you're ready to take the trip out to Korea.

Admiral Erly: Well, I'm trying to remember when we got word. I believe it was December 1951. We had been recommissioned almost 18 months. The *Owens* replaced a ship in DesDiv 261. DesDiv 221 was our normal division.

Paul Stillwell: Was that because you were faster in getting reactivated than the others?

Admiral Erly: No. Maybe it was because we volunteered for it. I'm trying to remember the facts. Let's see. We should look at that destroyer organization. We had the *Haynsworth*, *Henley*, *Owens*, and one other when we were activated as a division.

As I told you, I thought I had an eight ball. The files showed that she stood eighth in the squadron. And I might say that she stood first or second while she was under my command for over two years, not only in my division, but in being the "Tail-End Charlie," going out as a fill-in, a stranger, with the other division.

Paul Stillwell: We got Admiral Ray Peet's oral history, and he remembers taking over a ship like that, and he said that's the way he liked it because there was so much room for improvement.‡

---

* Vieques is a Caribbean island off the east coast of Puerto Rico. For many years the Navy and Marine Corps used it as a training site for amphibious landings and shore bombardment.
† USS *Moale* (DD-693) was an *Allen M. Sumner*-class destroyer commissioned 28 February 1944.
‡ See the Naval Institute oral history of Vice Admiral Raymond E. Peet, USN (Ret.).

Admiral Erly: Well, I can see what Ray is saying. Sure, you take one on the bottom and then you bring it up. But I really feel that when you commission or recommission a ship, you bring it to life and it develops and has a personality all of its own. Well, I really figured that this ship had been put to death, and I brought it back to life. You breathe this other life into it.

Paul Stillwell: Well, that's right. You didn't have to unlearn all the bad habits of the people there before.

Admiral Erly: Sure. But what Ray said is something, sure. You don't want to take a top ship and then drop a notch.

Paul Stillwell: What do you recall about the deployment itself, going over to Korea?

Admiral Erly: Well, I remember leaving Norfolk on a rainy, stormy day in January.[*] I was new to the division. There were three other skippers and myself and the squadron commander and division commander. He was double-hatted. The squadron commander always had the lower-numbered division.

The commodore had come from BuOrd, hadn't been to sea for a while, and he cranked us up to 18 knots.[†] We were heading for the Panama Canal. The sea was so rough that we started taking seas over the bow. We had waves battering mount 51. When you start battering mount 51, you better look out. You're going to be flooding its handling room and a few other things. So I got on the horn and said, "I am laboring. I recommend we slow down."

Well, I think he dropped to 15. I finally got him down to 12 knots, and we were riding comfortably. But not another skipper spoke up.

Paul Stillwell: How to make friends with your boss.

---

[*] The deployment began on 22 January 1952.
[†] BuOrd – Bureau of Ordnance.

Admiral Erly: But it had to be done. What the hell is the use of arriving if you're going to arrive there beaten up and can't do the job? There's no sense in getting there at all. You can't drive them that way. So that's the way we started out. I was the second section leader, because I was the senior skipper. I'm trying to think. The other skippers were Jimmy Dare, Charlie Carroll, and Jack Conger.[*]

This is where I should have looked at a schedule. The older I get, the more difficulty I have in recall.

I've picked up this joke, and I personalize it in saying that my wife kept telling me that I wasn't remembering very well. She got wondering, "Do you think you have Alzheimer's."

I said, "Oh, no."

"I want you to go to the doctor and get it checked out."

So I called my doctor up and went over there and said, "Hey, I can't remember a damn thing. I'm having trouble remembering, and I'm wondering if I have Alzheimer's."

Hal checked me over, and he said, "Oh, hell, no. You're fine, you're fine. All you've got is CRS. Don't worry about it."

So I came home and I told Lois, I said, "Jesus, I'm great. The doctor says not to worry about it, that I've just got CRS."

She said, "Well, what's CRS?"

I said, "Oh, my God, I forgot to ask him."

So then I had to call him up, and I said, "Hal, what in the hell is CRS?"

He says, "Oh, my God, Admiral, I'm sorry. I should have told you, but I thought everybody knew: "Can't remember shit."

You've heard that. [Laughter]

Paul Stillwell: No, I hadn't.

Admiral Erly: Had you figured it out?

---

[*] Commander James A. Dare, USN, commanded the *Douglas H. Fox* (DD-779) from September 1951 to September 1953. Commander Charles B. Carroll, USN, commanded the *Lowry* (DD-770) from 2 January 1952 to 27 January 1954. Commander Henry Jackson Conger, USN, commanded the *Laffey* (DD-724) from 10 February 1951 to 1 July 1953.

Paul Stillwell: No. So that's part of the problem.

Who was your commodore?

Admiral Erly: Can't remember that. Starts with a W, Whitehurst.

Paul Stillwell: We've just had a chance to pull out some reference books to look up dates, and you've got some details on the schedule for the *James C. Owens*.

Admiral Erly: Particularly during my command as we look at it, as I reported in August of '50, and you can see the real hurry-up with the gathering of a crew and trying to get spare parts and get ready for a recommissioning. We were recommissioned about a month later, on 20 September, and you can really see the hot breath breathing down on us. From there, we went into shakedown operations and ending up again in January of '51 undergoing overhaul at Charleston Naval Shipyard, and from that, again shakedown training at Guantánamo, followed by fleet exercises through the summer, and then off of Vieques and down in the Pacific operating area.

Somewhere along the way, I remember, on that exercise—and previously you asked how I kept in touch with the crew—I told them everything that I knew. I remember making one statement there. We were looking through op orders, and we were getting through one phase of the exercise and supposed to shift into another, and nowhere could we find out what task group we were going to join, and there were all kinds of, evidently, scuttlebutt rumors on the ship what was going to happen next. Well, I remember getting on the PA system and saying, "Okay, you guys, in all this scuttlebutt, now if anybody has any real concrete knowledge of what the hell we do next, come on up to the bridge and tell me."

But I finally shot a message off to the commodore, and we got in the right task group and everything fell in the slot.

Paul Stillwell: I'm sort of surprised, in view of this urgency, that it was more than a year before you deployed to Korea.

Admiral Erly: You've got to remember that the main Navy support for the Korean War came from the Pacific Fleet. And I think the basic contribution from the Atlantic, except for the *Missouri*, was DesLant's contribution of a destroyer division. The brunt of it fell on the Destroyer Force Pacific. And for this augmentation of coming back in, as you say, it took a while, and I felt actually fortunate that my ship got to Korea, because a lot of DesLant units never saw it. My feeling was, "Well, what the hell, if there's a shooting war, I want to have part of it."

Even in the *J. C. Owens*, we started out and trained very, very vigorously. The emphasis we adopted appeared right at the top of the plan of the day. It was "The more you train in peace, the less you bleed in war." That was always the way we trained, and that was the way we thought.

Paul Stillwell: It could be that your ship took some of the commitments that might otherwise have gone to ships that did go to Korea, that you released some to go around.

Admiral Erly: Probably. I'm trying to remember whether we were relieved on station by another LantFlt desdiv. Or it may have been a chop or a chop line somewhere, but there were always one in the pipeline, as I gathered.[*] I'm sure that DesLant history would probably indicate what they did towards the Korean War. I'm sure they've got it documented, and they well should. But I remember when we received the information that we were to go—and I'm sure that I volunteered to go—we were very, very happy. At least I was, and I think the ship's company was. They were looking forward to it, because this is what we had been training for.

Paul Stillwell: Well, the volunteering would explain how you became a fill-in on another division.

Admiral Erly: Yes. So we were recommissioned on 20 September 1950, and we didn't deploy until the 22nd of January of 1952. We encountered heavy seas heading for the Panama Canal, which slowed us down. We finally got to the canal and were grateful to

---

[*] "Chop" is short for change operational control.

get into Gatun Lake. There we anchored and had swimming call and a fresh-water wash down from the antennas to the waterline.

Then from the canal we chugged right along and came into San Diego, and were there about a week. We had a few minor repairs alongside the destroyer tender. I can remember my good friend Jim Dare in the *Fox* was moored outboard of *Owens*. He was moored to my starboard side and I was in closer to the tender. He decided to go out ahead from the nest, and as he was going out, his crew swung out the davits for his port lifeboat. As he went by me, my anchor yanked them off.

By this time, the squadron commander had already headed out. I did a little fast thinking, that here was a whaleboat, and he had no way of hoisting it aboard. The commodore, with the other destroyer, was standing out of the harbor. I called him on the radio and said, "Commodore, with your permission, I will pick up *Fox*'s whaleboat. It means that I will not be able to swing it inboard in case we run into heavy seas. *Fox*'s davits can be replaced at Pearl."

After delaying my departure about 15 minutes waiting for a reply, I was at the narrowest part of the channel, just off the Ballast Point, when I received the commodore's message: "Affirmative. Do so."

So I had to twist and turn in the narrowest part of the channel and go back and pick up that whaleboat and then proceed on. But again, if you can make a decision, why not make it fast?

Paul Stillwell: I can see that early on you didn't develop a lot of affection for this commodore.

Admiral Erly: Well, no. Why should I at this point? I guess I was a burr under his saddle, and I don't know. As you can see, this should have been a "Yes, by all means, do it." But I wasn't going to take the onus of running into heavy seas and losing my whaleboat because I couldn't bring it inboard. We delivered the whaleboat to Pearl. Everything went fine. We didn't run into those bad seas, and Jim Dare got his whaleboat back and got his davits fixed there.

Paul Stillwell: Were you in any sense treated as an outsider because you weren't a regular part of the division?

Admiral Erly: No, not that way. Actually, the four of us skippers, Dare and Jack Conger and Charlie Carroll and I, really became like a band of brothers. We'd get together, the four skippers, and have our shore parties and whatnot and look out after each other.

Paul Stillwell: Did you have a chance to run coordinated ASW tactics on the way out?

Admiral Erly: Not on the way out. No, but we'd done a lot of that before, and the creeping attack, two-ship attack. Earlier, I got in a two-ship coordinated attack going down there in Guantánamo. The exec in the other ship was running it from CIC, and it was putting us in extremis every bloody time.

So I got on the horn in the skipper of that ship and said, "Hey, look, you've got to be the safety officer here. I'm safety officer, too, but it takes two of us to tango if we're going to do this right. It's not working out right, and you can't do it from combat. You need Mark II, Mod II eyeballs to do this."

So we finally got to be able to do the dance together, but other than that it was just really horrible.

The same ship—this poor guy was a virgin to destroyers, Nev Shaffer out of '35.[*] They had Baker-Baker pilings where the battleships used to tie up in Gitmo, and we would go in alongside them.[†] The same ship, after one of our coordinated attack ASW sessions, we were returning to moor at Gitmo. I followed him in, and I was sort of laying back. He'd been assigned to Baker-Baker pilings. He had previously smashed a propeller guard there and gotten it straightened out by the Gitmo facilities. He went in and made a pass, and then he made many more passes. I was sitting back there waiting, and my heart was really bleeding for him. So finally I thought, "If I get in there first, then he'll have a better shot to come alongside of me." Because it was a tricky thing.

---

[*] Commander John Nevin Shaffer, USN, commanded the USS *Stormes* (DD-780) from 15 August 1950 to 21 January 1952. Later, as a rear admiral, he was Commander Cruiser-Destroyer Force Atlantic Fleet and Commander Naval Base Newport from July 1969 to July 1971.
[†] "Baker" was the word for the letter B in the phonetic alphabet of the period. BB is the designation for battleship.

There are pilings forward and aft, with open water between them. You had to line up and come in, and you didn't want your propeller guard to whap in against the after piling.

Paul Stillwell: Sort of like parallel parking a car.

Admiral Erly: Yes. So I sent a visual message, trying to sugar-coat it, and said, "Due to my angle of approach, do you desire me to make Baker-Baker pilings first?"

Back came, "Negative." So I waited, and then about five more attempts. Then I heard from him, "Your last BT, please."

So I went in and whammed her in there.

Paul Stillwell: First pass?

Admiral Erly: Oh, yes, because having had the *Phelps*, with a single rudder and with an extremely high bow, my God, I never had such easy handling as I had in the *J.C. Owens*. I figured no sweat, I could do it with my eyes closed, compared to what it was with the *Phelps*.

So we went in and tied up, and there were two destroyers on the other side of the piling. As I told you, when I taught at line school we had people from Ecuador, Chile, and Colombia. After they graduated, a lot of them were assigned to U.S. ships for shipboard training. Lois and I had entertained them. A good friend of mine was a Colombian officer in the adjacent destroyer. He yelled over to me in Spanish. Translated, what he said was, "Bob, he's going to cream your ship!" I might add that everybody in Gitmo Harbor had been observing this debacle of seamanship.

I hadn't thought of that. Oh, my God. So then he came in, and he missed a pass on me. Then he went back out and then he came in, and boy, I thought, man, he's got it cold. All of a sudden I heard him say, "Starboard ahead; full port back," and he really slammed it in. He crumbled my port Hedgehog a little bit and dah, dah, dah. But the worst thing was—the worst thing—his crew cheered when they finally got in.

God, so I thought, "Oh, the poor bastard."

So I waited a little bit and let things calm down. Then I went aboard, went up to his cabin, "Come on, we're going ashore and get a drink."

He looked up and he said, "You know, if I'd known it was going to be like this, I wouldn't have taken command."

I said, "Forget it. You're learning, you're learning, you're learning."

We went ashore and had a couple of drinks. Later he deployed and did well. In fact, he deployed before I did and did well with it, and then later became ComCruDesLant.

Paul Stillwell: We can put this down as a triumph over adversity and persistence and all that.

Admiral Erly: Yes, and he stayed with it. Nevin's a very smart guy. But I felt so sorry for him. But, as I say, this was his first. The *Stormes* was his ship. God, my heart just bled for him. When that crew cheered, that was—oh, what a devastating thing.

Paul Stillwell: But the point is that not everybody that comes to that kind of command has the same background.

Admiral Erly: That's right, and he didn't have it. He just didn't have it. But he got it. He went out there and did well in Korea and all the way along.

Paul Stillwell: What kind of duties did your ship have in those fleet exercises, plane guarding type things?*

Admiral Erly: We did plane guarding and ASW for various Atlantic task force exercises.

Oh, I know of something else that we did in this time frame—the DEW line.† The

---

* A plane-guard destroyer steams astern—or off on one quarter—of an aircraft carrier in order to recover aircraft crew members who go into the water.
† DEW Line – Distant Early Warning Line, a chain of radar sites built 1,200 miles from the North Pole in the early 1950s as a means of detecting Soviet bombers approaching the United States over the Arctic.

concept was Distant Early Warning line and radar pickets, DDRs out on station.* We were sent up off of Halifax. We were reporting all air contacts and this type of thing, and even some surface contacts. We were on the great circle route going across the Atlantic, and a lot of the big ocean liners would go by. We did that deal on independent duty.

Paul Stillwell: Let me ask you, how do you keep a crew motivated during that kind of dull duty?

Admiral Erly: Well, you go ahead with your training exercises, you hold tactical school for the officers. You keep doing the training bit. Remember what we had, "The more you train in peace, the less you bleed in war," and we kept preaching that all along.

Paul Stillwell: But you were missing the excitement of shooting or chasing a submarine or carrier.

Admiral Erly: I know. As I told you early on, at the end of World War II, when I decommissioned the *Phelps*, I had a serious thought: "Is it going to be any fun going to sea without the thought or thrill of being under air attack or submarine attack or surface attack? How's it going to be?" Those things were in my mind. How do you make it interesting, keeping them up?

You explain also to the crew in something like this, "Yeah, we're out here by all of our own, but look at what we're doing. We're evaluating the new concept of a possible defense for these United States. So we are making a contribution. We're just not out here going around in circles for nothing."

You had an area you had to stay in, which leads me up to one situation. The time of the year was in the hurricane season. We closely followed all weather reports, and I was plotting a hurricane that was coming up the coast. It was headed toward our patrol area. I remember I sent this message saying, "Unless otherwise directed, I am leaving station at zip, zip, zip and proceeding—" I wasn't going to wait and get caught in the

---

* The conversion to radar picket destroyer (DDR) was a reaction to the Japanese kamikazes of World War II. It involved the removal of torpedo tubes and the addition of a tripod mainmast forward of the number-two smokestack; the mast carried the SP early-warning radar.

eye. I also needed fuel. The only thing I got back from my operational commander was, "What are present conditions in your area?"

Well, it was calmer than hell. At the same time, I was breaking traffic like mad, and I saw where a carrier group was going to replenish from an oiler.* I got the oiler's position and beat the carrier group to the oiler. I wanted to top off fuel, just in case. I got alongside, and it was starting to blow just a bit. I was getting a drink from the oiler, and here came the carrier with an admiral, and I forget who the hell it was at this point. I got my drink and cleared the oiler. I received a message from the flagship; the admiral wanted to know whether I thought conditions were safe for the destroyers to fuel. I said, "I have just fueled, and I think it is safe."

I then peeled off to head on my way and asked permission to proceed on duty assigned, but I got pulled in. At least the admiral knew his stuff. He pulled me back in and put me in the screen.

Paul Stillwell: So he stole you?

Admiral Erly: Well, no. He was the senior on the spot. He realized here was a hurricane, and he was watching it. He really knew his business. I wish I could remember who it was, because I thought, "Okay, this is fine. The guy knows what the hell he's doing."

I also ended up then as the screen commander, because I was the senior one among the cans.† I think he had two cans, basically plane guard, so now we had three. We steamed for about two days, and we didn't really get the major impact of it the hurricane. He then released me to proceed on duty assigned.

Paul Stillwell: What was the advantage of including you in his group rather than letting you evade on your own?

---

* In this context "breaking traffic" means decoding classified radio messages.
† "Can" or "tin can" is Navy slang for a destroyer-type ship, because its hull plating is thinner than that of larger warships.

Admiral Erly: Well, I guess he felt the responsibility, being the senior officer present, in what could be a threatening situation and that he would probably have, with a meteorologist on board and a few other things, have more dope than what I could garner, then I would be safer with him. I imagine that was his reasoning.

Paul Stillwell: And then you presumably at that point told your regular boss that this had happened.

Admiral Erly: Yes, that I had joined task group umpty-ump.

Paul Stillwell: Well, that was a diversion. We were getting you on your way out to Korea. You got as far as Hawaii.

Admiral Erly: We haven't gotten there, but I was just saying about the Distant Early Warning line, and then we would turn our data in of the contacts and everything that we had. I'm sure that this was a determination on what were some of the stations that you then did assign the DDRs to for that. That had to be in September-October of '51 that we were doing that, and in January of '52 we deployed.

We came in and we went through Christmas leave, big Christmas party on the ship and this type of thing, and then we deployed. And onward to Korea. We got to Gatun Lake, as we were talking about. Then in on through the canal, and we got to San Diego, and then we got to Pearl. And I told you about the lifeboat episode.

In Pearl, I was just trying to think, that everybody had their little problems. The flagship managed to get going forward and cream a minesweeper with her bow. She had a little holdup, and they took care of that. And I'm trying to think. My friend, Jimmy Dare, had a problem.

We finally arrived in Yokosuka. We had a little post-voyage repair and then put to sea with the task group in screening. You were saying again earlier to me, how did you keep the morale of the troops up? Well, this business of doing squads right and squads left in the screen gets awful boring for all hands, including the captain. So I drafted a message to the task group commander and said, "The *James C. Owens* volunteers for any and all special missions." We got sent off for escorting a cruiser—I guess it was *St. Paul*—on some missions. We did that.

I'm trying to remember who the exec was on this ship, but the skipper was a submariner, and the exec was real hot on his escort, and that was a single escort, except once in a while we'd get a Korean patrol ship out there with us giving him ASW protection. I don't believe we had any—I'm trying—yes, maybe we had some gunfire support missions with that.

Another one we were sent on was up with a comint group on board, Russian-language-trained radio intercept people.[*] They came aboard, and we went up to patrol off of Vladivostok. I remember that very clearly, because I was thinking, "Goddamn it, here I'm sitting up here all by myself, and I can just be a big fat target. So I am not going to be overflown."

We were in a condition III watch, and an ammo load in the tray on the ready gun. If we had air contact, and it was threatening, I'd go to general quarters. This one I remember. All of a sudden this plane was boring in, headed right for us. It looked and tracked like a bombing run. Was it a Russian Badger?[†] I was going to throw a couple of rounds up there, and it turned out to be one of our observation planes. He saw those guns waving at him. Boy, he banked her off, showing his U.S. insignia. I also sent out a message then that, "I do not expect to be overflown by U.S. planes."

Paul Stillwell: And you weren't. [Laughter] What kinds of intelligence were you looking for with this interception team?

Admiral Erly: I really didn't ask them that, but I knew it involved whatever transmissions the Russians were making, and they were decoding, trying to translate—real hush-hush. We put them back in the emergency radio room. It was aft on the main deck. I didn't even go in the space when they were operating. They were on their own, so to speak, for what their mission was. I wasn't privy to that or what results they got. But they were all Russian-language students that were in there with the team.

---

[*] Comint – communications intelligence.
[†] "Badger" was the NATO designation for the Tupolev Tu-16 twin-engine jet bomber that was in service for the Soviet Union (and later Russia) from 1954 to 1993.

Paul Stillwell: What recollections do you have of working with Task Force 77, the carrier task force?

Admiral Erly: My recollections are, you did the refueling exercises and you did all the rest, and I found it could be boring as hell, really, just doing squads right and squads left and rotating positions. I used to have fun coming back to join that screen when I'd come back from some of these missions. It used to be a challenge, because we'd plot on radar, and normally I'd be joining up at night. We would come back and look and say, "Okay, where would we be assigned?"

I think my call sign was Keynote. I'd go up on the air and say, "This is Keynote rejoining. I am proceeding to station [I'd tell them the station I'm going to], unless otherwise directed."

Paul Stillwell: So you were writing your own orders.

Admiral Erly: Oh, sure, sure. Why not? Why not?

Paul Stillwell: Did you get taken away from that carrier force to go over and do any shore bombardment?

Admiral Erly: Oh, yes. I ended up as, say, the mayor of Songjin.* My job there was to look after the island right off the coast in which we had South Korean Marines and a U.S. Marine captain with them. We had to protect the island to make sure that North Korean troops from the beach didn't try to go over and take it. They had tried before. We had two .50-caliber machine guns, which I mounted up on the Hedgehog deck to cover each side and able to depress in order to fire on small boats. We had other automatic weapons, with which we equipped the crew to repel small-boat attacks. The concept was, your big stuff wasn't going to help you. In case of an attack by small boats, you would steam at high speed among them and take them under fire by automatic weapons.

---

* Songjin is a North Korean port city.

That meant all night long at different intervals, as we circled the island, we would fire star shells out just to make sure that no attack was coming in.* This took place every night, every night. At least the gun crews got exercise. Combat got exercise to make sure we stayed out on the circle. The captain got exercise because his sea cabin was right there for the gunfire the whole time. So that was a nightly procedure.

And then every 72 hours, I believe it was, we had to make a run to Chongjin, and this was to keep the blockade going.† In other words, it had to be done within a 72-hour time frame for the blockade to be declared to be legal or some qualification thereof.

Paul Stillwell: So this was under international law.

Admiral Erly: Evidently, yes. I didn't look it up, but I knew that I had to do it. Normally, you went up with an escort and tried to stay outside the 100-fathom curve. This was the safety measure to avoid moored mines. As you went in the Chongjin Harbor, it was something like a dog-ear, went up in like that. My standby ship and escort was an Australian destroyer, and its guns couldn't reach into Chongjin. So whenever we went up, *Owens* would have to go up in the dog's ear and do the shore bombardment.

Coming in, you always knew you had your own intercepts working. You knew you were being tracked by a fire-control radar. The escort ship was rigged to come in alongside, if you got hit or disabled, throw the lines over, and tow you out. That was the idea. It didn't happen. I was not fired upon there. We'd go up and throw in about 50 rounds, and then back on station at night to do the patrol around the island right off of Songjin.

Paul Stillwell: Do you have any speculation why you weren't fired at?

Admiral Erly: In Chongjin? No. No. Maybe we didn't stir them up enough, I don't know. But in Songjin, I used to give them hell, too, and I stirred them up. Where I really

---

* A star shell is a type of gunnery projectile that detonates in the air and provides a parachute flare for night illumination.
† Chongjin is a North Korean port city.

liked to get them was in their railroad marshaling yard. When they tried moving any of their trains or locomotive, we'd go in and knock them off the track.

Paul Stillwell: I'll bet you didn't have any trouble motivating the crew in those operations.

Admiral Erly: Oh, no, they were right with it. In fact, if you didn't watch it, they'd get going so hard and the gun barrels would get so hot they almost peeled the paint off of them. We moved in on Songjin, because we perceived some train movements. We were in a condition-watch status.

They opened up with everything they had, plus, I guess, throwing stone catapults. You heard this old adage, if you're being shot at, you want to steer for the last plume. There were so many plumes, it looked like the ship was just inundated. They shot everything they had, I think, from small arms to whatnot. I deliberated whether or not to go to GQ.[*] In a matter of seconds I went to GQ and radically maneuvered the ship, but we had six hits at least in the ship.[†]

Paul Stillwell: How big would you say the enemy guns were?

Admiral Erly: I would say about 3-inch. After all the hullabaloo and whatnot, we silenced some of the guns. But we had casualties, so we retired to seaward to take care of them and to evaluate the ship's damage.

I don't remember whether it was that day or the next day, the chief engineer, Jim Wilson, came up and said, "Captain we've got an unexploded shell in the top bunk in the officers' quarters aft."

Okay. So I went back. I said, "Everybody clear out."

I crawled up and I got this thing. It was about that long.

---

[*] GQ – general quarters, that is, battle stations.
[†] The ship sustained six direct hits while operating at Songjin on 7 May 1952. Three crew members were killed and five wounded. For details of the incident, see Malcolm W. Cagle and Frank A. Manson, *The Sea War in Korea* (Annapolis: U.S. Naval Institute, 1957), page 335.

Paul Stillwell: Two feet long, maybe?

Admiral Erly: Yes, about like that, and I would judge it was about a 3-inch size shell, or maybe a little bigger.

Paul Stillwell: Was that just the projectile part of it?

Admiral Erly: Yes, the projectile part of it, sure.

Paul Stillwell: Pretty good size projectile.

Admiral Erly: Oh, yes, it was a good-sized projectile. So I took it and gingerly—

Paul Stillwell: With all your EOD experience.*

Admiral Erly: Yes, with all my EOD experience. I figured, well, what the hell, I wasn't going to ask anybody else to do it. So I took the damn thing and I eased it over the side. So we took care of that. But I wasn't about to keep it to show to anybody to analyze, because you never know what the hell's going to happen with a piece of ordnance like that. It wasn't blind loaded and plugged, I'll tell you that.†

Paul Stillwell: What did you do with the bodies of those who were killed? Did you bury those at sea?

Admiral Erly: No, I got permission to leave station to rendezvous with the cruiser *St. Paul* to have some of their doctors come check our wounded. I hoped they would take my wounded so I could go back on station. They came and they took some wounded, but they wouldn't take the kid with the brain injury. We had him on the wardroom table. I tried to say, "Hey, why don't you take him? You can have a helo airlift him somewhere

---

* EOD – explosive ordnance disposal.
† BL&P – blind loaded and plugged, that is, inert dummy ammunition used for target practice.

to obtain proper neurosurgery." Oh, no, they didn't do it, and I really felt he wasn't getting the proper support. So then I started a run down to Pusan, South Korea, where we had our base, where the hospital ship was stationed. We got in there and transferred him to the hospital ship, but he didn't make it. I made a full-power run, but we started to run into a little rough water later in the night. So I just went into the hospital ship and landed him and the dead there.

I had had one shell that went through the after 40-millimeter mount and cut some wires, so that our 40-millimeter automatic battery fire control aft was disabled. So I got Warren, the chief fire controlman in, and I said, "What do you need to effect repairs?"

In Pusan Commander Herb Player, '38, was the base commander.[*] He had some supplies, and we got cable. So we immediately then started doing our own re-splicing to try to get that after 40-millimeter fire control battery back in operation.

I think that, in looking back on the engagement, I don't know what else we could have done that we didn't do. One thing that stands out so vividly in my mind was the stability of the 40-millimeter ammunition. I was standing right over the 40-millimeter magazine, right under the port wing of the bridge. An enemy shell went right into that magazine, didn't set a thing off. It also hit a ready tray on one of the after 40-millimeter mounts and didn't set anything off. So the 40-millimeter ammunition is very, very stable, and later on I will tell you another story about the 40-millimeter ammunition.

As I look back on this incident, I still feel that I wasn't properly supported by the medical team from the *St. Paul*. If they had taken off my dead and wounded, I could have been back on station immediately. My brain injury victim might have survived if he'd gotten to a neurosurgeon, and that's what was required. If the cruiser had taken him and heloed him somewhere where there were that type of expertise, instead of my taking about an eight-hour run at frantic speed trying to get him there, that might have helped. Other than that, the crew bounced back from that one. I had a thing. I told them when I took them out there I'd bring them back, and here I'd lost three of them. That got to me, and still gets to me, in fact.

Paul Stillwell: Did the other dead get transferred to the cruiser?

---

[*] Commander Heber Player, USN.

Admiral Erly: No, no. No, no, they didn't want the dead. No, we transferred our dead to the hospital ship, also, while we were there. I could have buried them at sea, but that was not needed in this case. We had a young hospitalman on board who had worked as a mortician. So we took that 40-millimeter magazine that had been hit, took the ammo out, and cleaned it up. We then used that as a mortuary and cleaned up the bodies.

Paul Stillwell: Then had to reinvigorate your crew, because that loss of life had to have an effect on them.

Admiral Erly: That's right. Again, we got all hands together and said, "Hey, we [unclear], but I'll tell you what. We're going to go back and we're going to really let them have it from now on." I really laid it on the line to them. They all bought it, and away we went charging, went back up on station.

Paul Stillwell: Did this counter-battery firing from the shore catch you by surprise when it hit?

Admiral Erly: Not really. It's always in the back of your mind. If I were positive I was going to get it, I would have been at full GQ, certainly.

Paul Stillwell: But you'd had so many times when you picked up their fire control radar and nothing happened.

Admiral Erly: Yes, well that was in Chongjin. I never picked up fire control radar in Songjin. This happened off Songjin, not Chongjin. Never.

Paul Stillwell: So you didn't get a fire control warning on this one?

Admiral Erly: Nope. No, I think they must have been using just visual fire control. Evidently, we had irked them enough that they were lying in wait. When they opened up, they exposed their gun positions. We also had a lot of white phosphorus then that we used. That really silences enemy fire. That was something else I learned early on in this shore bombardment business. Every time we replenished from the ammo ships, we requested white phosphorus, white phosphorus. It was a most effective counter-battery tool.

Paul Stillwell: What sorts of logistic support did you have during that deployment?

Admiral Erly: Oh, well, the oiler would come by and the ammo ships and this type of thing. You'd wheel off and top off and get your mail passed and this type of thing. When you were on the independent duty, yeah, you'd be on into the route. When I was OTC for other ships off Songjin, I had to draft operational directives.* So I designated Sam Collins, my exec, as the ops officer for the Songjin bit. I also passed the exec's job to the next senior officer, so we had some continuity.

Paul Stillwell: Did you go into port at all for upkeep and maintenance?

Admiral Erly: Oh, yes. Yes, yes. We'd go in with the idea that the squeaky wheel gets the grease. We would go in with a big list of work requests. Then as the tender started cutting you down, you'd know what you could let go and what you really wanted to get done, but you got their attention. In fact, I remember on one upkeep, it was just before we had to go up to Vladivostok. We went into Sasebo, Japan. It was Admiral Dyer's headquarters.†

Paul Stillwell: He was CTF-95, the blockading force.

Admiral Erly: Okay. He was down there in a destroyer tender as his flagship. We had sent in this long list of work items. The chief of staff came over and said, "The admiral said, 'What's wrong that this ship, the *Owens*, has so many material problems?'"

---
* OTC – officer in tactical command.
† Rear Admiral George C. Dyer, USN. The oral history of Dyer, who retired as a rear admiral, is in the Naval Institute collection.

I said, "Come on, sir. *J. C. Owens* has never missed a commitment. We're going to be out of here, and we're going to go on line. I'm getting everybody's attention because I want certain things done, and this is it. You can go back and tell the admiral that I haven't missed a commitment yet, and I'm not about to start."

That was just a question.

Paul Stillwell: And then you gave him an answer.

Admiral Erly: Yes. That was no problem. No problem. I had a very pleasant chat with the admiral.

Paul Stillwell: Did you have any disciplinary problems with the crew on liberty?

Admiral Erly: No, not really. But you would get run of the mill, things you would generally expect. No AWOLs or anything like that.[*] No, no. They were a pretty well welded-in crew.

Paul Stillwell: Once you had gotten past that initial problem with the shortage of talent, did the system replenish you regularly in people?

Admiral Erly: Yes, and then you made sure you got people off to school. DesLant had some schools and whatnot. Then you got moving—after that initial panic when I only had a little fireman step forward that felt he was competent to stand a boiler watch. Well, something else, when you go back to that. The ship had just been recommissioned, and, lo and behold, I was coming out. There was supposed to be a reception at the officers' club, and I smelled some smoke coming out of a ventilator. I didn't even have a damn screwdriver to get the screen off the ventilator to see what was inside. That got a little panicky too.

Paul Stillwell: How did you solve that one?

_____

[*] AWOL – absent without leave.

Admiral Erly: Oh, well, we found something to get the screen off. We got it off, and it was just an electrical malfunction and some insulation burning. We took care of that. But again, see, the tools, everything had been stripped. All tools. And, yes, everybody probably went home with a full footlocker of tools.

Paul Stillwell: Evidently. What kind of intelligence support did you have for those missions off Korea?

Admiral Erly: We did a lot of shore bombardment, and would be given coordinates. In some cases, Army spotting planes were telling us what we were doing. We were on call fire, and they were telling us what we knocked out. "You've knocked out this and knocked out that."

It would all be in the logs, if I wanted to get all the old logs of those missions, the number of rounds expended, number hits, what you destroyed on the beach. They were saying, "Right on, right on, great. You've knocked out this. Now shift fire," and so forth.

Paul Stillwell: Did you get warnings on various threats that you might face in the theater? I'm thinking, had the mine threat been eliminated by then?

Admiral Erly: Oh, hell, no. It was a real threat. This is what you always watched for. We went into that danger, particularly going into Wonsan.[*]

Paul Stillwell: The Wonsan was the one that had them bad early.

Admiral Erly: Oh, yes. We'd gone into what we called the war dance in Wonsan. We went into Wonsan with a cruiser and spotted loose drifting mines. You had lookouts all around, and then you would destroy them by gunfire. But you were also there being tracked back and forth by enemy radar. We had various sectors in Wonsan Harbor. We did that bit, too. The whole division was up there, actually, and doing the patrols, gunfire

---

[*] North Koreans mined their port at Wonsan on the east coast of Korea.

missions. We didn't get shot at Wonsan. As we left, I directed the gunnery officer to use white phosphorus and write "776," our hull number, on the mountainside.

Paul Stillwell: Having a cruiser with you probably helped in that case.

Admiral Erly: Oh, yes. It always helped. As we were almost at the end of our deployment, I got the last special mission to go back over to Songjin, but I went escorting a cruiser, and they turned me loose on Songjin, because I said, "Hey, I got a special message I want to deliver." And we went in and gave it hell.

Paul Stillwell: And if you mess with me, my big brother's going to deal with you. [Laughter]

Admiral Erly: That was good insurance. Not a peep.

Paul Stillwell: Anything else to mention about that Korean deployment?

Admiral Erly: Yes, I had something. I really felt that maybe the East Coast destroyers were much more "go get them," aggressive, and went in looking for it and trying to stir up a fight than our West Coast brothers.

Paul Stillwell: How would you account for that?

Admiral Erly: I don't know. I don't know. Maybe they the West Coast people had been out there so many times that they were willing to sort of run with the task force and do squads right and squads left. I don't know how to account for it.

But it seems like Jim Dare—and I'm trying to remember the other spot that we were in, I was up in there, that you would get shot at. He got shot at in there and I got a couple of lobs at me, but they were way off target. It's another one we used to go into and give gunfire support to our minesweepers; it wasn't Wonsan. There was another little area there, and you had minesweepers in there also, and you were covering for minesweepers and this type of thing. We were in there, too, on independent duty. I forget the name of the place.

Paul Stillwell: Did all this independent duty essentially solve your problem with the commodore because you didn't have to deal with him much?

Admiral Erly: Oh, I didn't have that much problem with him. He, of course, had to let me go too. So no, no.

Paul Stillwell: But you got past the initial difficulties.

Admiral Erly: Oh, yes. He thought I was probably one of his better destroyermen—the most seasoned one, anyway, let's put it that way. Jim Dare, it was his first destroyer command. Charlie Carroll was a submarine guy, and this was his break-in into the surface force. Then Jack Conger was the baby in the crowd, the class of '41, and this was his first command. No, the commodore and I got along. We got along fine.

Incidentally, prior to departing Korea we had the commodore's inspection, and we were a high outstanding. We were number one in the division, from the earliest days of inspection down in Guantánamo. The critique was staged in the wardroom. I ensured to have a microphone, and all inspectors delivered their remarks and comments on our drills, and the entire crew was cut in on all the proceedings. In some cases the inspectors may have been daunted by this requirement. But I wanted the entire ship's company cut in on our strengths and weaknesses.

Paul Stillwell: Well, you had an interesting trip home, going the rest of the way around the world.

Admiral Erly: Oh, yes. Well, we were showing the flag on the way home.

Paul Stillwell: What are the highlights you recall from that trip?

Admiral Erly: Well, the highlights for the crew, of course, would be when we were going down through the Malacca Straits. We had a tacit agreement. We all turned and went due south to get to the equator to have a crossing-the-line ceremony deal for the crew, so they'd all be shellbacks. Later we went to Ceylon, which is Sri Lanka now.

The commodore, you might think I don't like him, but I do. But I can't help but chuckle about how stupid you can be. Poor Conger came down with an awful fever or something, and I knew this, and we were all worried about him. He was in his bunk for damn near a month. We came down through Malacca Straits, I guess, and headed south for the equator crossing and the ceremony. Everybody sort of went their own way, and we joined up as we were going into Ceylon. It's tricky going in there. I had gotten there first and was sort of going to lead the way and whatnot, and I said to the commodore, "If you'd like, I will lead the way in," and then we got Form 18 and then negate Form 18.

"Yes, affirmative, Roger. Go lead it." Because it was a tricky entrance.

Paul Stillwell: He evidently had talked to the skipper in the meantime.

Admiral Erly: Well, the skipper wasn't even talking at this point, and I knew it. I don't know whether it was some smart-ass staff officer or not. You don't know when it comes whether it's the commodore or not.

It'll come out in the rewrite. But the crew got a big boot out of that. And as I recall, we had boxing matches on the beach, and they had quite a good liberty port at that time.

Paul Stillwell: Did you have any interesting liberty stops in the Indian Ocean or the Middle East?

Admiral Erly: The commodore went in at Bahrain, and I went up to a spot called Ras Tanura.[*] ARAMCO had a base there, and we tied up at the ARAMCO piers.[†] And then I went courtesy calling on the local emir for tea and so forth, and then he returned the call.

---

[*] Bahrain is an island nation in the Persian Gulf. It long served as the homeport for the flagship of the U.S. Middle East Force. Ras Tanura, Saudi Arabia, is a port on the Persian Gulf.
[†] ARAMCO – Arabian American Oil Company.

That was interesting. Then, of course, we felt right at home, because the head guy in ARAMCO had the best set of quarters, and they also had a little club and they entertained. They set up entertainment for the crew and for the officers and for the brass. The officers' mess returned a party to them. I guess we were there about, oh, four or five days. It was like being moored at a U.S. naval base.

Paul Stillwell: Sailors are sort of encumbered, though, in what they can do in a place like that because of the alcohol prohibition.

Admiral Erly: Oh, Lord, yes. And the heat. Goodness gracious. You've got to remember now, this was coming up July, late July, and it was hot over there. In those days, remember, ships did not have air-conditioning. When you think of what the crew had to live with and put up with and nary a whisper.

Paul Stillwell: They didn't really have a lot of choice.

Admiral Erly: Oh, no, no, no. But I meant, in comparison with what they have today—the air-conditioning, more privacy on their bunks, and the whole bit. They've come a great way, and it was needed. There's no sense in that type of hardship.

Then we left there and went into Aden, of all places.

Paul Stillwell: That was still British at that point, wasn't it?

Admiral Erly: Yes, still British at that point. Mainly a fuel stop there, as I recall. Basically we refueled, then out and then on through the Suez Canal. As I again was saying, that what stands in mind is the heat and monotony, and we were coming down through the Gulf of Aden and the Red Sea. If there was any breeze, it was from astern, so your relative motion was zero, which meant no breeze.

Paul Stillwell: Wiped it out?

Admiral Erly: Wiped it out, so there was no breeze. Then through the canal, which they enjoyed. Then we turned and went up to Turkey and had a good liberty stop at Istanbul, and back on down over to Greece. We went into Naples, Italy, and Villefranche, France.

Paul Stillwell: That part made up for the Middle East.

Admiral Erly: Yes, that made up for the Middle East, and they all had a ball there. And then finally the last stop coming out of there, as I recall, was Gibraltar.

Paul Stillwell: Did you hook up with the Sixth Fleet for any tictacs?[*]

Admiral Erly: No. I'm trying to think of what admiral entertained us skippers in Naples, and I forget what job he had. I think he was the service force commander. He had all the skippers over when we were in Naples, as I recall. Otherwise, they left us completely on our own. We were finishing up, and this was the better part, although I think in some ways, in retrospect, I would rather the trip through the Mediterranean and Middle East would have been when we were going out, because when you're coming home, you want to get home. I would have preferred to do that the other way.

Paul Stillwell: Was there a sense of anticlimax after you did get home and you were away from all this excitement?

Admiral Erly: Well, not really, because I got home just in time to really step off the ship and go to the Armed Forces Staff College. No leave. The BuPers detailer told me, "Oh, you'll get plenty of leave when you leave Armed Forces Staff College. I'm sorry."

I was hoping that my relief would have met me in Europe and I could have been relieved there, but no way was BuPers going to do that.

See, I was detached in August, so I had been with the ship just about two years—from pre-commissioning to recommissioning and deployment.

---

[*] "Tictacs" is a nickname for tactical maneuvering drills by a formation of ships.

I remember coming into port and about to make my last landing. The chief engineer said, "God, Captain, don't give me an emergency back."

We were coming into Norfolk, and I wouldn't take a pilot. I was the second section leader, so I would have been the third ship in coming up the head of the dock over here. I saw my wife on the tender and started waving. This distraction required that I order, "All engines back emergency full." It was one of the smartest landings I ever made.

Paul Stillwell: Why, because you weren't paying attention?

Admiral Erly: Yes, I doped off, but basically it was either that or go about 20 feet up into the concrete, because my berth was at the head of the dock.

Paul Stillwell: How did you get to Armed Forces Staff College? That doesn't sound like something you'd ask for.

Admiral Erly: No, I didn't ask for it. Some detailer sent me to it. But I'm glad I went. My office mate, actually, was an Army full colonel out of about the class of '39 from West Point. I was a commander. They had augmented so much more in personnel, so those guys were still there, and they were bird colonels. He went on to make general. But you met them, and then you had Air Force types. Some of the previous classes had had Canadians, though our class didn't. We had Coast Guard there, Marines, Air Force, and various branches of the Army. You had the ground pounder, communicator, Signal Corps. The course was preparing you for joint staff duty. That was the basis for the Armed Forces Staff College. An Army general in command, the Navy deputy was Rear Admiral McLean, and there was an Air Force deputy.[*] The flag secretary of it was Ebby Bell.[†]

---

[*] Rear Admiral Ephraim McLean Jr., USN, Deputy Commandant, 1951-53.
[†] Commander C. Edwin Bell Jr., USN.

Paul Stillwell: Well, the Navy had not really wholeheartedly embraced jointness in their staff. This is just a few years after the big fight with the Air Force.

Admiral Erly: This was August of '52. I don't know how long the school had been running.* They had two classes a year. I don't know what class I was, I've forgotten. But I found that it was interesting.

Paul Stillwell: What sort of curriculum did it have?

Admiral Erly: It basically taught you how to make a staff study, and you had to write one on a particular subject. I did mine on gunfire support.

We redid some of the—and analyzed. We wrote sample op orders. We were exposed to the various services. Say, the Marine Corps team from Quantico would come down and brief, and then you would have some other groups come into the auditorium and give us briefings, covering all aspects of warfare in groups. For instance, I would get up and explain underway replenishment in my particular group so the other services would know something about it. The Air Force would explain some of their missions and then the Army, and then, of course, we all worked on preparing operation orders and op plans, that type of thing.

Paul Stillwell: It sounds like a useful exposure.

Admiral Erly: Oh, yes, it was a very useful exposure. The way I found, it was actually, just the staff study alone, facts bearing on the problem, first defining the problem. Really, if you get too big a problem you're in trouble. So you really have to sharpen exactly what problem it is that you are doing in this type of staff study, and then the facts bearing on it and the objectives and all this, and then come out with a conclusion, or recommendations.

---

* The Armed Forces Staff College in Norfolk was established in 1946 and later incorporated into the National Defense University in 1981. In 2000 the school was renamed the Joint Forces Staff College.

Paul Stillwell: Well, I've heard, as a generalization, that the Army people going into that kind of thing were more adept because they had done a lot more of it.

Admiral Erly: Sure. I had not had any staff duty of writing plans or operations orders or anything else.

The net result was that at the end of the course, I don't think I got more than about four or five days of leave. A big amphibious operation was on, and I was ordered to the Amphibious Group Two staff with Admiral Rose.* I was going to be assistant ops and tactical officer. They wanted me on board the flagship when she sailed. So I stepped out of the Armed Forces Staff College and got my feet wet as an amphibian by immediately going on the exercise. Of course, I ended up as the senior watch officer, charged with setting up the watch bill. We were in two or three different flagships during this exercise, and each time I had to configure the flag plot, as we called it.

Paul Stillwell: Why did you move so much?

Admiral Erly: On various segments of the exercise the AGC was not available. When we started, we did not have an AGC, so we were quartered in a squadron commander's flagship, which was an APA.† It had more limited facilities than the AGC. The whys and wherefores of it at that point, I didn't know. But the same thing basically happened to me when I was an admiral and a phib group commander. I had shifted flag back to my old phibron flagship at one phase on account of the AGC not being available, and you needed to cover the exercise. But then I remember the ships, because I had to re-tailor things to go. I got my feet wet there.

Paul Stillwell: How much contact did you have with Admiral Rose?

Admiral Erly: A lot. A lot. I had contact with him there. Then when I went to OpNav, he came up later to OP-33 when I was in OP-33. Then when I moved to the front office,

---

* Rear Admiral Rufus E. Rose, USN, commanded Amphibious Group Two from May 1952 to April 1953.
† AGC was the designation for an amphibious force flagship; APA was the designation of an attack transport.

he came up to the front office as OP-03 Alfa. So I had quite a long time with Admiral Rose.

Paul Stillwell: What is your assessment of him?

Admiral Erly: I'd say he's a very brilliant man, and, damn it, he was good tactically too. I liked the way he could size up the situation and do something about it.

Paul Stillwell: Do you have any examples from your interaction with him?

Admiral Erly: Oh, well, I was just thinking, we had a sortie, and, lo and behold, some of your old brethren. Here came these lumbering LSTs, and he knew exactly what he wanted to do.[*] He rang up the proper—we ran up the proper tactical signals and maneuvered the heavies around them, which I thought right on.

I also remember, we arrived in San Juan or somewhere. He was a bear for mail. I remember I was with him. We were over searching through mail sacks to find our official mail. He was a jumpy, sort of nervous guy. I understand he has Alzheimer's now.

Paul Stillwell: I don't know.

Admiral Erly: Yes, that's what I've heard.[†] A lot of people didn't like Rufus. I got along with him fine, actually. I got along with him fine. You had to know your stuff, and damn well. I'll never forget. Here I was, brand new on the staff. What the hell did I know about? Oh, yeah, I did know about smokescreens, because I'd used smoke. But here we had the smoke plan, and here we have the staff in the ship, and he wanted to go over every segment of the operation order. So the chief of staff set up a briefing. I was to brief the smoke plan.

---

[*] The interviewer served in the tank landing ship *Washoe County* (LST-1165) during the Vietnam War.
[†] Admiral Rose died on 2 March 1992, a few years after this interview.

In those days I smoked, and it was hotter than hell. So I got up in front of the whole staff, and the admiral was sitting here and the chief of staff. I got out this big cigar and started blowing out smoke. There was a fan behind me, and I was looking at them and they were looking at me. I said, "See, when you lay smoke, you've got to take into consideration the prevailing breeze." [Laughter] This was the way I sort of opened up on the smoke plan.

Another guy on the staff was Kemp Tolley, the ops officer.* Frankly, there was the guy that hated Rufus. He hated Rufus's guts. You probably have heard him sound off. I don't know if you've interviewed Kemp.

Paul Stillwell: His assessment, I think, was that he thought Rose was a good staff-type officer, but not a good commander.

Admiral Erly: Well, I disagree with him. I thought he was a hell of a lot more of a tactical guy and a seagoing guy than Kemp. I don't think much of Kemp Tolley, frankly, as a tactician, or anything else, to get him to move off the damn dime. I was his assistant ops. You had to do most of his work for him. So now you hear another side.

Paul Stillwell: Indeed.

Admiral Erly: So I pinpointed who bad-mouthed Rufus, I guess.

Paul Stillwell: You did.

Admiral Erly: Okay. No, Kemp was something else again. He's a little out here, I think. He had one theory. The goddamn thing had never worked, and it haunted me. He tried to get it to work on this coast, came out here. This was running these underwater telephone lines. Well, hell, they never lasted more than about two damn minutes before somebody cut them and you lost that communication. It would have been a great idea if

---

* Captain Kemp Tolley, USN. The oral history of Tolley, who retired as a rear admiral, is in the Naval Institute collection. His interviewer was Dr. John T. Mason.

it worked. But it just never was workable with what we had. Maybe if you could do it with a laser beam or something that's not going to get cut, that would be something else, because you don't want to have to go over the air wherever the beach jumper unit or somebody can interfere.

But he came out here and did it, and wrote me ever so proudly, "Well, I've got it installed out here."

And I'm a son of a gun. I had big CPX exercise later on when I was a Pacific phibron commander, and damn if we didn't try using it up there.[*] He had sold it, and it was written into the plan. It didn't work worth a damn. Kemp thought he had really made a lasting contribution to amphibious warfare, which he hadn't.

Paul Stillwell: You really had to do a quick study on amphibious warfare, didn't you?

Admiral Erly: Oh, yes, yes, yes. Well, you get thrown the ball, you run with it. I learned a lot about it before I got through with it, because when Rufus left, he was relieved by Augustus Wellings, Gus Wellings, and he knew even less than I did.[†] I got along well with Gus, and then he was followed by H. P. Smith.[‡] So I had three in the phib group. Again, you say the Armed Forces Staff College training came in a good deal—we were working on the concept of not putting all your ships right off the op area due to the nuclear threat. We were also very worried about the mine threat when you went in, so it required the minesweepers to clear a path into the objective area and lanes in the transport area.

Well, in addition to this, you worried about your nuclear threat. Therefore, you didn't want any ships closer than about 3,000 yards to each other. That's a mile and a half, and when you figure that, plus you've got to figure the capacity of the minesweepers to sweep mines, so you had to have lanes. You didn't want to have too many ships in there. You kept them out to sea, out beyond the 100-fathom curve, and would call them in as you would need that echelon to unload, whether it was troops or needed supplies.

---

[*] CPX – command post exercise.
[†] Rear Admiral Augustus J. Wellings, USN.
[‡] Rear Admiral Harold Page Smith, USN.

That basically was called the sea echelon concept, which we in Phib Group 2 devised. The admiral bought it, and the Marines bought it, and it was then put into a naval warfare publication, NWP-22, as a standard doctrine. If I hadn't had that Armed Forces Staff College thing, I doubt if I would have been able to come out with that opus and to do what I did.

Paul Stillwell: What are your recollections of Admiral Wellings?

Admiral Erly: I got along famously with him. A kindly old man, I guess, is my basic observation. I didn't see any great operator or anything like that. He was only with us a short time. Of course, again, I was the senior watch officer. I had so much in contact with him.

In one case, I might have been a little abrupt. We were anchored off of that op area by Little Creek, and there was a landing in progress. This was at night, and then the flagship dropped one of its LCVPs into the water, and men were in the water and hurt.[*] Everybody was manning the rail, including some of my watch. I yelled, "Get back in here and plot the current, and direct the radar picket boats to search the area for any survivors." Everybody was hanging on the rail, looking, and we had things to do.

The old man was hanging over the rail too. That, I think, impressed him, and you know how something like that will impress somebody, that somebody's going to do something when something happens, instead of just standing there.

Paul Stillwell: Well, that was a typical reaction for you, wasn't it?

Admiral Erly: Well, basically. I try to react when things happen instead of just, say, gape. Let's do something.

Paul Stillwell: What are your recollections of Admiral Smith?

---

[*] LCVP – landing craft, vehicle and personnel.

Admiral Erly: Oh, a very polished gentleman, very courtly. Page could be a tough cookie when he needed to be. I'm very fond of him personally, and we still correspond at Christmas. When I go to Virginia Beach, he'll have a dinner party for us and this type of thing. We're very close to both him and his wife.

In fact, before he became the phib group commander, a big supporter of Page's was Slim Wooldridge, and we used to go up fishing.* Slim would take his stewards, and Page would come down from Washington. We'd meet at Cheatham Annex and have a fishing weekend. Wooldridge would supply the stewards and the chow and whatnot, and we'd just have a nice weekend in the quarters up there. So we knew Page and we knew Dee and we knew Dee's mother. We called her Mom Rogers. But when they came to the phib group, of course, I never presumed on that at all.

Paul Stillwell: How would you describe him tactically?

Admiral Erly: Oh, he'd been through the eye of the needle. He was a good sailor, good sailor.

We talked about Kemp. Page got so infuriated, I thought he was going to throw Kemp over the side. When the Guatemalan crisis occurred, we were having an amphibious exercise off of Little Creek. The day before our exercise was to end, Admiral Smith was directed to report to the CinCLantFlt headquarters. Admiral Smith took me and Lieutenant Commander Bill Hoppe.† We were briefed on the possibility of a Communist takeover in Guatemala, and Admiral Smith was directed to take the necessary steps to protect American citizens.‡

It ended up after that briefing—we'd left the flagship, with a small bag of clothes in hand. As an aside, I had planned a weekend trip to the Tides Inn in my boat, and Lois had it all stocked and ready to sail. I had to call her from CinCLantFlt headquarters and tell her to expect to see me in several weeks. We didn't know what was going to happen. We were en route in a matter of a short time in a Marine plane headed for Gitmo. When

---

* Rear Admiral E. Tyler Wooldridge, USN.
† Lieutenant Commander William E. Hoppe, USN.
‡ Jacobo Arbenz Guzman was President of Guatemala from March 1951 to June 1954, when he was ousted in a coup backed by the U.S. Central Intelligence Agency.

we got to Gitmo, Hoppe and I wrote a message op order that we sent out to forces being assigned to Admiral Smith. Then we took a destroyer as our flagship and headed for Guatemala.

We made a high-speed run to position ourselves on the Guatemalan coast. Mush Dornin showed up with his APA, all hot to trot for a landing if necessary.* Then an APD reported in.† A carrier came in, and I'm trying to remember which one. Bardy Bardshar was the ops officer on the carrier.‡ I remember going aft on the fantail of the destroyer while a helicopter lowered Bardy down; I grabbed his long spindly legs to pull him in. We briefed him on the proposed ops. Then the helo lifted Bardy back to the carrier.

A day or so later, we got the word, "Go." Admiral Smith ordered, "Execute my message op order." The op order had specified that the APD was to go to into the harbor, render assistance to friendly forces, and report on the situation. CinCLantFlt, having had our message op order for several days now, came out and said, "Oh, no, belay your execute. Keep all forces out of sight of land."

So we canceled the execute. A little later the APD reported back, "Wish to inform you that on receipt of your canceled execute, I was 300 yards from the pier. Everything appeared quiet and serene. I immediately backed down, twisted, and put to sea."

It appeared that the CinCLantFlt staff did not read our message operation order. They should have said, "No, keep your forces out of sight of land." They should have told us that bit of information after we put out our message op order.

As events unrolled, more LantFlt units reported to our opcon. Finally, the "Mount O" showed up, the *Mount Olympus*, with the rest of the phib group staff. Then as things quieted down, I know Admiral Smith was desirous of promulgating an operational summary and wanted Kemp Tolley, the staff operations officer, to get cracking on it. He had sent for Captain Tolley several times.

Knowing this, I went to Captain Tolley and said, "Sir, the admiral desires to talk to you."

Kemp ignored it.

---

* Captain Marshall E. Dornin, USN, commanded the attack transport *Mellette* (APA-156) in 1953-54.
† APD – high-speed amphibious transport.
‡ Commander Frederic A. Bardshar, USN, was operations officer of the carrier *Leyte* (CVS-32).

I said, "Captain Tolley, you had better talk to the admiral." Kemp could be obstinate at times. It was an inane situation—childish.

Paul Stillwell: How much work did you do with these special units like the beach jumpers and UDT and so forth?*

Admiral Erly: Oh, they were cranked into every operation, naturally. Phil Bucklew had the beach jumper unit at that time.†

Paul Stillwell: We got his oral history before that.

Admiral Erly: Oh, you had gotten it?

Paul Stillwell: Fascinating.

Admiral Erly: They called him Big Stoop. Did he tell you about that one?

Paul Stillwell: I don't remember that nickname.

Admiral Erly: Well, Buck had the beach jumper unit at that point, and he was good at it. And, of course, you needed the UDT. We didn't have SEALs in that time frame.‡ We just had the UDT, and, of course, you had to send them in to make the preliminary beach survey and remove any obstructions, and you needed their report and their clearance. To select the beaching area, all that information was needed for an amphibious operation. What I'm thinking is back—and maybe you might have seen it as a child—Edward R. Murrow's "See it Now."

---

* UDT – underwater demolition team.
† Commander Phil H. Bucklew, USNR. The oral history of Bucklew, who retired as a captain, is in the Naval Institute collection.
‡ SEALs are Navy personnel trained for sea, air, and land operations. In previous years similar individuals were designated as part of underwater demolition teams (UDTs). In addition to that specialty, the SEALs have a broader mission that includes commando-type operations ashore.

Paul Stillwell: I recall that.

Admiral Erly: We had completed an amphibious operation off Onslow Beach, North Carolina. Fred Friendly was the instigator of the "See It Now" series with Edward R. Murrow.* The crew from CBS had filmed this operation. They shot a series of film showing UDT ops, loading the LCVPs from the APAs, LVTs swimming out of the LSDs, boat waves headed for the beach—in fact, every segment except the sequences that lead up to the order "Land the landing force."†

I was designated to work with the film crew to recreate this sequence. They showed up on Sunday morning unannounced. I had to get Admiral Smith off the golf course to do a reenactment of "Land the landing force" in the flag plot of the *Mount Olympus*. That really shot my Sunday, for I was required to fly to New York that night to act as the technical advisor, starting Monday morning at the CBS studio with Fred Friendly. We had planned a cocktail party for Sunday evening, which I had to summarily leave for the airport with Red Ramage, one of our guests, driving me.‡

Paul Stillwell: The media were very much more pro-military at that time.

Admiral Erly: Yes, many had wartime service. Friendly had experienced clambering down a cargo net and loading into an LCVP. He recalled the heave of the sea and the fear that his hands would be stepped on by those following. Here is how they did the final editing. First the film sequences had to be cut and spliced for continuity with the script. Then and only then did Murrow play a part. He read the script, and it had to be dubbed into the film sequence. Edward R. Murrow was seeing all this unroll. He didn't see any of the actual operation at first. It was the magic of his delivery he could make you feel you were there seeing it now.

Paul Stillwell: But people at home could "see it now." [Laughter]

---

* Edward R. Murrow was a noted correspondent for many years for CBS radio and television. He became famous for his radio reports from London in World War II. He was director of the U.S. Information Agency from 1961 to 1964.
† LVT – landing vehicle tracked; LSD – landing ship dock.
‡ Captain Lawson P. Ramage, USN.

Admiral Erly: That was editing. Fred W. Friendly was an expert. Well, that was good publicity. In fact, after I commissioned the *Paul Revere*, we had our dependents day cruise. I got that film, and we showed it to the dependents to give them some idea of our mission, "Here's an APA, and this is what we do in an amphibious operation.

Paul Stillwell: That's a very exciting thing, with all these boats racing around and gunfire support and troops running out.

Admiral Erly: Oh, yes. Sure.

Paul Stillwell: Did you make any deployments in that phib group?

Admiral Erly: Not deployments per se. Exercises, yes.

Paul Stillwell: You didn't go to the Mediterranean?

Admiral Erly: No, no. Phib Group 2 didn't go. I'm trying to remember, in that time frame were we sending a phibron. Normally that fell to a phibron commander, the deployments with Marines to the Med. If a phib group commander was required, it would have been Phib Group 4, the operational phib group. We in Phib Group 2 were labeled the administrative phib group, and all LantFlt amphibs were under our admin control.

Paul Stillwell: Was there any tactical innovation during the time you were in that command?

Admiral Erly: Oh, hell, all kinds of them. As I say, we devised a sea echelon concept, how do you handle the minesweepers, how do you defend against nuclear and biological warfare and all this. I think Phib Group 2 was very instrumental in getting a lot of this incorporated in NWP-22, 22 Alfa, amphibious warfare doctrine.

Paul Stillwell: Did you get into the helicopters at all, or was that later?

Admiral Erly: Oh, no, we were into choppers well at this time. I'm trying to remember. It's my radiation reading, because I was also the nuclear warfare guy. I went to Camp Desert Rock when I was assistant ops in Phib Group 2. Went out to one of the nuclear tests, about a 75-kiloton deal at Camp Desert Rock in the Nevada flats.

Paul Stillwell: What are your recollections of that experience?

Admiral Erly: Oh, awesome. We were in a trench about, oh, 3,000 yards from ground zero, and, of course, were warned not to look at it. But when that thing went off, the old earth just felt like jelly, it was that bad. Then, in a matter of minutes, we were in to ground zero, and, of course, as we came in, they had sheep tethered at various spots, and as you got closer some already been blinded, and the closer you got in, the more they were dead.

About the same time, the Marine choppers followed up to take advantage of the shock effect for coming in. They were landing Marines in the area. So in this time frame, yes, the vertical envelopment concept was well along on its way, and we were using it.

Paul Stillwell: Did you have an LPH yet or what type of ship?

Admiral Erly: Oh, no, the LPH was not commissioned as yet.* We had a jeep carrier commanded by Eddie O'Neill that was being used as a helo deck.†

Paul Stillwell: Well, that was obviously a revolutionary way to approach amphibious warfare.

---

* The LPH concept developed in the 1950s as an amphibious assault ship that would deliver forces ashore by helicopters rather than boats. The USS *Thetis Bay* (CVE-90) was an escort aircraft carrier originally commissioned in 1944. In July her designation was changed to CVHA-1 and in 1959 to LPH-6. She tested the concept of vertical envelopment. The first U.S. Navy ship built for the purpose was the USS *Iwo Jima* (LPH-2), commissioned in 1961.
† Captain Edward J. O'Neill, USN, served as commanding officer of the escort carrier *Mindoro* (CVE-120) from April 1954 to May 1955.

Admiral Erly: That came along in this time frame, yes. I guess I was in on some of the ground floor of that, of which is commonplace now; it's standard procedure. Actually, it got to be SOP in some of the operations that I ran in the '60s. But here we're talking now, this is '53-'54, and the concept was still thinking in terms of using tactical nuclear weapons to take advantage of their shock effect.

Paul Stillwell: What was there concern for radiation in all of this?

Admiral Erly: Radiation was a concern, because we all wore dosimeters, and the readings were recorded. The radiation laboratory recently sent me my rad reading. The lab asked for an update of anything physical pertaining to radiation. So they're still following up on radiation and its effects. I don't feel that I had any adverse effects from it.

Paul Stillwell: Wouldn't there be a potential for harm, though, if you put those troops in right after you've set off one of those things?

Admiral Erly: Well, not really, because we went just before the time they put the troops in, and my rad reading wasn't that high.

Paul Stillwell: I see.

Admiral Erly: What I'm saying, there's a problem if it's a dirty burst or an airburst. This was a tower burst. If you have a ground burst, where you really contaminate all the earth, then you've got more of a lasting radiation factor. And you've got to remember, we were also thinking then, salt-water washdown. All ships were equipped with that. This was part of that, not only for fallout from atomic, but also for biological and chemical warfare, and you were thinking in those terms.

Paul Stillwell: That would certainly catch the enemy's attention with the tactical nuclear weapon and then a helicopter assault.

Admiral Erly: Oh, yes, yes. But the question then comes to mind, you're playing a little bit of this, a bit of who does what to whom. Now, how does he counter, and does something that was started tactical end up in a general nuclear exchange? That's what you all start to wonder. I don't know. Perhaps it would be better if they just outlawed nuclear weapons, period, and do away with them all. I think it would be a safer world. On the other hand, until we get something, solar power or some other power or power requirements as such, that I don't see how we can do away with nuclear power plants, though. Then if we start getting into philosophy on that, where do you end up?

Well, back to amphibious warfare. I've seen quite a few changes and, I guess, in the latter part of my career, I sure became an amphibian, there's no two ways about it. I really wet my feet. And one was Rufus Rose. I will say something else that drove probably Tolley wild, but I realized it was a lesson learned.

What I did as assistant ops, I'd take the op order—Admiral Rose demanded this. He wanted everything that could be predetermined ready, signals, anything, course changes, formation changes, etc., whether it was to go flag hoist, voice, encoded. I would sit down with the op order and have the communicator, the plans officer, myself, and we'd have the signal book and any of the tactical changes from the cruising formations, when we were going to change the type of formation, how were we going to enter the objective area.

The secret was, you started with the objective area, the landing area, and you worked backwards. So I came out with what ships had to be where and at what anchorages and had it drawn out. Then how are you going to get them there, what formations, and what events for various parts of the exercise, and had all of these various dated items printed up as a master gouge so pertinent changes could be entered. I had a cardex file in order, and if I had item—card number one—I would leave spaces so could have one alfa, one bravo, one charlie, if other things were going to come up.

So my watch officers, really, before they went on watch, could really thumb through and say, "Hey, this is what's happening in this time frame on my watch."

That I carried with me in doing my amphibious operations, and I made my people, my staff, do it. It was like pulling teeth the first time, but after they did it once, "Boy, boy, this is a great help."

Paul Stillwell: It was almost like having a script, wasn't it?

Admiral Erly: Well, it was more like, what you have really done basically, is war-gamed the damn thing. It can also possibly show you some flaws in the op order, that, "Oh-oh, this needs to be done," or "An addendum needs to go out to the op order for this," you see, up until "Away all boats," and the whole damn bit. And signals for air raid—anything you can think of. It'd cover every contingency.

Paul Stillwell: Communications are vital in that kind of an operation.

Admiral Erly: Yes.

Paul Stillwell: How reliable were they?

Admiral Erly: Well, with a beach jumper unit, it could get pretty damn screwed up when you tried to check up on the communicators, say. This is something else that you've got to watch. I set up a system where, in addition to the staff watch ops officer, I had a system for checking messages. Okay, the message was sent to communications at such and such a time. I want to know what time it was sent from communications, and is a reply required? And then if its got pending action on it, you kept it on the pending action file.

So communications is a key point, and again, Tolley's bit about if we could have had something that keeps you off the air and running the underwater phone lines, if it had worked, great idea. But it wasn't dependable. So you either had to go with voice or radio, and flashing light, flag hoist, you name it, the whole bit. The beach jumpers, of course, tried to disrupt your communications. They tried to get in and take over a net. You've heard them work, I'm sure.

Paul Stillwell: Use communications deception.

Admiral Erly: Sure. The best thing to do would be a silent landing, in my humble opinion. Goes by watch time; you're supposed to do such and such at such a time. Here it is; here's the op order; make sure your boats are there.

Paul Stillwell: What general observations could you draw about the quality of the people assigned to the amphibious force in that period? One of the stereotypes is that they were not of the quality that went, say, to the submarine force or the destroyers.

Admiral Erly: Oh, hell—well, no. It was pretty obvious the submarine force had something that an amphibious skipper didn't have. A submarine skipper can fire somebody off his sub just like that. And in the first place, to get to the sub he had to have a high GCT/ARI.[*] He had to have passed, I guess, a psychological test for stability and a few other things. So when you started looking at the requirements of manning a fleet submarine, the requirements of manning your big carriers and your flight deck crews, and you're looking at—well, I guess, an engineer is an engineer. But when you look at those requirements, then you looked at the destroyer requirements, who was getting the talent?

Paul Stillwell: And the amphibs and the service force were getting the leftovers.

Admiral Erly: Basically, that was part of the problem.

Paul Stillwell: So that's quite a leadership challenge.

Admiral Erly: Oh, yes, it is. Yes, it is. But I'll tell you, some of those young—again, you can have fun. I just think some of the LCVP and LCM, coxswains and responsibility they have of taking that craft in through the surf and unloading troops and equipment, and I take my hat off to them. I think that maybe in some cases their GCTs might not have been as high as the submarine or the aviation people. The kids did the job when they were called on to do it and, I think, did one hell of a good job.

---

[*] GCT – general classification test, a part of the battery of aptitude tests administered to Navy recruits. ARI is the mathematical part.

As I used to tell them, "We don't take anybody's backwash," and I'm talking as an amphibian now. I said, "My God, none of them can do what we can do. We're the force that projects our power right up on that enemy beach, and no one else can do it but us amphibians. So don't let these destroyer guys or these submarine guys or the aviators pull any of this hokey-pokey on you. You kids are it. You're the spearhead, and everybody else is just there to make sure you do it, and they're there to help you do it."

Paul Stillwell: It sounds like some good psychology. Well, it's a considerably different skill that's called for.

Admiral Erly: Oh, sure. Yes, absolutely, absolutely.

Paul Stillwell: And maybe the guy who thinks too much wouldn't be as good in that kind of job, because he dwells on the hazards.

Admiral Erly: I remember we had fun when I was going through refresher training. Well, that was later, when I had the *Paul Revere*, I would hop in a boat and go right on in with the rest of them as coxswain.

Paul Stillwell: That is a good way, leadership by example. What do you recall about the inspection function that the group staff carried out?

Admiral Erly: As Phib Group 2 in that time frame, we did not inspect ships.

Paul Stillwell: You probably endorsed squadron reports, didn't you?

Admiral Erly: Yes, squadron commander. But, of course, that would be more on the material side, and I don't think we went into the readiness side. I think that came along later, because if we had been doing that, I'm sure I would have been up to my eyebrows, and in this time frame, remember—I'm talking '53-'55—we were not doing that.

Paul Stillwell: Who measured that readiness? Was that the fleet training group?

Admiral Erly: The one that was basically interested in the ship's readiness was the phibron commander. He was the guy that was doing that. He was the one that observed or caused to be observed, whether or not they were going to get the assault boat insignia, if they got their boats loaded, if they were properly controlled and doing all the rest of these things. That was the phibron commander, not the phibron. Phib Group 4 was basically supposedly the operational side; it was just an operational staff. We had a material guy on our staff, and the Phib Group 4 didn't. We were writing the fitness reports of the phibron commanders; we didn't write them on the skippers. So Phib Group 2 was a combination of operational and administrative commander.

Paul Stillwell: Presumably, then, if some ship was a weak sister, it was up to the squadron commander to solve the problem.

Admiral Erly: Yes, and if he felt he couldn't, then he could have come to the phib group. As I say, the phib group did have a material officer. Now, whether we had any material funds, that's something else. I don't remember, and I didn't really get into that.

Paul Stillwell: Anything else to recall about that tour of duty?

Admiral Erly: Well, I found it very challenging, because here, again, it was a new facet of naval warfare opened to me, and I felt when I left it that I had made some significant contributions, i.e., the sea echelon concept, nuclear defense concepts, and this type of thing. Again, as I say, when I designed this principle of always planning ahead as far as you can, but always with the capability of adapting and changing as needed, was a very great device that I came up with, but I must say that I was directed to come up with it by Rufus Rose. Evidently, before I got there, he hadn't been able to get anybody to do what he wanted, so I don't know.

Paul Stillwell: Well, he certainly then had the foresight to recognize that there was a problem that needed a better solution than it had.

Admiral Erly: Yes, he sure did. And, as I say, that was a useful tool that I carried with me. It paid me in good stead.

Paul Stillwell: One of the criticisms of the Japanese in World War II is that they had these detailed plans, but they were so rigid that they couldn't adapt to changing circumstances.

Admiral Erly: In something like that, as I said, you left plenty of room. You could throw it away or not use it. It isn't apropos at this time, well, let's do this instead. But at least you had a framework to follow, and flesh it out as you went along, as other things develop or change.

Paul Stillwell: I think you told me previously that one of your next options at that point was exec of a cruiser, but you got steered otherwise.

Admiral Erly: Well, Page Smith seemed to think that I should go as an exec of a cruiser, and here I'd been, what, pushing a can for two years and been in the phib group for two years, basically, almost. This was four years, and I was so out of proportion with the rest of my classmates for sea duty and foreign duty that it was unbelievable. Let's see, in 17 years' service, I think I had had a little over a year at the General Line School, five months at the Armed Forces Staff College, and all the rest was either foreign or sea duty. I was in Venezuela for about two years, in Cuba for almost a year, and the rest was sea duty.

    Page thought the way to pay in promotion was exec of a cruiser, but Tiny McCorkle, who was OP-33 in Washington, felt I should go to Washington at this phase in my career.* I called him and told him that Page had said I'd go as exec of a cruiser. I said, "That's the way I was going to go if I could get it."

He said, "Okay."

We talked on the phone, and about three days later I got about a five-page letter from McCorkle telling me all the reasons why I was coming to Washington, why I was coming to OP-33.

Paul Stillwell: You didn't really have too much choice that way.

Admiral Erly: No, no. In fact, I would say from the time of when I got my second can, which I wanted, I wanted another destroyer, from asking for that and for the other, from that time on I never had any say on where the hell I was going, period. Nothing. It was a fait accompli before I could wiggle.

Well, I went to OP-33 in Washington, which again was a great learning experience. I think I told you before that I realized that it was essential that when I decommissioned *Phelps* at the end of World War II, I felt that really I probably should be a smart guy and go to Washington, but I opted to go enjoy life while the Navy was in a turmoil. So I got back to the scene of the crime, and I rapidly became impressed with the way one crossed one's T's and dotted one's I's in the preparation of official correspondence; that was the number-one priority of OpNav. I really felt that about one-third of the jobs in OpNav should be abolished immediately, and then about three months more you should take one-third more away, and then you might have a real competent working staff.

Paul Stillwell: You and Admiral Rickover would agree on that, then.[†]

Admiral Erly: It seems to me that people get so ingrained in the paperwork mill in OpNav that they lose the sight of what the hell they're there for, and their being there is

---

* Rear Admiral Francis C. McCorkle, USN, director of the Fleet Operations Division of the OpNav staff, 1953-55.
† Admiral Hyman G. Rickover, USN (Ret.), headed the Navy's nuclear power program for many years.

to try to help the fleet at sea and not just manufacture more OpNav instructions that will make life more miserable for everybody in particular.

That was, I'd say, my observation of my first months there. I must say that I was very, very fortunate in the jobs that I held. First, I was in OP-33, where I was sort of the admiral's right arm in what was going on in the various sections of OP-33, which gave me a good broad overview. I felt more at home in this particular setting, because we were concerned with ships' operations. They had a current setup where, in times of emergency, we kept track of the situation, of what was taking place. The oncoming OpNav flag duty officer would come up to our briefings in the morning, to be brought up to speed with what was happening operationally, and possibly something could happen on his watch that night. They required that the OpNav duty officer stay in the Pentagon.

When Admiral Arleigh Burke came in there, we really ended up coming up with an OpNav operations center, with duty captains standing the watch and keeping plots of everything that was going on.[*] But when I first went there, it was a rather crude setup, which was finally refined down the line, and part of it started during my tenure there. I was there from January of '55 to March of '58.

During that time, then I fleeted up and became head of the fleet organization section, which made me the official ship counter in the Navy. In other words, if anybody was going to quote the number of active ships that we had, they came from my shop. Of course, it had to be approved by 33, and then 03, who had the main say.[†] I found at this time that the number of carriers and how you counted them was in disarray.

Paul Stillwell: What do you mean by that?

Admiral Erly: Well, we were supposed to have 15, but actually we had about 17 or sometimes 18. I'm trying to remember. And then we had nine CVSs.[‡] So we had quite a carrier force. The total ship count—I'm saying warship count—manned by U.S. Navy sailors was around 1,010. I'm sort of digging that number. It was over 1,000.

---

[*] Admiral Arleigh A. Burke, USN, served as Chief of Naval Operations from 17 August 1955 to 1 August 1961. His oral history is in the Naval Institute collection.
[†] OP-03 – Deputy Chief of Naval Operations (Fleet Operations and Readiness).
[‡] CVS – an aircraft carrier specialized for antisubmarine warfare.

But the thing that plagued me most was how do you count the carriers and then still stay legal? I finally wrote this thing out for the CNO approval, that if a carrier was in for a long conversion overhaul, we'd take her off the line. We wouldn't count her as active, which she really wouldn't have been anyway. So that helped assuage my bit on numbers.

Paul Stillwell: Whom were you trying to satisfy? Congress?

Admiral Erly: Yes, Congress and the other services. The other services. And also, I think, in my time frame in being the ship counter and seeing in some cases, with the budget and other things that were going on, the thing that was getting us was not so much the number of ships we could man as it was the personnel ceilings imposed by Congress. I made it one of my aims at this point to try and get MSTS out of being manned by U.S. Navy personnel.[*] I felt that MSTS should be manned by civil servants, and that would give us the crews that were manning them to man our warships, because I could see that personnel was the crux. If you've got to get money and you're going to do it, how do you do it? What's the easiest thing you can control, sort of like a valve, open and close?

Paul Stillwell: Personnel.

Admiral Erly: Exactly, because your personnel costs, I think, roughly take about almost 58 to 59 cents of every budget dollar. So this is the way Congress was really limiting the size of the fleet. When they put a personnel ceiling on you, then, damn it, if you couldn't man the ships, what did you have to do? You'd have to put them in a reserve fleet. So I was looking for other bodies, and one was to get MSTS manned by civilians, which it is now, today.[†]

Paul Stillwell: Well, at least part of it was manned by civilians then.

---

[*] MSTS – Military Sea Transportation Service, a part of the Navy that operated ships for support functions.
[†] In 1970 MSTS was renamed MSC – Military Sealift Command.

Admiral Erly: Not that many. All the transports were manned by Navy crews. I think, maybe I figure ten or something vaguely sticks in my mind, or something in this nature in this time frame. I'm talking the time frame now, basically, about '53-'54.

But there was a tough old admiral who taught me navigation at the Naval Academy, and he had MSTS at this time.[*] But I felt that in that job down in OP-33 that I did do that. I got the carrier count stabilized out and then I started some of the other ones.

This business of home-porting. The issue of the flagship in the Sixth Fleet had come and gone and come and gone, and I finally got this letter. I think I had about 24 attachments to it and sent it up, proving the point that we should home-port the Sixth Fleet flagship in the Med. I expressed the thought that, hell, you could man it with volunteers, that people would to have a tour over there. Sure enough, it got approved, and the flagship has been home-ported there ever since. Well, one other thing was in that favor, I might add, that Arleigh Burke also wanted it, but wanted the ammunition to back it up.

Paul Stillwell: What were your supporting arguments?

Admiral Erly: Golly, we went from A to Z. We went from economy, continuity, for morale of the crew. You've done away with one deployment segment, so there's going to be more homeport time for everyone involved. Instead of having about two or three flagships in rotation, you've got it there and the permanency of it. Also, I would say from the operational benefits that would accrue to the staff instead of having to change from ship to ship and personality to personality.

As I say, there were just about 24 supporting arguments for it. But those were some that I remembered, the point. You're making me go back 35 years.

Paul Stillwell: What were the duties that you fell into when you initially got to OP-33?

---

[*] Vice Admiral Francis C. Denebrink, USN, served as Commander Military Sea Transportation Service from 1952 to 1956.

Admiral Erly: When I first went to 33, I ended up relieving a classmate of mine, Walt Stencil, who basically had taken over the job as sort of coordinating all the sections under the OP, if you would, the administrative assistant to OP-33.[*] Then I had a young assistant, who was a smart lad, and when the other section opened, the fleet organization section of OP-33 job came out and became available, I fleeted up to that. Then this administrative function went to this young lieutenant commander, and he was quite capable of handling it.

But I had a good oversight at this point, having had that job, of what went on in OP-33, and with then going down to—I think I was 333 Delta or something like that. I had to work with OP-34 and some of the other OPs in the building. I kept that job, I guess, about a year. I was a commander when I went down there. That was a captain's billet that I took. I was selected for captain in June of '55. I'm trying to think of some of my interactions. I was also home-porter. I had to designate homeports for the various ships, which brought me working with 05 and the carriers and this type of bit.[†]

Paul Stillwell: Was that in the fleet organization half?

Admiral Erly: Yes, that was in the fleet organization half.

I got there and said, "Hey, look, the carrier's going to go in for overhaul and she's going to be there for a year. If she's going to be there a year, we should change homeport. Give the families a break to be able to move."

Again, this all cost money, which you had to look at. I worked very closely with OP-90, which was the programming side of it. When it came to cuts or what ships were going to go out and this type of thing, I had to be in there with OP-90, working that out with OP-90.

Paul Stillwell: Who made those decisions?

---

[*] Commander Walter J. Stencil, USN.
[†] OP-05 – Deputy Chief of Naval Operations (Air).

Admiral Erly: Well, then they went with the basic decisions coming through them. Then the decision was going to come up between 03 and 05. Then it was going to be at the VCNO level and up to CNO, the final bit. The recommendations went up to CNO, and they got approved on that basis.

Paul Stillwell: Did the recommendations start in your office?

Admiral Erly: A lot of them in mine, a lot in 90.

Paul Stillwell: I would think that 90 would be more concerned about numbers and you would identify specific ships.

Admiral Erly: Well, no. I would not identify specific ships. You're going to have to leave that to fleet commanders, because when you get to the real nitty-gritty of it, the fleet commander's got to know which of the ships he should put out and which he wanted to keep. You had to get that input from the fleet commander.

Now, you also had the shopping list, which I didn't get into, not in this particular job. There was a committee that was chaired by 03 Bravo, and they came up and we had a committee. We had a shipbuilding end, which had an 03 or some designation or 34 designation. It came up for your shopping list of each year's new procurement.

Paul Stillwell: Was this the Ship Characteristics Board?

Admiral Erly: Yes, the Ship Characteristics Board, which was under 03 at that point. That was what I was looking for, yes. Then you were looking at that. When you were getting something new, you add that. And then you consider new items coming in on the line, and if a new item came in, does something have to go out, how are you going to man it, this type of thing. So you even had a BuShips representative on the Ship Characteristics Board. You had Hooper, I remember, coming over from BuOrd.[*]

---

[*] Rear Admiral Edwin B. Hooper, USN. The oral history of Hooper, who retired as a vice admiral, is in the Naval Institute collection.

But all this went into it. It seemed to me that the flails usually occurred on a Saturday and Sunday, because I remember being in there many times. We were meeting basically with 90, and we had some other inputs that came in—maybe somebody from 05. You wrestled the problems as they came up, and this was around your budget cycle and all your things that were going on. It was a real eye-opener.

Paul Stillwell: Do you remember any specific cases that were particularly interesting?

Admiral Erly: Or monumental decisions? Not really. Not really. You get struck so often with the panic button and you react and you go ahead and you come up with a solution, and then you discard that and go on and work on the next problem.

Paul Stillwell: Well, do you have any "unmonumental" examples?

Admiral Erly: No, not really, not at the moment. I'm having a little CRS (can't remember shit) problem.

Paul Stillwell: What do you recall of working with Admiral McCorkle?

Admiral Erly: Oh, well, I enjoyed working with Admiral McCorkle. I had first met him in DesLant, actually, when I was exec of the *Yosemite*, which was DesLant's flagship. Admiral Johnson had brought him in as his chief of staff.[*]

Paul Stillwell: Do you think that's the association that led to you getting ordered to come to OpNav.

Admiral Erly: Oh, from that and other assignments. We had kept contact through the time. He knew my destroyer experience and my background fairly well.

---

[*] Rear Admiral Felix L. Johnson, USN, commanded Destroyer Force Atlantic Fleet from 21 April 1948 to 25 August 1949. His oral history is in the Naval Institute collection.

Paul Stillwell: He was a man who was born to go to sea. What was he like ashore as an administrator?

Admiral Erly: I think he drove people nuts in the DesLant staff, but he didn't drive me nuts in Washington. But I remember in DesLant the place cards that were used for his goodbye party. Evidently he used to say, "Why?" and tack it on any paper he had questions about. I think that some of his staff he drove a little up the wall with it. He relieved Henry Crommelin, and I guess the staff probably needed a little yanking around at that point.* In OpNav I guess I was there with him only about maybe six months or so, not much more.

Then he was relieved by Admiral Savvy Sanders.†

Paul Stillwell: What recollections do you have of him?

Admiral Erly: He came up from the mine force. I have good recollections of him. I got along with him splendidly. Actually, he came up to OP-33 and then fleeted up to be 03 Bravo, and was 03 Bravo when I went up as 03 Alfa in the front office. Actually, I ended up with Admiral Theda Combs, and I relieved Art Gralla.‡

I remember something. I think I ought to tell this one. I was down there in 33. I labored long and hard on an opus about the battleship being the ship of the future. Savvy was OP-33 at that point. Well, he forwarded it to 03, who was Bob Briscoe.§ It went up to Arleigh, and I guess it died a natural death somewhere along the line, because if you'll recall, the chairman of the House Armed Services Committee was old Vinson, and I think he called Arleigh up there and said, "Hey, Arleigh, I don't want to hear the word battleship."

That's basically what happened. But here, as I sit here talking to you and there are four battleships on the line, I can't help but chuckle a little, and I think, "Well, Jesus

---

* Rear Admiral Henry Crommelin, USN.
† Rear Admiral Harry Sanders, USN.
‡ Vice Admiral Thomas S. Combs, USN, served as Deputy Chief of Naval Operations (Fleet Operations and Readiness) from August 1956 to November 1958. Captain Arthur R. Gralla, USN.
§ Vice Admiral Robert P. Briscoe, USN, served as Deputy Chief of Naval Operations (Fleet Operations and Readiness) from 1954 to 1956.

Christ, it only took 35 or 34 years to make your letter come true to some extent, to some extent."

Paul Stillwell: How did you envision them being used?

Admiral Erly: Oh, in that time frame, for their durability, for their ability to project gunfire well inland. At this point—in late '55 or early '56—we were not as missile oriented as we are now. I didn't have that type of armament in mind for her, but her basic ability to withstand damage and this type of thing. Also for that world of ours as to the showing of the flag and of national power and this type of thing was still an imposing deal. So that was part of the arguments. I didn't keep copies. I gutted all of my files when I retired. I kick my butt for it in some cases, but I just didn't want to be bothered with them. But that gives me a chuckle when I think back in that it took that long to say, "You're right."

Paul Stillwell: Did you find yourself frustrated in that environment in that you weren't doing the operating that you were so used to?

Admiral Erly: Yes, in some aspects. But then I tried to keep the thought of, "What the hell am I doing here?" in mind, and that was to try and help the fleet, the people at sea.

When I got up in OP-03A, I had one deal. To give you an idea of some of what I'm saying, that LSD mentality that seems to get people when they get mired in the Pentagon at that large steel desk. Up came this paper that had gone through the on-scene commander. Something had happened, maybe a collision, and there had been a court of inquiry. The on-scene commander recommended no further action.

Here some OP-30 guy in OP-34, the surface warfare area, came back up and said, "Oh, we think disciplinary action should be taken,"

I read the whole goddamn thing over and said, "Jesus, here is the on-scene commander. He knew what the local situations were, and he's recommending nothing." And here was some guy sitting behind a desk—a four-striper, about four years senior to me—recommending that my boss approve that we go ahead and slap the guy's wrist, from OpNav, far removed from the scene.

So I went down and said, "Hey, look, why don't you take another look at this? Here is the on-scene commander. I don't know what my boss is going to do, but I'm pretty sure he believes in looking out for the people at sea where he can, and I don't see where we're to sit here and try to override an operational commander and his recommendation, who was there and got the salt spray and inhaled it in his eyes and a few other spots. How about taking another look?"

He did another look and came back and backed off. So I did a lot of business as 03, where something would come up from one of the shops that I would not take it in to the boss. I'd look at it, and I'd, "Hmm." I'd go back and I'd take it to the admiral and say, "Hey, look, Admiral. Boom, boom, if you would do this and do that, I think that it will fly."

Art Gralla would do it a little differently. He'd write a little note to the boss and leave it on there saying, "Oh, no." I figured, hell, that's not the way to do it. Let's make the guy look good if we can.

Paul Stillwell: Well, you saved the boss's time too.

Admiral Erly: Oh, and saved the boss's time, sure. Why have him read the note if Bob's going to recommend against it anyway?

We had a going-away party for Fearless Freddy Warder.[*] He had OP-30, the submarine warfare. I had many of those that went back to his shop. He really appreciated what I had done. So when he was leaving, at his goodbye party he made damn sure he wanted me there.

Poor guy, I felt sorry for him. He had false teeth, and then we had this public speaking training, and we had this speech guy around. I remember Freddy was eliding a little bit. He would say, "Well, it's these damn false teeth."

Paul Stillwell: What impact on OP-03 did the advent of the nuclear submarines have?

___
[*] Rear Admiral Frederick B. Warder, USN.

Admiral Erly: Well, I remember Dennis Wilkinson showing up with the *Nautilus* down in Chesapeake Bay.* This was when I was in OP-33, and I went down aboard her. I remember I came back and said, "Boy, their housekeeping needs something done."

For the impact on 03 and its thinking, I happened to be in on the Ship Characteristics Board meeting when the concept of ballistic missiles afloat came up. President Eisenhower had ordered that he wanted some capability afloat. That caused the *Compass Island* and *Observation Island* to come into being, and more.† We took a quota of five Mariner hulls.‡ The concept was to put intercontinental ballistic missiles in those hulls, because at this point they wouldn't fit in a submarine because we only had liquid propellant. The thing that really brought on, not just the attack submarine and the things that came behind, but really for your deterrent force, your boomers, was that solid propellant. The *Observation Island* was just for test firing, and the *Compass Island* had the inertial navigational system. This type of research and development was ongoing. The development of the solid propellant made the remaining Mariner hulls available for the amphibious force. So we got the APAs *Paul Revere* and *Francis Marion* and the AKA *Tulare*. Originally all five were lined up to go as ballistic missile ships.

I remember J. B. Colwell, I think he was a captain at that point, and he was in BuOrd.§ I was in one session where somebody started raising objections regarding the feasibility of the conversions. J. B. is a real laid-back guy, because I worked for him later and loved the guy. In this meeting he started to show sparks and said, "Damn it, the President said we're going to have this capability, and we're going to get it." In this he was talking the liquid propellant and using those five ships to get that intercontinental

---

* Commander Eugene P. Wilkinson, USN, became the first commanding officer of the USS *Nautilus* (SSN-571), when she was commissioned as the world's first nuclear-powered submarine on 30 September 1954. The oral history of Wilkinson, who retired as a vice admiral, is in the Naval Institute collection.

† USS *Compass Island* (EAG-153) and *Observation Island* (EAG-154) were originally built as Mariner-class merchant ships. The Navy acquired them and commissioned them on 3 December 1956 and 15 December 1958 respectively. The role of the *Compass Island* was to research navigational methods other than the traditional ones in order to facilitate use by nuclear submarines. The *Observation Island* was a test ship for Polaris ballistic missiles.

‡ In the early 1950s the U.S. Maritime Administration developed the C4-S-1A Mariner-type break-bulk cargo ship, bigger and faster than those built in World War II. Each was 564 feet long, had a light-ship displacement of approximately 14,000 tons, and a top speed of 20 knots. Five went to the Navy, and the rest were used in commercial service.

§ Captain John B. Colwell, USN. The oral history of Colwell, who retired as a vice admiral, is in the Naval Institute collection.

ballistic missile capability to sea. Again, it was saved by the bell with the solid propellant.

Paul Stillwell: Did this Polaris program in the '50s become something of a preoccupation in OP-03?

Admiral Erly: Well, it wasn't so much a preoccupation in OP-03, because we knew that they had to be there, because it was a presidential edict. He wanted this capability at sea, and everybody knew it was a good deal. Then came the point—part of it, we had nuclear warfare under OP-03.

Then you start to worry, "Okay, now that this becomes this and it becomes an intercontinental ballistic missile, how do we keep the Air Force from grabbing hold of it?" This is some of the things that went on and some of the big questions.

Paul Stillwell: Admiral Burke had the answer to that with the Joint Strategic Target Planning Staff.[*]

Admiral Erly: Yes, and he put a three-star billet out there with that.

Paul Stillwell: How was that nuclear planning done before the Navy got into that organization? Was that done in OP-03?

Admiral Erly: No, there were two segments of this. OP-06 had a piece of this. See, we had OP-36, which was nuclear bit, and then there was an OP-60-something that also carried this nuclear bit. I think Bardy Bardshar ended up in that shop at one time, in the 60 bit.[†] Hal Bowen was down in OP-36.[‡] I think he was OP-36 Bravo, the nuclear part

---

[*] In August 1960, at the instigation of Secretary of Defense Thomas Gates, the Joint Strategic Target Planning Staff was established at Offutt Air Force Base near Omaha, Nebraska. The JSTPS is discussed in the Naval Institute oral histories of several officers who were assigned there: Admiral John J. Hyland, USN (Ret.); Vice Admiral Gerald E. Miller, USN (Ret.); Vice Admiral Kent L. Lee, USN (Ret.); Vice Admiral Edward N. Parker, USN (Ret.).
[†] Captain Frederic A. Bardshar, USN, served in the Strategic Plans Division of OpNav, 1956-58.
[‡] Captain Harold G. Bowen Jr., USN.

under 03, and I'll bet he's got something more on his debrief about what particular function they did there.

Paul Stillwell: Well, who did the targeting? Was that the fleet commanders?

Admiral Erly: I'm just thinking. I'm trying to think of what happened in the Sixth Fleet. There were Sixth Fleet targets, and there were profiles on targets. They had delivery and the pilots had to go through this. I'm trying to remember who drafted these things. I didn't really get in any depth, so I'm not really qualified to say that. But I know that it was there, and I know that it was done.

I don't know whether we delegated it to the fleet commanders to come up with this info or not. See, you would need all kinds of basic intelligence on the target, its characteristics and so forth and so on, and a profile, and how you going to fly it, and all this. Because I know the Sixth Fleet people, the pilots that were doing this had that type of brief. They were given specific targets and a target folder, and studied even to the way to approach the target and the release point and the whole damn bit. Again, trying to, I think, project and get a part of the nuclear money pie, that you had to say you had this capability. How real? I don't know.

Paul Stillwell: We'll never know.

Admiral Erly: Never know. And who had control of what? I think that in '60 it was well needed, because you could have had mutual interference over target, and that would have been a hell of a mess and a waste of nuclear weapons, if you were ever called upon to use them. I hate to say this, when we were talking tactical weapons, whether or not—if you get into the philosophy, can you use tactical nuclear weapons incisively or surgically without triggering an escalation is the scary bit, in my opinion.

Paul Stillwell: And presumably it's that precise fear that's kept them from being used ever since.

Admiral Erly: Well, how about the nuclear depth charge? Clancy used one.* [Laughter]

Paul Stillwell: Well, fortunately, Clancy hasn't been nuked in return.

Admiral Erly: Well, oh, boy.

Paul Stillwell: Did you work any with Commander Paul Backus on setting up the operational concept for Polaris?†

Admiral Erly: Oh, no, not I personally. But Paul used to appear here or there and yon, and in some of the meetings, and I remember him well, yes. But not closely. You've got to remember now that I was sitting up there in the catbird seat on the E-ring, too, you see.‡ I was not getting in on the real nitty-gritty side of it anymore. I'm the guy that has to carry the message to Garcia and go up in there and go in Don Felt's office on something that we've got to get signed off, you see.§

Paul Stillwell: What are your recollections of Admiral Felt?

Admiral Erly: Well, let's go back. You asked me about Savvy Sanders. He had moved up there and I came up there, and some of the stuff that would hit me, I'd start being very, very frank, and I'd write these notes that would go in to him before they went to the boss.

He came out one day and said, "Come on, Bob, let's take a walk."

---

* Author Tom Clancy wrote a number of novels that featured war scenarios.
† See the Naval Institute oral history of Commander Paul H. Backus, USN.
‡ The Pentagon has lettered corridors, going from A at the innermost to E at the outermost. E-ring offices, which go around the perimeter of the building, are considered the most prestigious.
§ In 1899 Elbert Hubbard wrote the essay "A Message to Garcia" about an incident in the 1898 Spanish-American War in which a messenger named Rowan demonstrated heroism in the face of danger by carrying a message to Garcia, the leader of insurgent forces in Cuba. The essay has been widely reprinted and quoted over the years.
Admiral Harry D. Felt, USN, served as Vice Chief of Naval Operations from 1 September 1956 to 28 July 1958. His oral history is in the Naval Institute collection.

We walked from the Pentagon on down, up to Arlington Annex and back.* His main topic was, "Okay, all right, I appreciate what you're doing, but don't put it in black and white. If some of the things that you're saying got to some of the aviation people or some of the other ones, they'd have your hide in a minute. Don't put it in black and white, but come in and tell me personally." That was his basic message.

Paul Stillwell: What kinds of things were you writing these messages about?

Admiral Erly: Well, I'm just trying to think. I wonder what had triggered me so vehemently. Oh, I know what it was, goddamn it! Yes. I worked my butt off, who should command an LPH, okay?†

Paul Stillwell: An amphibious assault ship that flies helicopters.

Admiral Erly: Right. Who should command it? Okay? Mine was 1100, who understands the helicopter capabilities and is knowledgeable in amphibious warfare; or an aviator who understands helicopters.‡ These fixed-wing guys are something else again when it comes to that. And amphibious warfare knowledgeable. Either one or the other one.

I remember what really got me irate. We'd go up, and Felt didn't even let that get to Arleigh Burke. He would just say, "No, it's going to be a naval aviator."§ That got me irate, I think, at that point.

The other was, we were told that we could not use, "It is believed that." Got to use, "It is." Felt. That's a true story. You think I'm making it up.

---

* The Arlington Annex was a large, multi-wing building near the Pentagon and the Arlington National Cemetery. It contained the headquarters of the Marine Corps and for many years had the Bureau of Naval Personnel also.
† The LPH concept developed in the 1950s as an amphibious assault ship that would deliver forces ashore by helicopters rather than boats. The USS *Thetis Bay* (CVE-90) was an escort aircraft carrier originally commissioned in 1944. In July her designation was changed to CVHA-1 and in 1959 to LPH-6. She tested the concept of vertical envelopment. The first U.S. Navy ship built for the purpose was the USS *Iwo Jima* (LPH-2), commissioned in 1961.
‡ At the time the 1100 officer designator was for unrestricted line officers who were not aviators.
§ Admiral Harry D. Felt, USN, served as Vice Chief of Naval Operations from 1 September 1956 to 28 July 1958. His oral history is in the Naval Institute collection. He was a naval aviator, and naval aviators wound up commanding the LPHs.

Paul Stillwell: No, I don't. I talked to Admiral Weschler, and he said there was a term for somebody who'd been mistreated was, "Have you been Felt lately?"* [Laughter]

Admiral Erly: I never had any trouble going in before Admiral Felt or anything, as long as you knew what the hell you were talking about. He is another one that if he could ever get you down, he wouldn't stop kicking. So, man, you had to stand up there and fire it straight.

Paul Stillwell: When did you make the transition to the E-ring in the front office?

Admiral Erly: Oh, I went to OpNav in January of '55. I was in OP-33 maybe a year to a year and a half in OP-33, then to 03A.

Paul Stillwell: Was Admiral Combs in the job then?

Admiral Erly: They had a reorganization in OpNav, and Libby was coming in. Admiral Libby was coming in to relieve Briscoe as OP-03, and I was going to be Libby's admin. But then they changed. Theda came in, and I still went up there.† Libby went to 06.‡

Paul Stillwell: What do you remember about the working style of Admiral Combs?

Admiral Erly: He was, I thought, real laid-back. I could see him now. We would have a get-together with all the other OPs—you know, 33, 34, 31, 36, the whole schmear—oh, about at least once a month, or maybe sooner if something came up. I'd prepare a little note for him, and he would take just a fast look and he would just talk and he'd have it, he'd catch it like that. He was fast. I could see where he would make a damn good front for testifying before Congress. He had that sincerity and projection.

---

* Commander Thomas R. Weschler, USN, was Admiral Burke's aide in the mid-1950s. The oral history of Weschler, who retired as a vice admiral, is in the Naval Institute collection.
† Vice Admiral Robert P. Briscoe, USN, served as Deputy Chief of Naval Operations (Fleet Operations and Readiness) from 1954 to 1956. Vice Admiral Thomas S. "Theda" Combs, USN, was in the billet from August 1956 to November 1958.
‡ Vice Admiral Ruthven E. Libby, USN, served as Deputy Chief of Naval Operations (Plans and Policy) from August 1956 to June 1958. Libby's oral history is in the Naval Institute collection.

I admired the gentleman, but damn it, it seemed to me whenever we'd have a flail, and don't ask me what specific, but whenever the panic button would be hit, it would seem he was up getting his goddamn flight time in, which leads me off on another favorite subject of mine that I'm saying they needed to do something about.

I voiced long and loud and said, "Jeepers, after you get a certain point, pay them the damn annuity. Don't make them go out there and punch holes in the sky and burn up valuable fuel that the young tigers need while these old farts don't need it. It's nice to get up in the wild blue yonder and relax and get a little extra pay, but let's give them the damn extra pay and let's use the fuel and whatnot for the young tigers." Now they're doing that.

While I was there, there was another pet gripe of mine that was going on, which I hated this business that when you went to a BuPers detailer, who would pull out a drawer, take a look, and say, "Oh, well, I don't know about that," for an assignment.

"Well—"

I was saying, "Look, these jobs, if you don't get them, if you don't get a major command, if you don't get the other commands and whatnot, you're finished, and it should be a damn sworn board. It shouldn't be a pick-up board from BuPers from the various sections doing this."

This was one of my crusades, that they be sworn boards, and now they are.

Paul Stillwell: You mean command screening?

Admiral Erly: Certainly. Before it wasn't.

Paul Stillwell: How would you describe Admiral Combs's ability and style in handling the paperwork flow?

Admiral Erly: Easy.

Paul Stillwell: It sounds like you made it easy for him.

Admiral Erly: Well, I had great help in the office, plus it went through 03 Bravo. So it had about a good two or three screenings before it got to him, so you better believe we tried to make it easy for him. All the way. That was our job. So all he had to do was take your pen and sign it. But you also got to defend it, maybe, up the way. Or if it was within your purview, sign and it goes out, and we could sign OpNav instructions, which we did. But some of the other, if it was a really sensitive matter, it would bounce on up to the Vice Chief or even to CNO.

Paul Stillwell: What recollections do you have of Admiral Burke from those years?

Admiral Erly: Oh, dynamic, hard working, and he put in some good hours, too, I must admit. But I sure remember that I felt sorry for him. He came in. He had called a conference of all captains in an auditorium, and evidently after he got there, and he'd been held up and been harassed a little bit in a Joint Chiefs of Staff meeting, and I think he was little short tempered then. But there happened to be some captain sitting down the front where he could see he was sleeping or something, and that got him madder yet.

Poor old Hi Massey.* I forget, something came up. And Hi was a captain, and I forget the exact exchange, but Arleigh just chewed his ass out one end up and down the other in front of the full audience, and it really wasn't meant that way. Well, I think Arleigh called him up the next day and apologized when it got explained. But it just goes to show that, no matter how you feel in front of a group, you should always not really let your temper get the best of you. But maybe this made Hi an admiral. I don't know.

Paul Stillwell: Did the OP-03 organization have any special role in the things in the Mediterranean back in that period, the Suez Crisis and the Lebanon matters?†

---

* Captain Forsyth Massey, USN.
† On 26 July 1956 President Gamal Nasser of Egypt announced that his country was nationalizing the Suez Canal Company. Israeli forces invaded Egypt's Sinai Peninsula on 29 October 1956. Britain and France then intervened militarily on behalf of Israel in an unsuccessful attempt to secure the Suez Canal, which was damaged and closed to traffic. Rather than support the British and French, the United States asked for a United Nations resolution to end the fighting. A cease-fire took effect on 6 November.
On 15 July 1958, at the request of Lebanese President Camille Chamoun, two U.S. Marine battalion landing teams went ashore at Beirut. Their mission was to support the government of President Chamoun, who was threatened by both civil war and the prospect of foreign intervention.

Admiral Erly: Oh, good God, yes. And all those, you might believe, as I was saying, any time of a crisis or you started moving forces around, 33 became in the picture, 03 came in the picture. So you wanted to have somebody on the operational side, which was 03, fleet ops, would come right in with the deal until we got the command center set up. Once the command center was set up and manned on a round-the-clock basis, I had gone by that time. You had duty captains and commanders ordered to it. There were a captain and a commander on watch, continuous watch, 24 hours a day. All that had been done previously by 33 personnel, pretty much.

Paul Stillwell: You said the setup was pretty crude when you arrived. What was the metamorphosis?

Admiral Erly: Well, in the metamorphoses, you got all kinds of plotting boards and displays and charts, the various areas of the world, and projection devices. You could move things and show where they were, say, in the Sixth Fleet, and you could make a projection where or why wherever the trouble spot was and what forces you had converging. You had intelligence inputs coming in and all the rest of them.

It wasn't this super arrangement you get in the mountains out there in Colorado Springs in the Air Defense Command, but it would compare well with, say, a big carrier flagship plot.

Paul Stillwell: Any specific crises that you remember being involved in?

Admiral Erly: Oh, boy. I'm just trying to think of some of the flame-ups. Lebanon happened after I left. The Suez, when we told the Brits and the French to back off, was one. Which in most cases, what you really do in a crisis basically is—CNO is not supposed to be an operator, per se. But then you start gigging the fleet commander to, "Hey, you better move something that way." Arleigh really felt that he was a fleet operator, really, which definitely is not CNO's role.

Let's see, I'm trying to remember, Tom Moorer called, and I'm trying to remember when*. Was he chairman of the Joint Chiefs, or was he CNO? I'm trying to think—Pueblo.† We had something happening down in the Caribbean, and I don't know whether it had to do with one of our intercept ships off Cuba or not. Tom wanted to know how long it would take us to get a carrier down in a certain locale, and I gave him the answer. I think this one must have had White House interest in it. I'm trying to remember the actual crisis part of it. But I think he was talking then as Chairman of the Joint Chiefs and was going to go back and say, "Yeah, we'll have a naval presence in so many hours."‡

And again, I think that's what happened. He came directly to the fleet commander, and would know that; whereas maybe, say, a chairman would go to CNO and say, "When?" and then CNO would go. But I think Tom, by knowing enough, having been CNO, where to go, I think he came directly. And he got me.

Paul Stillwell: Well, it's just past 4:00. Do you have any final thoughts on your years in OP-03?

Admiral Erly: I really feel that a naval officer will miss out on an important part of his career if he doesn't have a tour in OpNav. He should go back and see what's happening. It's not that OpNav—you've got to realize that some people think it's a sacrosanct organization. My point is, you get back there. Just because it's an OpNav instruction doesn't make it always right. I feel that they need to go there to understand really how things function.

As I say, I was rather disillusioned when I first got there. I just thought they were overstaffed, and I still do. I had another solution of this staffing. I said, "Okay, at 1700 go through the building, and every office that's closed—"

---

* Admiral Thomas H. Moorer, USN, served as Chief of Naval Operations from 1 August 1967 to 1 July 1970. His oral history is in the Naval Institute collection.
† USS *Pueblo* (AGER-2), an electronic intelligence ship, was seized on 23 January 1968 in the Sea of Japan by North Korean naval forces. The ship's crew members were held as prisoners until 23 December of that year. Of the 83 officers and men on board, 28 were intelligence specialists. Her commanding officer was Commander Lloyd R. Bucher, USN.
‡ Admiral Moorer was Chairman of the Joint Chiefs of Staff from 3 July 1970 to 30 June 1974.

Paul Stillwell: Is unnecessary.

Admiral Erly: Well, it may not be unnecessary, but check it out. Maybe they just do their work well and should go early. But it's that same old business where 10% do 90% of the work. This is what you run into. You run into it in OpNav; some OPs coast, and others work themselves to the bone. That's the nature of the beast, but it seems to me it should be streamlined more. Instead of growing more, it should be streamlined more. And less of a paperwork flow. You got so you really felt in some cases that how well you wrote a paper determined whether you were going to ever make the next rank. Well, I guess a naval officer, as John Paul Jones says, "Should be erudite and cultured," and all these personifications.

I think that a tour in OpNav is needed, more so, I think, than a joint tour. At least an officer should have an OpNav tour before they ever have a joint tour. Those are my final thoughts.

I'm glad that I was forced back to OpNav, really. It was time and it was a good time for me. And it probably had a lot to do with my making flag rank. I think some of that E-ring exposure, where you are exposed to a lot of senior officers and a lot are officers senior to you; I think it's beneficial.

I go back to one thing that I was going to tell you about. In discussing this same time in OpNav, I think I'd like to go on record with it about Red Ramage and the fitness reports. Red was OP-34 and had been assigned to the commander-to-captain selection board.* He cornered me and gave me hell for the way surface officers made out fitness reports. He said, "The reporting seniors are just killing your people's chances, and you'd better change it."

I don't know why he picked on me, maybe just because he knew me, and I liked him. But he was giving me a message, which I really took to heart and analyzed what he was saying, that I really think the 1100 officer reads the fitness report instructions and how to make out fitness reports and figure he's got to put so many here and so many there and all the rest, and he's really following the instructions to the nth degree. But I think that in some of the other warfare specialties they are not doing that. They say if the

---

* Rear Admiral Lawson P. Ramage, USN, directed the Surface Type Warfare Division in OpNav, 1956-58.

guy is good, we can have more than one who's truly outstanding. Then when you stack up the surface warfare against the air warfare and the submarine warfare, there is such a disparity between fitness reports, or was at that time, because Red will attest to that. I hope that that is not true today. I tried to do my best to inculcate in people making fitness reports that they do it adequately.

Paul Stillwell: In effect, the reporting senior is a one-man selection board?

Admiral Erly: That was what I would tell them: they are a one-man selection board. You want me to go on record as what I told you before, that before you take pencil in hand, you have to decide, if I were sitting on a selection board, would I vote for this officer because I consider him fully qualified for the next rank, or would I turn him down, or I don't know enough about him at this fitness report to either turn him down or to vote for him.

If you feel that an officer is not fully qualified, you should sit down and write a truly truthful report and call it as you have seen it, and mark him so. If you have not had a long enough period to observe him, so state in the report. However, if you have observed him and you consider him in all respects eligible and that he should be selected, then you should take up that pen or pencil and lie like hell.

Paul Stillwell: That's a good note to end on. We'll wrap up the session with that. Thank you very much.

Interview Number 5 with Admiral Robert B. Erly, U.S. Navy (Retired)

Place: U.S. Naval Institute, Annapolis, Maryland

Date: Thursday, 27 September 1990

Paul Stillwell: Admiral, last time we just had gotten you finished up on your tour of duty in OP-03 in the mid-1950s. Where did you go from there?

Admiral Erly: Well, I was very fortunate in leaving OpNav. I was assigned to APA-248, the *Paul Revere*, a Mariner hull that was being converted in Todd Shipyard in San Pedro, as my deep-draft command.* A lot of that, I think, was as a reward for all that drudgery back in the Pentagon.

I had called the captain detailer when I had my relief on board as OP-03A and said, "Hey, I've got my relief. How about a set of orders?"

He said, "Well, fine. What are you after?"

I said, "Well, I'm ready to take my cruiser." Then I held the phone away from my ear while I could hear the smoke coming out of it.

Then I said, "Okay, well, if you won't give me that, how about giving me the new attack transport that's coming on line, the USS *Paul Revere*?"

So he allowed as how he could do that.

Paul Stillwell: Why had you focused on that ship?

Admiral Erly: Well, first because it was a new prototype. It was to be a 20-knot APA, which was one of the first. At that point in time, as OP-03A, I knew what the shipbuilding and conversion program was. OP-03 Charlie or some such business had it,

---

* USS *Paul Revere* (APA-248), an attack transport, was the name ship of her class. She was commissioned 3 September 1958. She displaced 16,838 tons, was 564 feet long, 76 feet in the beam, had a maximum draft of 27 feet, and a top speed of 20 knots. She was armed with four 3-inch guns and carried a variety of landing craft for amphibious warfare operations. Originally she had been the SS *Diamond Mariner*, a commercial cargo ship launched in 1953 and operated for the U.S. Maritime Administration. The Navy acquired the ship on 14 September 1956 for conversion to an amphibious warfare ship.

and 03 Bravo was really the head of the shipbuilding and conversion program that set it up. So I knew what ships were coming on line.

Paul Stillwell: Well, you were really too junior at that point for a cruiser, weren't you?

Admiral Erly: Oh, hell, yes. [Laughter] But this was just the lead-in. I was just baiting the detailer, that was all, and I would have mentioned his name. I was very, very fond of him and knew him personally. He was out of the class of '32. He was a hell of a football player at the Naval Academy, Sam Moncure.[*]

But I knew what his reaction was going to be. But I also had some backing for it, and I had been in a phib group staff, remember. I had the qualifications to go back to the amphibs. I knew it was going to have a helo platform on it, and it was going to have all the latest boats, and it was going to be a fast ship. So that's why I was zeroed in on this. As I've mentioned before, I think the biggest challenge is taking a new ship or a ship out of mothballs and getting it started right. You know damn well when you finish that tour, either you've done a good job or you haven't. It's self-obvious.

Some skippers come along and the ship may be on the upward surge, and they ride it all the way up, and it wins everything in the fleet, you see. Well, that guy that's getting a lot of the honors really hasn't been the major contributor; it's been the people before. So those were the reasons that I opted to go that route, to get the *Paul Revere*. I must say, it was a challenge.

Paul Stillwell: Well, when you've got a ship that's new like that, the spotlight's on you, whether you do well or ill.

Admiral Erly: Oh, yes, particularly a new prototype, so to speak. You've got a lot of visitors, and you are under the magnifying glass.

Paul Stillwell: What were some of the specific challenges you did face? Where did you start?

---

[*] Captain Samuel P. Moncure, USN.

Admiral Erly: Well, where did I start? Remember, she was in the shipyard, and I also knew from my background in OpNav that after *Paul Revere* was coming along the *Francis Marion*, a sister ship that was to be converted.* I was determined that any modification or discrepancies found in *Paul Revere* would be passed to BuShips and the PCO of *Francis Marion* so that the other ships would not have that problem.

My first job, when I checked in as a prospective commanding officer, was to obtain office space there in the naval shipyard in Long Beach. Jimmy James was the shipyard commander at that point.† I also had to report in to the commandant 11th Naval District, who was in San Diego, and to the commander of Naval Base Long Beach. So I had a couple of bosses. I also had to write a monthly report back to CNO of what was going on in regard to the ship and its problems and started the conversion process. I was there first, and then I had a chief warrant machinist report, and then the supply officer, and then a warrant machinist. We had a little cadre there, while at the same time my PXO went on to San Diego, where he had started gathering a nucleus crew and putting them through training down there.‡ So this is the way it was working.

Paul Stillwell: What impressions do you have of Admiral James from that period?

Admiral Erly: I remember storming in with blood in my eye because he had, without consulting me, made an agreement with the Todd Shipyard that they could slip the commissioning date by a month or two. I felt that I as an interested party had been bypassed.

Paul Stillwell: You were indeed an interested party.

Admiral Erly: Damn interested party, because I had a lot to do. I had my people, and as I was saying, I knew I had a lot going. First, change orders. I had to look, and things were being done in the ship, such as the pelorus positioning on the wings of the bridge

---

* USS *Francis Marion* (APA-249) was commissioned 6 July 1961 with Captain David S. Bill Jr., USN, in command.
† Rear Admiral Ralph K. James, USN, whose oral history is part of the Naval Institute collection.
‡ PXO – prospective executive officer, Commander George B. Bush Jr., USNR.

and the location of the voice tubing to the helmsman and the officer of the deck that was going on in the ship and the engineering spaces. We were down there watching what was going on and trying to get change orders through which we thought were going to increase our efficiency over that which the ship's plans called for.

There were things going on that I didn't like, even the stowage of the Mike boats, because I ended up even early on starting to call and say, "This design is not going to work. You've got a battering ram there. You're going to smash your bridge to pieces in any type of a seaway trying to get that boat back on board and stowed—or even off, you're going to have problems."[*]

You could go on and on, even to the mundane things, as I was eagle-eyeing what was going on, of watching a guy laying linoleum, and they hadn't even bothered to clean the deck before they started to do this, with all the crud and stuff under it.

Paul Stillwell: This was a civilian yard worker?

Admiral Erly: Yes, civilian yard. I had my people prepped in whatever. I said, "As soon as we see something wrong, tell us." Then I'd go right to the Todd Shipyard manager."

Paul Stillwell: How much cooperation were you getting from the supship, the Navy representative?[†]

Admiral Erly: We worked with him. It was a lieutenant commander, and I can't recall his name now. But I kept singeing his butt, I might say, to follow through on these things that were going on and making sure it was getting back and a lot of this. A lot I would put in reports of some of the things that I found. I don't have any dossier or file on it, but I'm sure that somebody who wanted to dig into what was going on would see on my reports of what I thought the efficiency of the civilian yard and what the major problems

---

[*] Mike boat is the nickname for an LCM, a landing craft mechanized, because Mike is the word for the letter M in the phonetic alphabet.
[†] Supship – supervisor of shipbuilding, conversion, and repair. This is a naval officer who is the Navy's on-scene representative to monitor the progress of construction and repair of Navy ships at commercial shipyards.

were as I would generate my report and send it in.

In the back of my mind always was coming on that the other ship was coming, and as I was telling my people, "Whatever we can do and we find now, even if we can't get it corrected, it should be documented so when the contract is let for the *Francis Marion*, it'll save us money."

Paul Stillwell: Was the *Tulare* going along at about the same pace yours was?

Admiral Erly: Oh, no, the *Tulare* was in commission.[*]

Paul Stillwell: Had you been able to learn anything from that ship's experiences?

Admiral Erly: No, I had no record on her at all. She was going to be configured differently as an AKA, where I had to worry about a lot of troops on board and how I was going to feed them and the galley setup and all of this, and all the berthing spaces. The *Tulare* was mainly cargo and limited in troop-carrying capacity, compared to us.

Paul Stillwell: Well, your ship was substantially larger than the previous APAs.

Admiral Erly: Oh, Lord, yes.

Paul Stillwell: Did you have to have a different operating concept or, did you pretty much use what had been gone before?

Admiral Erly: Well, I think, Paul, really before we get into that, I was just trying to think of some of the things—you've brought up one that I'd like to stay with, your thought of Admiral James. As I said, I was working closely with the yard more of anyone to know, and not even being consulted by the yard or the other one. There was a civilian guy

---

[*] The attack cargo ship *Tulare* (AKA-112) was built at San Francisco by the Bethlehem Pacific Coast Steel Corporation as the *Evergreen Mariner,* converted in the building yard, and commissioned 12 January 1956 with Captain Donald W. Todd, USN, in command.

named Goodrich in the yard.* I got to be very friendly with him, though we had our little run-ins now and again. He went from Todd to Bath and turned out to be later your assistant SecNav or SecNav. He was running it. I'm trying to forget some of his people who were down that I worked very closely with, and then even with Goodrich.

As I felt Admiral James didn't cut me in properly, I was up there with fire in my eye, and I said, "It's part of my responsibility. I have reporting seniors, too, sir. I need to know if this is going in, and I should be a party to this because I have planning to do. I have to plan the commissioning. When is this going to be turned over? I have a lot to do on who's coming," and so forth and so on. I think he realized that there had been an omission.

Paul Stillwell: Did things improve after that?

Admiral Erly: Oh, yes. The channel of communication became better, because more and more, even for the turnover, for me to say, "Hey, I'm not about to take this ship the way it is, okay? They haven't done this; they want to move from the Todd Shipyard. You want to move it to the naval shipyard, and then they are still going to be doing it? I'm not going to be responsible."

See, I had a little whip hand in this, too, as this went on. Jimmy and I got along fine. He's a can-do guy, I must admit—you know, boom, boom, boom—and sometimes maybe got ahead of his troops.

Paul Stillwell: Did the finished product ultimately turn out pretty much to your satisfaction?

Admiral Erly: Eventually. We went out on sea trials, and even then—you know, away all boats, trying to do this and the other. Sure enough, what I'd been telling them all along, which I called the killer situation on the Mike boat stowage, we had to get that modified.

---

* James F. Goodrich was then general manager of the San Pedro branch of Todd Shipyards Corporation. From 1975 to 1978 he was chairman of the board of directors of Bath Iron Works. He later served as Under Secretary of the Navy from 29 September 1981 to 6 August 1987.

See, we went out and we operated, and then we went back with a whole list of items that needed correction. A great majority of the problems were involved with the handling of our boats, expeditiously and safely. Whoever drew up that design was dead wrong on that Mike boat nesting.

Paul Stillwell: It was just too close to the front of the superstructure?

Admiral Erly: Yes, yes, and the booms to handle it.

Paul Stillwell: Well, you were talking major step if you're going to move a boom, weren't you?

Admiral Erly: Oh, certainly. Certainly. And you've got that weight hanging. You've got a pendulum. That's a good way to knock down buildings. And what would it do to a ship's structure in any type of a seaway? Sure, that would be fine if you were an office building. It would have worked just great.

I'm trying to remember the work wish list. I'm sure that there were several hundred items that we came up with in our discrepancy list that we forwarded on to the CNO so they could have those as conversion items to be considered when the *Francis Marion* came on line so she wouldn't have all the problems that we encountered. I feel that we probably, with that attitude, saved the Navy a good deal of money.

As you well know, when you get a change order, this is what a lot of the civilian companies do, bid on something, saying, "Oh, there'll be the change orders, and this is where we'll nail them for the contract." That's where they make their money.

The other thing that I had a lot of fun doing, knowing, again, from my OpNav experience from where I was sitting, that there were an awful lot of new ships coming on line, new prototypes, and so I said, "Hey, let's write an OpNav instruction—a checklist of what you do when you commission a ship."

Paul Stillwell: There never had been such a thing?

Admiral Erly: No, no.

Paul Stillwell: That's amazing.

Admiral Erly: No, there had not been. All the ships that were commissioned, everybody had to go out and dig around for info.

Paul Stillwell: Reinvent the wheel.

Admiral Erly: Reinvent the wheel. So we listed it from A to Z and then sent it off, doing their work for them, and, sure enough, they came out with such an instruction. But again, this was with detail right along the line, with PERT charting, what you had to do to reach the end to have a successful commissioning.* And now when you see them, they do it with a flair, and I'm sure that that OpNav instruction has been perhaps upgraded for some of the things. Have you been to a commissioning recently?

Paul Stillwell: No.

Admiral Erly: Well, you do little things with flair, like I rehearsed this business to set the watch, and what we did at that moment was have the chief boatswain's mate pipe the call. It was not on the PA system, but I had boatswain's mates stationed all down the ship, and you could hear it picked up, passed along, see, all throughout the ship. There was a sound that would come back, and it was really—

Paul Stillwell: It sounds neat.

---

* PERT – Program Evaluation Review Technique, a system of milestones for tracking the progress of a program against its schedule. This was developed in the late 1950s for the Polaris ballistic missile submarine program.

Admiral Erly: Yes, yes. But you had to figure it in. I had more fun, also, on that, because we had Long John Sylvester, who was ComPhibPac, to talk.* There was Red Price, who was the naval district commandant's rep as comnavbase, was going to be there in Long Beach, and then Goodrich, who was turning the ship over from Todd Shipyard.† So what I did was sit down and make the scenario, and we wrote Sylvester's speech, Goodrich's speech, Price's speech, and we had it all so it would go in.

Paul Stillwell: So it wouldn't overlap.

Admiral Erly: It was great; everything just flowed. But, again, these are the things you have to plan and do, and we had it planned from A to Z. I don't know whether we wrote that one up or not as a suggestion. We might have.

Well, we were trying to do this, and that went over. We, of course, just like everyone else at this point, when we put it out, we'd invited Arleigh Burke.‡ We invited the Marine Corps Commandant at that time.§ We invited all the top people. We didn't get them, but got nice letters back, which we put in the commissioning brochure.

Now, then we got her commissioned and took off for shakedown training. The best I could wangle was to get to Acapulco and back for our shakedown. Underway training—again, a new prototype. Here I was in the midst of underway training, and I got a call from PhibPac, saying, "There's a big exercise being held up off of . . ." that area by the Hearst estate.** I'm trying to remember the Army fort up there on the coast. The caller said, "We want you to take a bunch of Navy league VIPs and go up there," and so I would be the host ship on display. Again, as I say, as you mentioned, being a new ship, you get other various jobs. I remember in San Diego, the Tenth Street Pier, that a big terminal when they were going to open it up and be a major port while we were there. I

---

* Vice Admiral John Sylvester, USN, served as Commander Amphibious Force Pacific Fleet from April 1958 to July 1960.
† Rear Admiral Walter H. Price, USN, was Commander Naval Base Long Beach.
‡ Admiral Arleigh A. Burke, USN, served as Chief of Naval Operations from 17 August 1955 to 1 August 1961. His oral history is in the Naval Institute collection.
§ General Randolph M. Pate, USMC, served as Commandant of the Marine Corps from 1 January 1956 to 31 December 1959.
** The Hearst Castle, long the residence of newspaper magnate William Randolph Hearst (1863-1951), is a historical landmark at San Simeon, California. The Army's Fort Hunter Liggett is near the California coast, midway between Monterey and San Luis Obispo.

was the first ship there and was sort of the backdrop for all of the big ceremonies. The commandant had gotten his bid in for us to do that. Those were just some of these unusual things.

Paul Stillwell: How well did this new ship work once you got her out and operated?

Admiral Erly: Oh, well, she was the queen of the seas; I might say that. It was just great having that 20-knot APA. I would think one of the things that I can't help but chuckle about, with coming in and out of port in San Diego, and here the destroyers would be coming up. As you're coming up on 1 SD and starting to head in, you'd see these destroyers would be coming along and say, "Hey, there's an APA. We'll just zoom right past them."[*] Well, about this time, see, I was making 20, and they didn't know what to make of all this.

Paul Stillwell: They thought you were going much slower.

Admiral Erly: Yes. So they never did pass us coming in. That was great having that speed. Her sea-keeping capabilities were just great. Her final boat handling was great, and, in fact, in our first time we went up for the assault boat E, and we got it on our first go-round.[†] She was a great sea boat, stable. Her accommodations for Marines and for the crew were, I think, outstanding in comparison with any other APA. The only thing that I didn't like—and I rebelled at from the word go—was the arrangement for the troop messing compartments. The design called for them to eat standing up. I got away from that and had them so they would be able to sit.

That was something else I would say about the *Paul Revere*, is I had my supply officer and his commissary officer come aboard early. I think I mentioned in some of the other interviews that I'd started this program in destroyers where I sent a personal birthday card and birthday cake to any crew member on their birthday. They were allowed to go to the head of the chow line and got a cake and a gallon of ice cream and

---

[*] 1 SD refers to a channel buoy.
[†] An "E," for excellence, is generally awarded to a ship or component of a ship as a result of top performance in competition with other ships during a given time period.

six of their buddies to take a table to go with them on their birthday. Early in the pre-commissioning detail I had a first class baker report. I had some contacts at the Hotel del Coronado, so I sent him down there to learn the ultimate in pastry, ice carving, and desserts.

I told the supply officer and whatnot that, "Okay, what we're going to do, we're going to win the Ney Award." And you know what the Ney award is.[*]

Paul Stillwell: As a matter of fact, it's named for a former supply officer in the USS *Arizona*.

Admiral Erly: Well, I'll be damned. I didn't know that.

Paul Stillwell: He had that job in the late '30s.

Admiral Erly: All right. Well, in this time frame—as I recall the competition—there was only one afloat award at that time, and not for fleets. But to make a long story short, if you plan well, you can do it, and we won it, and had only been in commission about eight months when we won it. But, again, plan it.

Paul Stillwell: What was involved in that planning? Does that mean you saved your money until you could really put on a spectacular show for the inspectors?

Admiral Erly: Oh, hell no. That wasn't it at all. No way you could do it. The way you did it was, number one, the quality of our chow was to be the same with our crew as it was when we took on 1,200 Marines. I felt that—and I preached to my people—"The mission of this ship is to transport troops, and unless we have troops on board, we're not carrying out our mission, and we're hand in hand with them. It's not those GD guys coming on board. They're coming on board because that is our mission." And that same

---

[*] The Captain Edward F. Ney Memorial Award was established in 1958 in recognition of food service excellence in Navy galleys. Captain Ney served as head of the Subsistence Division of the Bureau of Supplies and Accounts from 1940 to 1945. As a commander he was the supply officer of the battleship *Arizona* (BB-39) from July 1939 to November 1940.

thing for the birthday of Marines. When I had Marines on board, they got a birthday cake and ice cream from me, and they got seated.

I said, "If it takes us feeding 24 hours a day, I'll be goddamned if I'm going to have them stand up to eat."

Then we give the Marines a questionnaire asking for their comments and recommendations on the chow. I had stacks of these. The same way when we would give the red-carpet treatment when a Marine commander came aboard. We had Mugs Riley, one of our first Marines to visit, and some of the other ones.* We laid out the red carpet with side boys and all the frou-frou.†

And I requested to the Marine commander, "I want to address your troops." This is the pitch that I gave them: "We are a team. You are very essential, as we are. But we mesh and we are a team. We feel the mission of this ship is to transport you and get you there safely and provide you the materials that you need, and we want this to work. It is a team effort."

Those were the things that I built into what was going on in the ship in our relationship with the Marines. I think the selling feature that came out to the Ney Award inspection group was the Marines' satisfaction. Not to mention that I took my supply officers to Lindbergh Field at about 2330; we were out there to meet them.‡ We had adequate transport and made sure they got to the hotel. The next morning, instead of having them come by car to the ship, I made sure that my gig went around with a boat officer and picked them up and transported them down the bay to where we were moored at 32nd Street. They came aboard the accommodation ladder from seaward. I was just trying to get some salt-water flavoring into their thinking.

Paul Stillwell: I always thought that would be one of the great jobs to have in the Navy, to be on the Ney Award panel. [Laughter]

---

* Brigadier General Thomas F. Riley, USMC.
† Side boys are crew members stationed in two ranks at a ship's gangway on the arrival or departure of officers or officials for whom side honors are rendered. The number of side boys varies from two to eight, depending on the rank of the individual.
‡ Lindbergh Field is the commercial airport in San Diego.

Admiral Erly: Well, no, it wasn't. What they were really after wasn't the sample. They wanted to look at your menus, and they went through your reefers. They covered every aspect of food service. They checked on sanitation. They observed the preparation, the serving, and the cleanup, etc.

But our selling point was the fact that, "Here we do it for our crew, and we do it for the troops." And we won it. But I think the comical thing—and I've still got a clipping in one of my scrapbooks—we made *The New Yorker*.

Paul Stillwell: Oh, really?

Admiral Erly: Yes. They wrote a little squib that said, "USS *Paul Revere* has been declared the best general mess in the United States Navy." Get it?

Paul Stillwell: No.

Admiral Erly: "Been declared the best general mess," as in screwed up.

Paul Stillwell: Oh, I see, mess in another sense of the word.

Admiral Erly: Yes, not in eating, but just a mess. [Laughter]

Paul Stillwell: Did you have to wrangle with the shipyard at all to get the accommodation for the Marines to sit down to eat?

Admiral Erly: I got that as a change order. Got that as a change order.

Paul Stillwell: Was it standard practice for Marines to stand up in other APAs?

Admiral Erly: Oh, hell, yes, but I wasn't going to have it. I felt that everybody rated sitting down to eat.

Paul Stillwell: Well, especially if they were going to be on board for any length of time.

Admiral Erly: Oh, sure, but even for a short length of time.

Paul Stillwell: That ship, being as big as it was, offered some opportunities to spread out that the others didn't, which would help.

Admiral Erly: That was true, because the troop berthing compartments were much nicer. But that was something else that you had to watch, and particularly in the old ships, the tendency, when the troops weren't on board, for crew members to infiltrate some of those spaces. I mandated and enforced that troop spaces were troop spaces and were not to be used for anything else. We maintained those troops spaces right to par, period.

We were configured as a squadron flagship, which meant we would also have a troop commander on board, so we had very nice accommodations for a squadron commander and for a troop commander on board. That was something else that was not in the planning which I had to plan and worked very hard at. I'll never forget. Here I did all the planning, sent out a letter, and irked my squadron commander, who was deployed in WestPac. He hadn't even seen the damn ship, but he felt that he should have had a say in what I had assigned as squadron offices. However, I had given shelter to at least two different squadron commanders and had their input.

So I sent off this letter with all of my recommendations, and I got a message saying, "Cancel your letter so-and-so," which I did.

I carried out his order, but it was reinstated later.

Paul Stillwell: Who was this gentleman?

Admiral Erly: It was John Spangler, out of the class of '32.[*] Actually, I had known him casually back in Washington, but not in that sense, more on a social deal. As I say, that ironed out. John was a real fair guy in the long run. I guess he figured that, being the squadron commander, he knew what he wanted, and not knowing the ship. But he

---

[*] Captain John G. Spangler, USN.

accepted later on what was there, and that was probably—I was so used, I guess, in some ways of having brought this ship to life and doing everything that I'd been doing—

Paul Stillwell: It was your ship.

Admiral Erly: Yes, certainly. He was in line with what he did, but it perturbed me a little bit.

Paul Stillwell: Did you provide recreational facilities for the troops?

Admiral Erly: Yes. We tried to set up for deck tennis. We had some areas for exercise. There was a library, of course, a very nice library, and a rec lounge for them.

Paul Stillwell: In converting that from the merchant-type Mariner hull, you were putting more weight topside with the boats. How did you compensate for that in the stability considerations?

Admiral Erly: Well, in that hull there was no additional water or—oh, there was one other thing, of course. We had the self-contained tank for collecting sewage from the heads so you didn't put effluent into the bay.

Paul Stillwell: That was revolutionary for that time.

Admiral Erly: Oh, yes, this was unusual at that point, because we were commissioned in September of '58. Of course, now, everything's self-contained. You don't even dare burp.

Just as an aside, I'm just thinking, in my own 39-foot trawler, I had to display this new sticker of what can be tossed into the ocean. Any boat that's over 16 feet has to display this new placard, just like that thing about oil, discharging oil, that you have to display and comply with. The Navy is pretty well up on that, and was getting a hand on this back then.

Paul Stillwell: What more can you say about operating the ship, that trip to Acapulco and then getting into regular service?

Admiral Erly: Oh, in regular service, I'm trying to think the first operation that we went out on. We were flagship for Charlie Duncan, who was the phib group commander, and he had just recently been selected as a fresh-caught flag officer.* So we had, of course, being flag configured, here we were supposed to have been a phibron flagship, but we ended up as a phib group flagship on an operation.

Paul Stillwell: Did you have the communications to handle that?

Admiral Erly: Oh, yes. Our communications were adequate.

Paul Stillwell: Did they rival those of an AGC?

Admiral Erly: I would say they probably approached it to about 90%, what with teletypes and everything that went with it.

Paul Stillwell: You would need a fair amount of voice radio capacity too.

Admiral Erly: Oh, yes. Yes, yes. She had it all, single-side band and the whole schmear. I'm just trying to remember, did we use our friend Kemp Tolley's idea? The goddamn thing never worked—an abomination. He brought it out here, and he was so proud of it. He had this concept, you take this wire and you lead it out and you take it by boats from the AGC flagship to the phibron commander and this type of thing. The concept wasn't bad in that you weren't out over the air, so the beach jumper units couldn't come in and mess you up by trying to take over the circuit. But the problem was, if one of your boats would cut it or it would get fouled and break, and then you lost it. So it was never very substantial. He brought it out and had PhibRon 5.†

___

* Rear Admiral Charles K. Duncan, USN, Commander Amphibious Group One, 1958-59. The oral history of Duncan, who retired as a four-star admiral, is in the Naval Institute collection.
† Captain Kemp Tolley, USN, commanded Amphibious Squadron Five, 1954-56.

I remember when I was sitting back in OP-03A and Kemp writing me, "Boy, I've got it going out here. I make them do it in every exercise."

Well, when I got out here, of course, I inherited that too. It really never worked for any length of time. Of course, it's gone by the board. You had to make concrete weights to put on it to take the line down, try to keep it from being cut by the boats. You had to load the line and weights in the patrolling boats and pay it out to reach the other flagship.

Paul Stillwell: What impressions do you have from Admiral Duncan, from having him on board?

Admiral Erly: Oh, well, Charlie was really a very unassuming, very nice guy. I've always been impressed with Charlie Duncan. From the first time I ever met him, he was, I would say, almost like Oley Sharp.* We call him a perennial youth. Charlie still looks very, very young. He's out there in Coronado with me. We always just seem to hit it off.

I remember the first time I saw this young-looking fellow at a cocktail party, and I went over and said, "Hey, I'm Bob Erly."

And he said, "I'm Charlie Duncan."

I didn't know who the hell Charlie Duncan was. So that's when I first met him. This was when I had *Paul Revere*. The chief of staff was having a small cocktail party at his house, and Charlie and Sheila were there. And it went that way. I feel that Charlie has been a very good friend to me.

Paul Stillwell: He has an excellent oral history. It's one of the most thorough we have, because he explained everything in great detail.

What can you say about the quality of the officers and crew of the *Paul Revere*?

Admiral Erly: I would say that the only one that I had handpicked was my exec, George Bush, who was a reserve.

---

* Admiral U.S. Grant Sharp, USN (Ret.), whose oral history is in the Naval Institute collection.

Paul Stillwell: Not *the* George Bush?*

Admiral Erly: Not the George Bush, I don't think, or related to him. But he had been with me in OP-33 and had been in amphibs and wanted to go to sea from OpNav. Knowing that I was going to get the *Paul Revere*, he asked, "Could I be the exec?"

I said, "Yeah, George. Yeah, okay, I'll do it. But since you are USNR, you've got to work twice as hard as a USN."

He said, "I know that, and that's why I want to go with you."

He did a tremendous job. I was very pleased with George. In fact, so pleased, I was able to get him an LSD command. He had orders to that, on one hand, and then he had orders to inactive duty on the other. That happens.

If I digress a little about the poor USNR, and I used to tell them—and I'm still telling these youngsters—"Don't play the game as a USNR. Go USN if you possibly can. You can always then revert to USNR. But if you keep hanging on (and I saw this from some other incidents), pretty soon there will be a personnel cut. We're looking at the Cold War, and they're going to cut back. Who's going to take the cut?" The reserves on active duty are going to be cut, because it's the easiest way to go and the least expensive.

Paul Stillwell: Well, which set of orders did your exec carry out?

Admiral Erly: Well, I fired a message off to BuPers to get the proper detailer desks to talk to each other. He got his LSD command and went on to make captain.

Paul Stillwell: That's remarkable for a USNR officer to get a ship command.

Admiral Erly: Absolutely. Well, remember, I had learned how to write fitness reports. I'm not as good as Bud Zumwalt obviously was, but it worked for George.†

---

* George H. W. Bush was President of the United States at the time of this interview.
† Admiral Elmo R. Zumwalt, Jr., USN, served as Chief of Naval Operations from 1 July 1970 to 29 June 1974. His oral history is in the Naval Institute collection. He was adept at getting subordinates promoted.

Paul Stillwell: As we discussed earlier, a common perception was that the amphibs did not usually get the best people.

Admiral Erly: Hell, no, you didn't. You've got the floaters from hither and yon. I found some of these people—the incompetent—were jumping to get in anything. Some would get in a job, and they would get caught up within about six months to the year or so, and then they put in for a transfer before they really got the ax. Their outfit's about ready to cream them anyway, figure this is a way to get rid of a problem. So I had some of those, yes, definitely. But then I had some really solid, dependable people, and they all took the challenge of the ship and I think reacted well. If you make them think that they're the number one, and pretty soon people strive to be that.

Paul Stillwell: They rise to meet your expectations.

Admiral Erly: Oh, sure.

Paul Stillwell: How did the rotation work out with your officers of the deck under way?

Admiral Erly: Oh, well, again, that was training. Not only under way, you would want them to go alongside for a replenishment, and then, you know, this business of doing the man overboard and the Williamson turn and having the deck and out there doing the various exercises to give them a feel of the ship.*

Paul Stillwell: How did the ship handle alongside a pier?

Admiral Erly: Well, of course, with a lot of freeboard, you've got to be aware of current and that type of thing. Really, as bulky and as big as she was, you really needed tugs to

---

* Early in World War II, Ensign John A. Williamson, USNR, devised the man-overboard turn that came to be named after him. It involves turning about 60-65 degrees in one direction, then reversing the rudder so as to go down the reciprocal of the ship's original course. His description can be found in *U.S. Naval Institute Proceedings*, October 1979, pages 89, 92.

move her in and out of port. I wasn't about to make a destroyer landing with her with a single prop.

I think I told you in part of my destroyer bit, you never go charging in making 20 knots when you really don't know where you are. I remember when we made our first deal into Pearl in *Paul Revere*. Going into Pearl, as we were coming in, the navigator couldn't really tell me where we were. Here I'd been boiling in. We picked up Diamond Head, and we'd been coming in making about 18 knots. So all I did is, I backed her full and stopped and I said, "Until such time as you can show me the fix and give it to me, we're not moving."

Paul Stillwell: That got his attention, I'm sure.

Admiral Erly: Yes. [Laughter] I wasn't about to go blundering in, not against everything I preach. So I'm sure the object lesson got to him.

But she handled well. It was a good sea boat. We could go along in seas that would slow others up.

Paul Stillwell: One of the groups that was a beneficiary of your better seakeeping, although they may not realize it, were the troops who were not used to that sort of thing

Admiral Erly: Oh, absolutely.

Paul Stillwell: Did you deploy in the *Paul Revere* as skipper?

Admiral Erly: No. No, no. In fact, I felt I had her too short a time. Before I knew it, Admiral Bob Speck, who was ComPhibTraPac at that point, had gone to BuPers without talking with me and had got me ordered to his command.[*] Hell, I commissioned her in September, and I was pulled off in, I guess, June or July. They should have allowed me at least two years, but old Marshall Thompson, out of the class of '36, was the material

---

[*] Rear Admiral Robert H. Speck, USN, Commander Amphibious Training Command Pacific Fleet.

officer on PhibPac staff, and he had his name in the pot to relieve me.* Then all of a sudden I found out that I was being detailed over to PhibTraPac because Speck had asked for me. I was caught in a bind.

I tried to get Bob Speck to back off. Page Smith at this point was chief of BuPers.† I said to Speck, "Oh, well, Page Smith told me he would get me a spot over on a European staff somewhere after my sea duty."

Speck said, "Well, if you can do this, okay, I'll back off. But otherwise, I'm going to keep you."

Page wasn't that much help. Finally, Admiral Sylvester asked for me on his staff. I was relieved by Thompson in July '59. That was the one thing, again, when we did it. When I was relieved, we had the boat group pass in review. Remember, we were at 32nd Street there in San Diego, and, of course, this took some drill and whatnot.

We had the flight deck where we were having the ceremony, and, of course, I said, "Here's the whole thing. This is our whole reason for being, and here is a demonstration of it. This is our striking force, the way we are able to project our Marines, our troops ashore. And here they are. Take a look. Turn and here they are passing in review for you."

We had them with their colors and pennants. As they passed, they dipped their flags, and here they came in line, the mike boats and the papa boats and the whole deal.‡ No one had ever done that before, but, again, giving it a little flair and giving it a little thought. We had the Marines down from my change of command when I left. Brigadier General Mugs Riley, who is now a supervisor up in Orange County. He made quite a name for himself in retirement as a politician.§

Paul Stillwell: I didn't know that.

Admiral Erly: Yes. But that was a deal I'll never forget. They presented to me a birthday card signed by every member of the crew.

---

* Captain Marshall F. Thompson, USN, commanded the *Paul Revere* from July 1959 to August 1960.
† Vice Admiral Harold Page Smith, USN, was Chief of Naval Personnel, January 1958 to February 1960.
‡ Mike boats were LCMs, and papa boats were LCVPs—two types of amphibious landing craft.
§ The terminal at John Wayne Airport in Orange County, California, is named for Riley.

Paul Stillwell: My goodness.

Admiral Erly: Yes, when I left. I had a good crew.

Paul Stillwell: Anything specific to say about the enlisted men in the ship?

Admiral Erly: Well, that's what I'm talking about when I'm saying crew, the enlisted men. This same old business that I think that you have to do on a big ship as you do on a small ship. The captain cannot sit up in his ivory palace. He's got to circulate and go through various spaces. I'm not saying inspections. I'm saying he's just got to get out and walk through the ship.

Paul Stillwell: Be available for people to talk to.

Admiral Erly: Sure. Go down in the engine room, firerooms, go back to the pipefitters' shop and damage control centers, and do the whole schmear. Then, of course, your boat crews—if they don't function, you can't carry out your mission. Then if your people that are working the davits and getting the boats away don't do their job, the whole—it's just a question of teamwork.

Paul Stillwell: It's important for people to know that the captain cares and that he appreciates what they're doing.

Admiral Erly: Sure, sure. You have to build up that sense of belonging. I could see when you really have to move a ship out of its homeport to get that.

Paul Stillwell: How would you explain that?

Admiral Erly: Well, I would explain it, you've got to cut the shore ties, and then they've got to come together as a unit, as a being, the whole thing that makes the ship what it is. I think you heard me talk about that in destroyers, and I think it's the same in any ship.

It's when they stop thinking about the next liberty or stop thinking about, "Well, gee, I've got to be home by such and such a time," then you're in.

It's not like punching a clock, but think in terms of the ship, that you weld your team together, and that's so deadly important, in my mind.

Paul Stillwell: Well, that made it, I'm sure, particularly disappointing that you didn't get to deploy with that crew.

Admiral Erly: Oh, we didn't go for any length of time, but we did get to Acapulco; we did get to Pearl. We did get up there up north for that exercise. We did have exercises off Pendleton, but that was just out for a week. The longest we were gone, I would say, was about three weeks from homeport.

In comparison, I'm thinking in terms of shakedown training, that it's so much more effective when you send the ship down to Guantánamo to undergo your shakedown training. And what have you got? You've only got ship interest, basically. But here on the West Coast, your shakedown training, you come back in in the evening and drop your observers from the FltTraGru, and either you swing around the buoy or then you go back out.[*] But it's just that coming in and out with the beach beckoning isn't as effective or as efficient training use of time as what you get on the East Coast.

Paul Stillwell: Did you have troops on for any appreciable length of time?

Admiral Erly: Oh, no. No, no. The longest we had troops on in the time that I was there, because we didn't make a deployment in *Paul Revere*, was, I'd say for about two weeks.

Paul Stillwell: Well, anything else about that ship before we move on?

Admiral Erly: Well, no. I would just say, of course, she was making points of what a 20-knot SOA can do for you, when you're talking amphibious operations.[†]

---

[*] FltTraGru – fleet training group.
[†] SOA – speed of advance.

One other thing that I had some fun with was playing with some submarines when I had *Paul Revere*. When I was a phibron commander, and we had one of those sessions in the attack trainers, because I was getting ready to deploy. What I did with *Paul Revere*, was to use her to simulate a destroyer picket, put her out there making 20 knots, and it confused that submariner, who didn't know what the hell was going on. He thought it was a destroyer, because he wasn't used to an amphib that could make 20-some-odd knots. So he immediately considered it was an ASW type, or a destroyer type, rather than an amphib type. We led him way off and got the main body through.

Paul Stillwell: Of course, the drawback, if you have only one 20-knot ship, you can't do very much with only one.

Admiral Erly: Oh, no. But what I was going to lead up to is that we now have 20-knot LSTs. When I look at them, I say, "My, God, and to think that looks like prehistoric monster. Did you ever do right to go along with it?" And I would say, "Yeah, as I look back, it was the only way to go to get that 20-knot SOA," because what really made up your slow echelon was your old LSTs. Well, now those LSTs can stay up with the fast echelon.[*] Hell, you'd be lucky making five or six knots with some of those things.

Paul Stillwell: Well, of course, you were phasing into that era when the LPDs were coming along.

Admiral Erly: That's right, sure. LPDs, LPHs. I think the LPH went in, the first conversion from a CVE to an LPH went in in about '56-'57.

---

[*] USS *Newport* (LST-1179) was commissioned on 7 June 1969 as the lead ship in a class of 20 tank landing ships capable of 22 knots of speed. All 20 ships have since been retired from active service in the U.S. Navy. A few have been transferred to foreign navies. The ships of the class had "horns" that stuck out from the bow to facilitate moving equipment ashore. That differed from the old LSTs that went directly on to a beach to discharge material from the tank deck.

Paul Stillwell: They had the old *Thetis Bay*.[*]

Admiral Erly: Remember back about my statement when we were talking about the tour in OpNav who was going to command LPHs, and we tried to get it so either it would be a surface sailor with amphibious—with some knowledge of choppers, or an aviator with knowledge of choppers and amphibs. Felt himself sidetracked it, so that recommendation never got to Arleigh. Felt just said it was going to be a naval aviator, period.

Paul Stillwell: That had to be a letdown, then, when you went from command to a staff job.

Admiral Erly: Yes, as usual. I first went there as plans for about two months and then fleeted up to become ops, but that's what it was in. I was just filling in plans waiting for Burris Wood, who was out of '35 and was going to get an AGC.[†] I relieved him as N-3, the operations officer. That was with Admiral Sylvester.

Paul Stillwell: What are your memories of Admiral Sylvester?

Admiral Erly: A very brainy guy, laid back. I don't ever think I saw Admiral Sylvester really exercised. He just took everything in his stride, and nothing seemed to bother him. He pretty well bought his staff's work.

Paul Stillwell: Did you prefer going to that staff rather than to Admiral Speck's staff?

Admiral Erly: Oh, definitely. Yes, because in PhibTraPac Admiral Speck wanted me to take the naval amphibious schools, and I didn't like that. I much preferred being in the operational side of things.

---

[*] USS *Thetis Bay* (CVHA-1) was recommissioned 20 July 1956 and completed conversion to her new role as an amphibious assault ship on 1 September 1956. She was redesignated LPH-6 on 28 May 1959.
[†] Captain Burris D. Wood Jr., USN, commanded the amphibious force flagship *Eldorado* (AGC-11) from November 1959 to December 1960.

As it turned out, we had some joint operations after Admiral Speck was relieved by Admiral Duncan as ComPhibTraPac.* We worked in a joint exercise, a CPX.† Admiral Sylvester was to be the overall commander, and there was a major general in the Army up from Fort Lewis. Then there was, I think, a two- or a three-star Air Force type. Charlie was pulled out to be the chief of staff, and I became the J-3 on the exercise staff. We had an Army J-4 and an Air Force J-2, and it went on this way. Josh Cooper was the phib group commander and would function as such in the CPX.‡ We all went up to the Tacoma area, where we were running this exercise, and actually we had our CPX headquarters at Fort Lewis.

We had asked the phib group people to come up with some recommendations, and I'm trying to remember exactly what happened. But the crux of it was that Josh got his feathers up in a storm on account of a message that went out and called and asked me to come up to the flagship.

I said, "Sure."

I went on up. When I got back, Charlie got me in right away and he was junior to Josh.

Paul Stillwell: Well junior.§

Admiral Erly: Yes. And said, "Hey, Bob, I'm sorry I couldn't intercept you. I wouldn't have let you go up there. I wasn't about to have him browbeat you."

I said, "Oh, come on. I don't get browbeaten. But I appreciate your concern. I think I've got everything squared away, and we got his ruffled feathers smoothed down. So I think everything's going to be all right."

But that showed Charlie's concern for his people. He wasn't about to have me slapped around or being browbeaten if he could prevent it. I'm glad he didn't intercept me. It was just as well I went, because then we wiped this thing out and got back on a

---

* Rear Admiral Charles K. Duncan, USN, served as Commander Amphibious Training Command Pacific Fleet from 1959 to 1961.
† CPX – command post exercise.
‡ Rear Admiral Joshua W. Cooper, USN, Commander Amphibious Group Three. Admiral Cooper's oral history is in the Naval Institute collection.
§ Cooper's date of rank as rear admiral was 1 August 1955; Duncan's was 1 July 1959.

plane where we should be without a lot of bad feelings between staffs. But that, of course, elevated Charlie in my esteem.

Two years later that was followed by an actual exercise putting the Army troops ashore. That's what happened, believe it or not. I did the CPX as the J-3, and then two years later as a phibron commander I was up there executing an actual landing up in the San Juan Island area with the Fourth Infantry Division as the troops, Army troops.

Paul Stillwell: That's when you find out how good a planner you were.

Admiral Erly: Well, we'd had a different locale at that point. But that's what the basic format was for joint exercises: have a CPX and then you hot wash-up and then two years later have an actual joint exercise, and that's what had happened. Just from my continuity, I thought it was very productive and very helpful to me, going through a CPX and then actually doing it.

Paul Stillwell: Well, you really spent a period of time there in the amphibious world, as you were mentioning.

Admiral Erly: Well, let's see. I had the *Paul Revere*, and I think I reported in out here in March of '58. Then I left in July of '59 to go to PhibPac, and I left in January of '61 and went to a phibron.

That's another story, too. What I really wanted—being an old ship driver, my number-one selection was to get a cruiser. About maybe October of '60 I got a letter saying, "You are going to be detached in January or so to go to your major command."

Oh, boy, that sounded just great. It sounded just great. They didn't mention destroyer squadron, they didn't mention a phibron, and they didn't mention a cruiser. Normally they would mention. I thought, "Oh, man, I got it loaded and locked."

In, I think, late November I got a letter from BuPers that said, "You will be detached in January. Proceed and report ComPhibRon 5."

That didn't make sense, because our N-4 was Kerfoot Smith, out of the class of '33, but only the upper half was commissioned that year.* He came back later, so he was now running with the class of '35 for seniority. He had gotten a letter the same time I got mine saying I was going to PhibRon 5.

So I reached over and hit the damn squawk box, and I said, "Kerfoot, you son of a bitch. You got my cruiser."

Kerfoot came back and said, "Bob, I got humped."†

I wanted to crawl under the goddamn desk.

That was in 1960, and it tells you something that I had maintained for a long, long time, which I felt something was wrong. You went in to BuPers, and the detailer would pull out a little drawer and look at a card. They evidently at that time would meet with various BuPers department heads and make their list of who they thought should have major commands or who got what.

I had been very vociferous in saying, "Hey, it should be a sworn board," because if you don't get your major command, you're dead. You're not going to go any farther. It should be a sworn board that determines that.

That's the way it is now. But it wasn't then.

Obviously, a sworn board sat and said, "Hey, you go home, fellow." Where an unsworn board said, "Hey, fellow you got a major command." I think the proof's somewhere, isn't it? Anyway, I'm happy now for those that have followed, and it has been in effect for some time that the major command billets are selected by a sworn board.

Now, this brings you back to asking about Admiral Sylvester. I did see him perturbed. When the hump board first came up—I think you know to what I'm referring.‡ They went back, I think, to all the captains, and they took about 33 1/3% of each of the academy groupings and sent them home early, before completion of their 30

---

* As an economy measure, in 1933 only the top half of that year's Naval Academy graduating class received Navy and Marine Corps commissions the year of graduation. Some members of the class were subsequently commissioned in 1934 and 1935. Still others joined the reserve and served on active duty in later years. And some were commissioned in other branches of the service. N-4 was the code for the logistics officer on the staff.
† Captain Kerfoot B. Smith, USN, retired from active duty on 1 July 1961.
‡ Sometimes referred to as a continuation board or plucking board, it meets to decide which officers in a certain group will have to retire earlier than expected.

years of service. He sat on that first board, and I don't know how many classes they went through. He didn't get to my class. I think he got maybe three year groups.

When he came back from that, and I don't know how we happened to get talking about it, but he said, "Bob, it was a horrible experience. Every time I walk by a captain, I want to hide. You could get 2% easily. After that, you were really cutting into solid muscle." And he said, "Now when I walk down anywhere and see a captain, I just don't want to look him in the eye."

That really got to him that, just to keep the promotion zone open, a lot of very fine officers, in his opinion, were summarily ordered to retire. In my class, we lost about 33%, and a lot of them missed their 26-year fogy, which was a substantial pay raise, and went out with 25 years' service, about 33%.*

Later, when I had the phibron, I got this letter from BuPers everybody else had got. I held it up, and I could see it was a short paragraph, about five lines, and I said, "Oh, well, got it made in the shade." Because those that were sent home, they got this flowery letter of about two pages from BuPers saying what a great job they'd done. However, the other version, which I received, was just a curt announcement, "You have been retained."

Paul Stillwell: Short and sweet.

Admiral Erly: Yes. As I say, that really worried Admiral Sylvester, and I don't know, I guess it was the nature of the situation that commanded such drastic action. I gathered that when you keep promotion lines open—which I might add my own observation now. In some ways, that to keep them open and keep people younger, I sometimes wonder if we dip just too far down in the basket. So I'm saying, when they still have so much more to offer, and with the wealth and maturity and background, they've gone through the gamut because everything is on, as I might say, youth and inexperience. It's all relative in how you look at it. I've also said I thought Zumwalt could have been a great CNO if he had been properly brought along, if he had been given a numbered fleet, and then if

---

* "Fogy" is Navy slang for an increase in pay as the result of length of service.

they had brought him along the way Tom Moorer was brought along.* See, Tom had Seventh Fleet, and then he had CinCPacFlt and then he had CinCLant and CinCLantFlt and then CNO.† You get more maturity along the line. In many cases this is not happening today, and maybe they ought to backtrack. I don't think youth is always as important as maturity and experience.

Paul Stillwell: What were some of the major issues that PhibPac was dealing with at the time you were on that staff? Mostly running exercises?

Admiral Erly: No. Basically, we were looking at the Naval Warfare publications. I think OpNav was also interested in this, and we had both PhibPac and PhibLant looking at NWP-22, the basic amphibious warfare doctrine, along with the Marines. We were looking at the joint operations, how that was to go, that business of the change of command and all this business that you go through in amphibious operations. So your warfare documents revisions. We had set up a conference out here with the Lant people and examined a lot of these things and had little seminar groups working to come up with some of these things.

As I mentioned to you, the CPX, the exercises, and as N-3, again, I had to figure out ways to accomplish a fast reaction. We worked with the Marines at Pendleton, and we set up an exercise where we would just bank for a rapid deployment concept, a fast load-out, and get moving.‡ We had an exercise that we could trigger off by just releasing the message. Boy, and then the phibron had to get going. We liked to do it on a Saturday, or even hit them on a Sunday, just to check, see how you could respond. This was interesting.

That came out of a brainstorming session. I had gotten into reading this book on brainstorming techniques, so I used that with members of my N-3 staff. You know that old business of get in there and anything goes and afterwards you sort it out. This fell out of one of our brainstorm sessions of things to do.

---

* Admiral Elmo R. Zumwalt Jr., USN, became Chief of Naval Operations in 1970, when he was 49 years old, and retired when he was 53.
† Admiral Thomas H. Moorer, USN, became Chief of Naval Operations in 1967, when he was 55.
‡ Camp Pendleton is a Marine Corps base near Oceanside, California.

Paul Stillwell: How well did it work?

Admiral Erly: Oh, it worked fine. We found some weaknesses, which we shored up. It was a good exercise. It kept both the Marines and the Navy on their toes. The fact that you've got to be able to respond to every—did we ever have a conflict to respond to? Well, basically, yes. We had some fast load-outs that worked. In fact, I was already out there. I'm trying to remember what incident. But PhibRon 3 really went through that drill and out-loaded, because, hell, they came steaming into Buckner Bay out there with us.* This time frame was the Laotian crisis, if you can remember that.† That's what it was. She got deployed as far as Buckner Bay. So I would say, yes, it paid off.

Paul Stillwell: Did you have a lot of various contingency plans on the shelf for different types and sizes of emergencies?

Admiral Erly: Oh, certainly, yes, yes. What else did we do? Later we set up a command center there. That was when I was chief of staff to ComPhibPac.

But I was just thinking of this brainstorming technique, and I used it a lot in my career. Once I had it, I made up my own posters and would explain it and go over it, and it's amazing what you could come up with. I used it as N-3, I used it in the phibron, I used it as chief of staff of PhibPac, I used it in the phib group, I used it as the inspector general in Atlantic Fleet. I didn't use it per se in my Tower of Babel when I was over there in Portugal. But, surprisingly, some good things fell out from it.

Paul Stillwell: Well, especially if people get the idea they're not going to be inhibited.

Admiral Erly: That's right, yes. Well, say how can a commander go in and sit down with a lieutenant on a first date, one of those things. You take off your insignia. No

---

* Buckner Bay, Okinawa, was named in honor of Lieutenant General Simon Bolivar Buckner, USA, Commanding General Tenth Army in the Okinawa operation. He was fatally wounded by an artillery shell on 18 June 1945. The Japanese name for the bay was Nakagusuku Wan.

† There was unrest in Laos from about the time the administration of John F. Kennedy took office in the United States in January 1961. The United States supplied advisors and trainers for Laotian guerrillas.

insignias allowed. Anything goes and don't be polite. If you've got a thought, flash it or you're going to lose it. It'll never come out unless you spurt it out. And no matter how off the wall it is, it can always be tamed down and used. But, again, you don't apply any judgment and don't say, "Oh, hell, that won't work."

Any comment might trigger you to come up with a hitchhike on the idea or convert it to some other useful means as it goes along. The main thing is, you need a tape recorder, really, to pick it all up, it goes so fast at times. Then it's edited later. Then you put those that apply a judgment to some of them and see how they work. I'm sure you've gone through that, haven't you?

Paul Stillwell: Not in that formalized a process.

Admiral Erly: Well, I got it out of a book. I read the book, and it just struck my fancy. I said, "Well, let's explore this. Let's see what we can come out with."

Paul Stillwell: Do you remember any of the off-the-wall things that turned out to work?

Admiral Erly: No, not right offhand, but I'll think about it, and I might remember some tomorrow. One you might have thought was off the wall is that rapid deployment, as it first looked. There are so many reasons why you can't do it is what you have to overcome.

Paul Stillwell: There's always that for a new idea.

Admiral Erly: Yes.

Paul Stillwell: Was part of your job to plan for the introduction to the fleet of these new, more sophisticated types of ships?

Admiral Erly: Yes, because then you were also getting into the vertical resupply and the vertical replenishment, plus the vertical envelopment, which had been with us for some time. Here you were ending up where you were going to be able to even lift off some of your troops from the helo deck. Plus, our helo deck, I was just thinking, had an elevator, which is so important in your combat loading.* This is why all the amphib ships have a Marine combat cargo officer. Whether there's an APA, AKA, the things that are essential. Well, that was some of the essential things could also be airlifted from the ships. Along, as you say, with the LPH and LHA and everything that's coming along, that was a major issue.

Paul Stillwell: But you'd have to rewrite some of your doctrines to accommodate those.

Admiral Erly: Oh, sure. As I say, this was a continuing thing in your Naval Warfare Publications to keep them updated.

Paul Stillwell: How much did PhibPac have to do with the gunfire support part of the amphibious equation?

Admiral Erly: Well, since your landing force training unit was into that, which, of course, PhibTraPac and the Landing Force Training Unit come under PhibPac, yes, that was in there, basically your spotter training and that business.

The phib groups were required to have a section in their staffs that were basically concerned with the gunfire support, and as again, you can see where your vertical envelopment and all the planning had to tie in with your gunfire support. You sure as hell weren't going to be shooting in the objective area when you've got your choppers coming in to land troops. So you had to have the setup for the corridors and coordinate your gunfire, and also your air support. You've got to make damn sure that you've got to get all these coordinated, and at the schools, the NavPhib schools and at the landing force training unit, had courses there that covered these various aspects, and you had people on the staff that were versed in these fields.

---

* Combat loading involves putting the equipment and supplies needed first in an operation at the top of cargo holds so they can be off-loaded first. Items of later priority are farther down in the pile.

Paul Stillwell: Of course, you have a different relationship in that those ships don't belong to you the way the amphibs do.

Admiral Erly: That's right.

Paul Stillwell: So you have to coordinate with the gunfire commander.

Admiral Erly: Well, the point is the operational control, but they still follow the amphibious group commander's op order, and here is where your gunfire support and training people who are writing these sections have to know what they're doing. It's for implementation and to the gunfire support ships.

Paul Stillwell: But you would have to coordinate with CruDesPac to get those ships available when you need them for exercise.*

Admiral Erly: Oh, absolutely. They would make those available. Of course, by then your fleet commander has gotten into it for the various exercises and what units are designated. It comes out in your training schedule. Of course, then they have the training fleet that schedules all these.

Let's see, at this point in time I was still on PhibPac's staff as the N-3, and I was getting ready to be relieved and go out and take PhibRon 5. In the process, I was lucky to be given a month's leave, and so I opted to take that month's leave in Japan. The squadron had already deployed and was going to be there until June, and this was January of '61. So we went out and sopped up all we could about the Japanese, something I hadn't done before. For background I need to tell you more about my friend Rittenhouse, whom I'd encountered 20 years earlier as exec of the *Cassin*.†

I'm trying to think the best describe him. At some point, Arleigh Burke had sent him up to Mackinac Island, and there was a group there of young people who put on

---

* CruDesPac – Cruiser-Destroyer Force Pacific Fleet.
† By the early 1960s he was Rear Admiral Basil N. Rittenhouse Jr., USN.

shows and they traveled around.* They have an uplifting name, and I think it all stems from this Mackinac Island up the way. It was almost a religious type thing.

So Rit went up there, and as Rit reported to me, he told Arleigh, "You know, when I got there, I didn't have one drink of bourbon, and you know what that means, that the impact this must have had on me," because Rit really liked his toddy, as did his wife Vi. He partied so much, really, that his last job was out there with the Air Force as the Navy rep in that joint command outside of Tokyo, and evidently he was partying so much that one of his subordinates turned him in. He was called up to the naval hospital in Yokosuka, and he got one of those physical retirements.† When I went out to take the phibron, they were off somewhere.‡ Lois and I had his quarters at this air base out there for several days during our stay out there before I took the phibron.

Back to this group, Rit introduced me to the number-two guy in the Japanese, I guess you would say the police force, and they had the prefects throughout Japan. He was equivalent to a lieutenant general. The way Rit had gotten to know this fellow was through this Mackinac Island thing some years earlier.

Oh, this little fellow and his wife took to Lois and me. They took us to the sumo wrestling. They really showed us a great time. We said we were going to Kyoto, where the summer palace is. This was February or so out there, and I had this cap with earmuffs. Kyoto is great, evidently, in the spring because of the cherry blossoms. This is where the imperial palace and gardens are. So they left a message for me, "You go Kyoto. You stand on train platform. You wear cap." I spoke practically no Japanese, and he didn't speak very much English, but you communicated by this way.

Sure enough, we went, got off the train, and a rather large Japanese came up, introduced himself, and said, "I am Abraham," in very flawless English. He turned out to be our escort, and here he was with a big limousine. We arrived there on a national holiday. The gardens were closed, but Abraham had them opened for us. We went in, and he was very adept. He would say, "Now, you're in this Japanese garden," and so

---

* Admiral Arleigh A. Burke, USN, served as Chief of Naval Operations from 17 August 1955 to 1 August 1961. His oral history is in the Naval Institute collection.
† Admiral Rittenhouse served from December 1960 to October 1961 as Chief of Staff, Headquarters, U.S. Forces Japan. After service in the Bureau of Naval Personnel, he retired 1 January 1962. He died in 1973.
‡ Erly commanded Amphibious Squadron Five in 1961-62.

forth and so on. "Now I'm going to leave you. You just sit here and you enjoy."

So we were sitting there with no one else around, taking in the beauty of it, even in winter and cold, with the water moving. It was quite something. Then he dropped us off at a Japanese inn, with the futons on the floor and we had the seaweed for breakfast and the whole bit, including a hotsi bath.

That night the prefect of the province had a big party for us. I forget how many tatami mats were in this room. Shirley MacLaine had played a geisha in one picture.* The senior geisha was the one that had coached Shirley. The dinner they put on had untold numbers of courses. Also there were umpteen geishas waiting on us. There was the chief of the prefecture there, plus Abraham, plus myself, and Lois. That was it, and about a thousand-course dinner and the toast with the hot sake, the game playing that they do. We were really feted.

The next day, off on more sightseeing, as I recall, and as we were coming up to lunchtime, I said, "Abraham, where would you and the driver go for lunch if you were by yourselves?"

He said something.

I said, "Let's go."

We went for sukiyaki, and it was a typical spot. But then you got all the ambience of the working class and felt closer to the people.

So that was the lieutenant general. I told you the story that the only thing I salvaged from the *Cassin* at Pearl Harbor was my sword, and all the gilt had been burned off, the sharkskin was off the handle, and all there was the blade with my name on it, and the hilt was all charred. I said, "Well, I'm going to take this with me, and the first time I have a Japanese officer come on board to make a call and offers to give me one of those little dolls in a case, I'm going to pull this thing out and say, 'Here, fix it.'"

But my wife's a lot smarter than I am. She said, "You do that, it'll look just like any other Navy sword."

So I still have that charred piece of metal mounted on a holder in my den, with a little placard on it saying, "The sword of a lieutenant jaygee at Pearl."

I also have a Japanese doll in the case. [Laughter]

---

* Actress Shirley MacLaine starred in the 1962 film *My Geisha*.

Paul Stillwell: Giving him the sword would have been very ungracious after the hospitality you received.

Admiral Erly: Oh, the hospitality. Later, after I had taken over the phibron, I had him and his wife for dinner on the ship. We had a Polaroid camera for anybody came aboard, and we made him an honorary member of PhibRon 5. We bedecked him with all kinds of goodies, too, and did what little we could to return some of the things that they had done for us. But it all came about through Rit and his being sent by Arleigh Burke up to Mackinac Island to check out this cult.

Paul Stillwell: Well, you got the phibron command. This wasn't the cruiser you wanted, but certainly better than being humped.

Admiral Erly: Oh, yes.

Paul Stillwell: After your leave was over, then you got into it?

Admiral Erly: After the leave was over, I flew to Korea and relieved Shellabarger out of '33, as ComPhibRon 5.[*] The ship was at what was really the amphibious base of the South Korean Navy. I also noted there they had some of our LSTs and whatnot. The squadron had been over there carrying out a combined exercise with the Korean Navy. The flagship at that point was the USS *Calvert*.[†]

We went from Korea to independent ship exercises in *Calvert* to back making port visits. We were scheduled for phibron and PhibGruWestPac exercises later on in the summer.[‡] I'm trying to remember the time frame of the Laotian crisis, but I remember the ship was in a southern port, Kagoshima, Japan, on a ship visit.

---

[*] Captain Martin A. Shellabarger, USN.
[†] USS *Calvert* (APA-32) was a *Crescent City*-class attack transport commissioned 1 October 1942. She was originally the cargo ship *Deorleans* before the Navy acquired her on 30 September 1942. She was 491 feet long and displaced 14,247 tons at full load.
[‡] PhibGruWestPac – Amphibious Group Western Pacific, normally a rear admiral's billet.

As I said, my wife flew in to meet me, and we were staying at an old temple there. I'd had my chief of staff over that evening for dinner. My wife was scheduled to go over to Hiroshima the next day on an early train. I was going to go by ship.

Early in the morning we head a loud knocking on the door. I said, "Oh, that's our wakeup. It was 3:00 A.M., and the knocker was my chief of staff. He handed me an urgent dispatch from Com7thFlt directing PhibRon 5 to rendezvous in Buckner Bay and combat load the Marines for a possible landing in Laos.* So that meant that, boom, back to the ship, and as I told my wife, I said, "You're on your own. I may not see you for a while, period. Why don't you go see the Taj Mahal?"

So we went back to the ship and sent priority messages out to all the PhibRon 5 to rendezvous immediately in Buckner Bay and be prepared to load out.

Paul Stillwell: Were they fairly widely scattered?

Admiral Erly: Oh, yes, they were all over the place, port visiting and this type of thing, and sort of showing the flag around different ports. So we then headed out, and then as soon as we got in and got the combat cargo people from the Marines down, and with our combat cargo people, and then started loading the ships as they were coming. Then we headed down into the South China Sea and selected an area out of sight of land. We went into a holding pattern. We scheduled daily training exercises to offset the tedium of "Stand by to stand by." Also, the *Thetis Bay* joined up with us.

Paul Stillwell: How capable a ship was she?

Admiral Erly: She did her mission well. Later, after going around in circles out there, just sort of waiting, the situation in Laos diminished so that we weren't going to have to put people ashore. Then we joined up and had a SEATO exercise, with the landing on the island of Borneo.† *Thetis Bay* took part in it. We had some of the vertical

---

* Com7thFlt – Commander Seventh Fleet.
† SEATO – Southeast Asia Treaty Organization.

envelopment and a classical landing and then a critique. The Aussies and the Brits participated. It amused me to see the competition between them.

One of the highlights for me was that it brought back memories of the time when I was mayor in Songjin and had to run from Songjin to Chongjin to keep the blockade going during the Korean War. I had an Aussie ship with me then, and the skipper of that ship was in this exercise as the Aussie squadron commander. So he had me over for cocktails, and I had him over for movies and ice cream. So it was a reunion of some eight years later. That was one of the highlights of it.

Admiral Griffin, Com7thFlt, of course, came down for the critique.* The biggest kick I got was the seeming rivalry between the Brits and the Aussies.

Paul Stillwell: That's interesting.

Admiral Erly: Yes. The Aussie admiral and the British admiral were very competitive, one against the other, little digs here and little digs there whenever they could get one in.

So we had culminated in the load-out with the landing on Borneo. I had on board with me Willie Stiles, out of the class of '39.† He was the colonel in charge of our Marines. And damned if we didn't get there in the load-out, and then Brute Roeder was there.‡ He was the phib group commander, I was the phibron commander, and, of course, you know what happens when everybody starts to pull out after the critique. The junior gets the task of back-loading the troops and equipment.

I was there to complete the back-loading, and wouldn't you know, we had some young Marine lieutenant take a Jeep joyriding. It had been raining and whatnot, so things were slippery. He skidded off down a canyon. He returned to base camp to get a DUKW.§ In the process of trying to retrieve the Jeep, the DUKW skidded down the canyon. So we spent two days trying to salvage the DUKW but ended up stripping it and

---

* Vice Admiral Charles D. Griffin, USN, served as Commander Seventh Fleet from 7 March 1960 to 28 October 1961.
† Colonel William A. Stiles, USMC.
‡ Rear Admiral Bernard F. Roeder, USN, Commander Amphibious Group Three, 1960-61.
§ DUKW was the designation of an amphibious truck developed by the U.S. Army in World War II. The name was pronounced like that of an animal capable of operating on both water and land, the duck. Essentially the DUKW was a boat with wheels on the bottom.

left the remains to rust. We did get the Jeep back.

So whatever happened to the kid, I don't know. He was a young Marine second lieutenant going joyriding and held up the back-loading for two days and caused the loss of a DUKW. He should have been court-martialed.

During this exercise we tested the vertical envelopment concept and then the re-supply by choppers. The helicopters were provided by the *Thetis Bay*, skippered by Walt Curtis.*

Let's go back to when we were in the holding pattern off Laos. I would like someday to look it up in the Soviet reports. I'm pretty sure there was a Soviet submarine contact. We had a visual sighting on a periscope, and I knew damn well it wasn't any of ours. I had the *Calvert*, LSD, AKA, and APA—I'm just trying to think. I told them to all, "Energize fathometers."

We went into a retiring search curve that you would do, as if we had sonar, and I had everybody pinging with fathometers. We went to the datum point and dropped a smoke flare and did the whole damn bit, as if we were a division of destroyers.

Paul Stillwell: ASW with amphibs. That's clever.

Admiral Erly: Gave them something to think about.

Paul Stillwell: That's right.

Admiral Erly: That was one of the incidents that we had.

I remember one other thing we did. We had loaded out for the Laotian crisis, but then for the Borneo exercise we needed to make changes in the combat loading. This was done in the South China Sea, with the mike boats being loaded and hauling cargo. Thank God, it was flat calm, but we did it.

Paul Stillwell: Why didn't you combat load at Okinawa?

---

* Captain Walter L. Curtis Jr., USN, commanded the amphibious assault ship *Thetis Bay* (LPH-6) from 17 February 1961 to 18 February 1962.

Admiral Erly: We had already combat loaded for the Laotian crisis. But when you plan for a different scheme of maneuver on the beach, you've got to change your combat load.

Paul Stillwell: I see.

Admiral Erly: And this is what we did. That was a first.

Paul Stillwell: That's unusual, too, yes.

Admiral Erly: I would hope that the Russian submarine was around taking pictures of that. It was something new.

Paul Stillwell: What was it like getting into that role as a unit commander as opposed to the CO of an individual ship?

Admiral Erly: Well, you've got to think about all of your ships, because that brings up another little item. We had one of the oldest LSDs along with us, the USS *Oak Hill*.* It could make barely 15 knots. Now, here I was as a squadron commander, and what I wanted to do was get ahead of my predicted speed of advance so I would have time to run tactical evolutions I had in mind, special drills to generate unit cohesiveness. The flagship was the guide, and without signal I had the flagship slowly increase RPMs. Naturally, for the other ships to maintain position they had to also increase. This was a great maneuver to keep the squadron OODs on their toes, and they gained experience in maintaining steaming positions.

At first the *Oak Hill* was hanging in there pretty well, but after a while he started to drop back and back and back. I got this plaintive message, "Where are you going?" The CO felt all alone, so I went back with something to reassure him. My message read, "You may be the oldest and you may be the slowest, but I assure you, you're not the lowest in your squadron commander's esteem."

---

* The dock landing ship *Oak Hill* (LSD-7) was commissioned 5 January 1944.

Then when we would start to do tictacs, then he could catch up. But that was one of the deals. I should have brought along some messages that we had some fun with.

I told you when I was PhibPac ops we had generated a fast phibron load-out and deployment. Well, when we returned from the Laotian crisis and Borneo landing, PhibRon 3 showed up. We had quite a good little rivalry going with them. We had all kinds of messages flowing back and forth with rhetoric and rhyme, heroic rhyme, you know, "Hats off here to, and here is PhibRon 5 arriving, PhibRon 3 departing," all this stuff, which made for a lot of fun and kept things going, and sort of blowing your own horn at the same time. In summary, the brainstorming sessions that I had instigated in the PhibPac staff had paid dividends in readiness.

Paul Stillwell: Did you ever see an uglier ship than those early LSDs?

Admiral Erly: Well, but they were versatile, though, I must say that for them. However, the ugliest to me were the old LSTs.

Paul Stillwell: They even used LSDs as floating dry docks.

Admiral Erly: Yes. Oh, exactly, certainly. And the concept is incorporated in your newest, the LHAs.* Being able to ballast down and float out the LCMs and LVTs caused me to coin the phrase, "They spawn their lethal young." We ran the LSDs forever, and most of them on baling wire, similar to repairing the old four-piper destroyers.

I was trying to think of some of the other things that happened. Oh, yes. We were in Buckner Bay in the *Calvert*, and I lost the skipper of *Calvert* due to a heart condition.† When he went to get his physical down in Yokosuka, they turned him in with a heart problem. I had to have a replacement because the ship was sailing. So I took my chief staff officer, a commander who had been an ex-LSD skipper, and made him acting

---

* LHA is the designation of a type of amphibious assault ship. The first of the type, USS *Tarawa* (LHA-1), was commissioned 29 May 1976.
† Captain William J. Collum Jr., USN, commanded the attack transport *Calvert* (APA-32) from 21 July 1960 to 22 February 1961.

skipper of *Calvert*, with Seventh Fleet's okay.* He was skipper for about three to four months.

The squadron was now in Buckner Bay. Then the Seventh Fleet flagship, with Admiral Griffin embarked and with Schnitzel Schneider, my classmate, as CO, entered port.† The flagship moored to the only pier. The squadron was due to take on provisions the next morning.

Well, during the night the wind really increased, enough that it woke me and perturbed me enough that I woke Bull Durham, now acting as CO of *Calvert*. I said, "Hey, Bull, you'd better get steam up here. You could well drag and be in extremis. And I put out a message directing the rest of the squadron to get steam up, and be prepared to steam to the anchor or get under way if necessary." The windy conditions persisted, but in the early morning, in preparing also for the replenishment, there were quite a few Mike boats in the water, thank goodness. The wind had caused the flagship to be torn away from her mooring. She started snapping lines and ended up on a little shoal parallel to the beach. But we had enough mike boats in there, and I sent them over. They got on the other side of the *St. Paul*, the shoal-ward side, and we got her pushed back out. But if we hadn't had those mike boats in the water, it could have been a lot worse, and the *St. Paul* would have been driven farther aground.

I think it really was a Seventh Fleet cover-up. I don't think there was ever an investigation of this particular grounding. If it had been any other unit except the Seventh Fleet flagship, there would have been an official investigation.

Paul Stillwell: Looked like a grounding to you.

Admiral Erly: But because she was the flagship, and I don't know whether Schnitzel had protested tying up there or not, but as far as I was concerned, there should have been a full-blown investigation, and there never was because it was a flagship. Well, I call that a double standard in my humble feeling. I've never accosted Admiral Griffin and told him

---
* Commander Harold D. Durham, USN, was acting commanding officer of the *Calvert* from 22 February 1961 to 5 April 1961.
† Captain Frederick H. Schneider, USN, commanded the heavy cruiser *St. Paul* (CA-73) from October 1960 to 25 October 1961.

what my thoughts were, but if it had been any other ship, there would have been a formal investigation. To the best of my knowledge, there never was. And they had a classic picture out there. Here was this Marine who was on sentry duty. The ship was gone, but he was still there, stiffly at attention.

But, again, as for the poor old amphibs, I told Schneider later on, "What the hell, I saved your ass, and you didn't even have sense enough to say thank you."

Paul Stillwell: What was his response to that?

Admiral Erly: "Oh, well."

Paul Stillwell: Well, his successor in the *St. Paul*, Al Church, came to grief.[*]

Admiral Erly: Oh, it was *St. Paul,* that's right.

Paul Stillwell: He got blown into an aircraft carrier, I think, trying to make a landing at Yokosuka, and he did get burned for it.

Admiral Erly: That did it, yes. Well, Al's a hell of a nice guy. He was Mr. Franke's naval aide.[†] He'd been the assistant secretary.[‡] Actually there's an aside that he must have been financial affairs.

Paul Stillwell: Yes, he was.

Admiral Erly: Because Page Smith reported to him, and he became a great fan of Page's. In fact, how Al Church got the job of being his aide, they were somewhere and Franke said to Page, "This fine-looking officer and his beautiful wife, why can't I have someone like that for my aide?"

---

[*] Captain Albert T. Church, Jr., USN, commanded the heavy cruiser *St. Paul* (CA-73) from 25 October 1961 to 3 November 1962.
[†] William B. Franke served as Secretary of the Navy from 8 June 1959 to 20 January 1961.
[‡] Franke was Assistant Secretary of the Navy (Financial Management and Comptroller), 1954-57.

I think Page arranged that, and that's how Al got that job.

Paul Stillwell: As you say, Church was a nice guy.

Admiral Erly: Yes. And I think the class of '24 made Franke an honorary member. I guess Franke was really one of the perhaps well liked or beloved Navy secretaries that came along the way, with the common acceptance of all hands. The rest of them, for some reason Thomas and all the ones I've known have had some detractors, including Nitze.[*]

Paul Stillwell: Well, Gates has gotten high marks from whomever I talk to.

Admiral Erly: That's right. Gates was another one.[†] But I thought, for sheer affection, from what I got from a feeling that it was more went to the old man. Now, Gates was much younger. Franke evidently was a very fatherly, paternal type and a real down-to-earth gent. I had practically no personal contact, but this is what I gather.

Well, back to PhibRon 5.

Paul Stillwell: What became of your wife?

Admiral Erly: Oh, well, she went to see the Taj Mahal, and then we were able to later on get a trip to Hong Kong. She came home in April or May, and I got back in June of that year. That was a long deployment for the phibron. We were out for eight months.

As I said, I also became a phib group commander, ComPhibGruWestPac. We didn't keep an admiral out there all the time; it was only for specific exercises. Brute Roeder had come out as the phib group commander in the flagship. I remember that. They came steaming into Buckner Bay, and you're talking about losing an anchor. They did it in grand style. The *Estes* was the flagship with Paul Stimson in command.[‡] I was

---
[*] Charles S. Thomas served as Secretary of the Navy from 3 May 1954 to 1 April 1957. Paul H. Nitze served as Secretary of the Navy from 29 November 1963 to 30 June 1967.
[†] Thomas S. Gates, Jr., served as Secretary of the Navy from 1 April 1957 to 7 June 1959.
[‡] Captain Paul C. Stimson, USN, commanded the amphibious force flagship *Estes* (AGC-12) in 1961-62.

in my gig, waiting to board and pay my respects to the admiral after she moored. I noticed that she was making several knots as she let go the anchor. Suddenly the PA blared out, "Clear the forecastle!" The bitter end of the anchor chain came whipping out. Finally she moored with the other anchor. Thankfully, my UDT detachment was able to retrieve the anchor and chain. He was just going too damn fast, and he didn't have the backing power. So that's how the flagship arrived at Buckner Bay. She payed out the bitter end of that chain. I'm sure it's in the log. [Laughter]

Paul Stillwell: How did you avoid the temptation to still be the captain in the flagship?

Admiral Erly: It's troubling.

Paul Stillwell: Sounds like you gave some suggestions along the way.

Admiral Erly: You have to. I remember one incident with Goodfellow when *Paul Revere* was my flagship for an amphib op off Camp Pendleton.* As you know, timing is everything in an amphibious operation. All units must follow a strict time schedule in order to meet H-hour, boats off-loaded and troops and cargo loaded. The boats then formed in waves to hit the beach. This takes considerable time. We were coming in to the coast off Pendleton for a landing exercise. Ships had been released to proceed to assigned anchorages in the objective area. It was about 0400. *Paul Revere* just plodded along, and it was obvious to me, both as a phibron commander and past skipper that she would not make her H-hour commitment. I was up on the flag bridge, and I said, "*Paul Revere*, move out, move out."

Nothing was happening. I think the OOD had trouble waking Scott up. I just didn't get much more into it than this. But finally they got him out there, and he probably had a guilty conscience for not being on hand. There was no way he was going to get into position on time unless he was going to fly it. We had a little verbal exchange. He got the ship up to 20 knots, and it was able to meet its commitment.

---

* Captain Alexander Scott Goodfellow Jr., USN, was commanding officer of the attack transport *Paul Revere* (APA-248) from September 1961 to October 1962.

Afterwards, I called Scott in. I said, "Hey, Scott, let's get one thing squared away. What happened last night? You know you weren't where you should have been. And then your attitude wasn't what it should have been. You know you can't win in this. So let's forget this whole goddamn thing and start over." Scott never forgot it, and he felt very beholden to me, because he knew he was in the wrong.

The other case, I had Olsen as skipper of the flagship.[*] This was when we were going north. We were going up to actually do an exercise, and it turned out to be a shambles. Again, if you had to rely on morale, God, my morale wasn't the highest, but you had to keep everybody else's up. I had one ship that thought she had ruined her reduction gear, so she was dead in the water. We had to take her in tow, and the only ship available was the flagship. This was when I took *Calvert* and formed her 18 behind me, and when I got this other message from an AKA that was broken and just lying to, wallowing in the seas. The wind was blowing like hell, and the seas were very rough. What do you do?

I released *Calvert* and said, "Proceed with due caution for existing seas and wind conditions to rejoin the task group. Then I sent a message directing the *Paul Revere* to take the AKA in tow. The *Paul Revere* effected the rendezvous and made a destroyer-type approach to pass a towline. The strong winds rapidly pushed the ships together, and *Paul Revere* just narrowly missed colliding. She tried again with the same result. So I went down and said, "Hey, look, you're doing it going in parallel. What you need to do is to come in perpendicular and then turn short here as the AKA is drifting down. Then get your lines across that way, and you're not going to have any risk."

Now, that wasn't my idea. I had picked it up years before when Quiggle was skipper of "Mount O," and Rear Admiral Wellings was on board as phib group commander.[†] He was a salvage expert. Quiggle had banged the "Mount O" trying to take another ship in tow, and this is when the admiral said, "No, you want to do what the tugs do. You come up like this and then pass the towline."

---

[*] Captain Albert R. Olsen, USN, was commanding officer of the attack transport *Paul Revere* (APA-248) from August 1960 to September 1961.
[†] Captain Lynne C. Quiggle, USN, was commanding officer of the amphibious force flagship *Mount Olympus* (AGC-8) from February 1953 to September 1953.

Paul Stillwell: Since your hands don't show up on the tape, I'll say the first movement that didn't work was essentially a parallel approach, and you used the perpendicular instead.

Admiral Erly: Yes, and you want to come up perpendicular to the ship you're going to take in tow and then come around smartly.

Paul Stillwell: Make a hard turn when you get to its bow.

Admiral Erly: Oh, yes, yes. Make a hard turn, back her down if necessary, and then get your lines over. The first thing you really should do, and basically anyway, is to line up with the ship and determine relative rates of drift—particularly with dissimilar type ships. Now, here's *Paul Revere* and then here is the other one, with the different silhouettes, so they were going to drift at different rates. So you want to compensate for that. In other words, if *Paul Revere* was going to drift faster, she would come up here and then up, and wait as she's drifting down get her lines over. And if the other one's going to drift faster, do it a little short of the extension of her fore and aft lines. And we did that.

One other time I intervened—you say, when do you intervene? That same thing, earlier on the *Paul Revere* dropped an LCVP out of the davits. Crash! And here was this splintered boat. What do you do?

I went down and said, "Al, first thing you'd better do is get your crew at quarters to make damn sure there was no one in the boat. You want to make sure you've got all hands on board. You don't want to have lost anyone. Someone could well have been in the boat."

The main thought. Well, you really don't want to get in the ship's business, but when you think that you can give them some advice that helps, you've got to step in and do it. Otherwise, give them a free hand and stay out of their hair.

Paul Stillwell: It's a fine line to walk.

Admiral Erly: Oh, it's a fine line. But when it comes to safety of ship and safety of lives, you've got to do it. Or if you've got a mission to meet, you've got to step in to make sure they meet it if you see something going wrong.

You know, when you play by ear—I really had a bad one. We were having a landing off Pendleton. There's a place called Green Beach up there, and it's right by their damn clubhouse. The Marines want to always keep that in use as a Marine landing area so they can keep saying, "Oh, yeah, this is used for amphibious landings." Even though it was their bathing beach and recreation area.

We had this landing. Red Yeager was ComPhibPac at this time, and I was the phibron commander.* We went in there, and Red was in the flagship with Com1stFlt, Vice Admiral Melson.† Lo and behold, we kicked the operation off, and I was looking at this thing. I couldn't believe my eyes. The LVTs had hit the beach, and then the papa boats were going in, and saw that that were all broaching, broadsided up on the beach. The beach was littered with LCVPs. I couldn't believe what I was looking at.

I was cussing and saying, "Well, Jesus Christ, I could beach a papa boat better than these coxswains." Then I said, "Something's definitely wrong," and I directed the control ship not to dispatch any more LCVPs. This was holding things up, see. You had the whole beach practically littered now with papa boats.

I was sorting this one out and saying, "Well, there's only one thing we can do, is to get all the mike boats waterborne. I don't want any more papa boats hitting the beach. Let's keep this exercise going. We've got to get the embarked troops and their equipment ashore. Let's mate the papa boats and the LCMs and effect the transfer out here beyond the surf line."

That's what we did. This is what I directed the control vessels at the line of departure to get cracking on, and they did a superb job. About this time I got called away on the voice radio. It was Red Yeager. Here he was going to show his amphibs to Com1stFlt, and here they were sprawled up on the beach, and you can imagine, he was

---

* Vice Admiral Howard A. Yeager, USN, served as Commander Amphibious Force Pacific Fleet from July 1960 to March 1963.
† Vice Admiral Charles L. Melson, USN, served as Commander First Fleet from 14 July 1960 to 12 April 1962. Melson's oral history is in the Naval Institute collection.

anything but gentle. However, I can't blame him, and I agreed it was a devastating debacle that should not be repeated.

Paul Stillwell: What else do you remember about him?

Admiral Erly: Well, I think Red was a very controversial person. I thought he was very, very effective at public speaking, but I was sure glad to get out of the PhibPac mess. He had umpteen thousand stewards, I'll tell you, and I didn't want any part of that. And I was thinking in some of these cases of, what do you do with stewards and how they should be used and treated? I think some flag officers violated their use, and I think that Red was one of those that did that. When I had house stewards, I never took their per diem for food allowance. Many flag officers did. I think that was further proved when he lost Jean and when he was killed. He had his private quarters declared public quarters or something or other. He had WAVES stationed there that were taking care of his wife. As you remember, they died in his quarters.[*]

As an amphibian, I don't think he had the depth of knowledge, say, of Eph Holmes.[†] The guy was a real operator, I must admit that. He was an operator. What did I learn from Red? You can see I have no lasting affection. I would say he didn't inspire one to look up to or to set a standard for what one should strive. That's just my humble opinion. I think he was a skilled operator in more ways than one. He knew and used all the shortcuts he could.

Well, the lesson learned from that landing, I summarily went out and put out a direct order that there would be no landing craft on Green Beach by PhibRon 5 units unless directly approved by ComPhibRon 5. The directive further stated that LCUs and assist LCM beaching technique was the only way Green Beach could be used.[‡] The problem was that there were rock under there, and when the papa boats got in there and

---

[*] Rear Admiral Howard A. Yeager, USN, died at Great Lakes, Illinois, on 11 March 1967 while serving as Commandant of the Ninth Naval District. He was overcome by smoke inhalation when his quarters were on fire. Also dead as a result of the fire were two WAVES: 21-year-old Laura Jean Martin and 25-year-old Laura Mae Garrett. Firemen saved Admiral Yeager's invalid wife Mary Jean.
[†] Vice Admiral Ephraim P. Holmes, USN, served as Commander Amphibious Force Pacific Fleet from March 1963 to January 1964.
[‡] LCU – landing craft utility, larger than an LCM.

started to hold their position, you had to keep the engine going ahead. The whirling action of the propeller flipped the sand away and picked the rocks up. The rocks chewed the propeller blades off, so they had nothing to hold them perpendicular to the beach and surf, so they broached.

Paul Stillwell: Why had this not been discovered before?

Admiral Erly: That's what I was trying to find out. I remember vaguely somewhere in the dim recesses of my mind, I was against Green Beach. Nels Johnson was the phib group commander who was directing the exercise, and he was fresh caught coming in.[*] He had been chief of staff to Griffin out there in Seventh Fleet, and I didn't know, but I guess in past experience somewhere alone the line it had gotten buried. You look at the current beach survey, and it didn't show it. Do we blame the UDT for incomplete beach survey?

Paul Stillwell: Well, how did you find it out?

Admiral Erly: I found it out by going in there and beaching. Even with an LCM, you could see what was going on, and then after the fact saying, "Oh, this is what had happened." You could look at the props and figure it out, and you saw what was underneath this sand layer.

So you really would say that the initial beach survey that Johnson had to select these beaches, his staff—not my staff—didn't get it. So the end result of that was that that's what it was. They had to go with, "Don't ever land on Green Beach." And we had some news camera, TV camera, film it, and you could just see what was happening.

Something else I really didn't like was the planning, as I saw it. The LVTs ran too close to the waterline.[†] When I looked at the film, I thought to myself, "Did the coxswains really keep full throttle on there, or were they afraid of hitting the LVTs running up the beach in the surf line?"

---

[*] Rear Admiral Nels C. Johnson, USN, served as Commander Amphibious Group Three, 1961-63.
[†] LVT – landing vehicle tracked, an amphibian craft that could operate both on water and on land.

But that's basically what happened as they stood there grinding away. And you had to keep depending on the surf. The more the surf is—have you ever taken one of those boats in? Well, I have. I've landed them. I did that in the *Paul Revere* when I was skipper, going through refresher training. I jumped in an LCVP and took over as coxswain. I arranged with a lieutenant from PhibTraPac to blast the coxswain of that particular LCVP at the critique. The crew enjoyed it immensely when the instructor as the coxswain of Papa 24 had to stand up and explain his actions.

I was coxswain in the papa boat, and then we had the fellow from the landing force, the PhibTra schools, had him while he was a lieutenant, saying, "You want to be sure and criticize the hell out of papa boat so-and-so." And who was the coxswain of that one?" [Laughter]

But that built up the esprit. It's that old saying that you never ask a sailor to do something you wouldn't do yourself. Well, I pretty well knew what you had to do to keep from broaching. That's part of it. You've got to keep that power on there and keep your boat perpendicular to the beach.

Paul Stillwell: Well, there's no stern anchor as you have in an LST, so that's—

Admiral Erly: But then we had instituted the assist LCM beaching. Even then, because I wasn't even sure what was going to happen to LCMs, and I said that only LCMs would go. Well, that meant that you had to have two LCMs. One was loaded with troops and equipment. Then you had another with several hundred feet of line on it. The second one passed the bitter end of to the loaded LCM. The LCM went with him and he turned at the surf line and payed out towing line, keeping the loaded LCM from broaching by keeping tension on the towline. Then, if worse came to worst, he could pull him off. So you had to have enough towing line to get through the surf and be on the other side of the surf line. You didn't want to be in the breaking surf with the second LCM. Okay?

Paul Stillwell: You needed a lot of boats if you were going to do it that way.

Admiral Erly: Oh, yes, and that's going to slow down the operation. But that's better than losing all these boats, because you lost your main battery.

Paul Stillwell: Exactly.

Admiral Erly: Sure. You lose your main battery. That's what happened. *Magoffin* was the APA. They finally salvaged a lot of them, but, boy, they were up there, high and dry, I'll tell you. Very disconcerting, but how do you recoup? How do you keep the exercise going? We did, but we had to slow it down. It wasn't a full rate, but, damn it, we got the materials and troops ashore. The first damn thing to do was to get the remaining waves of papa boats unloaded, because I wasn't about to have them beach. So you've got to get your troops, and we got them. We got them, and then we started with the mike boats and LCUs, working them in there to get that stuff ashore.

Paul Stillwell: There are so many factors in an amphibious landing, you have to practice a lot to make it work.

Admiral Erly: Well, that's why you have rehearsal. You want your timing. That timing is so crucial of when the waves hit and when they touch down, because, remember, we were talking earlier about gunfire support and your air support, and all these have got to be coordinated, plus your vertical envelopment concept, and all these things. It's like everything that has to just be right on, or you can have a disaster. This business of trying to change H-hour at the last moment is like trying to make birth control retroactive. There ain't no way you're going to do it.

I was saying to be innovative. What I really got out of the PhibRon 5 job was that you try to think ahead. As I told you, I had devised a cardex file when I was in Phib Group 2 way back. So I had every possible contingency plotted. I had messages ready to go, the whole damn thing, and the big cardex file so you could change as other events occurred, so you weren't inflexible. But at least you had a structure of what to follow.

I would think, with computer science today, what a snap that would be to keep track of what was going on in an amphibious operation and be abreast of everything. It is a very challenging thing of all the considerations that you had to do. Remember, I say in an amphibious operation you work it backwards. You work it back from the ships are going to be off the objective beach, and when they have to be there. Then you go back and from that, and you make your cruising dispositions and then you bring her on back, including your replenishment rehearsals, and then back to your load-out. Do you see?

Paul Stillwell: Oh, yes.

Admiral Erly: It's a very complex operation, and a lot of people, unless they've been exposed, don't really grasp that. I think it's perhaps the most intricate operation that there is. I would say for that it was a good—then, even though you think you've got everything covered, what the hell do you do next, Coach? Like what was I to do? I sure as hell was not going to give up.

If it were an actual operation, and even if we just had the LVTs and the whatnot are on the beach, damn, you couldn't leave them to be gobbled up. You had to get the other ground troops ashore. How you going to get them in? Even if you can't get them in on that time scale, you've got to keep it going. A challenge. Then to be harassed in the middle of it, knowing you've got a problem, you don't damn well need to be told by your commander you have a problem and, "I'm unhappy with you," when you're trying to repair as much of the damage that you can.

I was just trying to think of other vignettes from that amphibious experience. Oh, well, as I say in the phibron, again, we used brainstorming and look at various problems. There wasn't any time to brainstorm what I was to do on that particular operation, everybody looking at the old man, what the hell's he going to come up with now? Very interesting.

I guess from there, the highlights—oh. Pretty well covered that trip north, but I'll tell you, as I was saying, taking the one ship in tow and we took it back off San Francisco, gave it to tugs, and then we went chugging up to rejoin. Then I got another jab in the gut. *Calvert* had suffered extensive structural damage and knocked off her forward gun mounts, flooded her forward peak tank in joining up with the task group—even in the face of my parting directive to her.

Paul Stillwell: Could this have been avoided if the skipper went slower? You're nodding yes.

Admiral Erly: Yep. I think it could have been avoided. He used too much speed. I really had no sympathy for him, because he still, even after I cautioned him, didn't slow down. When I detached him, I detached him with a, "Proceed with due caution for existing sea conditions. Arrive there in one piece." No sense in arriving wherever you're going all bent out of shape.

Too many people have a tendency, "Oh, isn't this fun." Bang, bang, bang, bang. No way.

We went on up on that exercise with Rear Admiral Hooper as the OTC.[*] I'll never forget. I had drafted a message and put it in context of a football game, and sent it out to the squadron. I included the OTC and ComPhibPac as info addees.

I said, "Boy, in the first half, we've really had our ass waxed and so forth, but by God, the second half is coming up and let's really get in there and hit the line. We'll be winners yet."

It had been one damn thing after the other. Got that message off. And I'll never forget, when we got into Tacoma and tied up, I went to the flagship and was walking up the gangway. Admiral Ed Hooper, the phib group commander, was waiting at the quarterdeck. I took off my cap and threw it up on the quarterdeck. I said, "Okay, Admiral, you've got the chance. You can throw it back."

Paul Stillwell: What was the point of that maneuver?

Admiral Erly: Well, the point of it, geez, I was just going to say, "If I'm not welcome, just throw it back at me."

Paul Stillwell: He doesn't strike me as the type of individual that would really go for a stunt like that.

---

[*] Rear Admiral Edwin B. Hooper, USN, served as Commander Amphibious Group One in 1961-62.

Admiral Erly: He went for it, believe it or not. He went for it.

Paul Stillwell: He was Mr. Dignified.

Admiral Erly: He went for it. He went for it. I think he probably had more empathy than you would think for the frustrations of the squadron commander and what I'd been through: the *Paul Revere* dropping a lifeboat, the AKA dead in the water, the *Calvert* damage, and so forth.

Something happened that required the Fourth Infantry Division to be ready for deployment.

Paul Stillwell: Was this from Fort Lewis?

Admiral Erly: Yes. We loaded out with them, and we were having a landing off the San Juan Islands. We even tried the telephone wire, old Kemp Tolley's wire between the flagship and the phibron commander. It lasted for about a half hour. Then, all of a sudden, we got orders to backload troops. This had to do with Berlin.[*] But we had to backload them, get them back to their post in a hell of a hurry, and we did that expeditiously and got all kinds of plaudits from the Army for doing it and this type of thing. So that eased some of the pain and strain.

So with the wash-up, there was General Truman. No, that was on the CPX when General Truman was up there.[†] He was an Army type that had the 4th Infantry Division and then went over and had the Army Continental Training Command, out of Fort Monroe. Got his third star back there. I remember having quite an argument with him, because remember, I'm CPXing now. When we CPX, what do you think we CPX?

Paul Stillwell: Southeast Asia.

---

[*] In 1961 the East German regime built a wall that separated the Soviet- and NATO-controlled sectors of the city of Berlin. It was a symbolic gesture at the height of the Cold War. A number of East Germans were killed in subsequent escape attempts. On the night of 9 November 1989 the East German government suddenly and unexpectedly opened the wall to permit free transit. The wall was subsequently torn down, this time a symbol of the easing of relations between the superpowers.

[†] Major General Louis W. Truman, USA, commanded the Fourth Infantry Division, 1958-60.

Admiral Erly: Yep. And Vietnam. Exactly. That's what we did. He vowed and maintained that he could not do the job unless he had tactical nuclear weapons. He kept requesting their use during the CPX and, of course, I felt no way were we going to use nuclear weapons. In this atmosphere, we're not going to start popping these tactical nukes because you never know where it'll stop once you start. Admiral Sylvester concurred. I had the damnedest time, continually saying no, but even after the exercise was all over—and he was a pretty good Joe at heart—at about 3:00 o'clock one morning, at his quarters, General Truman and I were still going at it. I said, "No way will it ever happen."

He said, "It's the only way it can happen."

Well, time has proven me right. That was an interesting sidelight from the CPX deal that came out of that. And we really had programmed and then showing what you could do in some of these exercises.

It brings to mind, also our current situation over there in Saudi Arabia.[*] My God, if we had war-gamed that damn thing. But the big black villain then was the Soviet Union coming down to get a warm-water port. That scenario had been war-gamed to death by every war college going, and continues in planning. So it should have been easy to dust it off. I'm sure they've got lessons learned coming out of this thing out of their ears. If they were going to have this situation again that they would forward deploy more supplies in other areas than what they'd considered. I'm sure they're looking at that.

But, again, the way you plan orients your thinking and maybe it sometimes stultifies it a little. You get [unclear] you go, but it should be a general guideline, any of them. You have to improvise and do something new or whatever to get the job done.

That's one thing that I think amphibious planning does for people. They plan, but you've also got to be prepared for the unexpected. You try to envision everything you possibly can, but sure in hell there will be something that you haven't thought of. But when it does hit, you've got to come up with a plan and do something about it. And I

---

[*] In January 1991, a few months after this interview, U.S. and Allied Coalition forces attacked Iraq to get it to retreat following its August 1990 invasion of neighboring Kuwait. The holding action in the meantime was Operation Desert Shield. The conflict itself became known variously as Operation Desert Storm and the Gulf War. Coalition forces won the war in February 1991.

think that same thing is what they are doing now. I think all military planners and the executors have to do it.

Paul Stillwell: Well, we might be vulnerable somewhere else now, because we have so much stuff stacked up over in the Persian Gulf.

Admiral Erly: Could happen. I guess we could sit here and dream up scenarios all around the world. I'm sure people are doing that right now in some of the think tanks, thank goodness. We're perhaps even over-committed. I'm wondering about our inventory right now. What have we got left if we had to deploy somewhere else? I'm also wondering now how much of our airlift is just committed to maintaining what you got over there. And if you brought up this thought of another contingency, say in Southeast Asia, and had to pull that airlift to go that way, what happens to supporting the people that you've got over there? Interesting isn't it?

Paul Stillwell: Yes, it is.

Well, what with both these positive and negative aspects of that tour as squadron commander, would you draw a balance? How do you think it came out overall?

Admiral Erly: Oh, I drew up something. I think overall, I am a great believer, I think you know, of lessons learned. For Christ's sake, if you do it wrong once, let's just don't do it again. Let's take every step we can to avoid that. Let's don't go around continually making the same errors or continually reinventing the wheel. I, as my dying gasp as a squadron commander, I came up with you name it, from just about everything for the amphibs, and sent a copy to PhibPac, do whatever he wanted to do with it. But in it I stressed the value of the amphibs, that we were the spearhead in war, and the only way we were going to get there, and we didn't take anybody's backwash, whether it be air, submarine, or any of the other surface sailors to build morale. I guess the thing was about that umpteen thick.

Paul Stillwell: Half an inch, maybe.

Admiral Erly: The concept of recognizing the individual, the birthday card, the birthday cake. I tried to put all those thoughts together which could be of help to an individual commanding officer, really not only coming to the amphibs, but any commanding officer, and left that as my parting shot, figuring that it could be of use and help some people to be a better CO, even, and to keep the amphibs' spirits high and this type of thing. I might say that I left and came back a year later and found that that publication, it was then being used, being handed out to PCOs coming into the amphibious force.

I took the phibron back to Southeast Asia in June of '62, and finally Paul Stimson relieved me in Yokosuka in July of '62. So I kept the squadron just about 18 months, and I would say I was about ready to move at that point. I had started out that deployment in *Paul Revere* as my flagship but shifted my broad command pennant back to *Calvert* in Pearl.

As we were getting ready for that deployment where I was going out, we had this escort convoy, and we had these convoy commodores. These were people who recently retired and had gone to convoy commodores' school. They wanted to use the amphib ships to play merchantmen. Well, I used *Paul Revere* to befuddle that submarine skipper. I fought this tooth and nail, and I said, "No way am I going to stand for taking this squadron out and the first night at sea have them exposed to submarine attack, with all the attendant stuff going on, operating under merchant signal procedure and convoy instruction procedures, after they have been in port for a series of several weeks preparing for deployment." I said, "You are asking for disaster, and no way will I be part of it."

You've heard me expound everybody's left-handed until they've been at sea for a couple of days. And then you go out on a new set of instructions that people have not exercised under or maneuvered under, and you've got a retired and a reserve staff that are supposedly running it. I said, "No way is that going to happen on my watch."

I was protecting the skippers. No way. I think you're just lining them up for disaster.

So we finally got the submarine people to say, "Well, we'll put it off until the second night."

So at least we had two days to shake down and maneuver under merchant ship signal books. I had a retired rear admiral, tombstone type, on board.[*] And you better believe that any damn thing he did, I was sitting right on his ass all the way. I wasn't going to allow him to endanger any of my ships.

Jimmy Thach was the ASW commander out there at Pearl, and I called on him.[†] Gil Slonim out of '36 was his chief of staff.[‡] It was Slonim who had been pushing for more convoy type of training for the escort commodores and staffs. Slonim tried to bait me, and Jimmy Thach just said, "No, I don't want to hear any of that. I understand Erly's viewpoint." Jimmy Thach was on my side. He was reading what I was saying, and we didn't have any undue incidents.

But this riding convoy had to break up. Instead of keeping the squadron together to meet the requirements, when we were about two or three days out of Pearl, we peeled off one group here and another group there on this bit. But they weren't going to be under any of this. They were operating under their own tactics.

That, I hope, is something that's been done away with. If you're going to have people do that, you ought to give them several days of work-up to do it. I think you've heard me expound before that there is nothing more crucial or the ship is never in a more dangerous position when she's coming out of overhaul or whether she's been in an extended upkeep period and not operating, because maybe you're only operating on about two of your six cylinders, and this is when you're liable to get nailed.

Paul Stillwell: Especially if you're not used to being a merchant ship.

Admiral Erly: Well, no. I'm being even more all inclusive in saying, "You give me a top-notch ship, even, and you let me let her sit along the dock for about six weeks or

---

[*] From the mid-1920s onward, officers who had received combat decorations received a one-grade honorary promotion, widely referred to as a "tombstone promotion," at the time of retirement. Although the individual still received the retired pay of his actual rank, he was authorized to assume the title and wear the uniform of the higher grade. The practice ended in 1959.

[†] On 1 March 1960, Vice Admiral John S. Thach, USN, became Commander Anti-Submarine Defense Force Pacific. It was later redesignated Anti-Submarine Force Pacific and still later as Anti-Submarine Warfare Force Pacific. He served in the billet until April 1963. His oral history is in the Naval Institute collection.

[‡] Captain Gilven M. Slonim, USN.

whatever, and when she gets under way, she's not at her top-notch rating. She's going to take two or three days, working up to be effective under her maneuvering rules, without new rules, even. So you just don't want to start operating under tactical signal books. You want time to bring them back up to their efficiency."

Shall we take a break? [Tape recorder turned off.]

Admiral Erly: I think at the end of the last tape we were just terminating my duty assignment as Commander Amphibious Squadron Five. At that time I had orders to the National War College, and I had to report in August to join that class.

We had a home in Coronado. Prior to my sailing with the squadron to the Far East, and knowing that I was going to the National War College, we had the place rented. But we were having what you would say one of these garage sales that are so prevalent in that area. In the process of the garage sale, a couple came in and asked Lois if she wanted to sell the house. She said, well, she didn't know, go see her husband who was inside.

So they came inside, and I said, "Sure, we'll sell it for a price." I pulled a price out of thin air, and they agreed. So in the process of a garage sale, we sold the house, much to the horror of the Coronado Bank of America manager, one John Schroder, who was so very, very upset. He said no one ever sells a house in Coronado. You hang onto it because the land out here is going to sell by the square inch.

I didn't, and the deed was done. So we had no house left here, and my basic feeling was that I wasn't going to be given a year's sabbatical in Washington, going to the National War College, and then be immediately transferred back to sunny California. I expected that I was going to put in durance vile either in the Joint Chiefs of Staff or OpNav.

So the house sold; I deployed to WestPac, and was relieved by Paul Stimson in Yokosuka, Japan. I wended my way to Mississippi to meet my wife, and then we went on to Washington and set ourselves up at the River House and I went off to being a schoolboy at the National War College.

I had been there about six weeks when I got a call from George Muse, the BuPers captain detail officer.* He said, "How would you like to be chief of staff of ComPhibPac?"

I said, "Not only no, hell, no. Go whistle Dixie. If you offer me chief of staff of Sixth Fleet or Seventh Fleet, yes, I'm ready and I'll go tomorrow. Let's go."

His answer was, "Well, Admiral Holmes, who is going to be ComPhibPac, wants you to be his chief of staff."

Admiral Holmes was OP-90 at that point.† I said, "Admiral Holmes, I gather, is here in Washington. I'm in Washington. And if he wants me to be his chief of staff, he'd better talk to me," and I hung up.

Then, I'd say within the day, I had a call from Eph Holmes, asking would I come over and see him and talk with him.

So I said, "Sure," and I went over.

I told him frankly that I'd had too much amphibious duty, and I didn't think it was a way to pay and promotion, but that if anyone knew anything more about the Pacific Fleet Amphibious Force than I did, I didn't think there was any such person alive.

Paul Stillwell: That was your fatal sentence.

Admiral Erly: Well, no. Well, but it was the truth. You call them the way you see them. That was the way I left it with Eph. Then I called Charlie Duncan, and I have a sneaking hunch that it wasn't all Eph's idea.‡ I have never pinned Charlie on this one, but I have a hunch from something he dropped later on that he felt that I really should be Eph's chief of staff. Eph had not been out there, he was not acquainted with that side of the world, and what scared Charlie, I think, more than anything else, that Eph was making noises about maybe taking Ebby Bell as chief of staff.§ Do you know Ebby?

---

* Captain George R. Muse, USN.
† Rear Admiral Ephraim P. Holmes, USN, served 1960-63 as Director, General Planning Group, in OpNav.
‡ Rear Admiral Charles K. Duncan, USN, served from 1962 to 1964 as Assistant Chief of Naval Personnel for Plans and Programs.
§ Captain C. Edwin Bell, USN.

Paul Stillwell: No. Was that a problem?

Admiral Erly: Well, it probably might have—Charlie might have sensed a problem. Ebby had had no amphibious experience. He ended up very successfully at one phase as OP-09D, was the programmer, submarine type, but not a nukey type. And a very alert and can-do individual. He was working with Eph in OP-90, and Ebby was a pretty good guy. I think that Charlie just felt that Eph needed some more solid backup than what Ebby would be able to provide, and I think that Charlie was pushing me because we had worked together in PhibPac. Oh, yes, he said, "You should take it."

A short time later, Eph had called and said, "Well, I'm telling BuPers I want you."

About this time, after I talked with Charlie, I just said, "Fine. Yes, sir," and let it go at that.

I had also checked it out with Rufus Rose. Rufus was then commandant of the Industrial College.*

Paul Stillwell: What did he say?

Admiral Erly: Basically, the same thing. He said it's better to go with somebody that's asked for you than not. He didn't think that the long amphibious experience would kill my promotional chances.

Paul Stillwell: Was there any implied promise from Duncan that, if you did this, he'd take care of you somehow?

Admiral Erly: Oh, no. He couldn't do that, and he wouldn't. I wouldn't expect him to. No, no. But, as luck would have it, both Charlie Duncan and Eph Holmes sat on the selection board when I was selected for rear admiral.

---

* Vice Admiral Rufus E. Rose, USN, with whom Erly had served in the 1950s, by then was commandant of the Industrial College of the Armed Forces in Washington, D.C.

Paul Stillwell: You never know how this luck's going to work out.

Admiral Erly: Oh, hell, no. Sure, because—I think we've discussed this before—for Christ's sake, for probably every one selected, there are two equally qualified, and it's just a matter of how you're profiled there and how many people on the board have really seen you operate. It's pretty hard to look at fitness report profiles and try to read from that. That's still just pros and graphs and things like that to translate that to a person in operation and getting the job done. So I think, again, a matter of luck. In my case, as I told my wife, "Hey, if I don't make it with that board, I would never make it."

It was Eph Holmes, Charlie Duncan, Hayworth, Gene Fluckey, and Brute Roeder.[*] So I already figured if, what, there are nine on the board, I had five votes already. I forget who some of the other ones were.

Paul Stillwell: Did you know Fluckey from somewhere?

Admiral Erly: Yes, I had run into Gene. I'm trying to remember where. I'm trying to think of some of the other members of the board at that point, too. As I say, it's a matter of luck.

Paul Stillwell: Well, before we get there, could you discuss your tour at the National War College, please?

Admiral Erly: Oh, I found it very interesting, with a chance to really get into the books and a sabbatical, and try to read everything they throw at you for the required reading. I also signed up for the George Washington University master's in international affairs and took the course on international organizations and other bits, and then wrote my thesis on the Monroe Doctrine, Rio Pact, and U.S.-Cuban relations.

I became a laughingstock at the National War College.

Paul Stillwell: How so?

---
[*] Rear Admiral Eugene B. Fluckey, USN.

Admiral Erly: Well, I went there in '62, and you recall the Cuban Missile Crisis.*

Paul Stillwell: I remember that.

Admiral Erly: Well, from my associations with the Cubans and my being shipmates and really knowing what was in them, I would have said, number one, that if any country would ever go Communist in our hemisphere, Cuba would be the last. That was one conviction I had. The other, I felt that the Monroe Doctrine, in some vague way, was still in force.†

In one of our first sessions, something came up from a speaker that later, in a discussion group that I was in, about the Monroe Doctrine. There was a State Department guy by the name of Dean, who I think has been until recently, oh, the last several years, had been ambassador, I forget, to either Argentina or Chile. Bob Dean was his name. He was a State Department student.

Dean said, "Okay, look, I'll research that, and the next meeting I'll come back and tell you whether or not the Monroe Doctrine is viable."

Well, he came back at the next meeting and said, "Nah, the Monroe Doctrine is not viable."

I didn't buy his analysis, and I set out to examine in depth whether or not the doctrine was still germane. So I selected the following title for my thesis: "Monroe Doctrine, Rio Pact, and U.S.-Cuban relations."‡ I ended up writing about U.S.-Cuban relations from '59 to the present, which was then in the midst of the missile crisis, with events changing daily.§

---

* The Cuban Missile Crisis was triggered in mid-October 1962, when a U.S. reconnaissance plane photographed a Soviet nuclear missile site in Cuba and the presence of Soviet bombers. On 22 October President John F. Kennedy went on national television to announce a naval quarantine of Cuba, to be implemented on 24 October. On 28 October Premier Nikita Khrushchev of the Soviet Union notified President Kennedy that he was ordering the withdrawal of Soviet bombers and missiles from Cuba.
† Promulgated on 2 December 1823, during the presidency of James Monroe, the U.S. Monroe Doctrine asserted that European powers were no longer to colonize or interfere in the affairs of independent nations in the Americas.
‡ The Inter-American Treaty of Reciprocal Assistance, also known as the Rio Pact, and the Rio Treaty, was signed at Rio de Janeiro, Brazil on 2 September 1947.
§ Fidel Castro took power in Cuba in 1959 and held it for many years. On 24 February 2008 he was replaced as President by his brother Raul and as First Secretary of the Communist Party of Cuba on 19 April 2011 by his brother.

I proved to myself, and I think to a lot of other people, that the Monroe Doctrine was still viable, but what Kennedy did may have amended it somewhat. I delineated some weaknesses in the Organization of American States and what needed some modifications of the Rio Pact where necessary. I am afraid that Lyndon Johnson, as I watched what happened in the Dom Rep a few years later, took every step that I said should be taken, and then he caught hell from the press, if you will recall.[*]

But that's how my World War II Cuban relationship influenced me 20 years later. My paper was cited as one of special consideration or merit and was circulated through all departments, and that's how, I think, some of the National Security Council people got a copy of it and said, "Hey, this looks like a good group. Let's follow this one."

It's amazing how what's happened there fills in somewhere else. A lot I attribute to President Kennedy and some of the things that he did that made it possible that now we have this Communist-controlled country sitting, what, 90 miles off our coast.

Paul Stillwell: Well, it was Communist before he got involved.

Admiral Erly: Well, it stayed Communist, because I feel that the debacle of the Bay of Pigs could have been avoided.[†]

Paul Stillwell: Right. Certainly that's true.

Admiral Erly: And it wouldn't have been that bloodbath. What we did was let Castro get further ensconced. The hope still breathes for some of these people there that they will one day see a free Cuba. I'm talking of my Cuban friends that are there in Miami and the

---

[*] On 28 April 1965 President Lyndon Johnson dispatched a 400-man expeditionary brigade to the Dominican Republic to protect the lives and property of American citizens caught in a military revolt in that nation. By 29 April, 1,600 Marines had landed, and by 7 May 6,000 Marines were ashore and another 2,000 offshore. They were followed by Army troops, bringing the U.S. combat presence by 11 May to more than 11,000 troops. Navy ships evacuated more than 4,300 civilians during the operation.

[†] In mid-April 1961 a force of 1,400 Cuban exiles, secretly trained by U.S. personnel in Guatemala, landed in the Bay of Pigs, on the southwestern coast of Cuba, in an attempt to overthrow Fidel Castro, that nation's Communist dictator. The invasion attempt was a disaster. President John Kennedy decided that U.S. naval intervention would worsen the situation, so ships and aircraft offshore were prohibited from taking part.

Cuban naval aide. But that paper was my biggest challenge, and I wouldn't let go or change, because the more I dug into it, the more I figured it needed digging into.

Paul Stillwell: That's great when you've got the President of the United States making your case for you.

Admiral Erly: Well, I'm not so sure that I made much of a case for—as things went along a little later about the Kennedy Doctrine, as I look at some of the things that happened later. I would have guessed you would have said on the basis of my paper I would have been a cum laude student, because it was judged one of the outstanding papers and was circulated through the State Department and through the military.

I updated my paper later, as an admiral when I had a phib group. But I didn't publish, because I thought somewhere along the line, if I published what my findings were, that it would turn off some of our South and Latin American neighbors to me personally for my views. So I didn't do it on that basis.

I even passed it to Admiral Libby and said, "Hey, Lib, will you look at this. What do you think? Should I or shouldn't I? Do you think if I do publish it, would it impinge on maybe my assignability in some role?"[*]

Well, as it turned out, would you believe it or not, maybe I should have published it, because my next duty was director of Pan American affairs and naval missions in MAAG in OpNav. So you just wonder.

But back to where we were. As I say, then I found out after being here on the East Coast, with the full thought that I would be here for several years and knowing full well very little chance of going back to California, here I had to turn around and we start getting the *Coronado Journal* and looking at houses for sale. We bought a house, sight unseen, on the same street where we lived before in Coronado. So when the end of the school year came, we had a house to go to back in Coronado, and it cost us $10,000 more to go back to town.

Paul Stillwell: Who were some of your classmates there at the National War College?

---

[*] Vice Admiral Ruthven E. Libby, USN (Ret.), whose oral history is in the Naval Institute collection.

Admiral Erly: Oh, Ralph Cousins, Bob Farrington, and Jack Slaughter.* We were the culls of our 1937 class. We were the last of the Mohicans. We were probably very, very senior to be there.

Paul Stillwell: Well, Zumwalt was there about that era, wasn't he?

Admiral Erly: Oh, hell, Zumwalt had been there a year before, and he came back and addressed our class.† His paper had been selected as one of the best the previous year. His thesis was on the succession in the Russian hierarchy. I guess Mouza must have helped him with it; I don't know.‡

Paul Stillwell: One of the benefits that graduates of that school have raised is that you get to meet people in other services and in the State Department and so forth, and these contacts are useful later on. Was that the case for you?

Admiral Erly: Yes. Well, I'm just trying to remember. Yes, in one case. He ended up as chief of the MAAG in Spain, an Army fellow by the name of Clark, who was one of my classmates.

Then Robin Olds was another, and Robin came to me at the war college to discuss some personnel.§ He was taking over one of the air commands somewhere, which I didn't know because I didn't think that happened in the Navy side. He had access to the personal files of all the people in his area, and he saw some of his officers that I had signed off fitness reports on who had worked for me in the J-3 staff when Admiral Sylvester was head of the joint CPX.

The other one is Bob, one of the State Department types, but I would say that is not really a multiple effect. If I had gone perhaps to the Joint Staff or something more of a nature, that might have been more productive and I might have run across more of

---

* Captain Ralph W. Cousins, USN, later four-star admiral; Captain Robert F. Farrington, USN, who retired as a captain; Captain John S. Slaughter, who retired as a captain.
† Captain Elmo R. Zumwalt Jr., USN, future Chief of Naval Operations.
‡ Zumwalt's wife Mouza was a White Russian whom he had met in China at the end of World War II.
§ Colonel Robin Olds, USAF, was a fighter pilot. He had a total of 16 aerial victories from World War II and the Vietnam War. He eventually retired as a brigadier general.

them. Yes, I met one classmate over in Brussels, a State Department type, and I'm trying to remember his name. In recollection, I had more encounters with State Department personnel than with any of the other services.

Then I'm sure other people have had a lot more success, particularly if they'd gotten to the joint arena. And that's where I really thought I was going to end up, but I didn't. So mine was happenstance later on. When I joined the international arena with NATO, I don't believe there was a soul over there in Brussels.

So I could see where it could be beneficial and with the give and take which you have. Some of the graduates were from other services and did very, very well in promotions. We still exchange Christmas cards with some of my classmates and, good Lord, that's been what, almost 30 years ago.

Paul Stillwell: What impressions do you have of Admiral Cousins from that period?

Admiral Erly: Well, he's a Naval Academy classmate. I'm very fond of Ralph. He always has a seemingly relaxed approach to life, and evidently the ability to get along with people. He was, what, Zumwalt's Vice Chief, and survived that, and then went on to CinCLant, CinCLantFlt, and SACLant.* On retirement he ended up over there with Newport News Shipbuilding. He learns his lesson well. He's handsome, well set up, well preserved, takes good care of himself, and projects well in front of an audience. He does that well. He was evidently recognized in the civilian world as he was in the Navy. Excellence comes to the top.

Paul Stillwell: What do you recall about guest speakers that came to the college?

---

* Admiral Ralph W. Cousins, USN, served as Vice Chief of Naval Operations from 30 October 1970 to 1 September 1972. He later served as Supreme Allied Commander Atlantic, Commander in Chief Atlantic Command, and Commander in Chief Atlantic Fleet from 31 October 1972 to 30 May 1975.

Admiral Erly: I thought most of them were outstanding. The one that I really felt sorry for, and I'm still trying to remember what happened, but Krulak just didn't hit the right note this particular day.*

Paul Stillwell: Counterinsurgency.

Admiral Erly: Oh, yes, counterinsurgency.

Paul Stillwell: That's surprising, because he's a very effective speaker.

Admiral Erly: I'd heard him speak at other times and he'd been very good, very good. But in this incident he just didn't come across. The Air Force Chief of Staff also blew his presentation because of his vulgarity.† The Air Force types were embarrassed for him.

I think the biggest thing in one of my classes, I was able to have personal contact with Eisenhower.‡ After the presentations, some students got to have a roundtable discussion with the presenter. I was working on my thesis, and I asked him how he felt about what was taking place in Cuba and what should be done. He felt that the U.S. was derelict in not really taking action once Castro came out and said, "I'm a Communist." He said, "We should have moved. That should have triggered us to do something right then and there."

And, of course, in my thesis I quoted him, not as President Eisenhower, but I said, "A high authority's evaluation of—" I worked that in as a direct quote to the ex-President Eisenhower.

Overall, the caliber of the speakers was outstanding. Dean Acheson did a great job.§ The year was also good for reflective thought. I must admit, I burned a lot of midnight oil in composing. Then after you've written it, the horror is, and I'm sure you

---

* Major General Victor H. Krulak, USMC, served in the early 1960s as special assistant to the director of the Joint Staff; his area of concentration was counterinsurgency and special activities.
† General Curtis E. LeMay, USAF, was Air Force Chief of Staff from 30 June 1961 to 31 January 1965.
‡ Dwight D. Eisenhower served as President of the United States from 20 January 1953 to 20 January 1961. During World War II he had been Supreme Commander of the Allied Expeditionary Force for the invasion of Europe. In the early 1950s, as a five-star general, he served as Supreme Allied Commander in Europe when the military portion of the North Atlantic Treaty Organization (NATO) was established.
§ Dean G. Acheson served as Secretary of State from 21 January 1949 to 20 January 1953.

know it, is being an editor, because after you get this thing and then you count the verbiage and realize you're going to have to cut a quarter and all the rest, and how you cut it and still maintain your gist, because you have the pride of authorship and everything else that goes in it.

Paul Stillwell: I know the problem.

Admiral Erly: I bet.

Paul Stillwell: The National War College is, for most people, a very broadening experience. Did your subsequent career assignments enable you to take advantage of that broadening?

Admiral Erly: Oh, yes, I think it's obvious, not so much in the strict confines of the duties as the captain, as the flag officer, I think, yes. But immediately I went back to the old rut of amphibious warfare and the daily problems that one encounters therein. This thought of global strategy and international policy and all of this sort of goes down the drain when you're in there doing the daily nitty-gritty that goes to keep an amphibious force, or a destroyer force, or whatever force, just running smoothly and keeping people happy and motivated and this type of thing.

I would say, yes, as a NATO commander, and I would say the studies and grasp that I had when I went as an admiral as director of Pan American affairs. Again, my studies there and my previous tours in Venezuela and Cuba, plus I had all been sort of brought back to me in that year at the National War College. So, yes, I think it paid dividends, but not in my immediate job. If I hadn't made flag rank and had retired, I probably would never have used any of it.

Paul Stillwell: Well, the people who get picked for that, there is usually a good expectation that they will make flag rank, isn't there?

Admiral Erly: They have a pretty good batting order. Of the four from our class—Ralph Cousins, Bob Farrington, and Jack Slaughter—two of us made it and two didn't.

Paul Stillwell: Did your class have a field trip?

Admiral Erly: Yes. I selected Europe. But two weeks prior to going, I rolled an ankle, and it went into a cast. I had the cast ripped off the night we got on the plane to go. I'd sent Lois off to Europe and she was to meet me in Paris. She was visiting with Admiral and Mrs. Page Smith in London.* Dee Smith and her mother, Mrs. Roger, were Lois's guides in her introduction to London.

The all-night trip on the plane with the leg down and then hobbling around Paris on crutches was tiresome. We saw the Lido show the first night, and it made for a long day.† The next morning my leg was swollen from the ankle to the knee. I was bedbound. We finally were able to find the Air Force doctor who accompanied our group. He took one look and prescribed bed rest with the leg elevated. The rest of the group shoved off, and Lois and I were hopeful that the swelling would abate and we could join up with the group. After a week it was obvious that would not be the case. The embassy made arrangements for an air evacuation to the States.

Paul Stillwell: How had you managed to hurt your ankle?

Admiral Erly: I was living in River House, and I came charging out one morning. I stepped off the pavement into the street. The street in the area had not been completely paved. Thus the street level was some three inches below the pavement curbing. Boy, when that pain hits you right in the gut, you know you've been had. I was the duty driver in a driving squad. So I went ahead, after the pain passed, got in the car, picked up the first passenger, and asked him to take over. I propped my ankle up on the dashboard to

---
* Admiral Harold P. Smith, USN, served as Commander in Chief U.S. Naval Forces Eastern Atlantic and Mediterranean (CinCNELM), U.S. Commander Eastern Atlantic, and Commander in Chief U.S. Naval Forces Europe (CinCUSNavEur) from February 1960 to April 1963.
† Lido is a famous Paris cabaret.

trying to keep the swelling down. He went directly to the dispensary at Fort McNair.* A cast was applied, and I hobbled to classes and attended to chores at home on crutches. Lois had already departed for London. So I was on my own. I had the cast cut off the day we left. So I missed the field trip. I spent most of the tour flat on my back.

Paul Stillwell: Not as much fun as touring Europe.

Admiral Erly: Oh, no. No, no. And I had opted for the European segment rather than the South American, Asian, and Middle East. Let somebody else see them.

Paul Stillwell: Well, anything else about the National War College?

Admiral Erly: I think that—as you've tried to point out—the value could be, I would say, in the joint arena. When the chips are down, it takes the combined effort of all our entities to be successful

I think basically people come out of the War College with that sensing that it is a full effort, and not only of the military, but I'm also saying that you can't divorce the State Department out of this either or some of the other federal agencies, because it all becomes one concentrated U.S. effort, and it takes all of our assets to realize our goals. It just can't be one entity. You can't expect the State Department to do it, because they don't have any power at all unless you have the military might to be able to back up with what you're saying. So I think that message comes through loud and clear.

Paul Stillwell: Well, another thing, you've got an insight into the mind-set of the other services.

Admiral Erly: Oh, sure. And I think there's some change. Actually, we had the

---

* Fort Lesley J. McNair, located in southwest Washington, D.C., is the site of the National Defense University, which includes, among others, the National War College and the Industrial College of the Armed Forces.

ex-chief of the Air Force. I think it was General White.* We would get a group together and chat with him, and things of that nature were going on. Actually, I was just thinking myself of what we ended up with on our last day of the term. There was Army, Air Force, there was the Coast Guard in there, a Marine, and about two Navy, and this was our close little group that we were having our own little good-bye get-together, and this gives you an idea of the camaraderie that was built up.

Paul Stillwell: Sure.

Admiral Erly: The other thing that sort of brought you together was that somewhere along the phase you changed personnel. There were several segments of the course, and you changed your discussion groups.

That brings up something about our good friend Ned Beach.† I love Ned, and I think he's a very talented guy, but you get Ned, and he's like a damn pit bull once he gets going. He would tend to monopolize the deal, and I had to say to Ned, "For Christ's sake, Ned, why don't you shut up once in a while and let somebody else get their input in?" I guess that's just his disposition, but you had to put him—because I was in one group with him and he was just too much, and that prevents some of the others that you want to get in or draw out to get their input in. You don't want it all one-sided.

Paul Stillwell: That's just his way.

Admiral Erly: Yes, I guess.

Well, I'll tell you, the war college is well worth the time, energy, and money. When I say time, because you're taking people out of their normal pursuits. Again, at that point they were also pushing the graduate degree, but I never did get mine. I never finished my master's. I got my thesis approved and then the credits, but I never got to

---

* General Thomas D. White, USAF, served as Air Force Chief of Staff from 1 July 1957 to 30 June 1961.
† Captain Edward Latimer "Ned" Beach Jr., Naval Academy class of 1939, wrote a number of books, most notably the submarine novel *Run Silent, Run Deep*. He served as President Eisenhower's naval aide and later commanded the nuclear submarine *Triton* (SSRN-586) during her circumnavigation of the earth in 1960. For a profile of Beach, see *Naval History*, Summer 1988, pages 62-64.

finish the course, because, bang, back to the trenches. If I'd had ended up in the Joint Staff or the OpNav, I'm sure I would have finished off. I could have been able to do it in six months.

In this time frame, too, they were really—everybody was, I guess, sort of looking and saying—in fact, we had a couple of Air Force officers in the course that were already PhDs. So there you go. I thought that maybe perhaps an advanced degree was another step up the ladder for potential promotion, and I'm sure selection boards, in some cases, look at it that way.

To sum it up, I would hope that they would keep the National War College and sort of keep its perspective the way it has been. After National War College, again, back to the trenches as chief of staff to Amphibious Force Pacific Fleet. I went out and relieved Don Wulzen, who had been selected for rear admiral.[*] He and his wife, I think, were very close to Admiral Yeager and Mrs. Yeager, and that's why he ended up as chief of staff out there, I gathered from Don.

Paul Stillwell: What was Admiral Holmes like to work for?

Admiral Erly: I liked working for Eph, except his hours were, not as bad as Arleigh Burke's, but pretty bad. So it meant that he liked to have people for breakfast at the mess, and we did some business there. It could be, well, 7:00, 8:00 o'clock in the evening sometimes leaving.

He was a detailist to some degree. Great powers of concentration. I remember I saw him work in the early 1950s when I was in Phib Group 2, and he was the N-3 officer on PhibLant's staff.[†] I'd been over in the PhibLant flagship, and there was all this distraction going on, and Eph was oblivious to it. He could just concentrate on what he was doing. Great powers of concentration. And I'd say very good at written expression. He just loved to get that pencil in hand. He just couldn't resist it, just couldn't resist it. He just loved it. Boy, he just loved to work with words and edit. Not that he bounced a

---

[*] Captain Don W. Wulzen, USN.
[†] As a captain Holmes served from 1953 to 1955 as operations, plans, and training officer on the staff of Commander Amphibious Force Atlantic Fleet.

lot of stuff back. He also liked to be in on the operational side of things. He wanted an operation center, so I set one up for him.

Paul Stillwell: Where was that, at Coronado?

Admiral Erly: Yes, at PhibPac headquarters. I'm just trying to think of how much we got afloat with him. We would fly out and observe some of the phib group operations. I'd go with him. We'd go out and spend a day or two when one of the ops was going on. He really liked to get into the nitty-gritty of things, wanted to have his finger on everything. And he had a very good sensing, you know, what would fly and what wouldn't fly.

I'm trying to remember one issue that—I didn't have to do it with him very often, but I have gone in to say, "Hey, Admiral, you don't want to send this message."

Paul Stillwell: Then he'd listen to that?

Admiral Erly: Yes, yes, and then say, "Why?" and I'd say why. I'd say, "Look, all you're going to do is irritate people. It isn't going to do a damn bit of good. Why don't we just let this one ease off?"

He'd listen. I think he appreciated it.

Paul Stillwell: Well, you had the benefit of having done a lot of those things before that he didn't.

Admiral Erly: Maybe.

Paul Stillwell: How quickly did he pick up the amphibious warfare business?

Admiral Erly: Oh, well, because he had had, I'm trying to think, an APA or AKA, and then he was on PhibLant staff as the N-3.[*] And then I think his next sea job, he was over

---

[*] As a captain Holmes commanded the attack transport *Sanborn* (APA-193), August 1952 to July 1953.

on the big staff and then had a cruiser. I remember when he came to OpNav when he first got selected. What the hell were we doing with him? Admiral Burke brought him up. This was when I was 03A. He was doing some type of a study for the CNO. And he was good. He's got a very logical mind, and keen. He's no dummy. Very smart. And I thought he did very well as CinCLant, CinCLantFlt, and SACLant.[*] I ended up as his fleet inspector general later on. I guess we can come to that later. That's why I ended up down there in the fleet.

He put in the hours, I must admit. He was, I guess, a miniature Arleigh Burke or comparable. I'm sure that if Arleigh was there until 10:00 at night, I'll bet you Eph was over in OP-90, I'll bet he was there too. So that's the kind of guy who really put in the hours, and I think he sure rated what he got.

Paul Stillwell: What were some of the issues you dealt with in that job as chief of staff? Perhaps they weren't as dignified to call them as issues. What were the things you'd help with?

Admiral Erly: Well, let's see. We had Bucklew, who, if you ever saw Caniff's strip, Big Stoop was in it.[†] You ever know the character Big Stoop?

Paul Stillwell: No.

Admiral Erly: Well, Big Stoop is supposed to be a great big old Chinese, and he was in this cartoon thing. But Phil Bucklew came in, and he was over in China masquerading as a Chinese. He had very black eyes, and if you did this a little bit to his eyes, and a great big—he was an oversized fellow. He'd played professional football.[‡]

When I first got to know Phil, he was heading up our beach jumper unit on the East Coast there when I was in Phib Group 2, and then he was out here in—I forget in

---

[*] Admiral Holmes served as Supreme Allied Commander Atlantic, Commander in Chief Atlantic, and Commander in Chief Atlantic Fleet from 17 June 1967 to 30 September 1970.
[†] Commander Phil H. Bucklew, USNR. The oral history of Bucklew, who retired as a captain, is in the Naval Institute oral history collection. From 1924 to 1946, Milton Caniff drew a syndicated comic strip called "Terry and the Pirates," in which a 9-foot-tall Mongol nicknamed Big Stoop was a character.
[‡] Bucklew played for the Cleveland Rams in 1937 and 1938 and for the Columbus Bullies in 1940-41.

what job. But when I came back as chief of staff, he was the executive officer to the commander of the naval amphibious base, and a commander. Buck was a reserve, I think.

Paul Stillwell: Yes, he was.

Admiral Erly: Yes, Buck was a reserve. So this business of special warfare was coming to the fore. Now we were talking about setting up the sea, land, and air (SEALs) service, and we're talking about setting up special warfare as a separate entity from the UDT. Well, where do you think it was first set up? In PhibPac we pulled Bucklew, when he was selected for captain, to head it up.[*]

So this was really the start of the special warfare, and now you know what you've got in this day and age, that I'm talking. This was back in '62-'63. The path of promotion for people in that field wasn't there. They weren't recognized. But if you see what's taken place today from what was there then, you'll realize what strides they have made. All I've got to look down the Strand when I go down there to see the buildings and the money that is going into that program for the special warfare deal.[†] They even have an admiral in the area there of special warfare. Now it is a recognized line of promotion and the rest of it. I would say that we in PhibPac, that Holmes and myself recognized this, and we sponsored and got it started. That was one issue.

Paul Stillwell: Anything else you want to say about Bucklew specifically and the qualities he brought to that job?

Admiral Erly: Well, Buck brought a lot of experience to the job, and he was sort of like a big old, paternal figure to the group, so to speak. In fact, I went to a ceremony at the Special Warfare enclave, where they named a building for Buck.[*] His stroke has impaired him considerably. I think he recognizes people, but you should tell him who

---

[*] The Naval Operations Support Group Pacific was established in 1963, made up of underwater demolition teams, beach jumpers, boat support units, and SEALs.
[†] The Silver Strand, or simply The Strand, is a seven-mile-long beach near the naval amphibious base headquarters in Coronado, California.

you are. I don't know how he's doing now. I've lost sort of contact.† This was about two years, or three years ago even, I think, he was out there for that. If it hadn't been for the UDT SEAL people, I don't think his wife would have been able to really handle it. They brought him out on a plane and this. He's highly regarded in the community. I don't know whether I ever made that Navy News or not, but I made some comments for the camera for that Navy News thing about the inception of SEAL teams and special warfare: where it got started, how Buck was the real first skipper of it, and his contributions to it.

He had sort of a leavening manner. You had to keep some of his young tigers in line. They wanted to jump this way and that way. I would say he's a good team player. Let's put it this way. He was probably the man for the job at the time, and with his vast background, he also—beach jumper units, too, I think, are part of that special warfare outfit now, too, you see, and he had that background.

Paul Stillwell: Well, the time was right for him.

Admiral Erly: Oh, sure.

Paul Stillwell: This was what President Kennedy was emphasizing.

Admiral Erly: Yes. Well, I'm not so sure whether Kennedy had gone or not at that phase, when we set it up, because we hadn't been there long when Kennedy was assassinated. What was the date?

Paul Stillwell: November 1963.

Admiral Erly: Okay, and I got there in July, August '63. I went '62-'63 to the war college, right? That's right, I got there in June '63, and I'm sure we set this up later.

---

* In 1987 the Naval Special Warfare Center in Coronado was named for Bucklew.
† Captain Bucklew died 30 December 1992, two years after this interview.

Paul Stillwell: Well, I've certainly got the impression it flowed from Kennedy's initiatives.

Admiral Erly: Well, oh, yes, he was into the counterinsurgency concept. That's where Brute Krulak really made a name for himself in DoD, wasn't it?

What other big issues did we deal with? Let's see. The 20-knot LST was one we had to buy at this phase, and we strongly supported it, even though with qualms and whatnot of that unholy rig, as I say, that looked like a prehistoric monster.

We discussed that at great length and said, "Well, if this is the only way we can get 20 knots, we'd better go get it and do it and support it."

Paul Stillwell: Were you involved in the task of putting those horn things up on a regular LST?

Admiral Erly: Well, it was the only way you were going to get the bivalve configuration. You couldn't have the clamshell bow doors that were common up to then, and that was the point. You had to come out with the pointed bow. That meant you were going to be grounding out that much farther out and would need causeways. That meant you had to carry the caissons to make the causeway. The causeway sections were going to be a must on every landing. You weren't going to hit the beach otherwise, because nowhere were the gradients of the beach going to permit you to do that. So that was part of the one.

What other big deals did we have going at this time? Oh, my Lord, I remember one. Again, this business of what beaches do you beach on? Eph was in Honolulu. I forget why he was out there on, but I got this frantic call from him. We had a phibron out there conducting a landing on one of the islands, I forget which one. The TV cameras were covering the landings, and here it was worse than my debacle.

What had happened, they beached, and the gradient was such that they were up about like this with the ramp down. The surf came in and, whoosh, right back in the well of the boats and flooded them. It was obviously an improper beach survey. That beach never should have been selected for a landing.

Eph was screaming, "What's going on?"

I wanted to say, "Goddamn it, Eph, you're a lot closer to the scene of action than I am."

But then I had to get out a flash message to the phibron commander and say, "Get a signal right off, care of CinCPacFlt to the admiral who is there, and bring him up to date." That was all I could do. Why he didn't do that from the CinCPacFlt headquarters, I don't know.

Paul Stillwell: Was this during the period that you were gearing up the amphibious force to go to Vietnam?

Admiral Erly: Not really, and I'm trying to think also in Admiral Yeager's time frame, we had made ComPhibGruWestPac a rear admiral's billet, to be home-ported in Subic.[*] Champ Blouin was the first admiral to be assigned that billet.[†] He had quarters at Subic, and so you needed a flagship out there for that. I never knew Champ, but I sure got a message when it was announced that I was being chief of staff. I got a private from him that said, "Thank God we're getting somebody that knows something about amphibs."

Paul Stillwell: He later became ComPhibPac himself.[‡]

Admiral Erly: Yes, he did, that's right.

A little hazy. I remember back-loading and really having to go to town and out-loading for Vietnam, but that was under J. B. Colwell.

Paul Stillwell: What do you remember about the business of running a staff?

Admiral Erly: Oh, again, a part of that business, I think, on running that staff, I got there, and for some reason or other Eph wasn't getting things moving with the staff. He was evidently frustrated. He was just champing at the bit.

---

[*] ComPhibGruWestPac – Commander Amphibious Group Western Pacific.
[†] Rear Admiral Francis J. Blouin, USN, served as Commander Amphibious Group One, 1961-63
[‡] Vice Admiral Blouin served as Commander Amphibious Force Pacific Fleet from July 1966 to May 1968.

So one of my first moves, I had to call the staff together and say, "Hey, look, let's get one thing straight around here. Your boss is one Admiral Holmes, and goddamn it, when he wants something and if it's within our purview, we're damn well going to get it for him. Now, let's get with the program, or if you can't get with the program, just let me know, and we'll move you."

I also instituted brainstorming various problems in that staff, which sort of welded them together, and then we started having a Friday happy hour to get the old camaraderie rolling and this type of bit, and that helped. I think then things sort of got rolling, and the staff was producing, and Eph got happier. As I say, we got him an operations center and we did other things, and we set up in the special warfare, a lot of things that just hadn't been rolling started picking up, and we got them accomplished. Even the little newspaper that they wanted to put out for the wives and whatnot, we even got that thing going.

Another thing that Eph wanted, jeepers, we got it going. I'm trying to remember where I saw this chief bandmaster now, Les. He says, "Do you remember me? I used to be the drum major."

We would have the colors ceremony and have the band and the honor guard for evening colors, taking off pretty much of the ceremony that the Brits had. We would invite civilians over for the ceremony, and then Eph would have them for cocktails afterwards, and with the drum major and the whole bit. Those were some of the things that, I guess, were above and beyond what one would normally expect.

What else did we do? Oh, inspections, yes. He got out and inspected a lot of ships and let them know that he was interested. We also tried to get more of the staff with the concept, instead of just being paper pushers and sitting on our butts on the beach, is try to get a flagship and then take a working staff aboard ship and just keeping a cadre on the beach, to get them going that way.

Paul Stillwell: How often did you do that?

Admiral Erly: Whenever we had ships available, and then on the big exercise, where ComPhibPac would go as CATF, commander amphibious task force, of course we had ships for that. Then our Marine counterparts from Pendleton would embark. Also, under

Red Yeager, we had started having quarterly get-togethers with our Marine counterparts. Under Eph, we continued that mixing of the top Marine commanders and naval commanders in get-togethers.

Once the Marines would lay on something and demonstrate, "This is tank warfare or this is a maneuver so-and-so," then we'd come back and show them a facet of Navy bit and entertain them on the site. Then we'd have an educational part and then a fun and games part of dinner and maybe golf—morning with the educational part and the evening, afternoon and evening, recreational part. Like we might go up to Twentynine Palms for the Marine bit out in the desert, or we would have them down to the phib base to go through our tac trainer and this type of thing.* It was mutual and it was, again, to know your counterparts, which was a good move, good move. And that was continued.

Then, of course, you always had that civilian orientation thing, where you take a bunch of prominent civilians out.

Paul Stillwell: SecNav guests.

Admiral Erly: Well, it's more than SecNav guests and also SecDef guests.

Paul Stillwell: Oh, I see.

Admiral Erly: Yes. So we'd get the amphibs in on that. I'm trying to think of the operations that we had at sea.

Paul Stillwell: Well, Silver Lance came along during that period.†

Admiral Erly: Yeah, I'm thinking Silver Lance, but I'm trying to remember whether Eph

---

* Twentynine Palms is a desert and mountain area in southeast California. It is the site of the Marine Corps Air Ground Combat Center.
† Silver Lance, a major fleet exercise, took place off the coast of California from 23 February 1965 to 12 March of that year. It comprised more than 50 ships and 65,000 men—one of the largest-ever Navy-Marine Corps training exercise.

was in Silver Lance, or whether it was J. B. Colwell.* I think we ended up having to divert some shipping and end Silver Lance early. We sent some ships out to WestPac early on. I'm thinking that was Silver Lance. I think J. B. was the commander at that point. Eph was there for a little over a year. I was with him just about a year, and then he went to the First Fleet.†

Paul Stillwell: Silver Lance was in early '65.

Admiral Erly: So Eph went to take the fleet command, J. B. came aboard, and I stayed on as his chief of staff. There again, there's a difference between daylight and darkness between the two. J. B. had no strain at all. He'd come in my office at 3:00 o'clock every day and say, "Bob, you got anything?" and then he'd go. He really left me to run the shop.

Paul Stillwell: Which you didn't mind.

Admiral Erly: No, I didn't mind at all. That was just fine.

Paul Stillwell: It must have been a real feeling of relief at that point.

Admiral Erly: Well, you learn to pace and to accommodate what needs to be done. Then again, that didn't lessen my hours by a hell of a lot, but it gave me a little more. Maybe I could get out of there by 6:00 or 6:30. But J. B. used to leave around 3:00 every day. He was a great pleasure to work with.

We were anguished over that LHA concept. It all looked good on paper, but how many do you have? But then you think you've got all these eggs in one basket. As long as you can protect it, you're in great shape. We anguished over the fact that the loss of

---

* Vice Admiral John B. Colwell, USN, served as Commander Amphibious Force Pacific Fleet from January 1964 to May 1965.
† Vice Admiral Holmes served as Commander First Fleet from 25 January 1964 to 18 July 1964.

one LHA could imperil the success of the amphibious operator. Finally we went along with it, saying, "Well, weighing all the pros and cons, at least you're getting something."*

As I mentioned earlier, the LHA encompasses the LPH, LSD, all in one. Plus you had the AGC concept. A big plus for it, also, was the medical facilities. I'm just surprised. I don't know where the LHA is out there at the moment. But as you saw, they had to call in *Mercy* and the other one, *Comfort*.† They are both out now—and manned with medical personnel m at the expense of Bethesda and Oakland naval hospitals.‡

I think that appealed to us from our experience of what we had seen even with *Princeton*, which was a CVA converted to an LPH, remember, well on.§ We were quite taken with how well you could handle casualties, and they could be heloed to the ship. This was looking pretty good, is what we were saying, looming up coming with Vietnam and that possibility.

Paul Stillwell: Do you remember being involved in preparing the reactivated LSTs to go over to Vietnam?

Admiral Erly: Not, really, no. I must have had some part in it, but I'm real hazy on it. Did we take those? I'm trying to remember, did we take those out of reserve fleet? I guess we had to.

Paul Stillwell: Yes. There were some, I think, reactivated at Philadelphia. They wound up getting home-ported out in Guam in the mid-1960s.

---

* LHA is the designation of a type of amphibious assault ship. The first of the type, USS *Tarawa* (LHA-1), was commissioned 29 May 1976.
† USNS *Mercy* (T-AH-19) lead ship of a class of hospital ships operated by the Military Sealift Command, went into Navy service on 8 November 1986 after being converted from an oil tanker. Her sister ship, USNS *Comfort* (T-AH-20), went into Navy service on 1 December 1987.
‡ This interview took place during the Desert Shield buildup to the Gulf War of 1991.
§ USS *Princeton* (CV-37) was an *Essex*-class aircraft carrier, commissioned 18 November 1945. She had a standard displacement of 33,000 tons, was 888 feet long, 93 feet in the beam, and had an extreme width of 148 feet. Her top speed was 33 knots. She had 12 5-inch guns and could accommodate approximately 90 aircraft. Later in her career she served as an antisubmarine warfare carrier (CVS-37) and still later as an amphibious assault ship (LPH-5).

Admiral Erly: Okay, I know who did this. Eph Holmes was now back as 090.* Single-handedly he brought back the APDs, he brought back a lot of LSTs, he brought back the LSMRs. He wrote them in, and I guess had a free ticket of doing it as 090. See, he was now back as the major programmer, having left the fleet. Now he was back in OpNav, sitting up there, and he was the guy calling the shots. He'd just come from a fleet and he'd just come from the amphib force, and he had a pretty good grasp of what was needed, but we didn't have what he was getting worried about. You use your APDs at the line of departure as your control vessels for the waves going in, see. So he got those recommissioned, and we had another ship—it wasn't an LSMR, but it was a rocket boat. It's the only one of its kind, and he even got that recommissioned.

Paul Stillwell: Well, there was one called the *Carronade*.†

Admiral Erly: The *Carronade*? Yes, I think it was. This amphibious augmentation was made, to my knowledge, without input from the phib force commanders. If you ever would get Eph's oral history. I'm sure he told me he didn't have time to go to his two phib force commanders to get a feedback. It was that tight a deal, that he had to come up with proposed amphibious units to be reactivated.

Paul Stillwell: I don't know how effective the rocket ships were, but they certainly were spectacular to watch.‡

Admiral Erly: If you were on the receiving end, I don't know. No.

That is another amazing thing. I had a youngster on my staff that I'd had in PhibRon 5, and then he was on PhibPac staff with me, named Roy McCoy. He ended up

---

* Vice Admiral Ephraim P. Holmes, USN, served as Director of Navy Program Planning, OP-090, from July 1964 to June 1967.
† USS *Carronade* (IFS-1) was an inshore fire support ship, commissioned 25 May 1955 to provide fire support during amphibious operations. She was decommissioned and placed in reserve on 31 May 1960. She was recommissioned on 2 October 1965 for the Vietnam War. The ship displaced 1,500 tons, was 245 feet long, 38 feet in the beam, had a maximum draft of 11 feet, and a top speed of 15 knots. She was armed with one 5/-inch/38 gun, two twin 40-millimeter guns, and eight twin Mark 105 rocket launchers.
‡ The interviewer saw the LSMRs firing rockets into South Vietnam in the late 1960s while serving in another ship in the same squadron.

with *Carronade*.* He got that as a command. He was out there, and so he was a sort of senior LSMR guy. Roy is quite a salesman, and evidently he got some reporter from *Time* magazine and really gave him the works. This article came out, "McCoy's Navy," in *Time* magazine.†

At this point, I had left PhibPac. I was sitting back in Washington as director of Pan American affairs; I was OP-62. God, I got this call from Roy, who said he was in deep, but deep trouble. His immediate boss had seen this *Time* article and was going to crucify him. He said, "What do I do?"

I said, "Sit tight."

So I got a copy of the article and went down to Rear Admiral Hank Miller, who was Chinfo, and said, "Hey, Hank, isn't this great? Look. Look at the publicity the Navy's getting. Jeepers, that kid ought to get a message from CNO telling him, 'Well, done.'"‡ And I also said, "Info his boss."

Sure enough, that's what happened.

Paul Stillwell: That was one way to get him off the hook.

Admiral Erly: That got him off the hook. But I still couldn't get off the hook from PhibPac, because I got selected for admiral in May of that year, of '65, and then took Phib Group 3, so I still had another year to do with PhibPac. So I'm really racking up the years, am I not?

In that job, it fell to me early on to develop doctrine for riverine warfare. There was an area there below Saigon in the Rung Sat area believed to have a concentration of Viet Cong.§ CinCPacFlt requested an amphibious landing to rout out the Viet Cong. Don Wulzen, who was ComPhibGruWestPac, said it couldn't be done. So it was bounced to Brute Roeder, who was then ComPhibPac. He directed me to work out an

---

* Lieutenant Commander Roy E. McCoy, USN, commanded the inshore fire support ship *Carronade* (IFS-1) from 1965 to 1967.
† "South Vietnam: McCoy's Navy," *Time*, 5 August 1966.
‡ Rear Admiral Henry L. Miller, USN, served as the Navy's Chief of Information from April 1966 to October 1968. His oral history is in the Naval Institute collection.
§ The Rung Sat Special Zone, also known as "Forest of Assassins," was mangrove swamp area at the delta of the Saigon and Dong Nai rivers.

operation plan to effect the landing. I was ComPhibGru 3. The PhibPac staff was desirous of changing the phibgru designation into something more appropriately depicting its mission. One suggestion was Commander Patrol Assault Forces. I said, "No damn way am I going to known as ComPatAssFor." [Laughter]

I'm trying to remember what name we did come up with, but it wasn't one that was going to have that acronym.* But I pulled my staff together and we beat to general quarters. We came up with a general plan for the Rung Sat landing and also came up with the basic concepts of riverine warfare. Then I flew to Vietnam to watch the operation. Jack Westervelt was the phibron commander who was conducting the landing with the *Princeton* as his flagship.† It was real eerie sitting up there in a chopper and watching your mike boats disappear in the mangroves at the riverbanks. We landed and found a Viet Cong hospital and convalescent area. It was obvious that the Viet Cong had gotten the word. They'd long since evacuated. There wasn't a shot fired in anger in that landing.

Paul Stillwell: What other observations do you have from over there in Vietnam?

Admiral Erly: Well, when I flew down, my first stop was Don Wulzen's flagship, the *Mount McKinley*. Bill Robinson was the special forces adviser on Don's staff. I had known Bill since 1959. He had a UDT team and then floated up as a SEAL. He was out there with Wulzen, and they were trying to do some of the special warfare bit. He was evidently under quite a strain, because at this point I remember Bill had a nerve ailment going on.

I talked with him and then I talked with people on their staff of what was ongoing. Bill seemed to think, for the special warfare types, that they had a definite role of infiltration and whatnot to play out there. I also had some trepidation of what some of the special warfare groups were actually doing.

Paul Stillwell: In what sense did you have trepidation?

---

* His other title was Commander River/Coastal Warfare Group.
† Captain John D. Westervelt, USN.

Admiral Erly: In one sense, there had been a warrant officer in the special forces unit who had been assigned to the phib base after his Vietnam tour. He felt that some of the things that the SEALs were doing were cruel and inhumane. We couldn't get any substantiation on that. Both Eph and I tried to look at that, and the answer was not there.

Paul Stillwell: Do you mean this was in the training or in what was actually being done in Vietnam?

Admiral Erly: What was being done in Vietnam. Not shades of My Lai, but things that shouldn't have been.[*] But, again, I guess when you put somebody into the enemy area, anyone in that area is an enemy. That may have been part of it. That just flashed through my mind when I was out there. Bill was telling me that they were on an ambush line at night in the mangrove. They were counting noses and all of the sudden they had one more than they should've had. They did not nail the infiltrator. Where did he come from? Who? You never got the right answer because it sort of dissolved, but you never knew where you were or what you were to encounter.

Paul Stillwell: Spooky.

Admiral Erly: Yes, spooky, eerie.

The other was—I'm trying to remember the base I went to. We had a base down the way and I flew into it. Now why was I there? We had something. I went down to check it out and spent the day down there and then flew back.

My orders said I had to fly at least in a twin-engine plane. I was not allowed to be in anything less. We came back in a Beechcraft, and we landed at Tan Son Nhut.[†] The

---

[*] On 29 March 1971 a court-martial convicted Army First Lieutenant William L. Calley, Jr., of premeditated murder of 22 South Vietnamese as the result of his platoon's massacre of civilians in the village of My Lai on 16 March 1968. On 31 March Calley was sentenced to life imprisonment; on 20 August his sentence was reduced to 20 years. On 19 March 1974 he was paroled.
[†] Tan Son Nhut was the name of the U.S. Air Force base at Saigon, South Vietnam.

damn controller brought a P2V right in the stern of us and it almost cut us in two.* The P2V ran off the runway to keep from doing just that.

So I went into the terminal and called up the control tower. I said, "Hey, who's your controller?" They had a Vietnamese controller. So I just said, "Aw, the hell with it. But this is stupid. Something like that shouldn't happen."

I'm thinking on that trip that I got in to see the number-one foot-slogger in the Marines, General Walt.† He had that reputation, number-one grunt, was out there as a major general at this point. We got a briefing from the Marines in all this when I was there.

Paul Stillwell: Did you have any contact with Admiral Ward, ComNavForV?‡

Admiral Erly: Yes, I saw Bub. He was ensconced there. I got a briefing from him. Brute Roeder and I went out. I'm trying to remember when we got the briefing with Walt and with Bub Ward. I guess Roeder and I went out together, because I was chief of staff while he was back there sitting on the selection board, but as soon as he came back, I had Partee Crouch right there, and he was ready to take over as my relief as chief of staff.§

Not only did we get briefing by the Marines out there, and by Bub, and we also went to where they were putting the airstrip in, Cam Ranh Bay. This was part of Brute's indoctrination or re-education of the area, and mine too. So I went along as the phib group commander and he was PhibPac commander, and we covered the Far East—Okinawa and then Japan and Vietnam.

---

* The Lockheed P2V Neptune was a land-based patrol plane that first entered an operational squadron in March 1947. In 1962 the aircraft was redesignated the P-2.
† Lieutenant General Lewis W. Walt, USMC, was Commanding General, III Marine Amphibious Force, 1965-67.
‡ On 10 May 1965 Rear Admiral Norvell G. Ward, USN, became chief of the Naval Advisory Group Vietnam; in April 1966 he got the additional title of Commander U.S. Naval Forces Vietnam when that command was created. He fulfilled the two roles until relieved on 27 April 1967. His oral history is in the Naval Institute collection.
§ Captain Partee W. Crouch Jr., USN.

Paul Stillwell: Who was putting together the package of riverine craft, like the Swift boats and the armored vessels and PBRs?*

Admiral Erly: And the hovercraft. That fell basically on PhibPac. I rode them all, even as a phib group commander. Then we established a training center up north in the Mekong Delta. Wade Wells, who had been chief of staff to PhibTraPac, was designated as the officer in charge.† Wade went on up and did a lot of the training with them up in the delta, and then Wade later on was out there with the Army.

See, the Marines said no way did they want to get tied down in riverine warfare. The Army got into it basically by default. Wade was quartered basically with the Army. And in this time we had all types of concepts of even taking floats out there and then building up floats and putting structures on the floats in the river to make those sort of operating centers.

This backbone of the riverine forces was the PBRs; they had water-jet propulsion. Also, there were the Swift boats. The swift boats were for coastal interdiction rather than in riverine warfare since their propellers made them vulnerable in the riverine environment. The PBRs, with no propellers, were ideal. They could turn in their own length. And, in fact, if you weren't strapped in and you laid that thing over while going at a good speed, it would throw you right out of the boat. I personally rode all the riverine craft, the PBRs, the Swift boats, and the hovercraft, just to get a feel for them. That was something else.

Just when you can say what do you get from riverine warfare, and still I just wonder if some day, if we might find ourselves up in the Amazon or some other place down in South America—one never knows—just how much of that capability is still with

---

* The Mark I PCF (patrol craft fast), known as the Swift boat, was built by Sewart Seacraft of Berwick, Louisiana, adapted from the design of Gulf of Mexico oil rig boats. The PCF was 50 feet long, 13 1/2 feet in the beam, and drew 5 feet. It was armed with three .50-caliber machine guns, one 81-millimeter mortar, and had a top speed of 25 knots.
The Mark I river patrol boat (PBR) was built for use in Vietnamese waters by United Boat Builders of Bellingham, Washington. The PBR was 31 feet long, 11 feet in the beam, and drew 2 feet of water. It was armed with three .50-caliber machine guns, one 40-millimeter grenade launcher, and had a design speed of 25 knots.
† Captain Wade C. Wells, USN. See Wells's article, "The Riverine Force in Action," in *Naval Review 1969*, edited by Frank Uhlig (Annapolis: U.S. Naval Institute, 1969), pages 47-83.

us. But it might be a thought that someone should keep it alive. Of course, your biggest proponent of any of the small boats and the hydrofoils and all that was Bud.*

Paul Stillwell: Yes. Well, he did use the PCFs in the rivers.

Admiral Erly: The Swift boats?

Paul Stillwell: Yes.

Admiral Erly: How far—well, I would think you're too big a target, myself. And from maneuverability. Of course, they had more firepower.

Paul Stillwell: Yes.

Admiral Erly: Yes, that would be a plus.

Paul Stillwell: Did you do any of the regular things that an amphibious group commander does? Ride around in an AGC?

Admiral Erly: Oh, yes, I had an AGC—I had *Mount McKinley* and *Eldorado*. I don't believe I ever got back in *Paul Revere* as a phib group commander. I was in the AGCs at that point, and I had exercises with the Marines. I'm just trying to think of memorable things.

I think the biggest one that I thought was trying to come up with riverine warfare—trying to come up with doctrine for Marine-Navy concept. But later, as I say, the Marines didn't opt for that type of warfare at all, and the Army did, to get a piece of the action, I guess.

---

* Vice Admiral Elmo R. "Bud" Zumwalt Jr., USN, served as Commander Naval Forces Vietnam/Chief of Naval Advisory Group Vietnam from 30 September 1968 to 14 May 1970. His oral history is in the Naval Institute collection.

Paul Stillwell: Well, and also, the Marines were entrenched up north, in the I Corps.*

Admiral Erly: Yes, yes, yes. And this was another extension they felt they didn't need at that point, I'm sure.

Paul Stillwell: What was the difference for you personally between being a flag officer after having been a captain for so long? Added clout? Prestige?

Admiral Erly: I really felt that I had more—what you get as a phib group commander is just assigned for a specific exercise. As a phibron commander, you could sort of cultivate more the band of brothers concept as a captain than you could as an admiral, because your forces were only those assigned to you by ComPhibPac for specific exercises. That was the difference. I thought it was a hell of a lot more fun being a phibron commander than it was being a phib group commander, just for that reason.

Paul Stillwell: Were there any benefits?

Admiral Erly: None that I—oh, well, the paycheck was larger. [Laughter] I can't say that I saw any more benefits per se or the fun of going to sea and the pleasure of carrying out exercises, I felt, were better as a captain, as it turned out. Now, if I'd been out there as ComPhibGruWestPac, it might have been more of a challenge than it was here.

I'm trying to think if I made any great contributions as a phib group commander, other than, as I say, the start of the doctrine for riverine warfare. I felt that in that we did make an imprint.

Paul Stillwell: Where did you start? Did you start with a blank piece of paper? Did you go back to the Civil War or what?

---

* South Vietnam was divided into four corps tactical zones. The northernmost was I Corps (pronounced eye). It ran from the demilitarized zone on the north, past Danang, and down to Quang Ngai Province at its southern limit. Included in it were Hue, Khe Sanh, Quang Tri, and Chulai. Because of their initial landing at Danang in 1965, the U.S. Marines operated largely in I Corps throughout the war.

Admiral Erly: We started, I would say, basically with a blank piece of paper and then filled in from what reference we could get on small boat operations and riverine and, as you say, even go back to the Civil War and what was done to the deals and to look at some of the concepts. You didn't want to go back to the *Monitor* and *Merrimac*, but you had to look at what was happening in small boat operations and what was available in the boats that you were going to put in there.

As I was saying, the LCVPs certainly didn't meet it for the type of warfare where you're going to do patrol and interdiction and keeping the waterways open. Still good for transportation of troops if you had to, but again, if you get into some of those waterways, where you got a lot of weeds and things like that, if you've got a prop vessel, you're asking for trouble. That's why a water jet was so effective in that area. Also, the LCVPs were built of plywood, laminated wood. A shoulder-held rocket launcher would have put them out of business.

I have really nothing profound to add to that at the moment. Maybe if I sleep on it, next year I'll come up with something.

It is 4:00 o'clock.

Paul Stillwell: Convenient breaking place.

Admiral Erly: Yes, let's break it.

Interview Number 6 with Admiral Robert B. Erly, U.S. Navy (Retired)

Place: Admiral Erly's home in Coronado, California

Date: Wednesday, 1 April 1992

Paul Stillwell: Admiral, it's a delight to see you on this coast after our earlier visits at the Naval Academy in Annapolis. The last time we were talking about your time in command of the amphibious group. Then after that you went back to Washington. Could you pick it up at that point, please.

Admiral Erly: Fine. I was just trying to sit here and thinking if we'd covered, really, I think the big highlights of the amphibious group, and I hope that I got it on the other tape. If I don't, for a little bit of levity, I think it might be an example of what our acronyms can get us in trouble with.

As a phib group commander, some of the people in PhibPac staff came up with the thought that, with the surface craft that we were having, particularly being developed for riverine warfare and whatnot, maybe that command should be known as Commander Patrol and Assault Force. I reared back and said, "No way am I going to be ComPatAssFor." [Laughter] So that did not come to pass.

Paul Stillwell: Well, that's similar to a situation Admiral Richardson told me a couple of days ago.* When NATO headquarters were being established over in Europe in the early '50s, they were trying to get an acronym similar to SHAEF, which was the Supreme Headquarters Allied Expeditionary Force, and one of the losing nominees was Supreme Headquarters International Team. [Laughter]

Well, back to Washington.

Admiral Erly: Well, back to Washington, where I became director of Pan American

---
* See the Naval Institute oral history of Vice Admiral David C. Richardson, USN (Ret.).

affairs and naval missions and MAAGs.* It was OP-63.

Paul Stillwell: How does one get diverted into that specialized a job?

Admiral Erly: Well, this was the point where I was paying my dues for having gone on a naval mission to Venezuela at the end of World War II in order to get out of the hurly-burly of the postwar shakedown. I had been a member of the first naval mission to Cuba in 1942. I think BuPers, in its infinite wisdom, took a look and said, "Okay, he's qualified."

However, the same mission background had led to a set of orders to Panama as commandant, with additional duty on General Porter's Southern Command staff.† General Porter decided he wanted a more senior admiral. Thank goodness, he saved me, because I didn't want that one.

Paul Stillwell: Why not?

Admiral Erly: I really felt that it would be out of the mainstream, and if I was going to continue to have a career and keep going, even as a flag officer, it wouldn't be sitting down there under a four-star Army general.

Paul Stillwell: So being in OpNav would be helpful?

Admiral Erly: Of the two, as it turned out, I was much happier being in OpNav. Again, that was the center of everything that was going on. In Panama you would certainly be isolated.

Since General Porter wanted a more senior person down there, he got Ralph Smith out of the class of '30, '31, '32, somewhere in there. I think before it was all over he'd wished he had gotten me, but we won't go into that.

---

* MAAG – military assistance advisory group.
† General Robert W. Porter Jr., USA, served as Commander in Chief, U.S. Southern Command, with headquarters in Panama, from February 1965 to February 1969.

Paul Stillwell: Did you have a facility in Spanish language?

Admiral Erly: Well, remember, I had four years of Spanish at the Naval Academy. I wasn't too sharp in it, but I continued the study through the years, and that's one reason I ended up in Cuba and got pulled off of the *Frazier* off Guadalcanal to go set up that first naval mission in Cuba. So my tour with the Cuban Navy really got my Spanish polished up to the point to where I started dreaming in Spanish.

Paul Stillwell: That's a sure tip-off.

Admiral Erly: Yes. So I did have the facility of understanding and speaking and being understood, even though I was never what you would say fluent in my pronunciation. I was always a gringo, which isn't all that bad, either.

Paul Stillwell: Why do you say that?

Admiral Erly: Well, I have found that U.S. officers with Spanish surnames and speaking Spanish got less attention than my gringo accent.

Paul Stillwell: Because people were making an extra effort to understand?

Admiral Erly: Well, no, just the other way. People would think, "Well, gee, this guy is speaking our language and so forth, and we're communicating. Isn't it great that he is really trying?" Whereas they expected the Spanish surname officer to be fluent.

So I think you got more recognition by not being superlative. Well, I couldn't be if I wanted to be, because I still elide even over English words, so what am I going to do with the other, either Spanish or Portuguese?

So I had a good language knowledge background. I can't think of anyone else who should have had the job in OpNav, although I didn't really want it. I would have much more preferred to be in OP-61, International Relations, something more dynamic than what I had to do. However, on reporting there, I started making my courtesy calls. I found that I was the senior U.S. naval delegate to the Inter-American Defense Board. That was one hat. I was also the senior U.S. member of the Brazilian, Mexican, and Argentine naval commissions. I was also the senior naval delegate to the Joint Board of Defense, U.S. and Canada. Therefore, I was required to attend all of these various meetings.

One of them, I say particularly with the Canadians, we had Ambassador Matthews who was the head of our team.* See, we had the State Department in the lead when we met with the Canadians. It got to be a little bit of a rat race trying to cover all the areas. Perhaps the two we spent the most time on were the Joint Board of Defense, U.S. and Canada and the Inter-American Defense Board. The latter met on a monthly basis at the OAS headquarters on 16th Street in Washington.† Vice Admiral Austin was the head of this board.‡

Come to think of it, when I had written my paper at the National War College, I had suggested that the Organization of American States should be strengthened in order to be effective. I had made recommendations for changes in the OAS charter and things of that nature.

I reported to Andy Jackson, who was OP-06.§ He had accepted me for the OP-63 billet and warmly welcomed me aboard. My predecessor had retired, having failed to survive the two-star retention board. So the billet had been vacant for a month or so. Then Wally Wendt relieved Jackson.** So I served under those two there.

Paul Stillwell: I'd be interested in your observations on both of those as leaders of the division.

Admiral Erly: Well, of course, Andy was the brainier of the two. I liked them both; let's put it that way. But Andy was sort of like a bubbly little cheerleader, Wally more

---

* H. Freeman Matthews, Chairman of the Permanent Joint Defense Board, Canada and the United States.
† OAS – Organization of American States.
‡ Vice Admiral Bernard L. Austin, USN. The oral history of Austin is in the Naval Institute collection.
§ Vice Admiral Andrew M. Jackson, Jr., USN, served as Deputy Chief of Naval Operations (Plans and Policy) from 13 July 1964 to 17 April 1967. His oral history is in the Naval Institute collection.
** Vice Admiral Waldemar F. A. Wendt, USN, served as Deputy Chief of Naval Operations (Plans and Policy) from April 1967 to June 1968.

reserved, but I thought both effective leaders in their own way.

Paul Stillwell: Wendt went on to four stars eventually.

Admiral Erly: Yes, Wally did. Andy, of course, had his three there and didn't get his fourth. His swan song was when he relieved Junior McCain as our ambassador to the United Nations.[*]

I've just been flipping through some fitness reports, signed by both of them. I'm trying to think of why he didn't get his fourth star. I know when Wally Wendt got his fourth star, the deputy in CinCLant—his name may come back to me—submitted his resignation because he felt he should have gotten those four stars before Wally did.

Paul Stillwell: Ashworth?[†]

Admiral Erly: Yes, Ashworth. You told me you had interviewed him. But that's what happened.

Paul Stillwell: Well, there's nothing shabby about finishing with three, either.

Admiral Erly: No, no.

Paul Stillwell: How did Canada get lumped in with the Latin American nations in this setup?

Admiral Erly: Let's clarify that. This was a joint U.S.-Canada board, period. That was a separate deal that I was lumped into. They were not lumped into the others. Let's see, I had myself and one commander. There were two Army types, two Air Force types, and the State Department outnumbered us. We had about four State Department. And that was matched by the Canadians.

---

[*] Vice Admiral John S. McCain Jr., USN.
[†] Vice Admiral Frederick L. Ashworth, USN, whose oral history is in the Naval Institute collection.

Paul Stillwell: What do you remember about your dealing with the State Department people?

Admiral Erly: It was fine. I had no problems with them at all. I'm trying to think, in all the times, whether we had any needy or meaty subjects. The U.S.-Canada board met about four times a year, as I recall. One time they would host, the next time we would host. They would host it in, say, the spring and summer, and we would host it in the winter months, basically, so they could get out of snowbound Canada. We had agendas. Our leader, of course, was Ambassador Matthews, and then one of their ex-Prime Ministers was their lead guy. So I would say that the military really was the backup for the State Department, backing up the civilians on such things as treaties and overflights. We had some military bases in Canada, this type of thing, that had to be ironed out.

Paul Stillwell: Could you draw any general conclusions on different ways that State Department people and military people would approach problems?

Admiral Erly: From that group, I think everything meshed nicely, so for their training, our training, and things that went, I never sensed any discord, because we worked together when we were there and we played together. They all had to put on their pants the same way we do. I didn't see any great difference in the caliber of the people in the State Department and what we had in the military. It just turned out we meshed well, and we were a good team.

Paul Stillwell: How pragmatic an approach did the State people take?

Admiral Erly: I'd say very much so.

Paul Stillwell: Do you remember any specific examples?

Admiral Erly: No. Maybe later, but at the moment, I am dredging this up now from almost 30 years ago.

Paul Stillwell: The United States went into the Dominican Republic in '65.* Was that one of the issues you dealt with?

Admiral Erly: Well, I didn't get back there until '66. Whether that raised any hackles in OpNav, I don't remember. But once you've said that, that was President Johnson, and as I think I told you before, on my paper that I wrote on the Monroe Doctrine, Rio Pact, U.S.-Cuban relations, I said in similar situations we should boom, boom, boom, boom, boom, do this and that, and this is what the President did and caught a lot of flak from the press.

He is dead now, but Jim Dare, who was a captain at this point, he was the phibron commander down there on the bitter end of that.† Jim and I had talked somewhat about what had taken place when he was there.

We did try to get the OAS involved, and we did try to get some of the members of the OAS to contribute forces. This was one of the things that I recommended: "Let's don't do it all unilaterally." Basically, what I was recommending then is what you saw in Desert Storm as the operation of an international coalition. So I'm making a comparison, using a worldwide versus an area organization, but basically doing the same thing, using that as a shield, if you would, or foil to cover us.

Paul Stillwell: Well, and more specifically—

Admiral Erly: Well, particularly in the OAS, trying to guard against this damn business that we are Yankee imperialists. If we could get all of the members of the Organization of American States participating, that blunts the criticism, and that was one of my big recommendations.

---

* On 28 April 1965 President Lyndon Johnson dispatched a 400-man expeditionary brigade to the Dominican Republic to protect the lives and property of American citizens caught in a military revolt in that nation. By 29 April, 1,600 Marines had landed, and by 7 May 6,000 Marines were ashore and another 2,000 offshore. They were followed by Army troops, bringing the U.S. combat presence by 11 May to more than 11,000 troops. Navy ships evacuated more than 4,300 civilians during the operation.
† Captain James A. Dare, USN.

Paul Stillwell: Well, did you see any lingering unhappiness when you came in after that Dominican operation?

Admiral Erly: No, I didn't get that at all, because part of my other job was to be the sea daddy to all South and Latin American attachés, so to speak. And we had what? We had the joint U.S. and Argentine board and also a Chilean one.

Paul Stillwell: Please describe that sea daddy role and how it worked.

Admiral Erly: Well, you sort of looked after them. Through the MAAG side of the house, military assistance, whatnot and purchases also had to come through my office in ONI. So you can see that I sort of felt—and it was turned over to me as such—that I was to be sort of the sponsor of these people. I was the one that laid on the big receptions. If there was a visiting CNO or minister of defense from one of these countries, it wasn't ONI, it was OP-63 that planned these things, set them up, sent out the invitations, did the whole schmear.

As you can see, the job was not mundane, and you were, again, like a juggler. You had the various commissions that you served on and the other things. You had your day-to-day requirements in OpNav. You had the area responsibility of the MAAG people in country. To wit, in Guatemala, when our Navy MAAG guy was assassinated, I wanted somebody in there, boom, right now. We were not going to be scared. I immediately got a volunteer into Guatemala as a replacement. I mean, things like these were going on.

Paul Stillwell: Attachés have that intelligence collateral duty or main duty as part of the reason they're there. Was there an interchange between those people and you on that? Did you give them briefings? Did they give you briefings?

Admiral Erly: No, no, no, no. Our MAAG people at that point did not have diplomatic passports. The intelligence people, the ONI, the attaché people, had diplomatic passports. That was the difference. You went with a special passport. You didn't have the carte blanche of the others, particularly when I was there. This was changed later.

I'm trying to remember when it was changed. General Porter, who was CinCSouth based in Panama, was trying to get, and pretty well succeeded, in doing away with naval missions per se and setting up MAAGs.

Paul Stillwell: What was the thinking behind that?

Admiral Erly: Well, he wanted to have control, because you had a contract as a member of the naval mission. You had a contract with the Venezuelan government, like when I went and the Venezuelan government paid me the extra stipend of, I think, about $190.00 a month. I was paid by the Venezuelan government; whereas the attachés were not. They had diplomatic passports.

Those had been a separate, I guess you'd say, a small treaty or pact that was set up when you had a naval mission or an Army mission, and it was separate and distinct from the attaché. As we all know, his primary deal there is to be gathering intelligence. The other way, if you're going to be effective in the military assistance group, you're not so much gathering intelligence as you are in trying to impart to them aspects of military science. You try to help them with their hardware, with their training, with their education, this type of thing. Although the attaché, at times, naturally, if you felt you had something that would help him, yes. But you tried to stay away from that, because you really didn't want to jeopardize, let's say, the image of the mission people as intelligence gatherers, which you were not. You were there basically on a training mission, and that was to be understood.

Paul Stillwell: Well, all those foreign attachés in Washington, since we have such an open society, wouldn't have too much trouble getting information.

Admiral Erly: I don't think any of them dug too deep for that. Some of those attachés and even some of the delegates to the Inter-American Defense Board, were really in exile. They could have been a little bit of a problem to the people in power in their various countries; they were stashed away safely out of country so they couldn't be fomenting revolutions.

Paul Stillwell: Well, there are worse places to be exiled.

Admiral Erly: Oh, yes, yes.

Paul Stillwell: We had provided leftover light cruisers to several of those South American countries in the early '50s. Did you have other hardware programs during your time?

Admiral Erly: Oh, yes, yes. Let's see, I tried to suck Argentina into some destroyers if we could have gotten them on the line in Vietnam.

Paul Stillwell: Now, why do you wink when you say that?

Admiral Erly: Well, that's the same thing we did for Korea. We were trying to get other nations involved in order to say that this was more than just a U.S. power strategy; that's all. We were in the fight against Communism. We would hope others would join in. That didn't fly. The Argentines were pretty hardheaded people from what I saw in some things.

Paul Stillwell: Well, and it would be hard to persuade them that it was in their national interest to support that kind of thing.

Admiral Erly: Oh, sure. But you've got to remember, in Korea, Ecuador had a frigate out there.

Paul Stillwell: Symbolic, at best.

Admiral Erly: Oh, sure. Sure. Also, the South Koreans, we'd given them some small escort ships. In fact, I had to operate with one when I was providing an ASW screen for a cruiser. You can be assured we kept a careful watch on him during any course changes and screen reorientation. They were out there, and when you had them out there, and if you had them anywhere near the screen, in the screen, when you were out with a cruiser or whatnot, you really tried to keep them off to one side.

Paul Stillwell: So maybe you weren't recruiting too energetically there for Vietnam.

Admiral Erly: Oh, it wasn't so much that. That came out of OP-61; 06 thought we might when we were looking at ways to get some other representation.

Paul Stillwell: What other kinds of issues came up in your job in your dealing with these foreign nations?

Admiral Erly: I'm trying to remember—particularly with Argentina, we were negotiating with something, and they got a little exasperated because it was going so slowly. I remember they sent a blistering message to the CNO. And then Dave McDonald called me up and said, "What the hell's going on here?"[*]

I don't remember all the machinations, but I was able to explain enough so he said, "Oh, well, we'll let it go."

Paul Stillwell: He had much bigger issues to deal with at that point.

Admiral Erly: Oh, yes. Oh, yes, yes, yes. Although, I must say that whenever we in OP-63 staged something, he and Mrs. McDonald would always appear and enjoy themselves.

Paul Stillwell: Staged what, like a party?

Admiral Erly: Yes. A lot of times we would have it over at Fort McNair or other places, even in the State Department building in Washington. Also, sort of under our aegis fell SoLant—the U.S. South Atlantic Force. Oh, and that was something else. Back to

---

[*] Admiral David L. McDonald, USN, served as Chief of Naval Operations from 1 August 1963 to 1 August 1967. His oral history is in the Naval Institute collection.

General Porter and going back to why he didn't want a junior admiral down there. He wanted an admiral down there, senior to ComSoLant. Now, you know the Southern Atlantic Command and what it does. In that time frame, Van Arsdall, out of USNA '34, was the commander.*

Paul Stillwell: It's goodwill force, mostly.

Admiral Erly: A goodwill force, and it goes south on a yearly basis to hold naval exercises as they go by each country.

Paul Stillwell: UNITAS.

Admiral Erly: Exactly.

Paul Stillwell: So he wanted a little leverage there?

Admiral Erly: Yes. He wanted the leverage more so his guy would be senior, and so he would have more impact as CinC of the Southern Command. He wanted Southern Command to have real, real control. He was a nice gent. I went through there and got to know them. We called him—on the side he was Mr. Peepers.†

Paul Stillwell: There was an old TV character by that name.

Admiral Erly: Yes. But he was really trying to strengthen—and he was the one who was really trying to do away with the naval missions, as they were not under his command. He wanted them all to be MAAGs, because MAAGs came under the Southern Command. The Navy commander down there, his Navy delegate, who was also commander of the

---

* Rear Admiral C. J. Van Arsdall, Jr., USN, served as Commander U.S. South Atlantic Force from March 1966 to March 1967.
† With his glasses, General Porter bore a passing resemblance to Wally Cox, the actor who played the title character in "Mr. Peepers." The program played in the United States from 1952 to 1955.

Navy base or Panama Canal, Com 15.* Com 15 was double-hatted on his staff. He wanted him, also, to be senior to SoLant, so when they came through with seniority it would be—

Paul Stillwell: Well, there are two interpretations you can put on that. One is that he was very much interested in promoting jointness and inter-their service cooperation, and the other is that he was an empire builder.

Admiral Erly: Yes. But then the question you almost would think, why wouldn't you leave something that had been in place for some 50, 60, 70 years or even more? I'm trying to remember how many years the naval mission in Brazil had been there.† I think it was one of the first we ever had. Why would he want to do away with that? Could it be empire building? Possibly. Or control. Or maybe he felt it was time for a change. Maybe he felt it would be more efficient. But the naval missions, you see, didn't report to him. They reported to OpNav. So he felt that he didn't really have the control that he wanted.

That's the way I see this business of seniority. Why was that so important? Because I don't think that seniority among rear admirals or vice admirals means that much. Not to me. Obviously it did to him. He was looking to make sure that his control would be extended.

Paul Stillwell: Do you recall any specific incidents about dealings with the South Atlantic Force?

Admiral Erly: Oh, with SoLant we had no problem. We always had them—I had to always slip them money for entertainment. There was a fund that I had of about $50,000, and so I'd allocate some to SoLant. They would stock up on presentos and things of that nature and also to be able to reciprocate on some of the things and parties that were held in connection with their visits to the various ports of call.

---

* Com 15 – Commandant of the 15th Naval District.
† Rear Admiral Carl T. Vogelgesang, USN, established the U.S. naval mission to Brazil in 1922.

Paul Stillwell: Hospitality.

Admiral Erly: Sure. Fritz Harlfinger was SoLant.[*]

Paul Stillwell: Oh, I see.

Admiral Erly: In my memory it was Van Arsdall first, and then he was followed by Fritz. Oh, and Fritz was relieved by Jim Dare.[†] I think that they all made a good impact. I think Fritz made a great impact when he was SoLant, because he figured it out. He put on his sword and he put on all of his medals and formally called on the San Juan mayor, who was a lady. She was really impressed, and Fritz enjoyed top billing thereafter.

Paul Stillwell: He tends to take over situations he gets involved in.

Admiral Erly: Yes. Well, I told you that one about Mendel Rivers, didn't I?[‡]

Paul Stillwell: Well, I don't know if it's the same story. I heard about Harlfinger escorting Rivers over in Italy.

Admiral Erly: Well, evidently Bill Wylie was the escort, and he's a real strait-laced guy.[§] It was Paris, of all places.

Paul Stillwell: Well, then this must be another story.

Admiral Erly: Well, now, it was in Paris and Mendel really got out of line and was grabbing things he shouldn't have and a few others. Bill got so exasperated with him, he

---

[*] Rear Admiral Frederick J. Harlfinger, USN, served as Commander U.S. South Atlantic Force March 1967 to July 1968.
[†] Rear Admiral James A. Dare, USN, was ComSoLant from July 1968 to February 1970.
[‡] L. Mendel Rivers (Democrat, South Carolina) served in the U.S. House of Representatives from 1940 until his death in 1970. He was chairman of the House Armed Services Committee from 1965 until his death and was credited with getting a great deal of military money funneled into his district in Charleston.
[§] Captain Joseph C. Wylie, USN. The oral history of Wylie, who retired as a rear admiral, is in the Naval Institute collection.

locked him in his room, wouldn't let him out, and sent a message in, "I'm not his escort anymore. Send me a relief. Get me out of here."

They sent Fritz over, and Fritz picked it up and went on. As I told you, when they went into Italy, Fritz had some contacts, so he was the one who got hold of this Italian guy and they got him an Italian bimbo, and that kept Mendel quiet.

Paul Stillwell: I heard it from the guy who was the U.S. shore patrol officer in Italy.[*]

Admiral Erly: Oh.

Paul Stillwell: So there's confirmation. It was the same visit, apparently.

Admiral Erly: Yes. But it started in Paris, see.

Paul Stillwell: I hadn't heard that part of it.

Admiral Erly: I remember Jim Dare going down to take over SoLant, and he knew that I'd had some dealings. I was then the Atlantic Fleet inspector general. This was around '68 that Jim was doing this.

I just made a tape for him, and the basic things I said were, "When you work with these people, be straight, above board, to the point. If you don't know, say so. Don't ever try to shade it. Call it straight, and you'll have no problems."

This is one of the things I found early on in my working with those people, and that's the way I've always worked. I said, "Don't try to be flimsy or phony, because they spot it in the instant because a lot of them are. You've got to be straight arrow all the way."

I think a lot of my ability to get along with them was just that. It was straight from the shoulder every time, and I felt that that helped relationships. Again, as I say, that business of you don't have to be superlative in the language. You've got to be

---

[*] See the Naval Institute oral history of Captain Alex A. Kerr, USN (Ret.).

outgoing, you've got to be friendly, considerate. Sure, just like you would be to anyone else.

Paul Stillwell: Right.

Admiral Erly: Sure. But even more so on that.

Paul Stillwell: And sincere.

Admiral Erly: Yes, yes.

Paul Stillwell: Anything else about that job to put on the record?

Admiral Erly: Well, I think one thing happened in the job that I ended up acting as CNO when we had those command post exercises with scenarios of nuclear exchange. We'd deploy to the mountain, and I'd end up acting as CNO. I was also airlifted to the *Wright*, which was the presidential command ship.*

At the end of that one, I sat down and wrote. I said, "This is all just well and good, but it seems to me that, if you're going to play these exercises and play them right, you should send those officers to do it that are going to be doing it." In other words, it shouldn't have been OP-63; it probably should have been 06 himself or some of the rest of them, and even the CNO. The Joint Chiefs would show for a short time and then leave it to the juniors to play out the exercise of a nuclear exchange. They ought to get them for more, because you're playing all these scenarios—what's going to happen, these are the estimates, and you've got all the services represented there, and you pull in people that aren't going to have anything to do with it.

Paul Stillwell: But you were really just testing procedures, weren't you?

---

* USS *Wright* (CVL-49) was originally commissioned in 1947 as a light aircraft carrier. In 1962, after a period in reserve, she was reclassified as a command ship, CC-2, and underwent conversation at the Puget Sound Naval Shipyard. She was recommissioned in her new role on 11 May 1963.

Admiral Erly: Well, more than that, because in some of it, when you start testing procedures and things develop, you are changing; you are setting precedent, whether you know it or not. You're even coming up with recommendations of the use of atomic weapons. I remember making a pitch there, recommending that we keep any nuclear fallout from South and Latin America. The rationale was that they would be our last refuge and things of this nature.

Paul Stillwell: Were these just U.S. CPXs, or were these other nations involved?

Admiral Erly: No other nations. This was U.S. solely.

Paul Stillwell: What was the relationship or dealing with Cuba during this period you were in OP-63?

Admiral Erly: Zilch.

Paul Stillwell: Earlier in the '60s, there had been all sorts of schemes about getting people back in there. Was that just being ignored by your time?

Admiral Erly: They were not a member of the Inter-American Defense Board. They were out of the OAS. Okay? While I was on the board, there wasn't any question of their ever being readmitted. If there was anything in the way of the dirty tricks department and whatnot, I was not cut in, and really didn't want to be.

Paul Stillwell: I think that was much more emphasized during the Kennedy administration.*

Admiral Erly: Oh, well.

---

* John F. Kennedy served as President of the United States from 20 January 1961 until he was assassinated on 22 November 1963.

Paul Stillwell: And Johnson had Vietnam to focus on by that point.

Admiral Erly: Yes. I think it was pretty much on the back burner.

Paul Stillwell: Was there any concern about Soviet activity either in Cuba or Latin America?

Admiral Erly: Oh, definitely. That was always a bugaboo. It wasn't so much trying to defend the Monroe Doctrine. It was trying to keep the Soviets and Cuba from spreading Communist influence throughout the Southern Hemisphere. That was always a concern. And, as you well saw, it was a concern to such a degree that you got Ollie North and his book and a few other things and the big hearings that fell out from it.[*]

As you can see, the country was—and I think is still—preoccupied with some of the cease-fires and whatnot. Of course, with what's happening in the OAS at the moment, that's not it. I don't know, I guess Castro is so beleaguered with lack of resources now that he is not a menace in the hemisphere, because to be a menace you've got to have resources, and you've got to have dough to be able to push it.[†] You've got to be able to get arms; you've got to be able to do other things to foment revolution or what have you.

Paul Stillwell: Well, the Soviets recognized him for the drain that he was.

Admiral Erly: Oh, yes.

Paul Stillwell: Cuba did provide some basing or at least support facilities for Soviet ships. Was that during the period you were in that job?

---

[*] Lieutenant Colonel Oliver L. North, USMC, a 1968 graduate of the Naval Academy, served on the staff of the National Security Council during the Reagan Administration. In the mid-1980s he had a key role in the selling of arms to Iran in order to raise money for Nicaraguan Contras.

[†] Fidel Castro took power in Cuba in 1959 and held it for many years. On 24 February 2008 he was replaced as President by his brother Raul and as First Secretary of the Communist Party of Cuba on 19 April 2011 by his brother.

Admiral Erly: Oh, I think the Soviets built quite a base in Cienfuegos, and it was, if you will recall—what year was *Pueblo*?*

Paul Stillwell: January 1968.

Admiral Erly: Well, we were running patrols off Cuba, and we wanted to be damn sure there wasn't going to be another *Pueblo* in that instance. So there were measures—strong measures—set up to make sure that wouldn't happen. I think it was more like an APD, a hell of a lot better ship than what *Pueblo* was. That was a concern. I don't think we knew at this time frame the amount of Russian troops that were there, and I think we found that out several years ago. We knew that Russian submarines were there.

Paul Stillwell: Right.

Admiral Erly: And you've got to realize, that's only roughly 90 miles from Key West, right across. Come to think of it, we were more interested when I went to my new job down in CinCLant/CinCLantFlt, down from sort of where I was sitting up there in OpNav as OP-63. I was just thinking, of course, I'd go every morning when we'd have the morning briefs.

Paul Stillwell: Are you ready to move on to that new job from OP-63?

Admiral Erly: Well, yes, I think we ought to move it. I'm just thinking if I have any other parting shots of what took place—you know, a great moment. Well, there was just getting the job done and sitting on those committees. Oh, yes, there were ship turnovers to friendly allies. Congress at times was looking with jaundiced eye at destroyer turnovers, but they didn't blink at a destroyer escort or an APD. In this time frame we turned over to Uruguay, Ecuador, I think Colombia, and we turned them over as basically

---

* USS *Pueblo* (AGER-2), an electronic intelligence ship, was seized on 23 January 1968 in the Sea of Japan by North Korean naval forces. The ship's crew members were held as prisoners until 23 December of that year. Of the 83 officers and men on board, 28 were intelligence specialists. Her commanding officer was Commander Lloyd R. Bucher, USN.

hot ships. Then when Zumwalt came along, the atmosphere had changed, and they were able to turn over destroyers and larger ships.

Paul Stillwell: You haven't mentioned Mexico at all. Did you have dealings concerning Mexico?

Admiral Erly: Yes, but not really—very cordial relations with the Mexican admirals and so forth. That little cigarette box is from one. They were staunch supporters of the OAS and hosted the Inter-American Defense Board. We traveled to Mexico, and they really laid it on lavishly. We were down there for one of their gritos, and we were guests in the presidential palace and this type of thing. I also had a close relationship with the Mexican naval attaché.

There was also the Mexican-American Commission, of which I was a member, but at that point in time they were not actively engaged in procuring any American ships, as such. We had a few inconsequential meetings. One of the big things, of course, that we had going, we had a Mexican naval officer at the U.S. Naval Academy teaching Spanish, and we had a U.S. naval officer at their naval academy teaching English. Now, Arleigh Burke had set that up early on.

There was one other item, before we leave, to which OP-63 was also tasked. There was a conference of the hemisphere CNOs, and my first job when I got to Washington was to go with Dave McDonald to Venezuela, where they were having this conference. Venezuela was the host. We had hosted it, I think, the year before at Key West. Thank goodness that didn't happen on my watch that we had to host it, because OP-63 would have been the prime one to set it up, and it took a lot of setting up. You had to allot berthing, plan the agenda, and so forth and whatnot. That was, I guess, a fruitful exchange, and I'm sure it still continues. I don't know when the last one was, but as a matter of record, I think we ought to try to look it up.

Paul Stillwell: Did it deal with anything substantive, or was it just getting to know each other?

Admiral Erly: No, it had a regular agenda, certain things to be done and so forth and so on. In this time frame, they also had—out of that had come this business of the translation of tactical documents into Spanish for the use by our Southern Hemisphere neighbors. You had a regular agenda, and there had to be some things to be voted on. I'm trying to remember. You might have to set up a little ad hoc committee to clarify some things, which I was a U.S. representative on one. This was more than just a get to know each other type of thing. The agenda had some firm items. I can't give you an example at the moment. But one was this business that they made officers available to various countries to set up on this translation, because what you had to watch—Castilian Spanish isn't the only answer. Each country uses different terms for some things. Then you had to get this group together to say, "Okay, this is the way it is," and buy it. So that was one fallout, that part of it.

Standardization, oh, yes, we were talking standardization of arms, munitions, source of supply, all of these that could have some impact, because if you've got a disparate force, and as you're going to say, from the OAS or whatever reason, how are you going to keep them supplied in bullets and spare parts unless you have some commonality? So this was one of the items that were discussed.

Paul Stillwell: This was still the period before Chile went Communist, so you didn't have that problem.

Admiral Erly: That's right, exactly. I think this was in the period where Chile was supposed to be in the model of the democracy, the most democratic one in the area, and with no dictator.[*] It's a changing scene.

With that thought, I guess we can leave Washington.

Paul Stillwell: Did your previous association with Admiral Holmes play a part in your

---

[*] From 1945 to 1970 Salvador Allende Gossens served in the Chilean Senate. After unsuccessful runs for the presidency in 1952, 1954, and 1964, he was elected in 1970 as the first Marxist President of Chile. In 1973 Chilean military leaders overthrew his government in a coup. His term as President was 4 November 1970 to 11 September 1973. He was shot and killed on 11 September 1973.

getting on his staff at CinCLantFlt?[*]

Admiral Erly: Oh, I'm sure it did. Yes. Certainly.

Paul Stillwell: What does an inspector general do?

Admiral Erly: When I got there, they had an inspection program. All subordinate commands were to be inspected, and that included all the type commanders, and it included commandants. It included the military, or the naval component of the U.N. I guess that was under the CinC's hat, because I remember inspecting Andy Jackson, because he'd gone up there and had that United Nations job.

In addition to that, we looked at fleet readiness, safety, did studies in depth, and came out with concrete recommendations in which we had the commander in chief sign to make it a current CinCLantFlt instruction or directive. We'd forward the study to concerned units for implementation, whether it was boiler operation to safety procedures, promulgated—we even looked at a SecNav instruction and called his attention to the disparities and corrections that needed to be made.[†]

When I got there, the precedent had been set that whenever the inspector general was junior to the commanding officer of the command inspected, the chief of staff would present the critique. My first inspection was the Atlantic Training Command. This was that business of seniority. It was commanded by a rear admiral, Jack Coye, class of '33.[‡] I was thinking, "Well, what in the hell is Ashworth going for?"[§]

Then I was scheduled within the month to inspect the Caribbean Command with the admiral based in Puerto Rico. My predecessor felt that a junior couldn't inspect a senior. The hell with that noise.

Ashworth got in the car, and I said, "Sir, do you want to go to San Juan for a vacation? Why are you going on that inspection?"

---

[*] Admiral Ephraim P. Holmes, USN, served as Supreme Allied Commander Atlantic, Commander in Chief Atlantic, and Commander in Chief Atlantic Fleet from 17 June 1967 to 30 September 1970.
[†] SecNav – Secretary of the Navy.
[‡] Rear Admiral John S. Coye, USN, whose oral history is in the Naval Institute collection.
[§] Vice Admiral Frederick L. Ashworth, USN, was Deputy CinCLantFlt.

He said, "Oh, well, so-and-so [I forget the guy's name] is senior to you."[*]

I said, "That doesn't make a damn bit of difference to me who's senior to me or not." And then I said the same thing here. "Why are you going to this thing? I'll do my job whether the guy is senior or junior; it doesn't matter a damn. We call them the way we see them, and that's the way it is."

He looked at me. We pulled up at TraLant headquarters, and here were Coye and his staff all waiting.

Paul Stillwell: Ashworth's classmate.

Admiral Erly: Okay. He looked at Coye and he said, "Bob's running this. I'll see you." [Laughter]

He didn't go to San Juan. From then on, I went on my own. It didn't bother me whether they had three stars or whatever; I did them all.

Paul Stillwell: Was there any awkwardness in that?

Admiral Erly: No! I never found it awkward. Maybe they did, but I didn't.

Paul Stillwell: Well, they knew you were representing a four-star admiral.

Admiral Erly: Oh, absolutely. That was my point. I should conduct myself accordingly, and they should too. My big pitch, what I tried to pitch, and not only tried, I was successful, I said, "Hey look, we're not here to hang you; we're here to help you. You damn well must have problems. Let's bring them out, and let's get them solved for you."

Paul Stillwell: Well, the classic line is that a staff should be a support, not a club.

---

[*] Rear Admiral Alfred R. Matter, USN, served as Commandant Tenth Naval District from 1967 to 1970. The billet included additional duty as Commander Caribbean Sea Frontier and Commander Antilles Defense Command.

Admiral Erly: Exactly. Exactly. I was very successful with that. I had no problem. I inspected Lloyd Mustin, went up and got DesLant, Service Force.* I hit them all. Plus hit Andy Jackson at the U.N. And Bill Wylie, the commandant up in Boston.†

But the inspector general's job was a good one, and I thought we made quite an imprint on morale, and our studies remedied many deficiencies.

Paul Stillwell: Do you remember any specifics? What kind of problems you found?

Admiral Erly: Yes. At this time, the inspection of nuclear safety had taken place, in that it was turned over to the CinCs. So we had a nuclear safety inspection team that did all the subs, and the leader's name was Captain Early.‡ So I went out with them, and I think it was the *Abraham Lincoln*. As soon as I boarded that boat, God, I could see the crew was walking on their heels. They'd been out getting ready for it. It's a wonder we damn well didn't have an accident, if you're going to scramble the reactor and do all this other stuff. Then I sat in on a critique, and they would start hammering on these. "That's wrong. That's wrong."

I said, "It's wrong? How do we help them correct it?" trying to push it the right way.

Paul Stillwell: Change the emphasis.

Admiral Erly: Oh, yes, yes. I wanted the team not to be hard and just cutting the legs off of everybody but to be part of the team in solving the command's problem areas.

Paul Stillwell: Well, some people take a delight in cutting other people down.

Admiral Erly: Well, this is what you have to watch against. I was able to turn that

---

* Vice Admiral Lloyd M. Mustin, USN, served as Commander Amphibious Force Atlantic Fleet in 1967-68. His oral history is in the Naval Institute collection.
† Rear Admiral Joseph C. Wylie Jr., USN, served a twilight tour from 1969 to 1972 as commandant of the First Naval District.
‡ Captain Paul J. Early, USN.

around.

I have another submarine memory, and I think it was the *Abraham Lincoln*, when we test-fired one of those missiles. It turned out to be a dud; it only partially fired. We could hear, "Dud, dud." Then what we heard was, "boom." It almost came back down the goddamn tube, honest. Then "Emergency surface, emergency surface." When we got topside and looked, you could see where it had hit on the ring of the tube that it ejected from. You would almost think that impossible. That thing was rattling around on deck and that was a great noise. I must admit—[Laughter]

Paul Stillwell: You must admit what?

Admiral Erly: That everybody sort of froze, I'll tell you. The klaxons went, and we heard, "Emergency surface. Get the hell up there, topside."

Paul Stillwell: When was that, do you recall?

Admiral Erly: That was in about '68 or '69.

The other one thing that I instigated in my many commands, and I did it down there with my people, was what we called brainstorming. We did a study for how you retain the people in the submarine force. They were having problems.

Paul Stillwell: It was a Navy-wide problem.

Admiral Erly: Well, in this case, the boomers had the problems.[*] The SSNs didn't have the problem.[†] You know what the problem was?

Paul Stillwell: Long deployments.

---

[*] "Boomer" is a nickname applied to nuclear-powered ballistic missile submarines.
[†] SSNs – nuclear-powered attack submarines.

Admiral Erly: No. The problem was, in the SSN you were doing derring-dos, and you were getting adrenaline, and you were in all these quite perilous situations at times. Where the boomer went out, and they were even scared to belch. About halfway through the deployment, the resignations started in. Sheer boredom.

Paul Stillwell: That's a problem that needs a creative solution.

Admiral Erly: Yes. Shorter deployments might well help it. I think now what's happening, and with the Trident missile, you don't have to be out as far.[*] You can sit in homeport and still be deadly. But that was the basic problem.

Paul Stillwell: Did you come up with any answers or suggestions?

Admiral Erly: When I talked to junior officers, they would say, "As I look at my commander, I realize that after umpteen tours of this sea duty, and then I'm going to be ending up where he is. You know, we're still out here doing it."

Again, that was that business of where you had to rotate them; you had not to keep them as long in the positions. Those were some of the things from the studies. The extra pay, they were already well into. The main thing was to not get them boomer assigned and stuck there forever. You had to move them around, because it was obvious that the challenge of the SSN and the much more flexible schedule, even homeport calls and whatnot, was more of a stimulating job than the SSBNs, although God knows they were deadly important at that time.

Paul Stillwell: How much did you work with Rickover's outfit in trying to deal with that problem?[†]

---

[*] The Trident I (C-4) submarine-launched ballistic missile, with a range of about 4,600 miles, was deployed in 1979 and phased out in the 1990s and early 2000s. The Trident II (D-5), with a range of about 7,500 miles, was deployed in 1990.
[†] Vice Admiral Hyman G. Rickover, USN (Ret.), was the long-time head of the Navy's nuclear power program.

Admiral Erly: We didn't work with him at all at that point. The CinCs had been assigned to take over the safety inspection program.

I told you that at one point that Admiral Holmes always had his flag secretary listen in and take notes when he got official telephone calls. Rickover came in, and the gist of it was he tried to put the pressure on Eph for something. And Eph said, "You son of a bitch, you're not going to blackmail me."

Paul Stillwell: Do you remember any other details?

Admiral Erly: No, I can't remember the other details of what the particular item was. But evidently Rick was trying to do that. Obviously, it was no love lost between the two.

Paul Stillwell: What else do you remember about Admiral Holmes from that tour?

Admiral Erly: A great detailist. He had a grasp, I think, of just about everything, and a workaholic if there ever was one.

Paul Stillwell: Well, you have to be, the way the command was structured then with three hats.

Admiral Erly: Yes, well, he seemed to enjoy it. At SACLant, he enjoyed that hat, and the CinC's hat, the Lant hat.

Paul Stillwell: CinCLant, SACLant, CinCLantFlt.

Admiral Erly: And he was CinCWestLant.

Paul Stillwell: And there was a different set of requirements in each job.

Admiral Erly: Oh, sure. Well, one was more almost like the diplomatic circuit; that was SACLant. That job required international liaison and trips. When he got over, I think, in

Norway where he was entertained by the King. He felt that was great. Eph was a good leader.

Paul Stillwell: Well, the person in the inspector general job can be especially useful in keeping him abreast of the pulse of the fleet.

Admiral Erly: I'm trying to remember when I got into so many facets. You know the Master Chief Petty Officer of the Navy?

Paul Stillwell: Yes.

Admiral Erly: We had one in the Atlantic Fleet before they ever had one in CNO, and I set up the selection process. I guess it was one of our studies that recommended that the master chief of the fleet be established.

Paul Stillwell: What about drugs? They were starting to rear their head at that point.

Admiral Erly: At that point, I don't react as recalling that as a specific problem at that point. In this time frame—I'm probably saying now we're '69-'70. I think our drugs really came to a crashing bit after our personnel came out of Vietnam. Isn't that where we got a lot of it started?

Paul Stillwell: Well, I remember about '68 in the Pacific Fleet one of the guys in our ship was using marijuana, and this was a highly unusual event. Four or five years later, that was widespread. It had gone from being unusual to almost commonplace.

Did you work with the Naval Investigative Service in that job?

Admiral Erly: No. Never during my time frame. Doc Abbot relieved me, and I became deputy for ops.[*] There was a boiler casualty in a destroyer during a Second Fleet

---

[*] Rear Admiral James L. Abbot Jr., USN.

exercise. Jerry Miller was the Second Fleet Commander at that time, and he wanted the fleet inspector general to do the investigation.[*]

I said, "No, way. No, way. That's a type commander. He should convene his own investigation. It's not the inspector general's job. That's not. If something falls out of this that you need the inspector general to look into afterward, that's something else. But you don't step in and do that. You're not really equipped. The type commander should have that expertise to go after it and come up with his report."

So from the investigative viewpoint, no, as I say, we put out quite a few studies, and then, of course, the command inspections that were done for all units. I think we were helpful. We were helpful.

I remember Bob Townsend, ComNavAirLant, didn't want to be inspected so soon after taking command.[†] He said, "I'd like to get things corrected before the inspection. Can you put it off?"

I said, "Well, sir, let us come in." And I told him the same thing that I said earlier, "Let's see what some of the problems you have, and let's see how we can get them on record and then get some help to solve them." And we did.

Paul Stillwell: Well, it may depend on part on the emphasis that you placed on it yourself, because sometimes you read about an IG being involved when there is a problem or an investigation, and maybe some are more energetic in that than others.

Admiral Erly: Yes. Let's see.

Paul Stillwell: You talked about the effects of those SSBN patrols. Did you see an effect on morale and retention from the East Coast ships that were diverted over to Vietnam to supplement the Pacific Fleet?

---

[*] Vice Admiral Gerald E. Miller, USN, commanded the Second Fleet from September 1970 to August 1971. His oral history is in the Naval Institute collection.
[†] Vice Admiral Robert L. Townsend, USN, served as Commander Naval Air Force Atlantic Fleet from 1 March 1969 to 29 February 1972.

Admiral Erly: No. I would think it would be the opposite. But when I say that, I didn't see it personally, but I'm saying what happened to me in the Korean War. I felt that it brought the ship closer together and so forth and so on to have that deployment, and the chance to get in another ocean and so forth. I felt that it would be a real chance for the morale enhancement that would enhance the fighting effectiveness of the ship.

Paul Stillwell: But it might be tougher on a family situation because of longer deployment.

Admiral Erly: Yes, sure. I trying to remember how long we were gone. I think we left in January and got back in August.

Paul Stillwell: Were the family ombudsmen a factor at that point yet?

Admiral Erly: No. No. The ombudsmen and more of that was one of the things, I think, came later with Bud Zumwalt.

Paul Stillwell: How were family-type problems dealt with back in the late '60s?

Admiral Erly: I would say basically the same way that they're dealt with now. Like Mrs. Erly, God, she's driven women to the hospital to have babies. You set up backups in your own ship at that point. You set up your own system to make sure that dependents were taken care of. Of course, again, to keep you advised and a big help was the American Red Cross to get messages through when ships were deployed.

That was something I used to always say to my wardroom, "You never write home about what Joe Doaks did. If you want to write what you did, that's fine, you write. But don't you write and say about what another member of the crew did or what or where or when. That's a no-no. You belong to the HPA, the Husbands Protective Association." [Laughter] Because that could really tear a wardroom apart, some guy sitting writing and so forth, and then it gets back, and yak, yak, whatever.

As I say, it has become more formalized now in the ombudsman, and I noticed that I went up to the change in the command in the *Peleliu* and the ombudsmen were introduced from the audience. Now, did the captain recognize his ombudsmen at this decommissioning?*

Paul Stillwell: Yes, very specifically.

Admiral Erly: Okay. See, it's much more formal, and as I think the change of commands now are becoming much more of a whole family concept than they used to be back in the time frame when I was there. And that's for the good. I think it's great.

Paul Stillwell: It's a very healthy trend.

Admiral Erly: Oh, sure. Certainly. Definitely. I'm all in favor of it. That recognition is essential. I think it's a great idea. It's more formal, and I guess they do solve problems and are helpful.

Paul Stillwell: Well, one advantage it has, it puts a systematic framework in place so it doesn't depend on the personality of the individual captain's wife or whatever.

Admiral Erly: Right, exactly. Much better.

Paul Stillwell: Do you remember any specific events that occurred during the time that you could especially cite? I don't know if the loss of the *Scorpion* happened during your time in that billet or not.†

---

* The battleship *Missouri* (BB-63) was decommissioned for the last time at Long Beach Naval Shipyard on 31 March 1992, shortly before this interview. Her last commanding officer was Captain Albert Lee Kaiss, USN.
† The submarine *Scorpion* (SSN-589) was lost with all hands while en route from the Mediterranean to Norfolk. She was last heard from on 21 May 1968. On 27 May she was reported overdue and on 5 June presumed lost with her entire crew of 99 officers and men. The wreckage was located on 30 October of that year. No definitive conclusion has been reached as to cause.

Admiral Erly: Yes, but I'm trying to remember. When was she lost? Remember?

Paul Stillwell: It was sometime in '68.

Admiral Erly: That's the one that was coming back from the Med, and we finally analyzed the traces on SOSUS and from that were able to determine the location, and we got divers and remotes and found her.* But nothing really comes to mind at the moment.

Paul Stillwell: Do you remember anything about Navy support of the space program?

Admiral Erly: Well, we had a headquarters at Breezy Point Naval Air Station there at Norfolk. There was our space outfit, which I also inspected. I didn't, except when something was going on on that for the recovery and this, it was a pretty stagnant operation, as I saw it as such. I wouldn't have wanted the job, because you didn't really have enough to do.

Paul Stillwell: A few peaks and lot of valleys.

Admiral Erly: Yes.

Paul Stillwell: You were mentioning that Admiral Holmes was interested in command centers.

Admiral Erly: Yes, I really became attuned to this when I was his chief of staff in PhibPac. We finally set him up a command center, and if we were having an exercise and everything, we had summaries of everything that was going on. He'd come down, and we'd brief him. Lo and behold, when I was his deputy for plans and operations in CinCLant and CinCLantFlt, we had the same deal. He wanted an up-to-date operations center, and we really put one there.

---

* SOSUS – sound surveillance system, a seafloor network of listening devices used by the U.S. Navy to detect noises from transiting ships.

At this point, we were getting into computers and all of it, and for the latest information, communications, all the data processing, and we set up a center for him. We even had the emergency cabin and whatnot for him if he had to spend the night. I lived in the compound, and, of course, whenever we had a crisis of any sort, I would head for the command center.

That reminds me, I was almost forgetting, in this job, too, I had to move from Breezy Point, where I had quarters as the inspector general, to come and live in the CinCLantFlt compound. The house was, I would say, about 150 yards from the command center, and we had the red phone, which of course tied us in with the whole—you know.

Paul Stillwell: The high command network?

Admiral Erly: Yes, it tied us in with Colorado, SAC, the whole bit, for any alerts and whatnot.* There would be an online circuit, and if the CinC was away, you had the red phone. You'd pick it up. If he came on, fine; if he didn't, you would come on line for CinCLant. Even on the golf course I had a portable phone, so you always lived waiting for the phone to ring or some other emergency to arise.

I think earlier we were discussing the *Pueblo*, and I mentioned the *Pueblo* because we didn't want another *Pueblo* down off Cuba. We would keep close, close track and always in communication with our patrol down there. If any threatening action was to be started, we had planes at the ready on the mat in Key West. We were all set to really move out to give any support if any of the Cuban patrol boats tried to intercept and do anything to our patrol craft. The skippers were well versed that there was not going to be another *Pueblo*.

Paul Stillwell: And there wasn't.

---

* The North American Air Defense Command (NORAD), an Air Force command based in Colorado Springs, was responsible for detecting and attacking Soviet bombers headed toward the United States. SAC – Strategic Air Command, based at Offutt Air Force Base near Omaha, Nebraska. It has since become a joint service command, Strategic Command, rather than Air Force only as it was then.

Admiral Erly: No. No. But several things got a little dusty down there. The APD would report being observed by Cuban patrol boats. We would go to a red alert but then ease off when the patrol craft left the area.

Paul Stillwell: Do you remember any specifics of those cases?

Admiral Erly: Well, yes. You got a report that patrol boats were closing in on them, and they'd go to GQ. Then they said, "Okay, they have circled. Now they've gone." So we could stand down.

The main thing is, then you flash the alert to Key West, "Stand by. We may have you airborne in short order."

Paul Stillwell: Do you remember what kind of rules of engagement there were for that operation?

Admiral Erly: The specific rules of engagement were, "You are not going to be taken, and use any means at hand that you can to prevent this."

Paul Stillwell: How did you get transferred into that job from being inspector general?

Admiral Erly: Because the officer in that job was transferred to OpNav, and the billet needed to be filled. I, at that point, had been about a year and a half as inspector general, and I'd really given it a shot in the arm. I was ready to take on other things.

Paul Stillwell: And Admiral Holmes obviously thought highly of you.

Admiral Erly: Yes. If he could have sprung me out of OpNav sooner, I would have had that job in the first place.

Paul Stillwell: That coincided about with the time that Admiral Zumwalt came in as Chief of Naval Operations.* What do you recall about his impact?

Admiral Erly: The Z-grams were sometimes hard to swallow, and I felt in some cases almost caused a circumvention of the chain of command.† Not so much that the Z-gram itself was at fault. It was that perhaps the intent or the reaction to it by some people made it at fault.

One particular incident I am recalling—it was told to me—was that some officer in town saw a dirty sailor in dungarees and so forth and so on, to take him to task and was told bluntly that, "Well, Admiral Zumwalt says it's all right, and who the hell are you?"

The officer didn't follow up on it, and that made me so mad. I would have said, "I'd be willing to court-martial the officer for permitting insubordination."

But this is one of the types of things that came out of it. I think some of the Z-grams were good, but some of them were damn arguable.

You know, you run into some things. Admiral Duncan—I'm just trying to think—came up with this concept of putting first class petty officers in chiefs' uniforms.‡ Well, I was against that, and we would go back and forth. And then along came Zumwalt, and he put everybody in a chief's uniform, which the people didn't want anyway.§

Getting into that one, I am told that BuPers had a study that really showed that the sailors wanted their bell-bottom trousers, and that Zumwalt was told this, but he still went ahead with the uniform change. I don't know. That is hearsay. But, as you can see, I

---

* Admiral Elmo R. Zumwalt, Jr., USN, served as Chief of Naval Operations from 1 July 1970 to 29 June 1974. His oral history is in the Naval Institute collection.
† Z-grams were consecutively numbered policy directives from Chief of Naval Operations Zumwalt that attempted to deal with such issues as enlisted rights and privileges, equal opportunity, and Navy families. Junior personnel viewed them much more favorably than did their seniors. See *U.S. Naval Institute Proceedings*, May 1971, pages 293-298.
‡ Vice Admiral Charles K. Duncan, USN, served as Chief of Naval Personnel from 5 April 1968 to 21 August 1970. The oral history of Duncan, who retired as a four-star admiral, is in the Naval Institute collection.
§ On 14 June 1971 Admiral Zumwalt, as Chief of Naval Operations, announced that enlisted personnel in the pay grades of E-6 and below would be converting over a period of time to a more officer-like blue uniform. Included would be jacket, tie, white shirt, creased trousers, and a combination cap with a visor. On 1 August 1977 the Navy announced that the uniforms for personnel below chief petty officer would return to the bell-bottom trousers, jumpers, and white hats that had been traditional prior to 1971.

still personally feel that what he tried to do, he overdid and I think it played hell with morale. I think it played hell with the respect for the chain of command. We are still trying to cinch back up to get to some degree of the discipline that we should have. How many years has it been--20?

Paul Stillwell: It has been 20.

Admiral Erly: A good 20. Well, so be it. As I say, I think it was fraught with good intentions, but he brought in too many young, naive advisers—let's put it that way—and they led him down the primrose path.

Paul Stillwell: Well, one of the objections was as much to the way these things were promulgated as to the content of them. The people in the mess deck might see them sooner than their skippers.

Admiral Erly: Yes, and as I said, it bred insubordination in some cases.

Paul Stillwell: Did you see any symptoms of that at your level in LantFlt?

Admiral Erly: Wouldn't permit it. No. Hell, if I looked out of my window and saw something I didn't like, I said, "Get them."

This business of beards. I looked at a CinCLant bandsman and I said, "Look, you look like a scraggly old goat, and if you can't grow a proper beard and have a neatly trimmed beard, you're not going to have one." There's nothing worse than a person who doesn't have a good beard try to grow one. That's what they look like.

You can go on and on in all of these things. An officer has to have his own sensing of what is right and honorable, and he must follow that regardless of whatever. And then if you're wrong, tough. You stand accountable. But you should be able to stand up and say, "This is it, and this is the way it's going to be," and try to carry out, as you see it, the orders of your superior.

Paul Stillwell: Did you see symptoms of racial unrest in the fleet during that period?

Admiral Erly: No, we didn't. I'm trying to remember. To prevent such things we set up a race relationship council. We had a black commander that sat on it, a Filipino chief, a Hispanic, a Navy female commander, etc. I think the black was a young naval aviator academy graduate that we pulled in specifically for this, to try and foresee any racial problems. I don't know whether the concept came from my study group or brainstorming group. But I ended up on all those special committees that we had set up, and in fact, I think we blazed the way for some of the things that CNO did later.

Paul Stillwell: Well, the Pacific Fleet had some virtual mutinies in the early '70s.[*]

Admiral Erly: Well, if you'll recall, we had not experienced them on the East Coast at this point. But I don't know whether we were looking in a crystal ball or why, but we moved ahead.

Again, this brings me up—Eph, I said, has a great shining sense of humor in some ways. At this time we were looking at monetary cutbacks. We were saying to base commanders was that money was tight, and self-help was needed everywhere. That was what we were saying to the base commanders. Well, then I said, "Gee that really goes fine." So I sat down and wrote Eph a little memo and said, "Hey, why don't we go with this and call it SHINE?"

Paul Stillwell: That was the acronym.

Admiral Erly: That was the acronym. Remember I told you about acronyms before. They come back to bite you.

Got a little note. This memo came back, said, "No."

---

[*] Racial disturbances broke out in the carrier *Kitty Hawk* (CVA-63) on 12 October 1972; in the oiler *Hassayampa* (AO-145) on 16 October 1972; and in the carrier *Constellation* (CVA-64) on 3 November 1972. See Captain Paul B. Ryan, USN (Ret.), "USS Constellation Flare-up: Was it Mutiny?" *U.S. Naval Institute Proceedings*, January 1976, pages 46-53. See also Gregory A. Freeman, *Troubled Water: Race, Mutiny, and Bravery on the USS Kitty Hawk* (New York: Palgrave Macmillan, 2009).

Then I took another look. SHINE.

Paul Stillwell: You didn't like that?

Admiral Erly: No. Don't you know why?

Paul Stillwell: No.

Admiral Erly: You're not from the South.

Paul Stillwell: That's true.

Admiral Erly: Do you know what a shine is?

Paul Stillwell: No.

Admiral Erly: Negro.

Paul Stillwell: Oh.

Admiral Erly: Sure. That was at one point, and I'd completely forgotten.

Paul Stillwell: I see.

Admiral Erly: That's why Admiral Holmes said no. So I personally felt that was bending over backwards. I would have gone with it, but he said no. We didn't call it SHINE.

He never explained, but then it was pretty obvious. Then I said, "Oh, my." As soon as he said no, I could see what he was thinking.

Again, on acronyms, be careful. But it shows his sensitivity, which I thought was, in this case, oversensitive.

I'd like to talk and my own personal feelings how, again, under Zumwalt that I—and this goes at a later date. This was when I was ComIberLant and chief MAAG Portugal. I had to leave and go over to Naples, along with Dick Colbert, who was CinCSouth, myself, the kid who had the Middle East force, who is now president of the Army-Navy Club in Washington.* And we had a black dental technician, a black lieutenant, and some others, and we were required to take this race relations deal, and it was a farce, in my humble opinion.

Paul Stillwell: In what sense?

Admiral Erly: In what sense? All it did was irritate most of us. Didn't come off with a message. They couldn't convey what it was, and I—

Paul Stillwell: Was this the confrontational approach?

Admiral Erly: No, I've forgotten. But they got up and talked, and you have a black dental technician and so forth, and they weren't that erudite, they were not that well versed. I felt most of us at this phase already had lived through quite a few things with the racial part, and we sure didn't learn anything. If anything, it might have exacerbated the situation rather than helping it.

Paul Stillwell: By having your nose rubbed in it.

Admiral Erly: Yes. It caused resentment. So I think that was wrong in that part of a program. It got completely out of hand, and as again I'm saying, whether Bud insisted that this was to be it or whether he was ill advised, but the execution of it stunk.

Paul Stillwell: I heard that same viewpoint in particular from an aviator named Spence Matthews.†

---

* Rear Admiral Rorbert J. Hanks, USN, served as Commander Middle East Force from 9 December 1972 to 20 February 1975.
† Rear Admiral Herbert Spencer Matthews, USN (Ret.).

Admiral Erly: Spence.

Paul Stillwell: Why do you grin so broadly when I mention his name?

Admiral Erly: Because I can see Spence now. He's got a stand on everything. He's very articulate, and he's come a long way, I think. I admire Spence in many ways, because when I first ran into him he was a yeoman striker, I think, in Opa Locka, Florida.*

Paul Stillwell: Yes, he came a long way.

Admiral Erly: Oh, yes. Kid's articulate. And, of course, he's that political type. He's on the Hill all the time. I like Spence. He's a member of the Naval Academy Foundation. That's where I see him.

Paul Stillwell: A real wheeler-dealer.

Admiral Erly: Oh, yes. There was another wheeler-dealer, and I'm trying to remember his name. Cut from the same bolt of cloth as Spence and really came up the hard way too. I don't know whether he was a naval aviator or not. I think he was also a naval aviator. The name escapes me, but they're both the same type. But I like Spence.

Paul Stillwell: Did you feel a sense of loss when Admiral Holmes was relieved by Admiral Duncan, that your patron was gone?†

Admiral Erly: Oh, Lord, no. No, no, no. Not at all, because I would say one patron was replaced by another.

Paul Stillwell: Well, what are your recollections of Admiral Duncan?

---

* This was in 1940, when Erly was undergoing flight training.
† Admiral Charles K. Duncan, USN, served as Supreme Allied Commander Atlantic, Commander in Chief Atlantic, and Commander in Chief Atlantic Fleet from 30 September 1970 to 31 October 1972. His oral history is in the Naval Institute collection.

Admiral Erly: Well, I am very, very fond of Admiral Duncan. I remember we hit it off from the first time I ever met him. I had the *Paul Revere* when I first really met Charlie, and I was his flagship for a while around 1958. Now here we are 14 years later. Also, Charlie was on the selection board when I got selected for flag. So we'd had a close relationship, and we still have a close relationship.

Paul Stillwell: What specific recollections do you have of him as the fleet CinC?

Admiral Erly: Oh, I think he did one hell of a good job, and I was real proud of him when he took over. He called all the staff together, and he got up, without a damn note, and talked for an hour, saying, "This is this and that." He's well organized, and Charlie's smart.

Paul Stillwell: He and Admiral Zumwalt had a good relationship, which is why he was one of the few relatively senior people that got good jobs after Zumwalt came in. Generally, Zumwalt was bringing in younger people.

Admiral Erly: Well, I didn't realize that. He got cross-threaded somewhere. Where? Do you know?

Paul Stillwell: No.

Admiral Erly: Because he didn't hold that job very long, when Ralph Cousins relieved him.[*]

Paul Stillwell: He had it for two years.

Admiral Erly: Well, that's not a normal tour, is it?

---

[*] Admiral Ralph W. Cousins, USN, served as Supreme Allied Commander Atlantic, Commander in Chief Atlantic Command, and Commander in Chief Atlantic Fleet from 31 October 1972 to 30 May 1975.

Paul Stillwell: I don't know.

Admiral Erly: I don't know either. But they didn't pin a medal on him when he left, did they?

Paul Stillwell: That I wouldn't know.

Admiral Erly: I was there at the change of command.

Paul Stillwell: Well, perhaps he did get cross-threaded.

Admiral Erly: I don't remember. He got cross-threaded somehow. I think I'll ask him the next time I see him. He's here in Coronado.

Paul Stillwell: One of the events of that period in the early '70s was a big drawdown in the size of the fleet, decommissioning a lot of ships. What do you remember about the impact of that on the Atlantic Fleet?

Admiral Erly: One thing that stands in my mind, again, that the squeaky wheel gets the grease. Everyone was coming back stating the impact on cuts and so forth and so on, except the amphibious force. So I took it on my own and called Lloyd Mustin and said, "Hey, look, unless you really lay it on the line of how you're going to be impacted, you're going to get impacted but bad. Everyone else is coming in screaming to high heaven. You'd better join the chorus."

It was like pulling teeth. You know where it really gets you, and I'm trying to think. The cutback is when they hit you on the personnel. When you get a personnel ceiling, then you can't man what you have unless you're going to reduce manning. That's where the cutbacks were coming, and I remember this one well. Chafee, from Rhode Island, was SecNav, and one of my prime targets was pulling the destroyer force out of Newport, Rhode Island, which we did.* We finally moved them down to Norfolk in trying to consolidate, and we also took personnel out of the staffs.

I remember calling in the CinCLant and CinCLantFlt staff and said, "Okay, give me a 25% cut across the board. And before you scream, I want to tell you this one. When you get your 25% cut, I want you to take a another look, because we may have to cut another 25%."

Paul Stillwell: Makes it more palatable.

Admiral Erly: Oh, sure.

Paul Stillwell: I gather Admiral Mustin joined in the chorus.

Admiral Erly: Oh, yes. Yes, yes.

Paul Stillwell: Were these complaints effective in getting the cuts reduced?

Admiral Erly: Well, what you were really after, you wanted to still end up with a balanced force. But if someone was going to stand mute and take it without a whimper, then the tendency of the powers that be was, "Well, let's go the easy way."

And it shouldn't. Everybody should have been weighed for what you want to end up with the right kind of force with, when you come with this stand-down that you're experiencing.

Paul Stillwell: Typically, the way those things work, the commitments don't get reduced when the forces do. So how did you in operations adjust to that?

Admiral Erly: Well, that is where you run into the tempo of ops. You tell personnel you're going to decrease deployment time, and they will have more time in homeport. You realize you're going to have this much time home. And what happens? The

---

* John H. Chafee served as Secretary of the Navy from 31 January 1969 to 4 May 1972.

deployment gets extended. That's when your reenlistment rate goes down, and that's when your morale plummets. This is what our friends on Capitol Hill should be told about the impact on what's going on.

I just listened to Colin Powell here last week, and I thought he made a masterful presentation.* In fact, I said to myself, "Well, I can see well how he's gotten as far as he's gotten, because he's really doing it." He didn't kowtow to the Senate Armed Forces Committee at all. He laid it on the line and stood right up to them all the way.

But what did they do? They took another big chop out of the defense budget. I'm a little worried that it appears that more and more of our so-called experts on the Hill don't have any really military experience. I don't think Sam Nunn has.† I don't know, I could be wrong. But if he has, it's never been touted about. I'm afraid, deathly afraid, of what we're going to end up with.

Paul Stillwell: Did you have to gap some operational commitments to try to cope with that shortage?

Admiral Erly: You've got to remember, as the Atlantic Fleet Commander he was responsible for overall operations and trying to meet commitments. What you really got, then, on those commitments, were your type commanders' inputs to make sure that the schedule and the whole thing was going to stay in sync. In some cases you'd have their recommendations for an early deployment or an extension of a deployment to meet it.

Basically, the ultimate referee, and if you're really hurting as the CinC, is on to CNO. That's the way it was then. I have no idea if they're still working in that same setup now. I'm sure they are. But, again, we had the type commanders. Of course, they have been supplanted by your naval surface forces and the air forces, submarine forces, and that type of bit.

---

* General Colin L. Powell, USA, served as Chairman of the Joint Chiefs of Staff from 1 October 1989 to 30 September 1993. In 2001 he became the first black person to serve as Secretary of State.
† Samuel A. Nunn, a Democrat from Georgia, served in the Senate from 8 November 1972 to 3 January 1997. He was chairman of the Senate Armed Services Committee from 1987 to 1994.

Paul Stillwell: Well, you mentioned when the machine wasn't running that you were involved in the studies that led to the consolidation of the Surface Force.*

Admiral Erly: Yes.

Paul Stillwell: What do you recall about that process?

Admiral Erly: Well, it became obvious to me that the type commanders had to go. Charlie Duncan, having been ComDesLant and ComPhibLant, was sold on the type commander organization. It was an anathema to him that we would have to do away with type commanders. It was a question of convincing him that, in order to meet some of this restructuring and saving personnel and saving duplication of effort, that we were going to have to eliminate some of the type commander staffs. I think he reluctantly had to buy it, because there wasn't any other alternative. So therefore, you saw the consolidation of the Service Force and the Amphibious and the Destroyer into the Surface Force. And, of course, the Battle Force had long since gone.

Paul Stillwell: Along with that was the idea of raising the professional standards for the amphibious people and the Service Force people to those of the cruiser-destroyer types and to give them more pride, and also set up the specialized surface warfare officer qualification.

Admiral Erly: Yes.

Paul Stillwell: That was a useful byproduct of the whole process.

Admiral Erly: Oh, sure. Certainly, the surface warfare insignia and everything that went with it was a great fallout.

---

* In 1975 the Cruiser-Destroyer Force Atlantic Fleet, Service Force Atlantic Fleet, and Amphibious Force Atlantic Fleet were merged into a new command known as Surface Force Atlantic Fleet.

Paul Stillwell: Well, it got away from the idea that these other people were second-class citizens.

Admiral Erly: Well, if you will recall, that was one of my big things when I was in the Amphibious Force as a phibron commander. That's when I said, "We don't take anybody's back draft. We're the spearhead. We're the ones that do it."

I think I even told you that writing back to PhibPac and saying, "Here I sit in Hong Kong Harbor, and my flagship enshrouded in darkness while everyone else bedecked with lights. We should be in the forefront. We should be bedecked with lights," and so forth, to raise morale.

I had prepared a brochure, giving just the shot in the arm to pass on to skippers, saying, "You've got to inculcate in your troops that we don't take the destroyers' backwash or the aviators or the submarines or anyone else." I had a pamphlet that was passed out.

Then all of this farther down the line, as you say, came out with the surface warfare designation. A good start for it was at the Surface Warfare Officers School that was started up in Newport, Rhode Island, all of this, again, to build the prestige. And now they've got the surface warrior bit, which they came along with, which is needed to get people in the surface forces to feel that they're comparable with the flashy aviators and the submarine people.

Paul Stillwell: Well, something like that can be a self-fulfilling prophecy. If you make people feel better about themselves, they will be better.

Admiral Erly: Sure. Sure.

Paul Stillwell: One of Admiral Zumwalt's initiatives during that period was the "Mod Squad," of having the skippers and other officers in destroyer-type ships of lesser rank than normal.[*] What do you recall about that initiative?

---

[*] In the early 1970s, as the result of an initiative by Admiral Zumwalt, Jr., USN, the Chief of Naval Operations, Destroyer Squadron 26 was designated to have officer billets filled by individuals one rank junior to the norm. The squadron was nicknamed the "Mod Squad" after a television program of the era.

Admiral Erly: I don't see anything startling about that. I'm sure that those people, you would call them the Mod Squad and so forth, but hell, I was 29 when I had my first destroyer, so you're not kidding me any about being early in command. They can do it, and sometimes do it better than some of the older ones, and that's what happened. Because mine, as you recall, was an offshoot of World War II, and they found that the older people just didn't have the stamina to be able to take the wear and tear. And it wasn't only in submarines or destroyers or planes; it was across the board. What I'm really saying, the older folks just didn't have the physical stamina to take what was required, and you needed the younger people in there who had the bounce.

Paul Stillwell: Well, I heard a suggestion last week, talking to a submariner, Slade Cutter, that the other attribute you got was that you didn't get the wisdom, caution, and common sense that come with age.[*]

Admiral Erly: True.

Paul Stillwell: You got hard-charging young guys.

Admiral Erly: Oh, exactly, and that's why you had a George Bush in aviation.[†] They wanted the 18-years-old that didn't think. You look at a group and say, "Hey, you got 25 of you here. Of the 25, only 24 are going to survive." And everybody's looking at each other and saying, "I feel sorry for these other 24," in that age group.

Paul Stillwell: What do you remember about the Zumwalt initiative on home-porting of ships overseas in Greece?[‡]

---

[*] See the Naval Institute oral history of Captain Slade D. Cutter, USN (Ret.).
[†] Future President George H. W. Bush was commissioned as a Naval Reserve ensign at age 20 and became a naval aviator with World War II service.
[‡] In 1973-74, the U.S. Navy home-ported six destroyers in the port of Elefis, Greece, near Athens. They were part of a plan that envisioned putting a carrier task force of up to 30 ships in the port. Before the remainder of the program could be implemented, it was cancelled because of strained relations between the United States and the Greek Government. See *The Washington Post*, 30 April 1975, page A2.

Admiral Erly: Oh, come on. Initiative, my butt. Arleigh Burke was the first proponent of home-porting overseas, and I firmly supported it. I think I mentioned before of getting the Sixth Fleet flagship home-ported in Villefranche. We had the opposition of the whole damn Navy. There were two people in favor of it—Bob Erly and Arleigh Burke. Bob Erly didn't amount to a damn, except he was the paper-pusher, but Arleigh Burke sold the goods as CNO, and was in favor of home-porting.

The business of the *Marias* and a couple of replenishment ships that we had over there in the Spanish ports, too, I thought was great. The home-porting cuts down that deployment requirement too. I felt that young, adventurous people would love to be home-ported overseas, and I think it's proved out.

Paul Stillwell: Well, I don't think the Greek one lasted. It has worked in Japan.

Admiral Erly: The concept that I thought you were after. Specifically about Greece, Greece would be no different, in my mind, from any other. You've got to recall, though, that they had, what, a terrorist group that was pretty much against sort of U.S. types in Greece. I recall an attaché being murdered over there by this outfit. I didn't think he was doing any great startling thing by picking on Greece any more than he would on Italy or anyone else. Remember when the French kicked us out, we ended up in Gaeta.* I'm sure that I would have been a strong sponsor for home-porting overseas. I think it is attractive to a lot of people. Would be to me.

Paul Stillwell: What other items fell under your purview as deputy for operations?

Admiral Erly: I mentioned the command centers, and we've gone through that. Oh,

---

* In 1966 and 1967 French Prime Minister Charles de Gaulle gradually withdrew his nation's naval and military forces from NATO because he believed the United States had too much control over those forces. He also demanded that all NATO headquarters, bases and troops be removed from France by April 1967, which was done. France remained a member of NATO politically but not militarily. The homeport of the Sixth Fleet flagship was moved to Gaeta, Italy.

Lord, I'll tell you what happened. Vieques was a bone of contention.* Commander Caribbean Sea Frontier based in San Juan, it was Bub Ward.† I was in two or three times a week talking, and he was having problems with our shore bombardment or Culebra, this type of thing, as you'll recall.‡

Paul Stillwell: What was the outcome?

Admiral Erly: I think in the final outcome they did open up parts of the area. I think once they got that training range in for the triangulation setup and some other things, I would think—I don't know what has happened to it now, whether it's completely gone or whether they're still having shore bombardment.

Paul Stillwell: I don't know.

Admiral Erly: I don't either. But once they got in that net of triangulation, you could have anchored targets out to sea and do it completely in international waters.

Paul Stillwell: One of the other things you mentioned when the machine wasn't running was being nominated for Com2ndFlt. What do you recall about that process?

Admiral Erly: Well, I don't know. See, the process is such that you aren't told. What happens, I gather, is that all three- and four-star admirals are polled periodically as to who they think should come up the line. When they get enough and then when they get them, the CNO and the chief of BuPers get together and then they have to submit—I'm told, now—three names to the Secretary of the Navy for the slot, and then the Secretary

---

* Vieques is a Caribbean island off the east coast of Puerto Rico. For many years the Navy and Marine Corps used it as a training site for amphibious landings and shore bombardment. In 2001 Puerto Rico's Governor Sila María Calderón Serra signed an agreement for the U.S. military to vacate the island. The U.S. departure began on 1 May 2003.
† Rear Admiral Norvell G. Ward, USN, served as Commander Caribbean Sea Frontier/Commandant Tenth Naval District from 1970 to 1973. Ward's oral history is in the Naval Institute collection.
‡ Culebra, an island in the Caribbean, is 17 miles west of Puerto Rico. In 1939, the U.S. Navy began using the island as a target for gunnery and bombing practice. That lasted until 1975, when the target practice moved to the island of Vieques.

supposedly, with the briefs on the three, makes the selection.

Paul Stillwell: Who were the other nominees?

Admiral Erly: I have no idea. I have no idea. If you can read through here, you can see where I was recommended for three for this, that, and the other. But you need more than just one—I gathered this from talking to Bob Townsend and some of the other ones.

Paul Stillwell: Well, this was when Jerry Miller got the job of Com2ndFlt.[*]

Admiral Erly: Yes. See, B. J. Semmes cut in, and I knew that I had been nominated because he intimated as much as that I was going to relieve him, but it never came to fruition.[†] And like poor old Clyde Van Arsdall who had ComCruDesLant.[‡] He had his bags packed to go get his three stars and he got shot out from under. That can happen. Charlie Duncan had called him. I happened to be up there when Charlie called him. He thought it was him. Charlie was chief of BuPers, and it didn't pan. Chafee had to be SecNav at that phase, and maybe he didn't give Van Arsdall the final upcheck.

Paul Stillwell: Well, that was at the point when Admiral Zumwalt was flip-flopping putting an aviator in Second Fleet, and Ike Kidd over in Sixth Fleet.[§] That may have been a part of it.

Admiral Erly: Yes, could have been. Could have been, but was the Secretary that made the final choice.

---

[*] Vice Admiral Gerald E. Miller, USN, commanded the Second Fleet from September 1970 to August 1971. His oral history is in the Naval Institute collection.
[†] Vice Admiral Benedict J. Semmes, Jr., USN, commanded the Second Fleet from April 1968 to September 1970. His oral history is in the Naval Institute collection.
[‡] Rear Admiral Clyde J. Van Arsdall Jr., USN, commanded Cruiser-Destroyer Force Atlantic Fleet from 1967 to 1969.
[§] Vice Admiral Isaac C. Kidd Jr., USN, commanded the Sixth Fleet from 29 August 1970 to 1 October 1971.

Paul Stillwell: Zumwalt was the choice as a younger CNO, I guess, for both Chafee and Laird, so he would be likely to go along with that way of thinking.[*]

Admiral Erly: And Warner. You know John Warner had Bud cached in his house until his appointment as CNO was announced.[†] They had brought him in from Vietnam. John told me this himself.

Paul Stillwell: Well, also, your not getting the fleet fits in with the idea of a youth movement.

Admiral Erly: Sure. I was the oldest of the 1965 selectees.

Paul Stillwell: Miller was several classes junior.

Admiral Erly: Well, I think probably the system's better that way. I was told after the fact, so you never—

Paul Stillwell: Don't get your hopes up.

Admiral Erly: Sure. Just as well. Just as well.

Paul Stillwell: Well, you can argue both sides of that question, whether it's better to have youthful vigor or more experience in a given job.

Admiral Erly: Yes. The point is that with this up-or-out concept, hell, what are they retiring at now, 54, 55, with still a lot left. I don't know. Is it a waste of talent? It could be or it could not. If you've got that many good people waiting behind, maybe it's best. Churn them out. Go. But there will always be that, won't it?

---

[*] Melvin R. Laird served as Secretary of Defense from 22 January 1969 to 29 January 1973.
[†] John W. Warner served as Under Secretary of the Navy from 11 February 1969 to 4 May 1972.

Paul Stillwell: Well, there will be that at no matter what age you put it.

Admiral Erly: Sure, that's what I'm saying. I'm just thinking that, as you know, I'm on the state board for the American Cancer Society and also for the unit board down here. I go up there and I'm on the nominating committee, and they're making a pitch we should have it for two years so you can really make an imprint.

I said, "Yeah, that's just fine. However, there are so many competent people standing in line waiting. Now, do we want to do that, or are we going to keep it at one?" So we kept it at one so that people can march through. So you could draw an analogy, I guess, to that.

Well, look at young Watkins. He's in the administration, isn't he?[*]

Paul Stillwell: And highly thought of, I gather, in that role.

Admiral Erly: Yes. Energy. Tom Hayward, I don't know what he's doing these days.[†]

Paul Stillwell: He's involved in promoting space ventures, including Japan and Hawaii. He lives out in Hawaii.

Admiral Erly: Oh. And Jimmy Holloway.[‡]

Paul Stillwell: He's involved in a number of essentially volunteer-type things, including the Naval Historical Foundation.

Admiral Erly: Well, I see he's also one of the drivers for your building, which I might say was a little ill timed after a lot of us had emptied our damn pockets out for the alumni

---

[*] Admiral James D. Watkins, USN, served as Chief of Naval Operations from 1 July 1982 to 30 June 1986. After his retirement from the Navy he served as Secretary of Energy from 1 March 1989 to 20 January 1993.

[†] Admiral Thomas B. Hayward, USN, served as Chief of Naval Operations from 1 July 1978 to 30 June 1982. His oral history is in the Naval Institute collection.

[‡] Admiral James L. Holloway III, USN, served as Chief of Naval Operations, 29 June 1974 to 1 July 1978.

building.* And then, God, when you're finishing paying that off, you're getting dunned for the Naval Institute building.† That was ill timed.

Paul Stillwell: More than a little ill timed.

Well, another argument on the relatively early retirement is that it gives an officer a chance for a second career in the civilian world.

Admiral Erly: Well, I wonder what Admiral Sides would say to that?‡ I don't know what age he retired, but I can't help but chuckle at one thing he said to me. He said, "You know, those guys aren't so smart in business." And he went out and got in with them.

Paul Stillwell: Yes, but he was smarter than most.

Admiral Erly: Yes. He was a great gentleman.

Paul Stillwell: Anything else you'd like to recall from that job at CinCLantFlt? Was there any overlap between that job and the other hats that the admiral wore?

Admiral Erly: I was just thinking, we had some symposiums there, and we had other things and we had brought in fleet commanders for exchange of ideas. I was sitting in the job, too, there, however, which under the SACLant hat I could see coming up. I thought would be an interesting tour was to relieve Gene Fluckey in Portugal, which reputedly was going to be a challenging job. So I put my hat in the ring, and was designated that I

---

* Alumni Hall is a multipurpose building at the Naval Academy. It was financed partly by government funds and partly by private donations. It was completed in October 1991. The seating capacity is 5,710 for basketball and 6,500 as a multipurpose auditorium.
† The Naval Institute was then in the process or raising funds to renovate and move into a wing of the former Annapolis Naval Hospital. The process took so long that the move wasn't accomplished until 1999.
‡ Admiral John H. Sides, USN, served as Commander in Chief Pacific Fleet, 30 August 1960 to 30 September 1963. He was 59 years old when he retired from active naval service.

was going to relieve him.*

Paul Stillwell: What was it about that job that appealed to you?

Admiral Erly: Well, it was going to be in the European side. I'd had South America. I thought it would be interesting to have a tour in Europe, and this was going to be in the NATO bit. It was going to be a joint staff. I thought it would be interesting. Also, Tom Moorer had been the principal architect of setting it up—he really had been when he was down there in CinCLant, SACLant.† And the manning tables called for a three-star, and I thought at my advanced age at about that point, I was 58, I figured that would be my final assignment.

I had survived the screening retention, which meant that I could serve until age 62. I felt I had also done my durance vile at CinCLant, and it was time to move on and let somebody else in there. I had discussed that with Admiral Duncan, and had found myself a relief, Leslie Sell.‡

I was getting ready to go to Portugal, which was going to be about five months of Portuguese language training at the Foreign Service Institute. Then I had another month of training to cover the MAAG side of the picture, not the NATO side. It was probably beneficial being double-hatted. However, the ambassador didn't much like that.

Paul Stillwell: Why not?

Admiral Erly: Oh, he felt that my IberLant duties would take too much of my energies away from the MAAG side.

---

* Rear Admiral Eugene B. Fluckey, USN, served as Commander Allied Forces Iberian-Atlantic Area and Chief, Military Assistance Advisory Group Portugal from 1968 to 1972.
† Admiral Thomas H. Moorer, USN, served as Supreme Allied Commander Atlantic, Commander in Chief Atlantic, and Commander in Chief Atlantic Fleet from 30 April 1965 to 17 June 1967. His oral history is in the Naval Institute collection.
‡ Rear Admiral Leslie H. Sell, USN.

Paul Stillwell: How proficient did you become in Portuguese?

Admiral Erly: Oh, I'd say almost equally as in Spanish, but I can't help but chuckle, because at the end of the course there was an oral examination. For my test there were three instructors and the department head. We talked about World War II and the possibilities of World War III and stocks and bonds, etc. This went on for well over an hour or two.

When it was all over and I got an excellent final mark, I asked why it was not perfect. I said, "Look, we covered half the waterfront and went from A to Z, nonstop."

They said, "Oh, yes, we covered all these. We sure did, but half of it was in Spanish."

Paul Stillwell: How much briefing did you get about the job from the State Department?

Admiral Erly: Fair. The ambassador, Ridgway Knight, came back.* I went over and called on him, and he gave me some background data. I also had six weeks of MAAG training under the State Department. I also, of course, went to OP-63 and OP-62 to see what we had for the Portuguese Navy. I hit the Army and Air Force. This was all programmed for the Portuguese Armed Forces. This was all on the MAAG side of the picture. On the SACLant side of the picture, for IberLant, I went down to Norfolk and was briefed on the NATO aspects. I would say I went over there fairly well armed, so to speak.

Proficiency in Portuguese, I could talk on the phone with the Portuguese and understand them. They could understand me. I feel that in any language, if you can do that, it shows you do have some mastery of the language. You can't use any body language. I felt the preparation was adequate, perhaps more than adequate. I could have done it much sooner in much less time, actually. That language training, it's slow, repetitive. In addition to many hours with an instructor, I spent many more hours listening to and recording tapes, both at home and at the Foreign Service Institute.

---

* Ridgway B. Knight served as U.S. Ambassador to Portugal from 30 July 1969 to 24 February 1973.

Incidentally, the pronunciation of European Portuguese is different from Brazilian Portuguese.

Paul Stillwell: In what way?

Admiral Erly: The Brazilian pronunciation has gotten to be an imitation of Spanish, almost pronounced the way it's written. Therefore, it's more melodious and has a lilting cadence. Whereas the Portuguese has the Gaelic R. It's harsher. And as the Brazilians say, they speak Portuguese with honey.

I think that's the influence of the flow and whatnot of Spanish. Like you say, "No" in Portuguese. You nasalize it so it sounds like "Naow. Likewise yes in Spanish is "Si." The Portuguese say they can understand the Spaniards, but the Spaniards can't understand them. When you listen to a Brazilian talking versus the European Portuguese, it sounds so melodious compared to the other.

Paul Stillwell: That job as IberLant was then quite new. What was involved in that? Fluckey really had set it up, hadn't he?

Admiral Erly: He had done a great deal of groundwork, because when I got there, they were recovering from bomb damage to the main headquarters building.[*] A terrorist group had also tried to bomb a transmitter site and a receiver site established in underground bunkers across the Tagus River. They did successfully bomb the administrative headquarters building. This occurred a couple of months prior to my arrival. When I got there they hadn't officially opened the headquarters, which was at an old fort installation in Oaris. It still had all the stuff underground and the tunnels underground for the ancient fort that guarded the entrance to Lisbon. They had built the administrative offices up above on a hill, and that's what they had bombed. They didn't get to the underground operations center. This underground center was really our

---

[*] The bomb damage to the headquarters building at Oeiras, Portugal, was on 27 October 1971. Despite the damage, the headquarters was commissioned on 29 October

operational control center. All radio and all telephonic communications, display boards, and other related items needed to visually display pertinent information.

When I took over from Gene, it was a bare shell—both the underground and the administration building. Also, the staff was not fully manned. The vice commander was a Portuguese commodore. The next senior was an RAF colonel who was the chief of staff.* We started fleshing out; we got our full complement. Then we had to get organized as an operational entity and set up a watch system and do all those things that had to be done in preparation for participation in the NATO exercises and CPXs.

IberLant had not run or participated in a big exercise. The biggest problem was communications. In the underground center we had relays so we could send to the transmitter station and also to receive from the receiver station across the River Tagus. And for the first, oh, I'd say, six to eight months, all the staff and administration were in the underground. Finally started moving the administrative side of things up to the topside building.

Boy, I was thinking about briefings. We had briefings for every audience—visiting VIPs, for the Portuguese War College, and even for the press, and for all the NATO ambassadors. For the latter it was a little bit of a dichotomy in command relationships, because on one hand, the U.S. ambassador was just an ambassador of a NATO country, and I was a NATO commander. And the other is, I reported to him as a member of his staff as chief MAAG.

Paul Stillwell: Did that ever cause any difficulties?

Admiral Erly: No, no it didn't for me. One of the last things I did as I retired was that I recommended that ComIberLant and Chief MAAG not—repeat not—be double hatted. I also recommended that IberLant be a three-star billet, as initially proposed by Tom Moorer when he was SACLant. They have been separate for some years. However, what has happened over there now is that the American is number two, because the U.S. Navy wouldn't come up with a three-star billet. Now they've got a Portuguese three-star who is CinCIberLant. And maybe that's the way it should be, I don't know. As I say,

---

* RAF – Royal Air Force.

IberLant was a U.S. deal. Tom pushed it. I was thinking that Ridgway Knight was also in favor of it.

Paul Stillwell: Any specifics on Ridgway Knight, his personality, his style of operating?

Admiral Erly: Well, you know who Ridgway was, don't you?

Paul Stillwell: No.

Admiral Erly: Do you remember Mark Clark lost his pants in that submarine landing on the French coast?

Paul Stillwell: Vaguely. I don't remember the details.

Admiral Erly: It was Mark Clark and Jerauld Wright, and they went ashore to meet with French loyalists.* They were landed on the beach in a rubber boat from a British submarine. They were there to establish French support for an invasion. Ridgway Knight met them on the beach. This was in Vichy, France. Ridgway's background, he was brought up in France. His dad was in the wine business over there, and he spoke French fluently and was working with the French underground. Very interesting character, actually. He had set up the meeting with Clark, Wright, and the French. After the meeting, in the process of getting back to the submarine, German patrol came by. Evidently, in getting Clark back into the rubber boat, he lost his pants. Later Ridgway got out of France and to the U.S. He was inducted as a lieutenant in the Army. Mark Clark tapped him as his aide. I remember the story he tells that Mark Clark could not stand Montgomery.† Whenever Montgomery showed up, Mark Clark would go to his

---

* In October 1942 Captain Jerauld Wright, USN, accompanied Major General Mark Clark, USA, on board the British submarine *Seraph* to Algeria, where they met secretly with Free French officials. Their aim, not achieved, was to get the French to welcome the Operation Torch landings in November 1942.
† Field Marshal Sir Bernard Law Montgomery (1887-1976) was a controversial British Army officer. In 1942 he commanded the Eighth Army during victorious operations in North Africa. He later commanded Allied armies in Northern Europe and commanded the British-occupied zone in Germany after victory was achieved in World War II.

trailer and go on the commode and wouldn't leave until Montgomery had left. And this is from Ridgway.

Paul Stillwell: What was he like as an ambassador?

Admiral Erly: I think he was a good ambassador, a good ambassador. He ran a taut ship. I remember I'd go to some of the meetings there, and he had these youngsters that were coming on board and who had to get up and make presentations, this type of thing. He ran a taut ship. From there he went to Brussels and then retired. Ridgway and I got along fine.

Paul Stillwell: What did your role as a NATO commander entail? Did you have any operational responsibilities?

Admiral Erly: Yes, we ran exercises. As I say, and we would run them out of the underground command post. We ran quite a few.

Again, this business of personal contact and what you can accomplish one on one is something else. I met the French admiral from Brest, and we hit it off quite famously. Lois and I traveled to Brest and were his guests. Then I entertained him down in Portugal. We were having this one exercise schedule, and the French were supposed to provide a couple of submarines, and all of a sudden I got a message they couldn't. So I sent a personal message to him and said, "The submarine withdrawal will cancel my exercise. Can you get this changed and assign a couple of your submarines?" Sure enough he did, on my personal intervention.

But I was just thinking about exercises, because in May of '74 is when they had their revolution. This had been brewing and this was part of all this terrorist bit, as you can see, to overthrow the government. Over my two-year period there had been several abortive attempts to overthrow the government. You would hear rumors of this and rumors of that, and so forth. Also, we were briefed by our embassy. I was personally threatened by phone calls, which I completely ignored. I'd still go ahead with my routine. I'd get out of my car and walk the Malecon and continue to do what I did.[*]

Then finally, it was a coup pulled off basically by the young military officers. We were having a big NATO exercise. I had Canadian aircraft at their Portuguese Air Force field. We had, let's see, Dutch, Norwegian, Brits, Canadian, U.S., we had the NATO standing force, all participating on this one exercise, minesweepers, the whole bit. We were sweeping the channel going out. This was all laid out in the operations plan and the pre-exercise briefings.

At the start of the exercise, I was going to have them at 8:00 o'clock muster on station, and we'd go down to the underground command post and pull the door closed. I got a call about 0500 from a Portuguese woman who worked in the MAAG office in Lisbon. She said, "Admiral, have you listened to the radio this morning?"

I said, "No."

She said, "There's a revolution and everyone is supposed to stay home. What do I do?"

I said, "Well, you call Captain Mosica [my MAAG deputy] and you tell him to direct all military personnel to go immediately to the MAAG headquarters, and direct all Portuguese civilians to stay home."

That was it. I hung up and called my NATO headquarters. A Portuguese commander had the duty. It had been planned to have all IberLant personnel report at 8:00. I directed, "Go ahead and start your recall now and get everybody on board soonest, because we're going ahead with this exercise. Also, tune in on the local radio station and note what is occurring."

Well, then I headed on down there to get everybody on board and do what we had to do. The ships had started out. The minesweepers had started their sweep, and then the surface ships were sortieing, but the Portuguese frigate did not. It was anchored off the Defense Ministry, and evidently the crew refused to get under way. This I found out later. But they also wouldn't open fire on the defense palace, either.

---

[*] "Malecón is a Spanish word for a waterfront embankment or esplanade.

As the day progressed, the NATO ships and aircraft were well into the exercise. The NATO Standing Force commander asked if ships were required to stand by to pick up their nationals.

I said, "No, the exercise continues. There have been no violent incidents. Will keep you advised."

Well, I had an augmented staff for the exercise as we were going to be standing watches around the clock. Among them were several Portuguese officers. About this time, we received a report that the rebels had closed all airports. We had ASW aircraft, Canadian, I believe, airborne from the Portuguese Air Force field close to Lisbon. I needed reassurance that the aircraft could be landed and refueled as necessary. So we drafted a message to the airfield requesting confirmation of their support. We got an affirmative reply. As time progressed, it looked like the ins were out, and I was saying, "Okay, I want to find out if whoever is in is playing this game, are they still in NATO? Are they still with it?"

The answer came back, "Oh, yes."

So in the midst of the revolution, the NATO exercise was running just fine.

About 9:00 o'clock that night, I threw a kidney stone. I had the nausea, I had everything that went with it. My IberLant medical officer was a young British lieutenant. He said, "You need to be hospitalized."

Well, the Portuguese had beat to general quarters. Even the reserves had been called up to man the Portuguese Naval Hospital. A Portuguese naval ambulance and a called-up reserve commander arrived at my headquarters at midnight. The commander suggested that I go out in a stretcher, but I declined.

I said, "No, I'm not going to lay down; it's too uncomfortable. I'm going to sit up in front with the driver," which I did, which gave me a firsthand view of what was taking place in Lisbon. The hospital was situated in the old part of Lisbon, up the hill.

Everything was quiet. Portuguese Marines were patrolling, but there was no shooting. Everything was quiet. It was a bloodless revolution.

I think the Portuguese commander doctor who rode in the back of the ambulance was wondering, "What the hell is he pulling?"

Upon arrival, I was assigned to the presidential suite. As I was sitting on the end of the bed, the doctor tapped me directly over my left kidney, and I went ten feet in the air. Then they put a painkiller drip in my arm. I was in misery.

When the pain abated in the morning, I went back to the headquarters until the pain came again. Then I went back to the hospital for more painkiller. We ran the exercise and finished it. I mentioned earlier that my staff was augmented for the exercise. One of the Portuguese augmentees, a Navy commander, was a primary conspirator in the revolution. He evidently paved the way to keep the exercise going and exercise aircraft flying. Two weeks later he was a four-star Navy admiral.

Paul Stillwell: I take it you eventually passed the kidney stone.

Admiral Erly: Yes. Finally what happened, after so many days, I started to run a fever. in about five. I figured, "Well, I must say Portuguese medicine is about 75 years behind our." So I flew over to Torrejón Air Force hospital, and I finally passed it there in about three days.* Boy, I don't want to have one of those again.

Paul Stillwell: What language was used in the IberLant headquarters for conducting the exercises?

Admiral Erly: English. Not French, English. And that's predominant. I think you'd find it most anywhere now, although I called it my Tower of Babel for lots of reasons. In the first place, not to mention the nationalities involved, but you had Army, Navy, Air Force, and we even had one U.S. Marine. And with all that, I always used to say our biggest problem in this Tower of Babel exists between—which two nationalities would you think?

Paul Stillwell: Portuguese and Spanish.

Admiral Erly: Didn't have any Spaniards, because they weren't in NATO at this time.

---
* Torrejón Air Force Base, near Madrid, Spain.

Paul Stillwell: Oh, I see.

Admiral Erly: The Americans and the Brits. You know why?

Paul Stillwell: No.

Admiral Erly: Well, they think they understood each other.

Paul Stillwell: Two civilizations separated by a common language.

Admiral Erly: Yes. Believe me.

Paul Stillwell: Oh, I do. What was the relationship between this command and NATO headquarters? How much interaction, how much planning together with them?

Admiral Erly: Actually, our immediate boss was SACLant. That's where the play went on. As I mentioned before, we were Tom Moorer's brainchild, and it came under his aegis as SACLant. He felt IberLant was basically for the safety of the convoys coming on down from the north and going into the Med. Our hand-off point was Gibraltar.

However, the IberLant area went on down, down the coast past Gibraltar, to our line of demarcation just off Madeira. Madeira, as such, was also in my domain. The chop line was a funny chop line from up from the border of Spain all the way down, and then going out to the islands, and then on down to Madeira. And Madeira, of course, and another island close aboard there, where there was an airfield and aviation fuel, which was an interim landing facility.

Back again, the infrastructure that the Portuguese made available for NATO was really staggering. Across the Tagus were fuel oil storage and fuel piers, a big ammunition depot, several airfields, not to mention just the complex encompassing my IberLant headquarters and communication transmitter and receiver centers.

And then what was going on in the island off Madeira. It was quite an investment when you saw the real estate they had made available for NATO. Now, how much of that infrastructure was paid for by NATO or by U.S., I can't answer. But they had made a sizable—just by the territory and terrain they had made available was quite staggering. When I would brief some of the other NATO people, it opened their eyes to how good an ally Portugal had been for NATO. I might say that in these installations, they were meticulously maintained. You could white glove them. Amazing.

Paul Stillwell: Was that the Portuguese influence?

Admiral Erly: Yes, yes, yes. Definitely. Because that was it. They were doing the maintenance.

Paul Stillwell: Was Salazar the guy that got ousted at that point?

Admiral Erly: No. Salazar had been ousted several years before. I'm trying to remember the Prime Minister at this point. The President was Admiral Américo Thomaz, and he was a spry old gentlemen.[*] I was calling him old, because in this time frame he was 20 years older than I was. Quite a charismatic man, actually.

They would have a meeting for all the—I guess this must have been under the MAAG hat where I would run into that at the palace. I guess on New Year's or Christmas Eve or something like that, you'd meet him, and he would be there and make the rounds. I also had the privilege of going shooting with him, and it was a spectacle out of the medieval times.

Paul Stillwell: In what sense?

Admiral Erly: In what sense, that I had two gun bearers, and I was on a stand, and then the beaters came in and they were all dressed in medieval costumes. They would beat and the doves would fly and the ducks would fly and the rabbits would jump. You were

---

[*] Américo Thomaz served as President of Portugal from 9 August 1958 to 25 April 1974. He was born 19 November 1894.

shooting like mad, and score was kept on each station. Of course, they gave the President the best station.

Then afterwards, in the field, lo and behold, most of the ministers would show up, and the rest of us were all in hunting gear. We would sit down to this banquet table, and the waiters in bow ties and tux, and we'd be served. The President sat at the head of the table, sort of as the great pater and keep the conversation rolling around and so forth. It was quite an experience.

Paul Stillwell: Was it something you undertook willingly?

Admiral Erly: I missed the first one because I had made a commitment to brief IberLant wives, the first time I was invited. I enjoyed it. It was the way to go. We started early morning with breakfast and a roaring fireplace, and then out on the stand. It was something you would envision that happened 100 years ago.

Paul Stillwell: Was the new regime as hospitable to the U.S. presence as the old one had been?

Admiral Erly: Oh, yes. They needed us. There wasn't any doubt about the presence, but they were all so leftist-oriented at that phase. They really were. I remember that I was flying to Spain to get rid of this kidney stone. It was a Portuguese plane and tuned in to Portuguese radio. Over the radio came the directive that all Portuguese activities were to have a minute of silence to honor Che Gueverra.[*]

Most of my friends were basically out. They did such things as this. Listen. My deputy was summarily retired. And how did they retire him and a whole slew of others? They had a selection board of a midshipman, an ensign, a jaygee, and up. They went up through the ranks like that, and that was the board that said which people were retired.

---

[*] Ernesto "Che" Guevara was a Marxist leader who was a key person in the Cuban revolution of the 1950s. On 8 October 1967 he was captured in Bolivia and executed the following day.

Paul Stillwell: Well, did it cause you problems having to deal with this leftist government?

Admiral Erly: It wasn't on the same basis. From the NATO side, as I told you, from the word go, and had proven that I ran that exercise right through the revolution, that come hell or high water they wanted to stay in NATO, number one. Well, right after the revolution, they lost their overseas possession, Angola. They went like a house of cards. They had already lost Mozambique spot several years before. It was taken over by the Indians. The islands coming up, they went. So they had lost all this, and then they had an exodus also coming in.

They opened all their prisons, practically let all the prisoners out, and then filled them with the secret police and with other political prisoners. They made a lot of people, boom, immediately—any opposition.

I'm trying to remember Fernando. When I went to Madeira, there was a brigadier over there, and we got very friendly. He was under my SACLant hat. He came back and he was the number-two security guy. They had him in the hoosegow.

Things that had happened, Américo Thomaz was sent off to Brazil. The Prime Minister evidently wouldn't order some things done, and the word was that Américo Thomaz called him a coward and a few other things to try to abort the revolution, because there really wasn't a shot fired. There was no bloodshed, really. But you had all these leftist-leaning people that were in there.

Within the week Mario Soares, a Socialist, came back and there was a big gathering, and I'm trying to remember the Communist's name. He came in and, God, he was met at the airfield. You never saw such an organization. However, he didn't get too far. Soares has been the President a couple of times, as a socialist.

But the Communist deal sort of ebbed, and this goes true to basically what happened—the same thing happened at the end of World War I. The same type of thing had happened in Portugal, and then the church and everything comes to the fore and those leftist elements get thrown out and it went the other way with Salazar and type of benevolent dictatorship, I guess you would call it. I have sort of lost interest. I kept up with it for a while. But I see that same trend is taking place, that the leftists went off and those people that were there are long since now gone, and it's sort of cycling back. But it played bloody hell, I thought. I felt like I had lost over two years of hard labor.

Paul Stillwell: Just because the people changed?

Admiral Erly: Yes, complete wipeout. Complete wipeout.

Paul Stillwell: Labor in what sense?

Admiral Erly: The making of contacts, the way to get things done, which door to knock on, so forth and so on. So it was all out the way.

Paul Stillwell: So you had to start over?

Admiral Erly: You bet.

Paul Stillwell: Did you get guidance from the ambassador or SACLant or both on how to react to this coup?

Admiral Erly: Nada. Nothing.

Paul Stillwell: Just common sense and your own devices?

Admiral Erly: Sure, sure.

Paul Stillwell: Well, presumably, if the United States had chosen to intervene, there would have been very overt guidance.

Admiral Erly: Sure. Sure. There was no way and there was no reason why the U.S. should intervene in that. As I say, there wasn't a drop of bloodshed. That's the revolution where the picture of putting roses in the end of rifles was on the front pages of newspapers.

Paul Stillwell: Why was Portugal so eager to remain part of NATO? Just for its own defense?

Admiral Erly: Well, I think with the infrastructure that was there, which meant jobs—

Paul Stillwell: So that was even a higher priority than national defense?

Admiral Erly: Well, no. What I'm really saying is this—what NATO was doing was bolstering the military. The military pulled the coup, and they weren't going to cut off the hand that was feeding them, the way I could see it, because NATO was funding these installations. That's hard cash coming in and, indirectly, funding the military.

Paul Stillwell: So the primary thing probably that Portugal contributes to the new alliance is its geographical position?

Admiral Erly: Yes. Well, its terrain too. Yes, sure. I'm trying to remember the islands down there, because when we would have our ASW planes—

Paul Stillwell: The Azores?

Admiral Erly: Well, we still have bases in the Azores. But when the planes would leave the Azores and go down the coast, there was an island, a Portuguese island they landed on and refueled. This was the way you could find out what in the hell was going on up and down the coastline, by those planes. It was sporadic, but in time of war it would have been essential.

Paul Stillwell: Did you have any responsibilities down along the west coast of Africa?

Admiral Erly: Yes. I'm trying to remember where my line ended. I'm trying to visualize the map, but it was down past Gibraltar. I would have been responsible for keeping those sea-lanes of communication open.

Paul Stillwell: Who would have had it farther south, ComSoLant?

Admiral Erly: I don't know.

Paul Stillwell: What do you remember about your responsibilities in the MAAG part of the job?

Admiral Erly: Well, again, the MAAG part of the job was trying to keep the Army, Navy, and the Portuguese Air Force happy with their demands and what they needed and what they could get. You've got to remember that with the Portuguese holding them down in Angola and Mozambique were basically populated by blacks. As you know, revolutionary black forces were ambushing and killing Portuguese troops. Our Black Caucus on the Hill was looking at any expenditures and military equipment to Portugal in this light.

I think one of them irked Tom Moorer as we were trying to update the Portuguese Navy's ASW capability.* Tom said he didn't know of any sonar that killed anyone. You had that Ron Dellums on the Armed Services Committee and the Black Caucus, which questioned any item on the Portuguese Army's wish list.† They were in a fight down there with the guerrillas, as you know, and most of those were black. So trying to keep them happy and seeing that we could meet their request for military assistance. They had our tanks, and they needed to get spare parts, etc. I was chief of the MAAG, and then I had a chief of section for each section, i.e., I had a chief Air Force section, who was a colonel; chief Navy section, full Navy captain; and chief Army section, who was a full

---

* Admiral Thomas H. Moorer, USN, served as Chairman of the Joint Chiefs of Staff from 3 July 1970 to 30 June 1974. His oral history is in the Naval Institute collection.
† Ronald V. Dellums, a Democrat from California, served in the House of Representatives from 3 January 1971 until his resignation on 6 February 1998.

colonel. Through them we had the shopping list for the military support and things that the Portuguese military required to be an effective force.

I remember that they were very, very touchy on protocol. I remember being overly encumbered with IberLant problems when a new head of our Army section was going to present his papers. The outgoing section chief had set this up without including me. I received a personal call from the Portuguese Army Chief of Staff, stating he would not receive them unless I attended. Thus my Army chief learned his protocol lesson early on.

Paul Stillwell: Did the requests or demands, or whatever they were, from Portugal typically exceed what the United States was willing to make available?

Admiral Erly: No. Normally the MAAG section chief hammered out the detailed items that they submitted to SecDef for approval prior to being submitted to Congress.

Paul Stillwell: Was it a matter of negotiation with Portugal?

Admiral Erly: No, it wasn't that much of a negotiation with Portugal. It was with the Armed Services Committees in Congress that had to approve funding for foreign military assistance.

Paul Stillwell: Were these outright grants or assistance rather than sales?

Admiral Erly: Let's don't forget that we had Lajes Air Force Base in the Azores. It was also a primary support base for our P-3 aircraft flying ASW missions that were tracking Soviet submarines. They certainly rated military assistance from us. In some cases they would pay; some was a military assistance program itself. You've got to remember that Portugal was not that rich a nation, per se. The main export was cork; number one income, tourism. They were trying to get into big ship construction there on the Tagus.

In addition, they were spending money like mad on their colonies. They had, what, in the Yellow Sea, they had an island there, and then Macao, the island off of Hong

Kong. Macao is self-sufficient. But Mozambique, Angola, and—damn, the islands, I can't remember, down the way—were not. Once you left Lisbon, even in this time frame, '72 to '74, you went back 100 to 200 years. That was life.

Paul Stillwell: That's a dramatic change.

Admiral Erly: Oh, yes, yes.

Paul Stillwell: Do you have examples of that?

Admiral Erly: Oh, well, yes. You would see the women dressed completely in black and barefooted and in the fields, and this type of thing.

Paul Stillwell: Horse and cart?

Admiral Erly: Oh, yes, definitely. Definitely.

Paul Stillwell: What was it like as a place for you and your wife to live?

Admiral Erly: Well, it's that old business of have and have nots. We had quite a large house in a place called Ranholas, which was just about two miles from Sintra.

It was really a summer manor home built by some French people, with a swimming pool and separate servants' quarters and down below at the front gate. The manor had two bedrooms, two baths down below, and above were two bedrooms, two bath, one great big master suite, large salon, living room, dining room, and kitchen. I'd say square footage, oh, about 2,600, 3,000 feet. Swimming pool down below on the terrace. On a clear day you could see the United States, but there weren't too many clear days. The clouds would come in. Gene Fluckey found that house for us. I think misery loved company, because he had bought and built a home in Sintra. It was a great house for the summer, but humid and cold during the winter. There was no central heating. It was a great summer house—period.

Paul Stillwell: Admiral Fluckey stayed there for a number of years, I guess.

Admiral Erly: Yes, he did, about five to ten years. I would call down from the golf course and say, "Gee, it's socked in up here. What are your weather conditions?"

"Oh, come on down. The sun is shining brightly."

It was about three to four miles down to the golf course, straight downhill. We were just up where the clouds would come in. Folklore was that one of the kings had said, "Well, this is the only place where you can have the winter in the summer." It would have been fine for a summer house, say, from about June to October. But then forget it.

Paul Stillwell: So what did you do, use space heaters the rest of the time?

Admiral Erly: Yes, we had to get space heaters. Lois hated it.

Paul Stillwell: Understandably.

Admiral Erly: See, I was out of there and moving and she was in the house, and it was miserable for her.

One other thing you had to get, I got a dehumidifier, and so help me, we could have made enough water for the household needs.

Paul Stillwell: That's a humid climate.

Admiral Erly: Oh, yes, definitely.

Paul Stillwell: How much interaction did you have with the common people of Portugal?

Admiral Erly: Well, I went to a local barbershop, and when we traveled, we'd interact. We had a maid and a gardener who were Portuguese. They lived in the little house down below. We inherited them with the house when it was rented.

Paul Stillwell: Did you have a chance to measure attitudes toward the coup?

Admiral Erly: The Portuguese were basically friendly people. After the coup and some of them, when they started setting up their little governing blocks and this type of thing, they sort of changed. We left in '74, and we went back in '76. We were driving down to the Algarve and we stopped in this one little spot en route, and here was this group. It was supposed to have been a little saloon, and they were sort of surly and were having some type of meeting. I saw a change that way within the two years. The rank and file did not benefit from the revolution. There are always, as you know, the haves and the have-nots, period. Remember, there had not been a shot fired during the revolution. Obviously the local citizenry were ready for the change that had been impending for some time.

Paul Stillwell: So it was just a different group?

Admiral Erly: I made the observation it was like the storming of the Bastille in the French Revolution. Some of my Portuguese friends were then incarcerated in the freed prison cells. Well, my previous deputy went, and I got a new deputy. At one point he was packing a pistol and recommended I do the same. He was upset with the revolution. It's a wonder he hadn't been retired. They tried to get him, but didn't. He submitted a reclama that was accepted by the junta. But then you've got to realize that most of the Portuguese officers had another job.

Paul Stillwell: No, I didn't realize that.

Admiral Erly: Yes, quite a few. They did it to survive since their military salaries were low. They needed two jobs, except when they were deployed.

Paul Stillwell: Or standing watch on exercise.

Admiral Erly: Well, a lot of the Portuguese officers on my staff had two jobs. Some of them tutoring, teaching, you name it. The basic military support for the coup came from the younger officers.

There was an immediate change of all service chiefs. The new Air Force commander was one of their youngest generals who had distinguished himself in Mozambique. He was something else again. But wherever he went or met with me or others, he said, "Well, this is the guy that's watching me." The guy being a junior Air Force officer had been a member of the coup.

I don't think they are any better off now than they were before. I haven't seen any indication. When we first went over there, the exchange rate was about 26 escudos to the dollar. Now I think it's something now about 400 to the dollar. As I still say, tourism was one of their big, big factors. And then after the revolution, for a while that messed things up, and I think they're trying to get that moving again. The graffiti and whatnot that was done on some of the public monuments and whatnot still has to be repaired. I think it set them back. It probably set them back about five or ten years.

Paul Stillwell: Well, your economy's not too solid if your two main industries are cork and tourism.

Admiral Erly: That was it. The Algarve you've heard me mention—

Paul Stillwell: Yes.

Admiral Erly: And that was a great buildup, building golf course after golf course, and the high-rise and time-shares, before we ever thought about it over here. See this time-share concept was very, very popular, and this is where it started, in Europe. Then it was in Portugal in the early '70s, and this is the way they were going, building time-shares like mad. And getting, I guess, a lot of the northern Europeans who were coming down there, because the Algarve is down inside the Med, and it's much warmer. And Portugal being about 300 miles long on the coastline here and just about 100 miles wide. A little country. A little country.

Again, there are people that have lots and then there are lots that have practically nothing. They were starting to build the middle class that worked for the government, the shopkeepers. But again, you might say, its location and its infrastructure, NATO infrastructure, made it very attractive. It kept, really, the, I think, military functioning. Otherwise, the country would not have been able to support its armed forces. Of course, there was the quid pro quo from the U.S.A. foreign military aid for the use of Lajes in the Azores.

Paul Stillwell: Well, any other thoughts to wrap up that tour of duty?

Admiral Erly: Well, that was my last tour of duty. I came back and went down and debriefed at SACLant and gave them some of my impressions of the revolution and Portugal.

The young Portuguese air officer took exception to some of the things I had to say and sent a message back to Portugal that I was doing this, that, or the other, which I didn't find out until I'd gone back to CNO and OP-63. The admiral who was running the military assistance, saying, "Hey, we want to get together with the attaché," and he had trouble. He said, "Gees, I don't know what's going on, Bob."

I finally got the picture of what had gone on. The Portuguese attaché was afraid to be seen with me because I was tainted, that I had damned their revolution, or words to that effect.

So I went on, took my physical exam, and said, "Oh, the hell with it."

I had been back. I had been having quite a few problems as an aftermath of that subarachnoid hemorrhage. You just don't walk away after you've spilled a lot of raw blood in the spinal column fluid without it taking some toll on you. My neurologist at the Bethesda Naval Hospital, I'd come back once with symptoms, and he said, "You've got to come back and we've got to do another angiogram."

I said, "Hell, no, I think—" I balked all the way, but I went back and had it again and all this stuff. I said, "You know I'm getting a little fed up with all this."

The doctor said, "You know, you'd be a lot better off if you retired. It well might add five years to your life."[*]

So I thought that over, and I said, "Okay, let's do it."

Paul Stillwell: Were you offered any other billets at that point?

Admiral Erly: I could have stayed on for another two years, actually. But he indicated the stress and the strain wasn't worth it. He said, "You've got enough problems as it is. Why do it?" So I took the physical. I was retired physically, which sure as hell helps on that income tax.

Paul Stillwell: Did you have any withdrawal symptoms leaving after 35 years as a commissioned officer?

Admiral Erly: Well, I went back to Portugal, and that's where I retired, in Portugal. You know, while I was there, Ridgway Knight was only there six months. And then I think the last six months I was there we had it. So what really happened, I was almost the ambassador pro tem, if you would, and was so regarded by the other ambassadors, because when I went back in '76, the Dutch ambassador said, "You going to call on the American ambassador?"

I said, "No, I'm just here on a personal visit."

"Oh, but you ought to call on him," and so forth.

I don't remember the ambassador's name.[†] He was later Secretary of Defense, and he was head of the National Security Council for the President under Reagan.[‡] I went in and talked with him. I was just going to pay a courtesy call, five or ten minutes, and, God, I was there for a couple of hours.

What was bugging the hell out of him was that he was afraid of a rightist coup coming up at this point. He had come from Brussels. He had quite a checkered career,

---

[*] Admiral Erly lived to be 100 years old.
[†] Frank C. Carlucci III was U.S. Ambassador to Portugal from 24 January 1975 to 5 February 1978.
[‡] Carlucci served as U.S. Secretary of Defense from 23 November 1987 to 20 January 1989. He was National Security Advisor to President Ronald Reagan from 2 January 1987 to 23 November 1987.

really. The Danish ambassador lived across the street from the American Embassy, so we were getting all the skinny. The guy had been divorced and had a redheaded secretary, whom he later married, a good-looking gal. But we were in on all that was happening at the American Embassy, before they got married. Oh, God, his name. If I said it, you'd know it. He was SecDef.

He was a Republican, yes. But in the interim, before he got there, there had been a lawyer who had come out of nowhere, out of New York. He was as surprised as anybody else to end up the last six months there.* Very nice gent. When he got there, he wasn't there more than a month. Then he went off to have a hip replaced. We enjoyed him.

In fact, Ed Miller, who had been ahead of Gene Fluckey over there, who just passed away, Admiral Miller was over visiting, and the ambassador wanted to have a great big going-away party.† I said, "No, I'd just rather not have that. I would like just a small dinner party with you and my deputy and the Millers." And that's what we had.

When we got back there, my deputy headed up a little deal and all this business and the young lieutenant was over and they had and so forth, and it was a hill of beans before the time he got. I guess that meant nothing to him.

Ralph Cousins had relieved Charlie Duncan about a year, I guess, before that, and Ralph's a classmate of mine. And as you see, he's trying to be a real good guy in here. He was recommending me to be commandant of the naval district in New Orleans. I think I might have mentioned that to him, if I wasn't going to get three stars, I'd go on and be the commandant in New Orleans because that was close to Lois's home town, and I might have settled there, if that had happened.

Paul Stillwell: Well, since it didn't, what did you wind up doing instead?

Admiral Erly: Well, didn't do a damn thing. We went back, I tried to talk Lois into doing Europe. We came back and went to Gulfport, Mississippi. This house was rented

---
* Stuart Nash Scott was ambassador to Portugal from 23 January 1974 to 12 January 1975.
† In 1966 Rear Admiral Edwin S. Miller, USN, became Chief, Military Assistance Advisory Group Portugal. In 1967 he gained additional duty as the first commander of NATO's Iberian Atlantic Area. He remained in those billets until he retired in 1968.

and was supposed to have been rented for the year. We'd been in Gulfport, oh, a month or two, and we got a letter from this Navy captain saying he could get quarters, he'd like to get out of the lease. We wrote back and said, "That's just fine. Just finish the month. You can't help but make money by being in quarters. Go."

So we came out to look at the property. We had been gone nine years and had to make a decision whether we were going to drop anchor here in Coronado or in Gulfport, and we finally opted to live here. I haven't done a damn thing since, except be a volunteer, like Jimmy Holloway.

Paul Stillwell: Well, it's nice to have that luxury.

Admiral Erly: Yes, yes. Looking back on the whole bit, of course, I was just thinking I should perhaps revise my biog. What did I do? You know, you get involved here one way and you get involved in another.

Paul Stillwell: Well, you've been on the Naval Academy Foundation.

Admiral Erly: Oh, yes. And don't forget, I was the western area vice president for the Naval Academy Alumni Association. I headed the chapter up here for several years. I was president of the Coronado Playhouse. I was chairman of the Coronado branch of the American Cancer Society. I was on the board of directors of the San Diego Unit. I'm on the board, and still am on the board, of the California cancer division board of directors. I'm on the board of directors of the Freedom Foundation of Valley Forge, the American Red Cross. What the hell else? Oh, there are a few more, but one thing or the other. Stay busy. I just find that I thought I was going to have time to sort of relax and do nothing, and I find that I'm still, now pushing 78, and I'm still pushing.

Paul Stillwell: Well, but presumably at a less-demanding pace than had you stayed on active duty longer.

Admiral Erly: No. Hell, I think it's probably more frustrating. However, I'm glad. I think at the moment, as I'm looking and seeing what's happening in the Navy that you were in, even, and the Navy that I was in, is not the same Navy today as it was then. This business of being an officer and a gentlemen and the perks that went with it just aren't there anymore. But I venture to say, I would do it all over again. I enjoyed every moment of it.

Paul Stillwell: Except possibly the kidney stone.

Admiral Erly: Yes. That's what's worrying me. I hope I'm not trying to throw another one.

Paul Stillwell: What are some of the satisfactions that come to mind as you reflect back on that career?

Admiral Erly: Oh, I think the biggest satisfactions of all were the ship commands, really.

Paul Stillwell: Because you can have a very direct personal influence that way.

Admiral Erly: Oh, absolutely, more so than others. You try in a multiple command, but it's not the same as an individual ship command. I had the phibron. I tried to cover all units and whatnot, but it's not the same. Phib group, same thing.

Paul Stillwell: You were even farther removed there.

Admiral Erly: Oh, sure, sure. Then the ship commands are too few and far between, but they were worth it when you had it. And the sense of accomplishment. I think, in a ship command particularly, when you commission it and get it going, you haven't picked up something that's on the upsurge, or even on the downsurge and stopped it or whatever, but if you commission it, or even recommission it, and see it come alive and take on personality and do well, I think it's a satisfaction that can't be replaced.

Paul Stillwell: One of your thoughts echoes something that I've heard from a number of men I've interviewed, that, "The Navy is not as good to be in now as it was when I was there."

Admiral Erly: Well, I'll bet you that from the time of John Paul Jones that has been so.

Paul Stillwell: Allegedly, when the second Marine joined the first one in the Marine Corps, the first one said, "Well, you know, it wasn't like this in the old Corps."

Admiral Erly: Yes, I guarantee. Well, let's put it this way. We're going to say, your children aren't going to have the same life you had.

Paul Stillwell: Certainly not.

Admiral Erly: And things are going to change. Or are changing. I think you can make that analogy between that and the service, or what happened, because it's a reflection of our society, and what we are. We are members of this society.

Paul Stillwell: But the system that you grew up in and grew to know feels comfortable, and so a departure from that feels uncomfortable.

Admiral Erly: Sure. Yes. Oh, absolutely.

Paul Stillwell: Any final valedictory thoughts?

Admiral Erly: Oh, I think for anything, in thoughts or whatever you're going to do, do it to the best of your ability. Don't hold back. Don't look back. Always look ahead. And don't accept something because they say it's always been this way. It doesn't necessarily mean it's the best way. Unless you grow and improve, you're going to degrade instead of upgrade. Those are the thoughts that I would like to leave that anyone is listening to this tape, that you've always got to have aims and you should always aim high, never low. That becomes QED.

Paul Stillwell: Well, Admiral, it has taken us several years to finish it, but I'm glad we did it. I'm grateful to you for contributing these recollections and grateful to Admiral Minter for recommending you for the program.* This, along with the career itself, is a legacy that will last for years to come. So I'm grateful for your contribution.

Admiral Erly: Well, I'm pleased to participate, and I'm sorry that, as I've gotten older, I may find that my memory is fallible. I was hoping if you'd do a draft, that perhaps I could amend or insert or something if things come to mind.

Paul Stillwell: You'll have that opportunity.

Admiral Erly: Good, because I think, as I see something, I'll say, "Gee, why didn't I say that." So I will look forward to doing that.

Admiral Erly: I find it very exasperating and people said, "Well, you can't type?"

And I say, "Hell, no, I can't type, because if I had to do anything, I always could dictate it." But that comes to your boys coming up. I hope you make them take typing.

Paul Stillwell: They are.

Admiral Erly: Good. At this time I would like to salute my lifetime partner, Lois, for her unvarying support throughout the years.† She was my biggest supporter and press agent and an essential part of my success. Her diplomatic handling of foreign dignitaries and U.S. officials rate her as an unsurpassed U.S. ambassador.

Paul Stillwell: Thank you, Admiral.

---

* Vice Admiral Charles S. Minter, USN (Ret.), is the subject of a Naval Institute oral history.
† Lois Erly died in 2004 after that couple had been married 60 years. He later married Thea Wallace.

Index to the Oral History of
Rear Admiral Robert B. Erly, U.S. Navy (Retired)

Abraham Lincoln, **USS (SSBN-602)**
Visited in the late 1960s by an Atlantic Fleet inspection team, 402-403

Advancement of Enlisted Personnel
As the result of manpower needs, individuals moved up much more rapidly during World War II than previously, 171-172

Alcohol
The ship's officers had a drinking problem when Erly reported to the destroyer *Laub* (DD-613) in 1944, 148
Effects of alcohol use on the part of Commander Escort Division 21 in 1944-45, 175-177

Algeria
British warships bombarded the French fleet at Mers-el-Kébir in July 1940 to keep it from falling into German hands, 153-154
In 1944 U.S. warships trained at Oran in preparation for an upcoming invasion, 159, 161-162

American Red Cross
Provided support to Navy families in the early 1950s, 210

Ammunition
Increase in ammunition capacity of the destroyer *Frazier* (DD-607) before she deployed in 1942, 126
Unexploded North Korean projectile hit the destroyer *James C. Owens* (DD-776) in May 1952, 231-232
In May 1952 a 40-millimeter ammo magazine on board the *James C. Owens* did not explode, even when it absorbed a direct hit, 233

Amphibious Force Pacific Fleet
In the early and mid-1960s participated in various exercises, 310-311, 314-315. 360
Development of amphibious warfare doctrine in the 1960s, 314-317
Origin of SEALs and Navy special warfare in the 1960s, 361-363
Push in the mid-1960s for development of 20-knot LSTs, 364
Exercises in the mid-1960s, 364-368
Role of the staff in the mid-1960s, 365-366
Buildup in the mid-1960s for the Vietnam War, 365, 369-370

Amphibious Warfare
A contingent from the battleship *New Mexico* (BB-40) made a disastrous practice landing on Maui, Hawaii, in the summer of 1938, 52-53

Operations and exercises under the aegis of Amphibious Group Two, 1953-55, 245-262

In the mid-1950s amphibious doctrine tied in with the use of helicopters and tactical nuclear weapons, 254-257

Question in the mid-1950s as to whether LPHs would be commanded by aviators or surface officers, 277, 309

Originally a merchant ship, the *Diamond Mariner* was converted to become the Navy attack transport *Paul Revere* (APA-248) in 1958, 273, 285-292, 299-308

Advantages of having 20-knot ships in the amphibious force, 307-309

Joint-service amphibious warfare exercises in the early 1960s, 310-311, 314-315

Development of amphibious warfare doctrine in the 1960s, 314-317

Operations in the Pacific in 1961-62, 321-345

Push in the mid-1960s for development of 20-knot LSTs and LHAs, 364

Exercises in the Pacific in the mid-1960s, 364-368

Amphibious Squadron Five
Operations in the Pacific in 1961-62, 321-345

Antiair Warfare
Antiaircraft guns on board the battleship *New Mexico* (BB-40) in the late 1930s, 46-47

Types of fuzes on 5-inch antiaircraft projectiles by ships at Pearl Harbor in 1941, 96

Erly set up antiaircraft batteries ashore at Ewa, Oahu, in the wake of the Japanese attack in 1941, 110-115, 125

In the early 1950s the destroyer *James C. Owens* (DD-776) served in the North Atlantic as a seaward extension of the DEW Line, 224-226

Antisubmarine Warfare
Patrols out of Pearl Harbor by the destroyer *Cassin* (DD-372) in 1941, 97-99

In 1943 the U.S. Navy upgraded two Cuban Navy ships and trained their crews for antisubmarine warfare, 136-147

Mission for the destroyer *Laub* (DD-613) in 1944 while on Atlantic convoys, 151-154

Among the subjects taught at General Line School in 1949-50, 196, 199

Training for the crew of the destroyer *James C. Owens* (DD-776) in the early 1950s, 214-215, 222

Use of amphibious warfare ships as decoys against submarines in the early 1960s, 308, 324-325, 343-345

Anzio, Italy
U.S. Navy gunfire support of the invasion and operations ashore in early 1944, 154-155

ARAMCO (Arabian American Oil Company)
Visited by the destroyer *James C. Owens* (DD-776) in 1952, 240-241

Argentina
    Negotiations with the U.S. Navy in the mid-1960s, 388-389

***Arkansas*, USS (BB-33)**
    Midshipman summer training cruise to Europe in 1934, 17-21

Armed Forces Staff College, Norfolk, Virginia
    Curriculum for students in 1952-53 emphasized staff work, 243-245, 248-249

Army, U.S.
    In 1960 the commanding general of the Fourth Infantry Division advocated the use of nuclear weapons in a war game, 340-341
    Operations in Vietnam in the mid-1960s included riverine warfare, 376-377

Ashworth, Vice Admiral Frederick L., USN (USNA, 1933)
    As Deputy Commander in Chief Atlantic Fleet in the late 1960s, 400-401
    Retired from active duty in the late 1960s when he was not selected for a fourth star, 383

Atlantic Fleet, U.S.
    In 1952 Destroyer Division 221 deployed to the Korean War zone and then completed a transit around the world, 217-221, 227-243
    Role of the fleet inspector general in the late 1960s, 400-410
    Establishment of a command center in the late 1960s, 410-411
    Impact of budget cuts in the late 1960s-early 1970s, 420-422
    Consolidation of three different types commands into Surface Force Atlantic Fleet in the 1970s, 423-424

Australia
    Visited by the destroyer *Cassin* (DD-372) in early 1941, 89, 92-93

Australian Navy
    Took part in a SEATO exercise in Borneo in the early 1960s, 322-323

Barbey, Vice Admiral Daniel E., USN (USNA, 1912)
    In 1946, as Commander Amphibious Force Atlantic Fleet, helped facilitate the transfer of the *LST-907* to the Venezuelan Navy, 183-186

Bardshar, Rear Admiral Frederic A., USN (USNA, 1938)
    In 1954 was operations officer of the aircraft carrier *Leyte* (CVS-32)
    Served 1956-58 in the Strategic Plans Division of OpNav, 274

Battleships
    In the mid-1950s House Armed Services Chairman Carl Vinson had no interest in keeping battleships in the fleet, 270-271

Beach, Captain Edward L., USN (USNA, 1939)
As a student at the National War College in the early 1960s, 358

Beach Jumper Units
Worked in collaboration with Amphibious Group Two in the mid-1950s, 252, 258-259

Bell, Captain C. Edwin, USN (USNA, 1939)
In 1962 was a possible candidate to be chief of staff to Commander Amphibious Force Pacific Fleet, 346-347

Bellinger, Rear Admiral Patrick N. L., USN (USNA, 1907)
Commanded Patrol Wing Two at Pearl Harbor during the Japanese attack in 1941 and its aftermath, 109, 111-112

Benson, Captain James F., USN (USNA, 1927)
Commanded the destroyer tender *Yosemite* (AD-19), 1946-48, 163-164, 194

Bent, Lieutenant Horace E., USN (USNA, 1940)
Helped train the crews of Cuban Navy ships in 1943, 142

Betancourt, Rómulo Ernesto Bello
Served as President of Venezuela from 1945 to 1948, 180, 182, 184-185

Blouin, Vice Admiral Francis J., USN (USNA, 1933)
In the 1960s served as ComPhibGruWestPac and later as ComPhibPac, 365

Borneo
Site of a SEATO amphibious warfare exercise in the early 1960s, 322-323

Boxing
In his youth Erly boxed for a National Guard team in Washington, D.C., 9-10
Erly boxed at the Naval Academy in the mid-1930s and helped coach, 14, 25
By members of the crew of the battleship *New Mexico* (BB-40) in the late 1930s, 33, 41, 43

Bradley, Lieutenant Commander Montgomery S., USNR
In 1944 served as temporary skipper of the destroyer *Phelps* (DD-360), 164

Brown, Lieutenant Elliott M., USN (USNA, 1931)
Was the first executive officer of the destroyer *Frazier* (DD-607), commissioned in 1942, 125, 129-130

Bucher, Commander Lloyd R., USN
Commanded the intelligence ship *Pueblo* (AGER-2) when she was captured by North Koreans in 1968, 135

Bucklew, Captain Phil H., USNR
    In the mid-1950s commanded a beach jumper unit that worked with Amphibious Group Two, 252, 361
    Had a major role in the origin of SEALs and Navy special warfare in the 1960s, 361-363

Budgetary Considerations/Issues
    In the mid-1950s Congress imposed ceilings on active Navy personnel, which also controlled the number of active ships, 265-269
    Cutbacks in Navy funding in the late 1960s-early 1970s, 420-422

Bulkeley, Rear Admiral John D., USN (Ret.) (USNA, 1933)
    Was very thorough over the years in his position as president of the Board of Inspection and Survey, 60

Bullis Preparatory School, Washington, D.C.
    Erly attended the school in the early 1930s to prepare for Naval Academy entrance exams, 5-9, 11-12

Bureau of Naval Personnel, Arlington, Virginia
    In 1942 arranged for Erly to serve as advisor to the Cuban Navy, 135-137
    In 1944 assigned Erly to command the destroyer *Phelps* (DD-360), 164
    In the 1950s and 1960s individuals were assigned to commands without sworn screening boards, 279, 311-312

Burford, Lieutenant William P., USN (USNA, 1923)
    Served as a company officer at the Naval Academy in the mid-1930s, 13

Burke, Admiral Arleigh A., USN (USNA, 1923)
    Impact on OpNav during his tenure as Chief of Naval Operations from 1955 to 1961, 264, 270, 280-281, 318-319, 361, 398, 426
    Sent senior naval officers to the Joint Strategic Target Planning staff for nuclear weapons, 274

Bush, Commander George B. Jr., USNR
    In 1958 served as the first executive officer of the attack transport *Paul Revere* (APA-248), 287, 301-302

Busik, Captain William S., USN (Ret.) (USNA, 1943)
    Served 1971-94 as Executive Director and President/CEO of the Naval Academy Alumni Association, 24

Calvert, **USS (APA-32)**
    In the early 1960s served as flagship for Amphibious Squadron Five during Pacific operations, 321, 326-327, 331
    Damaged during an amphibious exercise in the early 1960s, 338-340

Camp Pendleton, Oceanside, California
 As a landing site during amphibious exercises in the late 1950s-early 1960s, 307, 314, 330, 333-337

Canada
 Participation in the Joint Defense Board, Canada and the United States in the mid-1960s, 382-384

Carlucci, Frank C. III
 Served as U.S. Ambassador to Portugal from 1975 to 1978, 454-455

Carroll, Commander Charles B., USN
 Commanded the destroyer *Lowry* (DD-770), 1952-54, 218, 222, 239

***Carronade*, USS (IFS-1)**
 In-shore fire support ship that was recommissioned in 1965 for Vietnam Service, 370-371

***Cassin*, USS (DD-372)**
 Operations out of Pearl Harbor in 1940-41 emphasized readiness because of the possibility of war against Japan, 86-100
 For a time in 1941 she was flagship for Commander Destroyer Division Five, 86-87
 Deployment to the South Pacific in early 1941, 87-90, 92-93
 Gunnery practice in 1941, 94-96, 122-123
 In dry dock at Pearl Harbor when the Japanese attacked in December 1941, 97, 100-105, 123
 Guns from the damaged ship were used for an antiaircraft battery on Oahu, 110
 Enlisted crew members worked on salvage after the attack, 110-112, 119

Ceylon
 Visited by the destroyer *James C. Owens* (DD-776) in 1952, 240

Chafee, John H.
 Served 1969-72 as Secretary of the Navy, 420-421, 429

Chalbaud, Carlos Delgado
 From 1945 to 1948 served as Venezuelan Minister of Defense, 182, 186, 188

Charleston Naval Shipyard, Charleston, South Carolina
 Reactivated a number of mothballed destroyers in 1950, 203-209, 211, 219

***Chicago*, USS (CA-29)**
 Made a cruise to Australia and New Zealand in early 1941, 97

Church, Captain Albert T. Jr., USN (USNA, 1938)
　　In the early 1960s served as commanding officer of the heavy cruiser *St. Paul* (CA-73) after having been aide to the Secretary of the Navy, 328-329

***Clark*, USS (DD-361)**
　　As flagship of Destroyer Squadron Five in 1939-40, 73

Clay, Captain James P., USN (USNA, 1922)
　　In the summer of 1944 served as ComDesLant representative in the Mediterranean, at Oran, Algeria, 159, 161-164
　　Served as chief of staff to Commander Destroyer Force Atlantic Fleet shortly after World War II, 162-163, 194

Colbert, Admiral Richard G., USN (USNA, 1937)
　　A Naval Academy classmate of Erly, he did public speaking as a member of the Quarterdeck Club in the mid-1930s, 25-26
　　As a flag officer served on the SACLant staff in the late 1960s and as Commander in Chief Allied Forces Southern Europe in the early 1970s, 26, 417

Cole, Lieutenant Otis R. Jr., USN (USNA, 1936)
　　Served in the submarine *Cachalot* (SS-170) during the Japanese attack on Pearl Harbor in 1941, 103

Collins, Commander Samuel L., USN (USNA, 1939)
　　Served as executive officer of the destroyer *James C. Owens* (DD-776) in the early 1950s, 175, 210-211
　　In the 1960s was chief staff officer to Commander Amphibious Squadron Five, 211

Collisions
　　The destroyer *Laub* (DD-613) collided with the light cruiser *Philadelphia* (CL-41) off Anzio, Italy, in May 1944, 155-160

Collum, Captain William J. Jr., USN (USNA, 1938)
　　In 1961 had to give up command of the attack transport *Calvert* (APA-32) because of a heart condition, 326

Colwell, Vice Admiral John B., USN (USNA, 1931)
　　While serving in the Bureau of Ordnance in the mid-1950s was involved in the development of the Polaris ballistic missile system, 273-274
　　Served 1964-65 as Commander Amphibious Force Pacific Fleet, 365, 367-368

Combs, Vice Admiral Thomas S., USN (USNA, 1920)
　　Served 1956 to 1958 as Deputy Chief of Naval Operations (Fleet Operations and Readiness), 270, 278-280
　　Put in flight time as a senior officer to qualify for flight pay, 279

Commercial Ships
    In 1937 various battleships, including the *New Mexico* (BB-40), sent out picket boats when Japanese merchant ships were in the harbor, 90
    In 1943 Erly rode from the South Pacific to San Francisco on board the Matson liner *Hawaiian Merchant*, 137-138
    In transatlantic convoys, 1944-45, 153, 166-170
    Proposal in the 1950s to send Polaris ballistic missiles to sea in Mariner-class merchant hulls transferred to the Navy, 273-274
    In 1958 the Todd shipyard in San Pedro, California, converted the merchant ship *Diamond Mariner* to become the Navy attack transport *Paul Revere* (APA-248), 286-292, 299

Communications
    On board the destroyer *Conyngham* (DD-371) in the late 1930s, 67-69
    Decoding of messages on board the destroyer *Cassin* (DD-372) in 1941, 87
    In 1952 the destroyer *James C. Owens* (DD-776) patrolled off Vladivostok to obtain communications intelligence, 228
    Capability on board the attack transport *Paul Revere* (APA-248) in the late 1950s, 300

***Compass Island*, USS (EAG-153)**
    Used in the 1950s to research navigation methods, 273-274

Conger, Commander Henry J., USN (USNA, 1941)
    Commanded the destroyer *Laffey* (DD-724), 1951-53, 218, 222, 239

Congress, U.S.
    Erly's father was able to obtain favors in the 1920s and 1930s because of his connections with congressmen, 1-4
    In the 1950s imposed ceilings on the number of Navy personnel, 265
    Representative Carl Vinson was not in favor of keeping battleships in the fleet in the 1950s, 270-271
    Cuts in the Navy budget in the late 1960s-early 1970s, 420-422
    Concerns on the part of the Black Caucus in the early 1970s about military aid to Portugal, 447

Convoys
    Escorted between the United States and the Mediterranean by the destroyer *Laub* (DD-613) in 1944, 148-154
    Escort of transatlantic convoys by the destroyer *Phelps* (DD-360) in 1944-45, 153, 166-170, 173-178
    Convoy commodore escort in the Pacific in 1962, 343-344

***Conyngham*, USS (DD-371)**
    Short-changed in receiving food from a vendor in the late 1930s, 58-59
    Operations in the Pacific in 1938-39, 60-78, 91

Engineering plant, 59-60
Damage control, 61
Messing and berthing, 62-65
Ship handling, 66-67
Enlisted personnel, 62-67, 79
Communications, 67-69
Gunnery, 71
Speed of 39 knots, 76
Tendency to roll, 76-77
At-sea operations in the aftermath of the Japanese attack on Pearl Harbor in 1941, 106-108

Cooper, Rear Admiral Joshua W., USN (USNA, 1927)
In the early 1960s commanded Amphibious Group Three, 310

Corrigan, Dr. Frank P.
In the late 1940s, as U.S. ambassador to Venezuela, argued against provided guns to the Venezuelan Navy, 185-187

Cousins, Admiral Ralph W., USN (USNA, 1937)
Student at the National War College in the early 1960s, 351-352, 356
Overall career success, 353
Served 1972-75 as Commander in Chief Atlantic Fleet, 419-420, 454-455

Coye, Rear Admiral John S. Jr., USN (USNA, 1933)
In the late 1960s served as Commander Training Command Atlantic Fleet, 400

Craig, Lieutenant Commander James E., USN (USNA, 1922)
Commanded the destroyer *Conyngham* (DD-371), 1939-40, 69, 71, 106
Killed on board the battleship *Pennsylvania* (BB-38) when the Japanese attacked Pearl Harbor in December 1941, 105

Cramer, Ensign Shannon D. Jr., USN (USNA, 1944)
In May 1944 helped deal with the aftereffects of a collision between the destroyer *Laub* (DD-613) and the light cruiser *Philadelphia* (CL-41), 157

Crawford, Lieutenant Commander David S., USN (USNA, 1919)
Commanded the destroyer *Conyngham* (DD-371), 1938-39, 93

Crouch, Captain Partee W. Jr., USN (USNA, 1939)
In the mid-1960s served as chief of staff to Commander Amphibious Force Pacific Fleet, 374

Cryptography
Decoding of messages on board the destroyer *Cassin* (DD-372) in 1941, 87

Cuba
    As a National War College student in 1962-63, Erly focused on U.S.-Cuban relations and the continued relevancy of the Monroe Doctrine, 348-350, 354-355

    Not involved in the Inter-American Defense Board in the mid-1960s, 395

    U.S. concern about Soviet activities in Cuba in the mid-1960s, 396-397

    In the wake of the North Korean seizure of the USS *Pueblo* (AGER-2) in 1968, the U.S. Navy took precautions to make sure none of its ships would be seized near Cuba, 397, 411-412

Cuba **(Cuban Sloop)**
    In 1942 was upgraded by Todd Shipyard in Galveston for antisubmarine duty, 139-147

Cuban Navy
    In 1943 the Gulf Sea Frontier command oversaw the upgrading of two Cuban Navy ships for antisubmarine service, 136-147

Culpepper, Ensign Frank M., USN (USNA, 1939)
    Fleeted up to serve as engineer officer of the destroyer *Cassin* (DD-372) in 1941, 87, 91

Cummings, Lieutenant Damon M., USN (USNA, 1931)
    Served on the staff of Destroyer Squadron Three in 1941, 108

Cutter, Ensign Slade D., USN (USNA, 1935)
    Was married in the mid-1930s even though not officially allowed to, 44

Damage Control
    Training on board the battleship *New Mexico* (BB-40) in the late 1930s, 31

    Training on board the destroyer *Conyngham* (DD-371) in the late 1930s, 61

    Training on board the destroyer *Cassin* (DD-372) in 1941, 123

    Firefighting after ships in dry dock at Pearl Harbor were hit by Japanese attackers in December 1941, 102-104, 116-118

    Removal of paint from the newly commissioned destroyer *Frazier* (DD-607) in 1942 to minimize fire hazard, 126

    On board the destroyer *Laub* (DD-613) after she collided with the light cruiser *Philadelphia* (CL-41) in May 1944, 155-160

Daniel, Lieutenant Commander Henry Chesley, USN (USNA, 1924)
    Commanded the destroyer *Conyngham* (DD-371), 1941-42, 106-109

Dare, Commander James A., USN (USNA, 1939)
    Commanded the destroyer *Douglas H. Fox* (DD-779), 1951-53, 218, 221-222, 227, 238-239

    Commanded an amphibious squadron that landed Marines in the Dominican Republic in 1965, 385

Commanded South Atlantic Force, 1968-70, 392-393

Depth Charges
Posed a hazard on board the destroyer *Laub* (DD-613) in 1944 after she ship survived a collision, 157

Desert Shield
Military buildup in the Persian Gulf region in the aftermath of the Iraqi invasion of Kuwait in August 1990, 341-342

Destroyer Division 221
In 1952 deployed to the Korean War zone and then completed a transit around the world, 217-221, 227-243

Destroyer Force Atlantic Fleet
In the late 1940s the tender *Yosemite* (AD-19) was flagship of for the destroyer type commander in addition to her role in servicing destroyers, 162-163, 192-196
Provided crew members to the destroyer *James C. Owens* (DD-776) in 1950 to fulfill shortages, 206-207
Sent a division of destroyers to the Far East for the Korean War and around the world, 217-221, 227-243

Distant Early Warning (DEW)
In the early 1950s the destroyer *James C. Owens* (DD-776) served in the North Atlantic as a seaward extension of the DEW Line, 224-226

Dominican Republic
In April 1965 President Lyndon Johnson sent an expeditionary brigade to the country, 350, 385

***Douglas H. Fox*, USS (DD-779)**
In 1952 deployed to the Korean War zone and then around the world, 218, 217-221, 227-240

***Downes*, USS (DD-375)**
In dry dock at Pearl Harbor when the Japanese attacked in December 1941, 102-105, 116-117
Guns from the damaged ship were used for an antiaircraft battery on Oahu, 110, 125

Duncan, Admiral Charles K., USN (USNA, 1933)
In 1958-59 commanded Amphibious Group One, 300-301, 419
Commanded the Amphibious Force Pacific Training Command, 1959-61, 310-311
Served in the Bureau of Naval Personnel, 1962-64, 346-347
Sat on the selection board that picked Erly for rear admiral in 1965, 347, 419
As Chief of Naval Personnel in the late 1960s, suggested a change in enlisted uniforms, 413-414, 428

Served 1970-72 as Commander in Chief Atlantic Fleet, 419-420, 432

Durham, Commander Harold D., USN
In 1961 took over temporary command of the attack transport *Calvert* (APA-32)

Dusinberre, Commander Henry W., USN (USNA, 1923)
In the late 1940s was executive officer of the destroyer tender *Yosemite* (AD-19), 192-194

Dye, Midshipman Willard J., USN (USNA, 1937)
Erly's Naval Academy roommate previously attended Bullis Prep, did not graduate from the academy, 8, 12-13, 15-17

Dyer, Rear Admiral George C., USN (USNA, 1919)
Based in Sasebo, Japan, during the Korean War, 235-236

Eisenhower, President Dwight D. (USMA, 1915)
As guest speaker at the National War College in the early 1960s, 354

Enlisted Personnel
In the crew of the battleship *New Mexico* (BB-40) in the late 1930s, 32-33, 38, 40-46
On board the destroyer *Conyngham* (DD-371) in the late 1930s, 61-67, 79
At Opa Locka, Florida, in 1940, 82-83
On board the destroyer *Cassin* (DD-372) at Pearl Harbor after she was damaged by the Japanese, 110-112, 119
In the crew of the new destroyer *Frazier* (DD-607) in 1942, 127-128
Two enlisted crew members were killed in a collision of the destroyer *Laub* (DD-613) in 1944, 159-160
In the crew of the destroyer *Phelps* (DD-360) in 1944-45, 171-172
Abundance of chief petty officers in the crew of the destroyer tender *Yosemite* (AD-19) in the late 1940s, 38
In the crew of the destroyer *James C. Owens* (DD-776) in the early 1950s, 205-208, 211-214, 219-220, 231-236
As part of the Navy's amphibious forces in the 1950s, 259-260, 303
Sailors and Marines on board the attack transport *Paul Revere* (APA-248) in the late 1950s, 293-299, 303-307
Change in the style of enlisted uniforms in the early 1970s, 413-414

Erly, Rear Admiral Robert B., USN (Ret.) (USNA, 1937)
Parents, 1-6, 11
Siblings, 2-5, 10
Wife Lois, 1, 119, 151, 179-181, 184-185, 188-189, 204, 210, 218, 243, 250, 319-320, 322, 329, 356-357, 408, 450, 455, 459
Boyhood in Washington, D.C., 1-11
Service in the Naval Reserve in the early 1930s, 5-10
As a Naval Academy midshipman, 1933-37, 11-30, 33-34, 117

Served 1937-38 as an ensign in the battleship *New Mexico* (BB-40), 29-44, 90, 55-59, 122

Served on board the destroyer *Conyngham* (DD-371) in 1938-39, 41, 58-79, 91, 122

Flight training in Florida in 1940, 79-85

Service on board the destroyer *Cassin* (DD-372) in 1940-41, 86-105, 116, 122

Temporary assignments around Pearl Harbor in late 1941-early 1942, 105-120, 125

In 1942 was in the crew of the destroyer *Frazier* (DD-607), 120, 124-135

In 1943 advised the Cuban Navy on behalf of Commander Gulf Sea Frontier, 136-147

For a few months in 1944 was executive officer of the destroyer *Laub* (DD-613), 148-164

In 1944-45 commanded the destroyer *Phelps* (DD-360), 153, 164-179

Served in the U.S. naval mission to Venezuela, 1946-48, 179-190, 387

As executive officer of the destroyer tender *Yosemite* (AD-19) in 1948-49, 162-163, 213

In 1949-50 was an instructor at the General Line School, Newport, Rhode Island, 191, 196-202, 213-215

Commanded the destroyer *James C. Owens* (DD-776), 1950-52, 57, 170-173, 203-243

In 1952-53 was a student at the Armed Forces Staff College, 242-245

Served on the staff of Commander Amphibious Group Two, 1953-55, 245-262, 331

From 1955 to 1958 was in the Fleet Operations and Readiness section of OpNav, 262-284

Commanded the attack transport *Paul Revere* (APA-248) in 1958-59, 254, 260, 285-307, 336

In 1959-60 was on the Amphibious Force Pacific Fleet staff as operations officer, 309-310

Commanded Amphibious Squadron Five, 1961-62, 301, 308, 321-345

As a student in 1962-63 at the National War College, 348-359

Served 1963-65 as chief of staff to Commander Amphibious Force Pacific Fleet, 197, 200-201, 359-361

In 1965-66 served as Commander Amphibious Group Three and Commander River/Coastal Warfare Group, 371-378

Served 1966-68 in OP-63 as coordinator of inter-American affairs, naval missions, and MAAGs, 379-399

In 1968-69 was Atlantic Fleet inspector general, 399-410

From 1969 to 1972 served as Deputy Chief of Staff for Plans and Operations on the Atlantic Fleet staff, 406-431

Final active tour, 1972-74, was as Commander Iberian Atlantic Command and Chief of the MAAG in Portugal, 417, 431-453

Post-retirement activities, 433, 455-459

Estes, USS (AGC-12)

In the early 1960s served as flagship for ComPhibGruWestPac, lost an anchor in Buckner Bay, Okinawa, 329

Ewa, Hawaii, Marine Corps Air Station
U.S. planes were shot down there during the Japanese attack in December 1941, 100-101
Erly set up antiaircraft batteries ashore at Ewa in the wake of the Japanese attack in 1941, 110-115

F4B
Fighter plane used for flight training at Opa Locka, Florida, in 1940, 82

Fahrion, Rear Admiral Frank G., USN (USNA, 1917)
In the early 1950s, as ComDesLant, inspected the newly recommissioned destroyer *James C. Owens* (DD-776), 211-213

Felt, Admiral Harry D., USN (USNA, 1923)
Personality of while serving as Vice Chief of Naval Operations, 1956-58, 276-278, 309

Fernández, Captain Braulio, Cuban Navy (Ret.)
Served as commanding officer of the Cuban Navy sloop *Cuba* during World War II, 140, 142
Talked with Erly in the late 1940s about retaining the U.S. naval mission to Cuba, 186-187
Moved to the United States after retiring from the Cuban Navy, 140, 146-147

Fire
Firefighting after the ships in dry dock at Pearl Harbor were hit by Japanese attackers in December 1941, 102-104, 116-118
Removal of paint from the newly commissioned destroyer *Frazier* (DD-607) in 1942 to minimize fire hazard, 126

Fire Control
Of torpedoes on board the destroyer *Conyngham* (DD-371) in the late 1930s, 70-73

Fitch, Lieutenant (junior grade) Graham N., USN (USNA, 1923)
Died in 1927 in the sinking of the submarine *S-4* (SS-109), 3

Fitness Reports
While serving on a selection board in the mid-1950s, Rear Admiral Lawson Ramage observed that surface officers did not rate their subordinates highly enough on fitness reports, 283-284

Fletcher, Captain Frank Jack, USN (USNA, 1906)
Commanded the battleship *New Mexico* (BB-40), 1936-37, 50-51
As a flag officer during World War II, 51-52

Flight Training
At Pensacola and Opa Locka, Florida, in 1940, 79-85

Fluckey, Rear Admiral Eugene B., USN (USNA, 1935)
Sat on the selection board that picked Erly for rear admiral in 1965, 347
Served as Commander Allied Forces Iberian-Atlantic Area and Chief, Military Assistance Advisory Group Portugal from 1968 to 1972, 431
Retired to Portugal after his Navy service, 449-450

Food
On board the destroyer *Conyngham* (DD-371) in the late 1930s, 51-64
In the late 1950s the attack transport *Paul Revere* (APA-248) received the Ney Award for outstanding food service, 294-297

Foreign Service Institute
In the early 1970s provided Erly with five months of Portuguese language training, 432-434

***Francis Marion*, USS (APA-249)**
Originally a merchant ship, she was converted to become a Navy attack transport in 1961, 287-291

Franke, William B.
Served as Secretary of the Navy from 1959 to 1961, 328-329

***Franklin D. Roosevelt*, USS (CVB-42)**
Future crew members received training on board the destroyer *Phelps* (DD-360) in the summer of 1945, 179

***Frazier*, USS (DD-607)**
Built at Bethlehem Steel in San Francisco, commissioned in July 1942, 120, 124-126
Increase in ammunition capacity before deploying in 1942, 126
Operations in the Pacific in 1942, 127-135
Enlisted crew members, 127-128
Radar capability, 127

French Navy
Interaction with NATO's Iberian-Atlantic Command in the early 1970s, 437

Friendly, Fred
In the early 1950s oversaw the production of a "See It Now" television program about amphibious warfare, 253-254

Fullinwider, Lieutenant Ransom, USN (USNA, 1926)
Served in the crew of the battleship *New Mexico* (BB-40) in the late 1930s, 35, 39

Galpin, Captain Gerard F., USN (USNA, 1920)
In 1942 served on the staff of Commander Gulf Sea Frontier, 138-139, 147

Gates, Thomas S. Jr.
Served as Secretary of the Navy, 1957-59, 329

General Line School, Newport, Rhode Island
In 1949-50 taught professional subjects to former Naval Reserve officers to bring them up to part with their regular Navy counterparts, 191, 196-202, 213-215

German Navy
U.S. antisubmarine doctrine in 1944 for dealing with deep-diving U-boats, 151-152

Goodfellow, Captain Alexander Scott Jr., USN (USNA, 1940)
In 1961-62 commanded the amphibious warfare ship *Paul Revere* (APA-248), 330-331

Goodrich, James F.
In the late 1950s was general manager of the Todd Shipyards facility in San Pedro, California, 289-290, 293

Gralla, Captain Arthur R., USN (USNA, 1934)
Served in the Fleet Operations and Readiness section of OpNav in the mid-1950s, 270, 272

Greece
In the 1970s the port of Elefis served for a time as the base for U.S. destroyers, 425-426

Griffin, Vice Admiral Charles Donald, USN (USNA, 1927)
Commanded the Seventh Fleet, 1960-61, 323, 327-328

Guantánamo Bay, Cuba, Naval Base
Training site for Cuban Navy ships in 1943, 142-143
Training for the crew of the reactivated destroyer *James C. Owens* (DD-776) in 1950, 209, 212-215, 222-224, 239

Guatemala
U.S. naval forces went to the vicinity of Guatemala in 1954 in anticipation of a possible Communist takeover, 250-251
U.S. military assistance advisory group officer was assassinated there in the mid-1960s, 386

Gulf Sea Frontier
In 1943 this command oversaw the upgrading of Cuban Navy ships for antisubmarine service, 136-140

Gunnery-Naval
  Turret operation on board the battleship *Arkansas* (BB-33) in 1934, 20-21
  Firing by the battleship *New Mexico* (BB-40) in the late 1930s, 46-49, 55, 122
  By the destroyer *Conyngham* (DD-371) in the late 1930s, 71, 122-123
  Practice by the destroyer *Cassin* (DD-372) in 1941, 94-96, 122-123
  Practice by the destroyer *Conyngham* (DD-371) in 1941, 107-108
  Erly set up antiaircraft batteries ashore at Ewa, Oahu, in the wake of the Japanese attack in 1941, 110-115, 125
  By the destroyer *Frazier* (DD-607) in 1942, 127, 131-134
  In the Cuban warships *Cuba* and *Patria* in 1943, 140-141
  Training and in combat by the destroyer *James C. Owens* (DD-776) in the early 1950s, 206-207, 229-238
  Shore bombardment for amphibious landings in the early 1960s, 317-318

Habitability
  On board the battleship *Arkansas* (BB-33) in the mid-1930s, 18
  On board the destroyer *James C. Owens* (DD-776) in the early 1950s, 213, 241
  In the attack transport *Paul Revere* (APA-248) in the late 1950s, 294-298

Hanks, Rear Admiral Robert J., USN (USNA, 1946)
  Served as Commander Middle East Force, 1972-75, 417

Harlfinger, Rear Admiral Frederick J. II, USN (USNA, 1935)
  In the mid-1950s escorted Representative Mendel Rivers in Europe, 392-393
  Served as Commander South Atlantic Force in 1967-68, 392

Hartz, Lieutenant William H. Jr., USNE
  In 1944 served as executive officer of the destroyer *Phelps* (DD-360), 164-166

Hawaii
  A contingent from the battleship *New Mexico* (BB-40) made a disastrous practice amphibious landing on Maui in the summer of 1938, 52-53
  Operations out of Pearl Harbor in 1940-41 emphasized readiness because of the possibility of war against Japan, 86-100
  Japanese attack on Pearl Harbor in December 1941, 100-105, 116-118
  Erly set up antiaircraft batteries ashore on Oahu in the wake of the Japanese attack in 1941, 110-115

Hay, Lieutenant Commander Alexander G., USN (USNA, 1934)
  Commanded the destroyer *Laub* (DD-613) in 1943-44, 148-150, 154

***Haynsworth*, USS (DD-700)**
  Operations in the Atlantic in the early 1950s, 211-212, 216

Hazing
Example of hazing in the mid-1930s in Bancroft Hall, the midshipmen's dorm at the Naval Academy, 23-25

Hedgehog
Antisubmarine weapon on board the destroyer *James C. Owens* (DD-776) in the early 1950s, 215

Helicopters
Used for inter-ship transfer in 1954, 251
In the mid-1950s amphibious doctrine tied in with the use of helicopters and tactical nuclear weapons, 254-257
Involvement in a SEATO exercise in Borneo in the early 1960s, 322-324

Holmes, Admiral Ephraim P., USN (USNA, 1930)
Personality and working style, 359-361
In the mid-1950s was on the staff of Commander Amphibious Force Atlantic Fleet, 359-360
Served in the early 1960s as Commander Amphibious Force Pacific Fleet, 346-347, 359-361, 364-367
From 1964 to 1967 was OP-090, Director of Navy Program Planning, 370
Sat on the selection board that picked Erly for rear admiral in 1965, 347
Served 1967-70 as Commander in Chief Atlantic Fleet, 399-400, 404-406, 410-412, 415-416

Hooper, Rear Admiral Edwin B., USN (USNA, 1931)
Commanded Amphibious Group One in 1961-62, 339-340

Hoppe, Lieutenant Commander William E., USN
In the early 1950s served on the staff of Commander Amphibious Group Two, 250

Iberian-Atlantic Command (IberLant)
Role in the North Atlantic Treaty Organization in the early 1970 as a subdivision of the Supreme Allied Command Atlantic, 431-453
Terrorist bombing of the command headquarters in 1971, 434-435
NATO exercises in the early 1970s, 437-440

Intelligence
In 1952 the destroyer *James C. Owens* (DD-776) patrolled off Vladivostok to obtain communications intelligence, 228

Inter-American Defense Board
Activities in the mid-1960s, 381-382, 387-388, 395
Cuba not included in the mid-1960s, 395

Iowa (BB-61)-Class Battleships

In the mid-1950s House Armed Services Chairman Carl Vinson had no interest in keeping battleships in the fleet, 270-271

Italy

U.S. Navy gunfire support of the invasion of Anzio and operations ashore in early 1944, 154-155

The destroyer *Laub* (DD-613) collided with the light cruiser *Philadelphia* (CL-41) off Anzio in May 1944, 155-158

Temporary repairs to the *Laub* at Naples, 158-161

Jackson, Vice Admiral Andrew M. Jr., USN (USNA, 1930)

Served 1964-67 as Deputy Chief of Naval Operations (Plans and Policy), 382-383

In the late 1960s was U.S. Navy representative to the United Nations, 402

Jacobs, Captain Walter F., USN (USNA, 1906)

Commanded the battleship *New Mexico* (BB-40), 1937-39, 40-42, 51-52

James, Rear Admiral Ralph K., USN (USNA, 1928)

In the late 1950s commanded the Long Beach Naval Shipyard, 287-290

James C. Owens, USS (DD-776)

Reactivated from mothballs by the Charleston Naval Shipyard and recommissioned in September 1950, 203-209, 219, 235-236

Enlisted crewmen in the early 1950s, 205-208, 211-214, 231-236

Operations in the Atlantic in the early 1950s, 57, 205-208, 211-220, 222-227

Gunnery, 206-207

Ship handling in the early 1950s, 170, 242-243

Deployment to the Western Pacific and then around the world in 1952, 217-221, 227-243

In 1952 patrolled off Vladivostok to obtain communications intelligence, 228

Korean War combat, 229-239

Crew members killed and wounded by North Korean gunfire in May 1952, 231-235

The ship was transferred to the Brazilian Navy in 1973, 175

Reunions of former crew members, 168-169, 174-175

Japan

In 1937 various battleships, including the *New Mexico* (BB-40), sent out picket boats when Japanese merchant ships were in the harbor, 90

Erly hated the Japanese for years after the 1941 attack on Pearl Harbor but later softened, 119-120, 319-320

Erly and his wife enjoyed great hospitality in Japan in early 1961, 319-310

Japanese Navy

Attack on Pearl Harbor in December 1941, 100-105, 116-118

Proficient in night operations during World War II, 90

Johnson, Commander Frank L., USN (USNA, 1930)
In July 1944 became the first commanding officer of the destroyer *Purdy* (DD-734), 147

Johnson, President Lyndon B.
In April 1965 sent an expeditionary brigade to the Dominican Republic, 350, 385

Johnson, Rear Admiral Nels C., USN (USNA, 1934)
Commanded Amphibious Group Three, 1961-63, 335

Joint Defense Board, Canada and the United States
Activities in the mid-1960s, 382-384

Keliher, Commander Thomas J. Jr., USN (USNA, 1916)
In 1941 commanded Destroyer Division Five with the *Cassin* (DD-372) as flagship, 87

Kennedy, President John F.
Association with Cuba during his presidency in the early 1960s, 349-351
Interest in counterinsurgency, 363-364

Kimmel, Admiral Husband E., USN (USNA, 1904)
As Commander in Chief Pacific Fleet in 1941, 96-97

King, Ensign Thomas Starr Jr., USN (USNA, 1936)
Served as a junior officer on board the battleship *New Mexico* (BB-40) in the late 1930s, 37

Kitts, Captain Willard A. III, USN (USNA, 1916)
As Pacific Fleet gunnery officer in 1941, assigned Erly to set up antiaircraft batteries ashore on Oahu, 110-112, 125

Knight, Ridgway B.
World War II adventures, 436-437
Foreign Service officer who was U.S. ambassador to Portugal, 1969-73, 432-437, 454

Korea, North
In 1952 the destroyer *James C. Owens* (DD-776) bombarded North Korean ports and was hit by counter-battery fire, 229-238

Korea, South
In 1952 the destroyer *James C. Owens* (DD-776) off-loaded dead and wounded crewmen at Pusan after being hit by North Korean projectiles, 232-233
In-port repairs to the ship, 233
A South Korean warship operated with U.S. forces during the Korean War, 388-389

Joint amphibious exercises with the U.S. Navy in the early 1960s, 321

Korean War
The onset of the war in 1950 led to the reactivation of mothballed ships and recall of reservists, 203-208
In 1952 Destroyer Division 221 deployed to the Korean War zone and then completed a transit around the world, 217-221, 227-243
Role of the destroyer *James C. Owens* (DD-776) in 1952 in patrolling and shore bombardment, 229-239
South Korean ship operated with U.S. forces during the Korean War, 388-389

Krulak, Major General Victor H., USMC (USNA, 1934)
As guest speaker at the National War College in the early 1960s, 354

Lander, Lieutenant Commander Robert B., USN (USNA, 1937)
In the late 1940s served as an advisor to the Venezuelan Naval Academy, 187

Laning, Lieutenant Commander Caleb B, USN (USNA, 1929)
Served as executive officer of the destroyer *Conyngham* (DD-371) in 1941, 107-108

Laos
A crisis in this nation in 1961 prompted the dispatch of U.S. amphibious warfare ships to the scene, 321-325

***Laub*, USS (DD-613)**
In 1944 escorted convoys between the United States and the Mediterranean, 148-154
Collided with the light cruiser *Philadelphia* (CL-41) off Anzio, Italy, in May 1944, 155-158
Temporary repairs at Naples, Italy, 158-161
Two enlisted crew members were killed in the collision, 159-160

Leave and Liberty
For junior officers in Southern California in the late 1930s, 36-37, 53-54
For the crew of the destroyer *James C. Owens* (DD-776) in an around-the-world cruise in 1952, 241-242
Erly and his wife enjoyed great hospitality in Japan in early 1961, 319-321

LeMay, General Curtis E., USA
As guest speaker at the National War College in the early 1960s, 354

LSMRs
Role of rocket-firing ships in the Vietnam War, 370-371

***LST-907*, USS**
In 1946 the U.S. Navy transferred the ship to Venezuela, where it became the training ship *Capana*, 182-184

Long Beach, California
    In 1937 various battleships, including the *New Mexico* (BB-40), sent out picket boats when Japanese merchant ships were in the harbor, 90

***Magoffin*, USS (APA, 199)**
    The ship's landing craft had problems with a rocky beach during an amphibious exercise at Camp Pendleton in the early 1960s, 333-337

***Mahan* (DD-364)-Class Destroyers**
    In the 1930s the ships had glass bridge windows, susceptible to damage by gunfire, 107, 141

Mandelkorn, Lieutenant Robert S., USN (USNA, 1935)
    Commanded an antiaircraft shore battery at Ewa, Oahu, in the aftermath of the 1941 Japanese attack on Pearl Harbor, 115

Marine Corps, U.S.
    Detachment on board the battleship *New Mexico* (BB-40) in the late 1930s, 46
    In the mid-1950s amphibious doctrine tied in with the use of helicopters and tactical nuclear weapons, 254-257
    Marines on board the attack transport *Paul Revere* (APA-248) in the late 1950s, 294-299, 305-307
    Development of amphibious warfare doctrine in the 1960s, 314-316
    Involvement in a SEATO exercise in Borneo in the early 1960s, 323-324
    Cooperation with Amphibious Force Pacific Fleet in the mid-1960s, 366-367
    Marine operations in Vietnam in the mid-1960s did not include riverine warfare, 374-377

Mariner-Class Merchant Hulls
    In the mid-1950s were considered as Navy missile-launching ships, later put to other Navy uses, 273-274

Marinke, Commander Charles A., USN (USNA, 1938)
    Served as chief of staff to the reserve fleet commander in Charleston in 1950, 208

Markham, Captain Lewis M. Jr., USN (USNA, 1925)
    Commanded Escort Division 21 n 1944, 166, 175-178
    Effects of alcohol use, 175-177

Martineau, Lieutenant Commander David L., USN (Ret.) (USNA, 1933)
    In 1943-44 commanded the destroyer *Phelps* (DD-360), 164

Massey, Captain Forsyth, USN (USNA, 1931)
    Received a public chewing-out from Admiral Arleigh Burke in the mid-1950s, 280

Massey, Lieutenant Lance E., USN (USNA, 1930)
Served as senior aviator on board the battleship *New Mexico* (BB-40) in the late 1930s, 34
Son Lemuel, 35

Matthews, Rear Admiral Herbert Spencer, Jr., USN (Ret.)
As a young enlisted man at Opa Locka, Florida, in 1940, 83, 418
In the early 1970s objected to the tone of racial-awareness meetings, 417-418

McCorkle, Rear Admiral Francis D., USN (USNA, 1926)
Served 1948-49 as chief of staff to Commander Destroyer Force Atlantic Fleet, 195-196, 269-270
Served 1953-55 as director of the Fleet Operations Division of OpNav, 262-263, 269-270

McCoy, Lieutenant Commander Roy E., USN
Commanded the inshore fire support ship *Carronade* (IFS-1), 1965-67, 370-371

McDaniel, Lieutenant Commander Eugene F., USN (USNA, 1927)
In 1943 commanded the Sub Chaser Training School at Miami, 143

McDonald, Admiral David L., USN (USNA, 1928)
As Chief of Naval Operations in the mid-1960s made a trip to Venezuela, 189, 398
Concerned about relations with Argentina in the mid-1960s, 389

Medical Problems
Treatment of destroyer *James C. Owens* (DD-776) crew members wounded by North Korean gunfire in May 1952, 231-233
Erly missed most of a National War College field trip in 1963 to Europe because of a sprained ankle, 356-357
Erly had a painful experience in 1974 with a kidney stone, 439-440
Disability retirement for Erly in 1974 because of a subarachnoid hemorrhage, 453-454

Melson, Vice Admiral Charles L., USN (USNA, 1927)
Commanded the First Fleet, 1960-62, 333

Mers-el-Kébir, Algeria
British warships bombarded the French fleet in July 1940 to keep it from falling into German hands, 153-154

Metz, Captain Earle C., USN (Ret.) (USNA, 1910)
In the mid-1940s served in the section of OpNav that supervised naval missions to other countries, 180

Mexican Navy
Relations with the U.S. Navy in the mid-1960s, 398

Military Assistance Advisory Groups (MAAGs)
U.S. relations with Latin American nations in the mid-1960s, 386-387, 390-391, 397-398
U.S. MAAG officer was assassinated in Guatemala in the mid-1960s, 386
U.S. mission in Portugal in the early 1970s, 435, 447-449

Military Sea Transportation Service (MSTS)
In the mid-1950s a number of its ships were operated by active-duty U.S. Navy crews, 265-266

Miller, Rear Admiral Edwin S., USN (USNA, 1933)
Served 1966-68 in a two-hatted billet in Portugal, 455

Miller, Vice Admiral Gerald E., USN (USNA, 1942)
Served 1970-71 as Commander Second Fleet, 406-407, 428-429

Miller, Rear Admiral Henry L., USN (USNA, 1934)
Served 1966-68 as the Navy's Chief of Information, 371

***Mindoro*, USS (CVE-120)**
In the mid-1950s was used to test the feasibility of helicopters in amphibious warfare, 255

Missiles
Proposal in the 1950s to send Polaris ballistic missiles to sea in Mariner-class merchant hulls, 273-274

***Missouri*, USS (BB-63)**
Her crew was beefed up for deployment to Korea in 1950 by drawing on destroyer crews, 205

Moncure, Captain Samuel P., USN (USNA, 1932)
In 1958 detailed Erly to command the new attack transport *Paul Revere* (APA-248), 285-286

Monroe Doctrine
As a National War College student in 1962-63, Erly focused on U.S.-Cuban relations and the continued relevancy of the Monroe Doctrine, 348-350, 354-355

Moorer, Admiral Thomas H., USN (USNA, 1933)
In the mid-1960s, as Supreme Allied Commander Atlantic, pushed for the establishment of the NATO Iberian-Atlantic Command, 432, 435-436
Served as Chief of Naval Operations 1967-70, 40, 313-314

As Chairman of the Joint Chiefs of Staff, 1970-74, 282, 447

Mount Olympus (AGC-8)
In the early 1950s served as flagship for Commander Amphibious Group Two, 251, 253, 331

Murrow, Edward R.
In the early 1950s, as a CBS correspondent, narrated a "See It Now" television program about amphibious warfare, 253-254

Muse, Captain George R., USN (USNA, 1938)
In 1962 was a captain detailer in the Bureau of Naval Personnel, 346

Mustin, Vice Admiral Lloyd M., USN (USNA, 1932)
Served 1967-68 as Commander Amphibious Force Atlantic Fleet, 402, 420-421

Naples, Italy
Site of temporary repairs to the destroyer *Laub* (DD-613) in 1944 after she was damaged in a collision, 158-161
Target of air raids in 1944, 161

National War College, Washington, D.C.
As a student in 1962-63 Erly focused on U.S.-Cuban relations and the continued relevancy of the Monroe Doctrine, 348-350, 354-355
Members of the class that attended in 1962-63, 351-359
Guest speakers, 354
Erly missed most of the field trip in 1963 to Europe because of a sprained ankle, 356-357

Naval Academy, Annapolis, Maryland
Plebe summer in 1933, 11-12
Academics in the mid-1930s, 13, 27-28
Summer training cruises in the mid-1930s, 13, 17-21
Unauthorized absences by midshipmen in the mid-1930s, 15-17
Comparison of honor code era with the 1930s, 22-24
Activities in the mid-1930s in Bancroft Hall, the midshipmen's dorm included mild hazing, 23-25
Extracurricular activities, 25-26
Ways of teaching leadership, 28-29
Value of training and experience at the academy in the mid-1930s when later applied in the fleet, 26-27, 116-117
Graduation of the class of 1937, 30
Alumni association activities in California in the 1980s-90s, 24, 456

Naval Academy Alumni Association
Erly served on the board for a number of years after retiring from active naval service, 24, 456

Naval Gun Factory, Washington, D.C.
Site of Naval Reserve drills and training in the early 1930s, 7-8

Naval Reserve, U.S.
Influx of newly trained reserve officers into the fleet in 1941, 87, 91-92

A large portion of the crew of the destroyer *Phelps* (DD-360) comprised reservists near the end of World War II, 171-172

In 1949-50 the General Line School at Newport, Rhode Island, taught professional subjects to former Naval Reserve officers to bring them up to part with their regular Navy counterparts, 191

The onset of the Korean War in 1950 led to the recall of reservists to active duty, 203-208

Naval Reserve officers on active duty were vulnerable when cuts were made in personnel strength, 302

Naval Special Warfare Center, Coronado, California
In the late 1980s was named in honor of Captain Phil Bucklew, 362-363

Navigation
On board the destroyer *Laub* (DD-613) in 1944, 150

Among the subjects taught at General Line School in 1949-50, 196

The fleet auxiliary ship *Compass Island* (EAG-153) was used in the 1950s to research navigation methods, 273-274

On board the attack transport *Paul Revere* (APA-248) in the late 1950s, 304

Navy Relief Society
Provided support to Navy families in the early 1950s, 210

New Mexico, **USS (BB-40)**
Modernization of the ship in the early 1930s at Philadelphia, 48

Emphasis on conservation of water and electricity to cut down on fuel consumption in the late 1930s, 29-30, 54-55

Operations in the Pacific in 1937-38, 29-59, 90, 122

Operation of SOC floatplanes for spotting and scouting, 32, 34-35

Enlisted personnel in the crew in the late 1930s, 32-33, 38, 40-46

Junior officers' mess, 34-36

Crew members made up various athletic teams in the late 1930s, 40-42

Overhaul in the Puget Sound Navy Yard in the late 1930s, 40-43

Celebration of Christmas in division compartments, 43-44

Marine detachment in the late 1930s, 46

Antiaircraft guns in the late 1930s, 46-47

Turret operations, 47-49, 55, 122

Participation in war games, 49-50, 56-57
Disastrous practice amphibious landing in Hawaii in the summer of 1938, 52-53

News Media
In the early 1950s the CBS network ran a "See It Now" television program about amphibious warfare, 253-254
Time magazine coverage of the inshore fire support ship *Carronade* (IFS-1) in Vietnam in 1966, 370-371

Ney Award
In the late 1950s the attack transport *Paul Revere* (APA-248) received the award for outstanding food service, 294-297

Night Operations
By U.S. warships in the years leading up to World War II, 122-123
By the destroyer *Frazier* (DD-607) in 1942, 130

North Atlantic Treaty Organization (NATO)
Role of the Iberian-Atlantic Command (IberLant) in the early 1970 as a subdivision of the Supreme Allied Command Atlantic, 431-453

Nuclear Power Program
Atlantic Fleet nuclear safety team visited the ballistic missile submarine *Abraham Lincoln* (SSBN-602), 402

Nuclear Weapons
In the mid-1950s amphibious doctrine tied in with the use of helicopters and tactical nuclear weapons, 254-257
Targeting of U.S. nuclear weapons in the 1950s and 1960s, 274-275
In 1960 the commanding general of the Fourth Infantry Division advocated the use of nuclear weapons in a war game, 340-341
Factor in command post exercises in the mid-1960s, 394-395

OP-03 (Fleet Operations and Readiness)
Role of in the mid-1950s, 262-284
Erly's assessment that OpNav was overstaffed, 263-264, 282-283
Establishment of an OpNav operations center in the mid-1950s, 264, 281
Tabulation of number of active ships, 264-268

Oak Hill, **USS (LSD-7)**
Western Pacific deployment in the early 1960s, 325-326

Obermeyer, Midshipman Jack A., USN (USNA, 1937)
Stood number one of the 323 graduates in the Naval Academy class of 1937, 27

Observation Island, **USS (EAG-154)**
Used in the 1950s to test Polaris ballistic missiles, 273-274

Officer Candidate School, Newport, Rhode Island
Began operation in 1951, during the Korean War, 202

O'Hare, Lieutenant Commander Edward H., USN (USNA, 1937)
As midshipman, shipboard officer, in flight training, and World War II combat, 80-82, 84

Okinawa
Buckner Bay was a staging point for amphibious warfare ships operating in the Western Pacific in the early 1960s, 322, 326-328
Grounding of the heavy cruiser *St. Paul* (CA-73) in 1961, 327-328
The flagship for PhibGruWestPac lost an anchor in Buckner Bay in the early 1960s, 329-330

***Oklahoma*, USS (BB-37)**
Summer training cruise for midshipmen in 1936, 19-21

Olds, Colonel Robin, USAF (USMA, 1943)
As a student at the National War College in the early 1960s, 352

Olsen, Captain Albert R., USN (USNA, 1938)
In 1960-61 commanded the attack transport *Paul Revere* (APA-248), 331

Ombudsmen
Useful for Navy families in the 1970s and beyond, 408-409

O'Neill, Captain Edward J., USN (USNA, 1931)
In the mid-1950s commanded the escort carrier *Mindoro* (CVE-120) during tests of helicopters in amphibious warfare, 255

Opa Locka, Florida, Naval Reserve Air Base
Site of fighter plane training in 1940, 80-84

Oran, Algeria
In 1944 U.S. warships trained at Oran in preparation for an upcoming invasion, 159, 161-162

Organization of American States (OAS)
Activities in the mid-1960s, 382, 385-386, 398

Orr, Ensign Ellis Burton, USN (USNA, 1936)
In the late 1930s served as commissary officer in the destroyer *Conyngham* (DD-371) before leaving for Submarine School, 58-59

P-2 Neptune
Near collision with a Beechcraft plane at Tan Son Nhut airbase in Vietnam in the mid-1960s, 373-374

Padgett, Lieutenant Commander Lemuel P. Jr., USN (USNA, 1920)
In the 1930s served as a battalion officer at the Naval Academy and later as gunnery officer of the battleship *New Mexico* (BB-40), 33-34

Panama Canal
Destroyer Division 221, including the *James C. Owens* (DD-776), went through the canal in early 1952 en route to Korea, 220-221, 227

***Patria* (Cuban Training Ship)**
In 1942 was upgraded by Todd Shipyard in Galveston for antisubmarine duty, 139-140

Patrick, Lieutenant Commander Goldsborough Serpell, USN (USNA, 1929)
In 1942 was on the staff of Commander Destroyers Pacific Fleet in Hawaii, 131-132

Patrol Wing Two
Commanded patrol plane operations out of Pearl Harbor in the wake of the Japanese attack in December 1941, 109-112

***Paul Revere*, USS (APA-248)**
Originally a merchant ship, she was converted to become a Navy attack transport in 1958, 273, 285-292, 299
Commissioned in September 1958, 292-293
Operations in the Pacific in the late 1950s-early 1960s, 291-294, 300, 331-332, 336, 343
In the late 1950s received the Ney Award for outstanding food service, 294-297
Enlisted personnel in the late 1950s, 293-299, 303-307
Communications capability, 300
Ship-handling qualities, 303-304, 331-332
In the early 1960s was involved in an amphibious exercise at Camp Pendleton, California, 330-331, 340

Pay and Allowances
In the 1950s Vice Admiral Thomas Combs flew on a regular basis to qualify for flight pay, 279

Pearl Harbor, Hawaii
Naval operations out of Pearl in 1940-41 emphasized readiness because of the possibility of war against Japan, 86-100
Japanese attack on military installations at Pearl and environs in December 1941, 100-105, 116-118

Erly set up antiaircraft batteries ashore on Oahu in the wake of the Japanese attack, 110-112

Pendleton, Camp
See: Camp Pendleton, Oceanside, California

Pennsylvania, **USS (BB-38)**
In dry dock at Pearl Harbor when the Japanese attacked in December 1941, 103-105, 118-119
Supplied uniform parts to Erly after his were lost in the attack, 121

Pensacola, Florida, Naval Air Station
Site of flight training in 1940, 79-80

Personnel
Retention problem for nuclear submariners in the late 1960s-early 1970s, 403-405

Peterson, Lieutenant Mell A., USN (USNA, 1930)
Served on board the destroyer *Cassin* (DD-372) in 1941, 86-87

Phelps, **USS (DD-360)**
Modernization yard periods in 1944-45, 164-166, 173
A large portion of the crew comprised reservists, 171-172
Escort of transatlantic convoys in 1944-45, 153, 166-170, 173-178
Ship handling in 1944-45, 169-170, 223
Captain Lewis M. Markham Jr. was embarked in the ship in 1944-45 as Commander Escort Division 21, 166, 175-178
Limitations in antisubmarine warfare, 215
Served as a training ship in the summer of 1945, 179
Decommissioned in November 1945 and scrapped soon afterward, 178-179
Reunions of former crew members, 168-169, 174

Philadelphia, **USS (CL-41)**
Collided with the destroyer *Laub* (DD-613) in 1944 off Anzio, Italy, in May 1944, 155-160

Phillips, Rear Admiral William K., USN (USNA, 1918)
Served as Commander Destroyer Force Atlantic Fleet, 1947-48, 195

Pirie, Lieutenant Commander Robert B., USN (USNA, 1926)
Flight instructor at Opa Locka, Florida, in 1940, 80, 83

Placette, Radarman First Class Harold, USNR
In the late 1960s began organizing reunions of former crew members of the destroyer *Phelps* (DD-360), 174

Player, Commander Heber, USN (USNA, 1938)
In 1952 commanded the naval facility at Pusan, South Korea, 233

Polaris Ballistic Missile System
Proposal in the 1950s to send Polaris ballistic missiles to sea in Mariner-class merchant hulls, 273-274

Porter, General Robert W. Jr., USA (USMA, 1930)
Served as Commander in Chief U.S. Southern Command from 1965 to 1969, 380, 387, 389-391

Portugal
In the early 1970s the Foreign Service Institute provided Erly with five months of Portuguese language training, 432-434
Role of the Iberian-Atlantic Command and U.S. military assistance advisory group in the early 1970s, 434-453
Portugal made considerable contributions to NATO in the early 1970s, 441-442
Change of government as the result of a bloodless revolution in 1974, 437-440, 443-446, 451-452
In the early 1970s cork and tourism were the main pillars of the national economy, 448-449, 452-453
Military pay was so low that most officers of the Portuguese armed forces had other jobs, 451-452

Price, Rear Admiral Walter H., USN (USNA, 1927)
In the late 1950s was Commander Naval Base Long Beach, 293

Price, Commander William M., USN (USNA, 1936)
Engineering duty officer who was stationed at the Charleston Naval Shipyard in 1950, 204-205

***Princeton*, USS (LPH-5)**
Former attack carrier that served in the 1960s as an amphibious assault ship, 369, 372

Promotion of Officers
Promotion exams were phased out after World War II, 199-200
While serving on a selection board in the mid-1950s, Rear Admiral Lawson Ramage observed that surface officers did not rate their subordinates highly enough on fitness reports, 283-284
Continuation boards in the early 1960s selected some officers for early retirement in order to keep promotions moving, 313-314

Propulsion Plants
Emphasis on conservation of water and electricity to cut down on fuel consumption by the battleship *New Mexico* (BB-40) in the late 1930s, 29-30, 32, 54-55

Engineering plant in the destroyer *Conyngham* (DD-371) in the late 1930s, 59-60

Steam engineering was among the subjects taught at General Line School in 1949-50, 196-197

Inadequate initial manning in 1950 to operate boilers in the recommissioned destroyer *James C. Owens* (DD-776), 205-209

Boiler feedwater problems in the destroyer *Haynsworth* (DD-700) in the early 1950s, 211-212

Public Relations

The battleship *New Mexico* (BB-40) visited various West Coast ports in the late 1930s to publicize the Navy and boost local economies, 53-54

***Pueblo*, USS (AGER-2)**

Intelligence ship that was captured by North Koreans in 1968, 135

In the wake of the *Pueblo* incident, the U.S. Navy took precautions to make sure none of its ships would be seized near Cuba, 397, 411-412

Puget Sound Navy Yard, Bremerton, Washington

Overhauled the battleship *New Mexico* (BB-40) in the late 1930s, 40-43

Pusan, South Korea

In 1952 the destroyer *James C. Owens* (DD-776) off-loaded dead and wounded crewmen at Pusan after being hit by North Korean projectiles, 232-234

In-port repairs to the ship, 233

Quiggle, Captain Lynne C., USN (USNA, 1930)

Commanded the amphibious force flagship *Mount Olympus* (AGC-8) in 1953, 331

Racial Issues

In the early 1970s ships in the Pacific Fleet were hit with racial disturbances but not those in the Atlantic, 415

Racial-awareness meetings in the early 1970s, 415-416

Radar

Used by U.S. battleships in the period shortly before World War II, 95-97, 124

Installed on board the new destroyer *Frazier* (DD-607) in 1942, 127

Equipment on board the destroyer *James C. Owens* (DD-776) in the early 1950s, 214-215, 225, 229

North Korean radar in 1952, 230, 234, 237

Radio

On board the destroyer *Conyngham* (DD-371) in the late 1930s, 67-69

Decoding of messages on board the destroyer *Cassin* (DD-372) in 1941, 87

In 1952 the destroyer *James C. Owens* (DD-776) patrolled off Vladivostok to obtain communications intelligence, 228

Capability of the attack transport *Paul Revere* (APA-248) in the late 1950s, 300

Ramage, Rear Admiral Lawson P., USN (USNA, 1931)
While serving on a selection board in the mid-1950s, observed that surface officers did not rate their subordinates highly enough on fitness reports, 283-284

Ramsey, Commander Logan C., USN (USNA, 1919)
On the staff of Commander Patrol Wing Two in the wake of the Japanese attack on Pearl Harbor in 1941, 112

Raymer, Ensign Jackson H., USN (USNA, 1938)
Served in the destroyer *Conyngham* (DD-371) in the late 1930s, 59

Refueling at Sea
Experiments involving the battleship *New Mexico* (BB-40) in the late 1930s, 58
In the early 1950s, in the North Atlantic, the destroyer *James C. Owens* (DD-776) refueled as a hurricane was approaching, 226-227

***Reina Mercedes*, USS (IX-25)**
Former Spanish warship that served as a prison ship at the Naval Academy in the 1930s, 12, 15, 23

Richter, Lieutenant Commander Henry E., USN (USNA, 1924)
Commanded the reactivated destroyer *Roper* (DD-147) in 1940-41, 75

Rickover, Vice Admiral Hyman G., USN (Ret.) (USNA, 1922)
Heavy emphasis on fuel consumption as assistant engineer officer on board the battleship *New Mexico* (BB-40) in the late 1930s, 29-30, 54
Relationship with Atlantic Fleet Commander in Chief Ephraim Holmes in the late 1960s, 404-405

Riley, Brigadier General Thomas F., USMC
In the late 1950s visited the newly commissioned attack transport *Paul Revere* (APA-248), 296, 305

Rittenhouse, Rear Admiral Basil N. Jr., USN (USNA, 1928)
As executive officer of the destroyer *Cassin* (DD-372) in 1941, 86, 105, 119
In 1943 was destroyer detailer in the Bureau of Naval Personnel, 136, 151
In the early 1960s served on the staff of U.S. Forces Japan, 318-319, 321

Riverine Warfare
Development of doctrine in the mid-1960s for application in the Vietnam War, 371-378

River Patrol Boats (PBRs)
Developed in the mid-1960s for service in Vietnam, 375

Rivers, L. Mendel (Democrat-South Carolina)
    Questionable activities when traveling in Europe in the 1960s, 392-393

Rockets
    Role of rocket-firing ships, IFS and LSMRs, in the Vietnam War, 370-371

Roeder, Rear Admiral Bernard F., USN (USNA, 1931)
    Served as Commander Amphibious Group Three, 1960-61, 323, 329
    Sat on the selection board that picked Erly for rear admiral in 1965, 348, 374
    In the mid-1960s commanded Amphibious Force Pacific Fleet, 371-372, 374

Roessler, Commander Anthony C., USN (USNA, 1931)
    Commanded the destroyer *Laub* (DD-613) in 1944-45, 154, 177

Rommel, Commander Herbert F. Jr., USN
    Commanded the destroyer *Haynsworth* (DD-700), 1950-52, 211

Rose, Vice Admiral Rufus E., USN (USNA, 1924)
    Assessment of as Commander Amphibious Group Two in 1952-53, 245-247, 257, 261-262

Royal Navy
    British warships bombarded the French fleet at Mers-el-Kébir, Algeria, in July 1940 to keep it from falling into German hands, 153-154
    Took part in a SEATO exercise in Borneo in the early 1960s, 322-323

SOC Seagull
    Operated by the battleship *New Mexico* (BB-40) in the late 1930s for spotting and scouting, 32, 34-35

Safety
    Emphasis on safety when operating 12-inch-gun turrets on board the battleship *Arkansas* (BB-33) in 1934, 20-21

***St. Paul*, USS (CA-73)**
    Korean War operations in 1952, 228, 232-233
    Wind blew the ship aground in Buckner Bay in 1961, 327-328

Sanders, Rear Admiral Harry, USN (USNA, 1923)
    Served in the Fleet Operations and Readiness section of OpNav in the mid-1950s, 270, 276-277

San Diego, California
    In 1939-40 served as homeport for active destroyers and upkeep site for destroyers in reserve, 73-76

In early 1952 Destroyer Division 221 stopped at San Diego en route the Korean War, 221

Homeport for the attack transport *Paul Revere* (APA-248) in the late 1950s, 305

Construction and growth in the 1980s, 74

Sasebo, Japan
Site of upkeep and maintenance during the WestPac deployment of the destroyer *James C. Owens* (DD-776) in 1952, 235-236

Saudi Arabia
Visited by the destroyer *James C. Owens* (DD-776) in 1952, 240-241

Schneider, Captain Frederick H. Jr., USN (USNA, 1937)
Commanded the heavy cruiser *St. Paul* (CA-73) in 1960-61, 327-328

SEALs
Origin of SEALs and Navy special warfare in the 1960s, 361-363
Questionable operations in Vietnam in the mid-1960s, 372-373

Security
Mishandling of classified material on board the destroyer *Phelps* (DD-360) in 1944, 165-166

Selection Boards
While serving on a selection board in the mid-1950s, Rear Admiral Lawson Ramage observed that surface officers did not rate their subordinates highly enough on fitness reports, 283-284
In 1960 a continuation board selected a number of captains for early retirement, 312-313
In 1965 a board selected Erly for rear admiral, 347-348

Sell, Rear Admiral Leslie H., USN (USNA, 1943)
In 1944 served on the staff of the ComDesLant representative in the Mediterranean, 159
In 1972 relieved Erly on the Atlantic Fleet staff, 432

Shaffer, Rear Admiral J. Nevin, USN (USNA, 1935)
Commanded the destroyer *Stormes* (DD-780) from 1950 to 1952, 222-224
Commanded Cruiser-Destroyer Force Atlantic Fleet from 1969 to 1971, 222

***Shaw*, USS (DD-373)**
Set afire by the Japanese attack on Pearl Harbor in December 1941, 103-104, 116-118
Guns from the damaged ship were used for an antiaircraft battery on Oahu, 110, 125

Shea, Lieutenant Commander Daniel F. J., USN (USNA, 1923)
  Commanded the destroyer *Cassin* (DD-372) in 1941, 86, 93, 105-106, 119

Ship Characteristics Board
  Role of in the mid-1950s, 268, 273
  Proposal in the 1950s to send Polaris ballistic missiles to sea in Mariner-class merchant hulls, 273-274

Ship Handling
  On board the battleship *New Mexico* (BB-40) in the late 1930s, 50
  On board the destroyer *Conyngham* (DD-371) in the late 1930s, 51-64
  On board the destroyer *Phelps* (DD-360) in 1944-45, 169-170, 223
  On board the destroyer *Douglas H. Fox* (DD-779) in 1952, 221
  For the destroyer *James C. Owens* (DD-776) in the early 1950s, 170, 242-243
  Problems for the destroyer *Stormes* (DD-780) during training at Guantánamo Bay, Cuba in the early 1950s, 222-224
  Qualities of the attack transport *Paul Revere* (APA-248) in the late 1950s-early 1960s, 303, 331-332

Shore Bombardment
  U.S. Navy gunfire support of the invasion and operations ashore in early 1944, 154-155
  In 1952 the destroyer *James C. Owens* (DD-776) bombarded North Korean ports and was hit by counter-battery fire, 229-238
  Shore bombardment for amphibious landings in the early 1960s, 317-318

Sides, Admiral John H., USN (USNA, 1925)
  Went into the business world after his Navy retirement in 1963, 431

Simulators
  Used as training aids at the General Line School in 1949-50, 199

Sixth Fleet, U.S.
  Home-porting of the fleet flagship in the Mediterranean in the 1950s, 266

Slaughter, Captain John S., USN (USNA, 1937)
  Student at the National War College in the early 1960s, 351-352, 356

Slonim, Captain Gilven M., USN (USNA, 1936)
  Served as chief of staff to Commander Anti-Submarine Warfare Force Pacific in the early 1960s, 344

Smith, Admiral Harold Page, USN (USNA, 1924)
  In the early 1950s commanded Amphibious Group Two, 248-251, 253, 262-263
  Served as Chief of Naval Personnel, 1958-60, 305
  In the early 1960s served as CinCNELM in London, 356

Smith, Captain Kerfoot B, USN (USNA, 1933)
　　In 1961 was forced into retirement as the result of continuation board, 312

Smith, Ensign Russell H. "Snuffy," (USNA, 1935)
　　As an ensign had already become a turret officer by 1936 on board the battleship *Oklahoma* (BB-37), 21

Solar, Boatswain's Mate Adolfo, USN
　　Served in the crew of the battleship *New Mexico* (BB-40) in the late 1930s, 32-33, 38
　　Killed on board the battleship *Oklahoma* (BB-37) at Pearl Harbor in 1941, 32-33

Sonar
　　On board the destroyer *James C. Owens* (DD-776) in the early 1950s, 214-215

Songjin, North Korea
　　In 1952 the destroyer *James C. Owens* (DD-776) patrolled off the city and at times bombarded it, 229-235, 238

South Atlantic Force, U.S.
　　Operations in the mid-1960s, 389-392

Southeast Asia Treaty Organization (SEATO)
　　Staged an amphibious exercise on Borneo in the early 1960s, 322-323

Southern Command, U.S. (SouthCom)
　　General Robert W. Porter Jr., USA, served as commander in chief from 1965 to 1969, 380, 387, 389-391

Soviet Union
　　In 1952 the destroyer *James C. Owens* (DD-776) patrolled off Vladivostok to obtain communications intelligence, 228
　　U.S. concern about Soviet activities in Cuba in the mid-1960s, 396-397

Spangler, Captain John G., USN (USNA, 1932)
　　Commanded an amphibious squadron in the late 1950s, 298-299

Special Warfare
　　Origin of SEALs and Navy special warfare in the 1960s, 361-363
　　Operations in the Vietnam War in the mid-1960s, 372-373
　　Promotion opportunities for Navy practitioners have improved since the 1960s, 362

Speck, Rear Admiral Robert H., USN (USNA, 1927)
　　In the late 1950s tried to recruit Erly for the ComPhibTraPac staff, 304-305, 309-310

***Stark*, USS (FFG-31)**
　　Hit by Iraqi missiles in 1987, 134-135

State Department, U.S.
In the late 1940s took a position against supplying guns to the Venezuelan Navy, 185-187
Involvement in the mid-1960s in the Joint Defense Board, Canada and the United States, 384

Stiles, Colonel William A, USMC (USNA, 1939)
Commanded a contingent of Marines involved in an amphibious exercise in Borneo in the early 1960s, 323

Stimson, Captain Paul C., USN (USNA, 1936)
In 1961 Commanded the amphibious force flagship *Estes* (AGC-12) in the Western Pacific, 329-330
In 1962 took command of Amphibious Squadron Five, 343, 345

***Stormes*, USS (DD-780)**
Ship-handling problems during training at Guantánamo Bay, Cuba, in the early 1950s, 222-224

Sub Chaser Training School, Miami, Florida
In 1943 trained the crews of Cuban Navy ships, 143

Swift Boats (PCFs)
Developed in the mid-1960s for service in Vietnam, 375-376

Sylvester, Vice Admiral John, USN (USNA, 1926)
Served 1958-60 as Commander Amphibious Force Pacific Fleet, 293, 309-310
As president of a continuation board in 1960, 312-313

Tactics
U.S. antisubmarine doctrine in 1944 for dealing with deep-diving German U-boats, 151-152

Tank Landing Ships (LSTs)
Push in the mid-1960s for development of 20-knot LSTs, 364

Tan Son Nhut Air Force Base, Saigon
Near miss by aircraft in the mid-1960s, 373-374

Television
In the early 1950s the CBS network ran a "See It Now" program about amphibious warfare, 253-254

Terrorism
Terrorist bombing of the IberLant command headquarters in 1971, 434-435

Thach, Admiral John S., USN (USNA, 1927)
Commanded Anti-Submarine Warfare Force Pacific in the early 1960s, 344

Theobald, Rear Admiral Robert A., USN (USNA, 1907)
Commanded Destroyer Flotilla One at the time of the Japanese attack on Pearl Harbor in 1941, 108-109

***Thetis Bay*, USS (LPH-6)**
Amphibious assault ship that took part in a SEATO exercise in Borneo in the early 1960s, 322-324

Thomaz, Admiral Américo
Served as President of Portugal from August 1958 to April 1974, 442-444

Thompson, Captain Marshall F., USN (USNA, 1936)
Commanded the attack transport *Paul Revere* (APA-248), 1959-60, 304-305

Todd Shipyards Corporation, San Pedro, California
In 1958 converted the commercial ship *Diamond Mariner* to become the Navy attack transport *Paul Revere* (APA-248), 286-292, 299

Tolley, Captain Kemp, USN (USNA, 1929)
In the early 1950s served on the staff of Commander Amphibious Group Two, 247-248, 250-252, 257-258
Devised a plan for using underwater telephone lines in amphibious exercises, 247-248, 258, 300-301, 340
In 1954-56 commanded Amphibious Squadron Five, 300-301

Torpedoes
U.S. destroyers made simulated torpedo attacks against the battle line during war games in the late 1930s, 49, 70, 122
On board the destroyer *Conyngham* (DD-371) in the late 1930s, 70-73
New magnetic exploders in torpedoes on board the destroyer *Cassin* (DD-372) in 1941, 87-88, 90-91

Townsend, Vice Admiral Robert L., USN (USNA, 1934)
Served 1969-72 as Commander Naval Air Force Atlantic Fleet, 407

Truman, Major General Louis W., USA (USMA, 1932)
As commanding general of the Fourth Infantry Division in 1960, advocated the use of nuclear weapons in a war game, 340-341

***Tulare*, USS (AKA-112)**
Commissioned as a Navy attack cargo ship in 1956 after being converted from a commercial hull, 289

Turrets
    Operation of on board the battleship *Arkansas* (BB-33) in 1934, 20

Uniforms-Naval
    Erly had to replace his Navy uniforms after his previous wardrobe was destroyed during the 1941 Japanese attack on Pearl Harbor, 120-121
    Change in the style of enlisted uniforms in the early 1970s, 413-414

Van Arsdall, Rear Admiral Clyde, J. Jr., USN (USNA, 1934)
    Served 1966-67 as Commander South Atlantic Force, 390, 392
    In 1967-69 was Commander Cruiser-Destroyer Force Atlantic Fleet, 428

Van Leunen, Lieutenant (junior grade) Paul Jr., USN (USNA, 1934)
    Served in the destroyer *Conyngham* (DD-371) in the late 1930s until he left for Submarine School, 59

Venezuelan Navy
    From 1946 to 1948 Erly served as part of the U.S. naval mission to Venezuela, involved in training, liaison, and providing advice, 179-190, 387
    In 1946 acquired the former USS *LST-907* and renamed her *Capana*, 182-284
    Hosted a conference of hemisphere CNOs in the mid-1960s, 189, 398-399

Vieques
    Island that was a bone of contention in the 1970s because of the Navy's use of it for target practice, 427

Vietnam War
    Buildup in the mid-1960s on the part of Amphibious Force Pacific Fleet, 365, 369-370
    Role of rocket-firing ships, IFS and LSMRs, 370-371
    Development of riverine warfare doctrine in the mid-1960s for application in Vietnam, 371-378

Vinson, Representative Carl, (Democrat-Georgia)
    As Chairman of the Armed Services Committee in the mid-1950s, did not favor keeping battleships in the active fleet, 270-271

Virden, Lieutenant Commander Frank USN (USNA, 1927)
    Served as the first commanding officer of the destroyer *Frazier* (DD-607), commissioned in 1942, 125-126, 129-134

Ward, Rear Admiral Norvell G., USN (USNA, 1935)
    Served 1965-67 as Commander U.S. Naval Forces Vietnam, 374

War Games
    U.S. Navy encounters at sea in the late 1930s, 49-50, 56-57, 122
    In 1960 the commanding general of the Fourth Infantry Division advocated the use of nuclear weapons in a war game, 340-341
    Command post exercises in the mid-1960s, 394-395

Warder, Rear Admiral Frederick B., USN (USNA, 1925)
    Served in the Fleet Operations and Readiness section of OpNav in the mid-1950s, 270

Washington, Midshipman Thomas, USN (USNA, 1887)
    In the early 1930s served as Governor of the Naval Home in Philadelphia, 5

Washington, Midshipman Thomas Jr., USN (USNA, 1938)
    Tutored by Erly's brother-in-law before entering the Naval Academy in 1933, 5

Weather
    Effect of Santa Ana winds on the destroyer *Conyngham* (DD-371) in the late 1930s, 76-77
    Operations in fog by the destroyer *James C. Owens* (DD-776) in the early 1950s, 57
    Operations in heavy seas by the *James C. Owens* in the early 1950s, 217-218, 225-227
    Wind blew the Seventh Fleet flagship *St. Paul* (CA-73) aground in Buckner Bay in 1961, 327-328

Webb, Hamilton W. "Spike"
    As boxing coach at the Naval Academy in the mid-1930s, 14-15, 25

Wellings, Rear Admiral Augustus J., USN (USNA, 1920)
    In the early 1950s commanded Amphibious Group Two, 248, 331

Wells, Captain Wade C., USN
    Role in connection with riverine warfare in Vietnam in the 1960s, 375

Wendt, Vice Admiral Waldemar F. A., USN (USNA, 1933)
    Served 1967-68 as Deputy Chief of Naval Operations (Plans and Policy), 382-383

Westervelt, Captain John D., USN
    In the mid-1960s commanded an amphibious squadron in the Vietnam War, 372

White, General Thomas D., USAF (Ret.) (USMA, 1920)
    As guest speaker at the National War College in the early 1960s, 357-358

Whitehurst, Lieutenant Edson H., USN (USNA, 1930)
    Served as chief engineer of the destroyer *Cassin* (DD-372) in 1941, 86-87, 91

Wilkinson, Commander Eugene P., USN
    In the mid-1950s took the newly commissioned nuclear submarine *Nautilus* (SSN-571) into the Chesapeake Bay, 273
    Was very thorough in inspecting the submarines he commanded in the 1950s, 60

Wonsan, North Korea
    Bombarded by the destroyer *James C. Owens* (DD-776) in 1952, 237-238

Wootten, Lieutenant Charles T., USN (USNA, 1920)
    While stationed at the Naval Academy in the 1920s tutored Erly to prepare him for entrance exams, 3, 7-9
    Served as executive officer of the Naval Home in Philadelphia in the early 1930s, 5

Wright, Commander George C., USN (USNA, 1925)
    In 1944 was chief of staff to the ComDesLant representative in the Mediterranean, 159, 163-164

Wright, Lieutenant William D. Jr., USN (USNA, 1923)
    Served on board the battleship *New Mexico* (BB-40) in the late 1930s, 35

Wulzen, Rear Admiral Don W., USN (USNA, 1935)
    Selected for flag rank while serving in the early 1960s as chief of staff to Commander Amphibious Force Pacific Fleet, 359
    In the mid-1960s was Commander Amphibious Group Western Pacific, 371-372

Wylie, Captain Joseph C. Jr., USN (USNA, 1932)
    In the mid-1950s escorted Representative Mendel Rivers in Europe, 392-393
    Twilight tour as Commandant of the First Naval District, 1969-72

Yeager, Vice Admiral Howard A., USN (USNA, 1927)
    Commanded Amphibious Force Pacific Fleet, 1960-63, 333-334, 359, 365, 367
    Died in a house fire in 1967, 334

***Yosemite*, USS (AD-19)**
    Served in the late 1940s as flagship of Commander Destroyer Force Atlantic Fleet, in addition to her role in servicing destroyers, 162-163, 192-196
    Abundance of chief petty officers in the crew in the late 1940s, 38, 193-194
    Underway period to enhance combat readiness, 193

Zumwalt, Admiral Elmo R. Jr., USN (USNA, 1943)
    As a student at the National War College in the early 1960s, 352
    Commanded U.S. Naval Forces Vietnam, 1968-70, 375-376
    As CNO in the early 1970s, introduced widespread changes, 62, 413-414
    Emphasis on youth in the Navy, 313-314, 419, 424-425, 429

www.ingramcontent.com/pod-product-compliance
Lightning Source LLC
Chambersburg PA
CBHW082221090526
44585CB00020BA/2133